COMPANION TO MEDIA AND HUMANITARIAN ACTION

COMPANION TO MEDIA AND HUMANITARIAN ACTION

Editor

Farrell Dabney

Socialy PRESS
AN IMPRINT OF SCITUS ACADEMICS

Companion to Media and Humanitarian Action

Edited by **Farrell Dabney**

This Book is Printed on Acid-Free Paper. ♾

ISBN: 978-1-68117-808-0

Library of Congress Control Number: 2017938838

Socialy Press

(An Imprint of Scitus Academics),

616, Corporate Way, Suite 2, 4766,

Valley Cottage, NY 10989

www.scitusacademics.com

Notice

Printed in United States of America.

PREFACE

The different components that make up civil society, such as social movements, trade unions, NGOs, and the media, often interact in a way that generates or motivates actions or reactions that impact the state of a conflict. Any attempt to capture the vigor, complexity, and idiosyncrasies of interaction among government policymaking institutions, humanitarian organizations, and the media will suffer form oversimplification. Interactions among the three are complex. Governments not only make policy but also have their own implementing humanitarian agencies. Many governmental and private humanitarian organizations seek to influence the processes and results of public policy formation. All implementing agencies are subject to decisions reached by policymakers and may be subject to media scrutiny. All those with an interest in humanitarian crises, whether governmental, intergovernmental, or private, share analytical and operational problems. Whether a disaster is conveyed in the media and how this is done depends on numerous criteria, which are infrequently publicized to the recipients and especially the persons involved in the disaster. Major disasters such as the Haiti earthquake in 2010 or the triple disaster in Japan in 2011 are events that are picked up by the media worldwide and can create fear, compassion and feelings of powerlessness in the recipient. The media bring images, as well as emotions, to our living rooms. This is important for NGOs because of the power of the media, where competing commercial companies are particularly prominent due to circulation or audience.

Companion to Media and Humanitarian Action explores the interconnections between media, old and new, and the humanitarian challenges that have come to define the twenty-first century. It introduces the complex humanitarian arena in which the news media, humanitarian institutions and government policymakers interact. We analyze each of these institutions with reference to its agendas and interests, its range of responses to humanitarian crises, and its limitations. It presents various frameworks for analyzing the timing, level and degree of news media impact on government policymaking and humanitarian action. It examines the relationship among the news media, government policymakers and humanitarian organizations. Studies of media practices and content analysis and evaluation of media coverage and representations of humanitarian emergencies and affairs offer further insight into the ways in which strategic communications are designed and implemented in field of humanitarian action.

TABLE OF CONTENTS

1

OPTIMIZING SOCIAL MEDIA IN HUMANITARIAN CRISIS RESPONSES

Mark J. Mullaney

Macalester College

ABSTRACT

The genesis of the internet has led to a new technological age that is quickly connecting the world. The enormity of the internet's potential is difficult to fully comprehend, even for the innovators who developed it. Over time, some internet "mainstays" have begun to gain wide acceptance as fundamental building blocks allowing for improved and meaningful interaction. Some of these mainstays include search engines, online marketplaces, and the topic of this essay: social media websites. There are certainly many advantages to social media sites, but some aspects of social media—such as anonymity and a lack of proper verification methods—are leading to skepticism among the academic community over how to optimize its use for the greater good of society. This essay will look in-depth at how social media use can improve responses to humanitarian emergencies.

In order to further the academic dialogue concerning social media in humanitarian situations, this paper will first evaluate past related literature. Because social media is such a recent phenomenon, most research related to it is still in its infancy, and the research that has been published is mainly focused on observations during particular humanitarian crises. This paper will evaluate the sparse literature that does exist concerning social media and humanitarianism, which can be divided into three main debates: the trustworthiness of social media sources, the difficulties of implementing social media in crisis situations, and the ways we can analyze social media data and testimonies. Additionally, this paper will analyze several recent crises where social media played a notable role in the response efforts. The case studies— the 2010 earthquake in Haiti, and election fallouts in Iran (2009) and Kenya (2008)—give a diversity of locations and types of crises. In analyzing the academic framework and case studies, this paper will break down humanitarian communication into four levels: within, without, outside looking in, and inside looking out. It then will describe how each category is affected by social media. This leads to a section on the general and situational barriers to integrating social media in humanitarian responses. By looking at the potential of social media and the barriers to implementation, this paper puts forth three prescriptions for optimizing social media in humanitarian responses:

1. Establish an information aggregation website that can receive data from numerous sources and quickly process and analyze it in real time.
2. Encourage humanitarian actors to involve local groups in crafting communications strategy with the available resources.
3. Focus future research on social media postings and how to identify and respond to trends during humanitarian responses.

These actions will make responders more coordinated with each other and more agile in reacting to information as it comes in. By improving our understanding and use of social media, we can respond quicker and avoid being reliant on slower-moving "official accounts", perhaps saving more lives as a result.

BACKGROUND

The term "Social Media", much like the websites the term denotes, is constantly changing and fluid in its purpose and composition. The label has been used for a large number of internet entities, so much so that the uniting thread between them is fairly simple: instant communication and interaction. This can mean a lot of things, but the real upstart of social media as a widespread phenomenon is linked to a specific change in thinking about the internet, termed by electronic information design consultant Darcy DiNucci as "Web 2.0" (DiNucci, 1999). This idea of shifting away from centralized websites and towards user-generated content slowly pushed the internet towards what we know today as social media.

There are many types of social media websites, varying greatly in style and purpose but nonetheless underneath the umbrella of sites that enable user-based sharing and communication. Social networking sites like Facebook and Twitter allow users to amass "friends" or "followers" who will see and be allowed to comment on user activity. "User activity" can include simple thoughts on the day, links to photos and videos, articles from other websites, and much more. Content hosting sites like YouTube and Photobucket are similar in nature, but focus more on clean display of content. They allow users to upload videos and photos for anybody to see.

Another notable social media category is the information exchange-focused web world, typified by sites like Digg, Reddit, and Stumbleupon. Such sites' users identify intriguing and relevant items on the internet—articles, videos, etc.—and allow users to vote them "up" or "down" depending on whether they feel it should be more or less prominently displayed.

Social media has not been without its critiques, as cultural observers have come to question its effect on depth of thought and attention spans. The natures of sites like Facebook and Twitter capture tiny bits of life in 140-character bits and pieces. The most watched YouTube videos are rarely longer than a couple of minutes, perhaps because its layout includes "suggested videos" and encourages flipping between endless arrays of short, easy-to-digest media content. Considering the characteristics of traditional news media, which itself relies on short sound bites and flashy production values to keep viewers from flipping the channel, the case can be made that social media websites foster an anti-critical atmosphere in modern society to an even further degree (Rodgers, 2005).

Despite its flaws, it seems certain that social media will only become more widespread, accessible, and important in the workings of society as technology continues to grow. In response, scholars have begun to research the ways in which social media may help in humanitarian emergencies as a way of improving overall responses to crises. While this research is in its infancy, it has clustered around certain specific barriers that exist for using social media in humanitarian crises. This next section will address the three main academic debates on social media and humanitarianism: evaluating the trustworthiness of social media sources, incorporating social media in crisis responses, and interpreting and using social media data and testimonies.

LITERATURE REVIEW

One of the primary concerns associated with social media is the reliability of the information that is transmitted. Because social media's primary attribute is immediacy, it is impossible to have a verification mechanism that would be able to evaluate the truthfulness of every tweet and status update. However, this should not be considered reason enough to avoid relying on social media information—there is simply too much potential within social media to ignore. Scholars have taken different approaches to understand and adapt to the reliability gap in social media.

Determining how to analyze and use the waves of social media data commonly found during humanitarian crises is a big step in utilizing social media to its full potential. The difficulty is how to assess the quality of information—whether good or bad, intentionally misleading or not—in a situation where massive amounts of data are pouring in. According to one study, the answer is found by use of "everyday analytic skills" typically used during crises; these skills may be improved with practice and could be supplemented by the development of "analytical support tools," (Palen, Vieweg, & Anderson, 2011). They say that the importance of developing such tools cannot be understated, as "people will increasingly incorporate information from digital sources into decision making and assess it against the local circumstances they experience," (60). This study focused primarily on how amateur social media reporting can lead to better understanding of the situation among responding organizations. While the ability to process reliability from an organizational standpoint is important to improve future humanitarian responses, it also only accounts for one level of the social media interaction sphere. As risk communication specialist Nathan Huebner described in a recent Social Media roundtable, "Social media is obviously about more than how we reach out to the public and educate the public…it's about the public talking to us. It's also about the public talking to the public," (Currie, et al., 2009). Despite the difficulties of social media data verification, there are nonetheless many other aspects of social media that are also important and rely less on unverified accounts of crises.

Another concern with social media reporting is the way that medium and circumstances can affect message. Schultz, Utz, and Goritz recently completed a public relations study on how variances in message and medium affected reaction and response to crisis situations (2011). Their findings indicated that the medium of a message has specific, consistent effects in three measures: reputation, secondary crisis communication, and reactions. Meanwhile, an identical message across different media does not have the same uniform effects. The study illustrates that social media is viewed with a unique understanding of credibility—perhaps one of less official reputation, but nonetheless seen as timely and reactive to the issues of the moment.

This unique view of social media's credibility has a direct effect on crisis managers' ability to control messaging. In the wake of the Virginia Tech shooting of 2007, public relations officials from the school found it difficult to control the message of traditional media coverage, largely because newspapers and television news networks were more likely to use "citizen generated content" during the first stage of the crisis, and more likely to use non-official sources than official sources for overall coverage (Wigley & Fontenot, 2010). Several implications arise from this conclusion. First, social media allows for peoples' gut reactions to an incident before it has a chance to get framed by public relations officials. Second, greater value has been placed on the experiential details of crises as opposed to official facts and figures. Third, skepticism about overly-polished PR statements may lead people to seek out unofficial sources, despite the lack of verification mechanisms.

While social media may offer certain advantages over other information sources, its benefits can only be helpful if it is implemented properly. Many challenges exist for integrating social media within humanitarian responses, especially in areas with less technological development and in crisis situations that result in internet and power failures. However, if the proper means are used, "It speeds up communication, and, for all practical purposes, it speeds up awareness," according to American Public Health Association Executive Director Georges Benjamin (Currie, et al., 2009). This section will look at the opportunities presented by social media, the difficulties of implementation, and some of the unique ways people have started to use social media to improve humanitarian responses.

At the 2009 National Association of Government Communicators roundtable on social media in times of crisis, one of the few points that all participants agreed upon was that social media undoubtedly presents an opportunity to improve crisis communication.

While the public has flocked to the Internet and smart phones with access to online content, the emergency community has only begun to catch up. Yet, as the survey data suggests, there is a definite trend toward adoption—and more importantly, toward strategic implementation. (Currie, et al., 2009)

Participants found that one of the key benefits of social media is the ability to send critical information immediately to as many people as possible. Further, military research has shown that in times of crisis, information-sharing reduces fear because of a feeling of connectedness (Woodcock, 2009). That study goes on to point out that the decentralized nature of social networks is actually a strategic advantage, as it is much more difficult to completely shut down.

Despite these advantages, there is no clear path to implementing social media in humanitarian responses. The NAGC roundtable identified four main difficulties of social media integration: Private/Public Partnerships, Evaluation/Metrics, Capacity/Resources, and Social Media/Communications Strategy (Currie, et al., 2009). Partnerships can be difficult to come by, especially for international humanitarian crises, because of the ad hoc nature of responses as well as potential distrust of international actors. Evaluation poses difficulties because of the massive amount of immediate data verification necessary. Resources are problematic because of technology failures during natural disasters and potential state-sanctioned internet outages to prevent communication with the outside world, not to mention developing countries without internet access. Finally, a specific strategy must be formed and executed to assure maximum benefit—an unlikely prospect without serious thought about the methods of integration. Woodcock laments, "Unfortunately, public safety officials have not embraced Web 2.0 technologies and are missing a great opportunity to engage the public and harness its collective power. With virtually no capital investment, public safety agencies can create an innovative partnership by capitalizing on tools the public uses everyday," (2009). While U.S. military officials may be behind in implementation, other groups have already begun to use social media constructively in crisis situations.

A notable advance in the use of social media can be found in the National Institute of Health's crisis mapping research (NIH, 2010). Headed by Dr. Rebecca Goolsby, their project analyzed different online crisis maps, where people were able to report incidents and contribute to an aggregated map of these reports. Goolsby notes that the basic technology—most prominently, texting—for this type of mapping is widely available, stating, "New communication pathways are changing the less wired world," (2010). She also addresses the reliability questions of social media, arguing that it is "reliable on the aggregate" because the large sample size negates any false "outliers". As maps become more established and reliable, they tend to become "community projects" that participants take ownership of and pride in.

Other groups, large and small, have integrated social media into their work as a way to improve humanitarian responses. Software engineer David Kobia was recently named the "Humanitarian of the Year" by Technology Review for his work on a software program, "Ushahidi," that allows users to upload news reports, facilitating later analysis and improvement upon responses (Greenwald, 2010). The technology has already been used in Sudan, Gaza, Haiti, and during the BP oil spill. Other scholars have researched how implementation of social media within NGO's often is divided into three stages: technology stage, mutual infusion stage, and service-led stage (Chang, Liao, Wang & Chang, 2010). This roadmap for social media implementation will certainly be adjusted in years to come, but provides a basic blueprint for how to go about incorporating it.

The data surrounding social media will continue to grow due to frequency of use and increased incorporation, but another difficulty of social media is how to navigate through this constant, often unfiltered mass of information. One proposal for doing so is the creation of the Crisis Oriented Search Engine (COSE), a program that collects and stores social media information during times of crisis (Novinger, 2010). Because social media sites only save so many pieces of activity, much of that data can be lost during emergencies because of high traffic volume. By saving this activity, we can look back and see minute-by-minute the type of information we received from everyday citizens, which may lead to better future synthesis of data.

The recurring theme of social media data analysis in the military and humanitarian arena is the fact that information-sharing is beneficial for all involved. In 2002, the Worldwide Civil Affairs Conference endorsed the idea of information sharing between humanitarian and military groups as "essential", stating that "Location and networking capacity of the military informationsharing function is critical to effective coordination," (US Institute of Peace). Since that conference, social media exploded in popularity and curiosity about real-time crisis data sharing led to Exercise24, an emergency simulation where social media and cloud computing technologies were stressed in order to improve reactions. Social media technologies "equip the average citizen with the power of observation", and then empower them to upload those observations and compare them to the aggregation of other social media reports in order to choose the best course of action (Howe, 2010). The study's final conclusion reiterates our earlier stated points about the multiple levels of social media communications:

It is important that information sharing in a crisis occurs between individuals within government, between government employees and communities of interest, between researchers and government data, between the government and its citizens, and between governments of different countries. (Howe)

Sharing is most important because of the need for compiling as much information as possible to reach accurate conclusions. The social media boom is still extremely new from a research standpoint, and optimal use will require transparency and information-sharing in order to "synthesize the information into readily understood situational awareness models," (Howe).

To further establish that information sharing, research of social media aggregations, and piecewise implementation are necessary to optimize use of social media, this paper will now turn to several recent case studies where social media activity was particularly notable. These cases, Haiti during the 2010 earthquake, Iran during their 2009 election, and Kenya during their 2008 election, will illustrate how social media was used and the ways that social media might have been employed more successfully. This discussion will lead to an analysis of social media in specifically humanitarian crises, showing its effects, negative consequences, and potential for better implementation.

CASE STUDIES

The earthquake that devastated Haiti in early 2010 combined many of the worst elements of humanitarian crises, as massive destruction and confusion rocked the island nation that had already been suffering from a lack of resources and infrastructure. Social media played a crucial role in the multi-faceted response efforts, connecting victims to aid workers, military officials to humanitarian NGOs, and concerned witnesses to the appropriate avenues for helping.

This emergency serves as a clear example of how many distinct lines of communication are facilitated by social media. In addition to increasing access to news coverage, internet technology also expanded opportunities for volunteers, enhanced on-the-ground operations, and improved military-NGO coordination. Crisis mapping was better, quicker, and more widely available than in previous emergencies. Outsider participation was encouraged through Facebook and Twitter campaigns, as well as with simple fundraising efforts, where one could donate $10 to Haiti simply by sending one text message. The U.S. military worked with the World Food Programme to line up deliveries of aid shipments. Even ordinary citizens sitting at home could contribute to relief efforts by monitoring Twitter for missing person's reports and recording descriptions in a database. Though these efforts may have been somewhat linked to Haiti's geographic proximity to the United States, the fact remains that many aspects of the social media response efforts made a crucial difference in the alleviation of suffering (Slaugh, 2010).

Despite the successes of the social media response, there was still room for critique over the ways social media was and wasn't used. According to one study, both NGOs and news media organizations used social media well for information dissemination and disclosure. However, one shortcoming was the way that these groups did not capitalize on the two-way nature of social media (Muralidharan, Rasmussen, Patterson & Shin, 2011). Perhaps because of the dubious understanding of user report credibility, that information was underutilized. The same study also found that nonprofit social media transmissions generally conveyed a positive perspective, while news media reports carried a more negative tone. This is particularly surprising since it runs in contrast to one of David Rieff's criticisms of humanitarian aid organizations in 2002's A Bed for the Night: that they are overly reliant on hyper-negative portrayals of humanitarian crises as a way to influence donors.

An example of social media use in a complex political emergency can be found in the wake of Iran's 2009 Presidential elections, suspected by many to be election fraud. The Iranian government used 20th century tactics to try and stop a 21st century social movement. In 2005, there were over 700,000 Persian language blogs, 60,000 of which were updated on a frequent basis (Mottahedeh, 2010). After the 2005 election, the Iranian government made a concerted effort to centralize the national media, a mistake considering that, as mentioned earlier, social media is a naturally decentralized entity. The 2009 election was marred by charges of fraud, and many took to Twitter to decry their outrage. Despite the Iranian government's efforts—cutting out SMS messaging and the Internet for a week after the elections—protests grew stronger, and pictures and videos of the discontent still made it to the web.

The Iranian election fraud most prominently highlighted how the "small stories" told on social media can galvanize the public to substantial action. Two examples prove this: the killing of Neda Soltan and the arrest of Majid Tavakoli. Neda Soltan, known throughout the world simply by her first name, which means "voice" or "calling", was an Iranian protester killed by gunshot at a rally (Mottahedeh). A video of the incident spread across the internet and became a symbol of the struggle against an anti-democratic Iranian government. Her story inspired many to speak up against the increasingly brutal rule of Mahmoud Ahmadinejad.

Majid Tavakoli was a student activist who also opposed the apparent election fraud in Iran. After giving a speech on the controversy, he was arrested, and a photo of him in a hijab—a traditional veil worn by females—was released by officials. Though the photo was intended to discredit Tavakoli as a coward who attempted to flee in women's clothes, the photo was imitated by many social media users as a sign of solidarity. Many people also tinted their Twitter and Facebook "profile pictures" a shade of green, the opposition movement's colour, to form a social media "sea of green" against the Iranian election fraud.

Once again, social media was employed in a humanitarian crisis, leading to results that could not have been achieved before the advent of Web 2.0. In previous generations, an authoritarian regime cutting off media and communications efforts may have quelled the outrage about election fraud. However, thanks to the connectedness of today's technology, and the inspirational stories of several protesters, the world's eyes turned to Iran. That being said, the social media campaign simply wasn't enough to bring about actual political change to the region. Political circumstances, international alliances, and fears over Iran's destructive capabilities all contributed to the inaction after the election. However, indications exist that change is possible in the future, as several other social media-influenced revolutions have taken place across the Middle East, confirming the importance of social media coordination in present day political movements.

Kenya's 2008 post-election crisis was similar in nature and in social media response to the Iran situation. The election, a closely contested race between incumbent Mwai Kibaki and opposition party candidate Raila Odinga turned to chaos after Kibaki was declared the winner amid Odingas claims that the electoral commission had "doctored the results," (Makinen & Wangu, 2008). The confusion deepened when internal security minister—and Kibaki ally—John Michuki imposed a ban on live broadcasts and SMS messaging, "in the interests of public safety and tranquility," (Reporters Without Borders, 2007).

Again, as in Iran, citizens actually became empowered by the traditional media limitations, using social media to organize, discuss, and report their personal experiences. The usual social media suspects were again in action: Facebook and Twitter for organizing and spreading awareness, YouTube and Flickr to distribute images from Kenya, and active crisis maps to show citizens where it is safe to be (Makinen & Wangu). A difficulty in these efforts is that Kenya does not have a large population with internet access—only 3.2%, according to Makinen and Wangu. They suggest that mobile phone technology may be more effective in less developed countries. The advantage of text messaging is that many more Kenyans have access to such technology; a difficulty is that there exists no centralized "text message board" where everyone can look at the aggregation of messages to determine the best course of action.

These three case studies have shown how social media has already made an impact on humanitarian crisis responses. Haiti showcased how many levels of communication can be facilitated through social media. Iran and Kenya both illustrate how traditional media shutdowns no longer can keep news from being transmitted. However, all three situations could have been executed better, and through more research and analysis of how past crises incorporated social media, the future of social media in humanitarian responses can be more effective, more efficient, and more catered to each specific situation.

ANALYSIS

To analyze the ways that social media change how to execute humanitarian crisis responses, this paper will first look at the different levels of communication affected by social media. Highlighting examples from the case studies in each level, this paper will determine which levels of communication are particularly strong or weak in specific types of crisis. This will lead to a discussion of the negative consequences of social media and the most significant difficulties with integrating social media within humanitarian responses. This paper concludes with a number of prescriptions for improving the ways that social media gets used for crisis response.

One of the biggest impacts that social media have had in recent humanitarian crises is with visibility and how the world sees a crisis. This first category, the "outside looking in", is exemplified in the Haiti earthquake response as well as the political unrest in Kenya, Iran, and more recently, Egypt. Observers are able to get quicker, more colloquial descriptions of a crisis because social media users are reporting in real time how the situation is affecting their lives. Especially in times where political entities attempt to silence traditional media sources, social media is strong because of its decentralized nature. Even when the internet itself has been shut off, other technologies such as text messaging have been employed to show the world what is happening. Just as the advent of televised news pulled people closer to war-ravaged countries, social media connects humanity in an even more direct manner, leading to an even deeper level of dedication to humanitarian causes.

The second level of communication facilitated by social media is the "inside looking out" sphere, where victims and citizens of affected countries contact the outside world. The ability to tell the story of those on the ground experiencing the crisis is important for a variety of reasons. On a personal level, victims gain a sense of empowerment in being able to show the world what is happening to them. Especially in complex humanitarian emergencies, victims tend to feel surrounded and without allies, and the mere idea of others listening to their problems can be meaningful. Additionally, the "inside looking out" communication level can help aid organizations know what areas are most in need, leading to a more efficient distribution of assistance. When every victim has a defined role to play in a time of crisis, they are more likely to stay engaged instead of falling into complacency. In the Iran and Kenya case studies, this selfreporting was an extremely important role, since it was the only source for information on the unrest. Rebecca Goolsby's analysis on crisis mapping offers a similar conclusion, arguing that communities take pride and ownership of their crisis maps, leading to a united populace.

Communication within a humanitarian crisis is critical for a successful response. As observed earlier, most responders agree that a policy of transparent information-sharing is important to help coordinate aid distribution. While the "inside looking out" communication level is important for identifying high-need areas, it isn't enough if that information is hoarded by one group. A major success on the "communication within" level can be found in the Haiti case study, as the World Food Programme worked in conjunction with the U.S. military to distribute food aid quickly and efficiently in the highest-need areas. Also from Haiti, the personlocation initiative—where volunteers would monitor social media feeds and record mentions of missing and found people—made it much easier to unite separated families. Especially in countries with little to no infrastructure, social media are helpful in keeping communication lines open.

The final level of communication—communication without—is most relevant for fundraising and spreading awareness about humanitarian crises. Many options are available for outside actors who want their personal networks to know (and care) about an emergency. Facebook and Twitter posts are the most obvious resource, especially since we know that those venues often flare up during important global events, the most recent example being the flurry of internet activity after the announcement that Osama bin Laden had been killed by U.S. forces. Beyond this, there are many other avenues to spread awareness: social media applications that solicit donations, YouTube and blog posts describing the importance of recent events, NGO websites that facilitate discussion about response efforts, emails to corporations that typically supply aid in emergencies, and countless other humanitarian internet sites. A valuable aspect of this communication level is that technological infrastructure is established across the affluent world, so social media and internet fundraising efforts have the potential to be extremely effective.

It would be ignorant to assume that the advent of social media yields only positive consequences, especially considering how powerful and versatile modern technology has become. After all, if the "good guys" can use communication to alleviate suffering and improve response efficiency, then the "bad guys" can communicate ways to impart suffering. The recent roundtable on social media and risk communications detailed one example of the unintended negative consequences of modern technology, describing a terrorist attack in India that was facilitated by a number of media and internet resources.

The 10 gunmen, well armed with assault rifles and grenades, Richard Kolko [chief of the FBI's National Press Office] pointed out, 'were experts in communications as well.' Media outlets unintentionally interfered with police efforts by pinpointing for the terrorists where law enforcement was arriving by helicopter. Meanwhile, the terrorists had effectively used tools such as Google Earth maps and photos to scout a location before the deadly attack and used a GPS device to navigate across the Arabian Sea. (Currie, et al., 2009)

In that particular instance, social media were also their undoing, as text messages, tweets, and Flickr photos were the first images of the attacks available to the world. The lesson remains: terrorists and combatants are able to take advantage of social media. Terrorist networks like AlQaeda have long been known to operate as a decentralized entity with "hubs" in different locations; it would follow that they may benefit from decentralized communication methods.

Another negative aspect of social media, partially addressed by Goolsby's "aggregation" theory, is that every post cannot be individually verified and processed. This can lead to false information, whether it is misinformation or disinformation, and a lack of legitimate reliability. It also means that reaction time to social media reports cannot be quite as "instant" as with verified sources. For example, with the recent killing of Osama bin Laden, there was actually a nearby onlooker who posted an account of the operation on Twitter as it was happening (Gross, 2011). Had Pakistani officials, or Al Qaeda sympathizers, for that matter, been able to instantly assess that information, they could have investigated the operation much earlier and perhaps changed the end outcome. This is not so much a "negative consequence" of social media as it is a reality about the venue. For now, we must analyze social media posts in large volume, spotting common trends in order to determine the truth.

In addition to the negative consequences of widely accessible social media, there also exist a number of fundamental roadblocks that currently prevent full integration of social media in humanitarian responses. Different roadblocks affect different levels of communication, and identifying how to eliminate or work around these roadblocks within each level will ensure that responses maximize the potential of social media. This section will focus on several significant roadblocks, analyzing their characteristics as we lead into prescriptions for expanded use of social media.

The most basic barrier preventing full use of social media is the lack of technological infrastructure in many areas of the world. The United States is undoubtedly the center of the social media universe; some argue that the main reason why Haiti received elevated social media attention is because of its geographic proximity (Muralidharan, Rasmussen, Patterson & Shin). While Western countries have incorporated the internet within daily life, many developing countries have little or no access to social media. Equally problematic, these countries often have much more pressing problems to deal with than spotty internet access. Expanding internet access to the entire world is a difficult task that requires an immense amount of upfront investment costs. It is likely that one day the entire world will be "online", but without massive funding from the Western world, that day remains far in the future.

Even for countries with an established internet infrastructure, consistent internet access during a time of crisis cannot be guaranteed. In the case of natural disasters, internet access is often wiped out by the emergency, perhaps even leading to greater confusion from people who rely on internet sources for disaster information. For complex humanitarian emergencies, as we've seen in Iran and Kenya, authoritarian figures may shut off internet access intentionally to prevent opposition groups from organizing. In either case, most of the established social media outlets are not accessible, making it much more difficult to communicate.

Many of the other main concerns for social media integration have already been addressed and repeated in the literature review and case studies. Not only access, but also reliability, information-sharing, social media use instruction, and data analysis are all major concerns that manifest themselves because of the unprecedented level of connectedness associated with social media. The expert roundtable on Social Media and Risk Communication identified four categories of issues that need resolution to ensure full integration: Public/Private Partnerships, Evaluation/Metrics, Capacity/Resources, and Social Media/Communications Strategy. We will use that framework to offer prescriptions for social media implementation in humanitarian crisis responses, exploring how those four categories interact with the four levels of communication.

Addressing relationships between public and private entities in humanitarian responses is mainly related to the "without" and "outside looking in" levels, as the main concern is how different actors interact with each other. Several of our case studies confirm that in times of crisis, information-sharing is a mutually beneficial way for NGOs, militaries, and IOs can coordinate and identify particular areas of need. Furthermore, aggregating social media data helps analysts identify trends and create more accurate reports of the "on-the-ground" situation. This can lead to creation of better crisis maps that can in turn be distributed to crisis victims. To strengthen Private/Public Partnerships, I advocate for the creation of humanitarian databases, administrated by an independent organization, specifically in charge of processing and redistributing critical information as it rolls in.

Scholars have already proposed a number of ways to evaluate and measure social media data and its helpfulness in humanitarian interventions. In the long-term, mechanisms like Ushahidi and the Crisis Oriented Search Engine (COSE) are outstanding resources for evaluating how humanitarian crises unfolded and what actions had the most positive impact. This is clearly the "without" communication level, as outsider groups analyze how they intervened and what can be improved. The greater difficulty is the "in the moment" evaluation—a more complex relationship that involves the "inside looking out", "outside looking in", and "without" levels. Hypersensitivity to small bits of information can lead to mistakes, but waiting too long for confirmed trends is equally problematic, as the fear of being wrong may lead to hesitance during life-saving opportunities. An information-sharing database is again key, as is past humanitarian response research. If we hone our "everyday analytics" by evaluating other crises and understanding trends, we will be able to respond quicker when trends are starting to present themselves.

Capacity and Resources are substantial barriers to social media integration in developing countries. Situated in the "within" and "inside looking out" communication levels, the reality is that very little can be changed in relation to resources once a crisis is underway. The long-term solution is obviously to get the entire world on the internet, but such a task is easier said than done. In the immediate future, humanitarian actors must recognize the resource limitations and take measures to compensate for the lack of certain social media outlets. Cell phone technology is much more commonplace in the developing world, and text messaging is very similar to Twitter and Facebook status updates, only directed to a specific phone number. By establishing and publicizing a "reporting hotline", responders can still aggregate victim reports and go about trend-spotting in a similar way to social media. It may even be possible to have a television feed with this information, perhaps even synthesized into a "crisis map" or another easily-digestible transmission.

Social Media and communications strategy is the most variable of the four challenges, as it depends on a number of situational factors including number of actors, severity of threat, and availability of resources. It is difficult to offer standardized prescriptions for communication strategy, but the main focus must be on giving agency to the local population. Even though this is situated in the "outside looking in" communication level, the ability of local officials and groups to understand and redistribute information is more important than the outsiders' organizational goals or priorities. If the message isn't relevant or maximally beneficial to its recipients, not only will it not be processed or distributed, but it may jeopardize future lines of communication. Because of this, local actors must be involved as much as possible in the communication strategy, to ensure that the information distribution is effective.

CONCLUSION

The social media explosion of the last decade has had remarkable effects on many aspects of everyday life. Just as humanitarian crises became "closer to home" with the advent of televised news, social media has once again cut down the space between victims and witnesses. But while the potential for social media to help facilitate humanitarian response is great, there has been a degree of skepticism from scholars and humanitarian actors about its immediate usefulness. This essay has identified three main concerns related to social media: reliability of data, implementation within responses, and analysis of social media data.

Our case studies, the earthquake in Haiti and political unrest in Iran and Kenya, highlighted how multifaceted social media can be in impacting humanitarian crises. Response to the Haitian earthquake was extremely strong, and information sharing and cooperation between NGOs and states helped reunite family members and allocate food aid to the areas with the greatest need. Iran and Kenya both showed how social media gives victims agency and empowers them to organize and unite in spite of an authoritarian government. Overall, these cases highlighted how there are many ways social media can contribute to humanitarian responses, and how even if resource shortcomings limit certain avenues of communication. We identified four levels of communication that occur during humanitarian crises: within, without, inside looking out, and outside looking in. Each is unique, involves different actors, and can be helped by social media in different ways.

We concluded with several prescriptions for the future of social media in humanitarianism. First, we advocated for establishing an information aggregation website that can receive data from numerous sources (social media websites, NGOs, IOs, military groups)

and quickly processes and analyzes them in a manner similar to the "Ushahidi" software program. Second, we encourage humanitarian actors to involve local groups in crafting a communications strategy. Despite the potential lack of social media resources at the crisis site, it is nonetheless important to stay linked in any way possible in order to ensure that all crisis communications are situation-appropriate and that credibility is not lost due to improper messaging. Finally, this paper strongly endorses future research on social media postings and their relation to humanitarian responses. There is a massive amount of data stored from recent humanitarian crises, and an equally massive amount of potential links and trends that can be identified. By evaluating timelines that incorporate social media data, timing of humanitarian responses, and local activity, responders can be better prepared for future crises and understand how the events correlate with one another. It is through practice, preparation, and familiarity that social media can be used to the fullest in humanitarian responses. Social media can be an extremely effective tool in these situations, and by optimizing its use, responders can better uphold the humanitarian imperative and alleviate suffering for more victims of humanitarian crises.

WORKS CITED

1. Chang, Y.-J., Liao, R.-H., Wang, T.-Y., & Chang, Y.-S. (January 01, 2010). Action Research as a Bridge Between Two Worlds: Helping The NGOs and Humanitarian Agencies Adapt Technology to Their Needs. Systemic Practice and Action Research, 23, 3, 191-202

2. Currie, D., Fouse, D., Tinker, T., Association, A. P., Booz, A. &., University, G. W., et al. (2009). Social media and risk communications during times of crisis. McLean, VA: Booz Allen & Hamilton.

3. DiNucci, D. (1999). Fragmented Future. Design and New Media , pp. 32, 221-2.

4. Expert Round Table on Social Media and Risk Communication During Times of Crisis, Currie, D., Fouse, D., Tinker, T. L., American Public Health Association., Booz, Allen & Hamilton., George

Washington University., ... National Association of Government Communicators (U.S.). (2009). Social media and risk communications during times of crisis. McLean, VA: Booz Allen Hamilton

5. Goolsby, R., & National Institutes of Health (U.S.). (2010).Crisis maps and social behavior: How information from people will change crisis planning. Bethesda, Md: National Institutes of Health

6. Greenwald, T. (January 01, 2010). Humanitarian of the year: David Kobia, 32: software that helps populations cope with crises: Ushahidi.(INTERNET). Technology Review (cambridge, Mass.), 113, 5.)

7. Gross, D. (2011, May 2). Twitter user unkowingly reported bin Laden attack. Retrieved May 2, 2011, from CNN.com: http://politicalticker.blogs.cnn.com/2011/05/02/twitter-user-unknowinglyreported-bin-laden-attack/?iref=allsearch

8. Howe, A. W. (2010). Social cloud media and crowdsourcing in emergency management: An analytical review of Exercise24. San Diego, Calif: San Diego State University

9. Mäkinen, M., & Wangu, K. M. (January 01, 2008). Social Media and Postelection Crisis in Kenya. The International Journal of Press/politics, 13, 3, 328-335

10. Mottahedeh, N. (January 01, 2010). Green Is the New Green: Social Media and the Post-Election Crisis in Iran, 2009. New Politics, 13, 1, 65-68.

11. Muralidharan, S., Rasmussen, L., Patterson, D., & Shin, J.-H. (June 01, 2011). Hope for Haiti: An analysis of Facebook and Twitter usage during the earthquake relief efforts. Public Relations Review, 37, 2, 175-177

12. Novinger, M. T. (2010). COSE: Crisis Oriented Search Engine. (Masters Abstracts International, 48-5.)

13. Palen, L., Vieweg, S., & Anderson, K. M. (January 01, 2011). Supporting "Everyday Analysts" in Safety- and Time-Critical Situations. The Information Society, 27, 1, 52-62

14. Reporters without Borders. 2007. "Kenya: Government Imposes 'Dangerous and CounterProductive' News Blackout."

15. Rieff, David. A Bed for the Night: Humanitarianism in Crisis. New York: Simon and Schuster, 2002

16. Rodgers, R. (2005), New media effects: Do formats organize networks?. Complexity, 10: 22-34.

17. Schultz, F., Utz, S., & Goritz, A. (March 01, 2011). Is the medium the message? Perceptions of and reactions to crisis communication via twitter, blogs and traditional media. Public Relations Review, 37, 1, 20-27

18. Slagh, C. (2010). Managing chaos, 140 characters at a time: How the usage of social media in the 2010 Haiti crisis enhanced disaster relief. Georgetown University, USA.

19. Wigley, S., & Fontenot, M. (June 01, 2010). Crisis managers losing control of the message: A pilot study of the Virginia Tech shooting. Public Relations Review, 36, 2, 187-189

20. Woodcock, J., & Naval Postgraduate School (U.S.). (2009). Leveraging social media to engage the public in homeland security. Monterey, California: Naval Postgraduate School

21. Worldwide Civil Affairs Conference, & United States Institute of Peace. (2002). Good practices: Information sharing in complex emergencies : report from a roundtable on humanitarianmilitary information sharing : 2001 Worldwide Civil Affairs Conference. Washington, DC: U.S. Institute of Peace

2

EROSION OF TRUST IN HUMANITARIAN AGENCIES: WHAT STRATEGIES MIGHT HELP?

Saroj Jayasinghe

Department of Clinical Medicine, Faculty of Medicine, University of Colombo, Colombo, Sri Lanka

ABSTRACT

Aid agencies (AAs) provide a range of humanitarian and health related assistance globally. However, the trust placed on them is eroding. Evidence for this includes accusations of a decline in their humanitarianism, and the increasing number of conflicts with host states. An analysis of the concerns expressed yields two possible reasons: a relative lack of transparency of their work and weak accountability mechanisms. This is further supported by the existing milieu: an absence of internationally accepted instrument or mechanism to check the credentials of INGOs and an opaque system of close links between some of the INGOs and their donors. The article suggests two global strategies to tackle these issues: (a) Increase transparency by establishing a global register of aid agencies. This should have basic information: their main goals and activities, countries they are active in, number of employees, annual turnover of funds (updated regularly), principal financing sources and nature of links with donors. This could also be available as printed manual that should be freely available to client countries. (b) Ensure accountability by developing templates of fair legal instruments (to facilitate and regulate work), and a set of generic rules and procedures of engagement for the interactions between agencies and client states. These should be institutionalized within the regulatory frameworks of countries and included in the Codes of Conduct of NGOs.

Keywords: aid, philanthropy, trust, transparency, accountability

Aid agencies are organisations that are dedicated to distributing aid. At an international or global level, three categories can be identified: those functioning within governments (such as United States Agency for International Development [USAID] that is an institution within the US federal government) or between governments (e.g. United Nations Development Programme [UNDP] that is a global network linked to the UN) or 'independent' private organisations known as International Non-Governmental Organisations (INGOs). All these organisations play increasingly important roles in distributing development aid and humanitarian assistance. In recent times, the scope of work of these agencies, especially that of INGOs, (including medical philanthropists) have included an expanding circle of interests in the health arena: providing health care to the needy to responding to humanitarian crises to providing comprehensive packages of health services to administrative regions in developing countries 1.

The initiatives of INGOs are often supported by the international community, the WHO, and donors 12. However, in the recent past, there have been serious concerns on their conduct and a sense of mistrust developing among different stake holders. Evidence of mistrust includes accusations of compromising humanitarian ideals, eagerness for profits and media coverage and embracing political and religious agendas. The relief effort in 2010 in Haiti prompted an editorial of the *Lancet* (aptly titled *Growth of aid and the decline of humanitarianism*) to note that some organisations are driven by publicity and profit motives that compromise humanitarian ideals 3. It stated that '... large aid agencies can be obsessed with raising money through their own appeal efforts. Media coverage as an end in itself is too often an aim of their activities. Marketing and branding have too high a profile. Perhaps worst of all, relief efforts in the field are sometimes competitive with little collaboration between agencies...'. There are also increasing number of reports of conflicts and strains between INGOs and developing countries. Some of the conflicts indicate a perception among host governments and other observers that certain INGOs have hidden agendas 4. Events in Haiti in 2010, Sudan in 2009, in Iraq and in Southern Asia after the 2004 tsunami, illustrate the possible consequences of such a view. In Haiti, NGO workers were arrested for child trafficking during the relief efforts. Sudan accused the INGOs of conniving with the International Criminal Court to issue an arrest warrant for President Omar al-Bashir on charges of war crimes and crimes against humanity. This led to the expulsion of 10 prominent INGOs (e.g. Oxfam) that Sudan defended at the UN saying that they had transgressed from their mandate and dared to challenge Sudan's sovereignty 5:http://news.bbc.co.uk/ 2/hi/africa /7925509.stm[cited 25 October 2011].. In Iraq, faith-based NGOs were suspected of unfair proselytisation under cover of their humanitarian assistance, partly substantiated when certain Christian relief agencies announced their intention to mix humanitarian aid in Iraq with evangelisation 6Lampman J. A crusade after all? Plans of come Christian to evangelize as they offer aid pose dilemma for Iraqi reconstruction. Chris Sci Monitor. April 17, 2003. Available from:http://www.csmonitor. com/2003/0417/p14s01-lire.html[cited 25 October 2011].. A similar accusation was made after the tsunami of December 2004, when some faith-based NGOs were accused of attempting to blackmail vulnerable communities to enter their faith to receive aid 7.

ROOT CAUSES FOR EROSION OF TRUST

What are the root causes for this erosion of trust of humanitarian agencies, especially the INGOs? The answer is provided in part by analysing the concerns expressed in relation to the above events: the 2004 tsunami, the conflicts in Iraq and Sudan and the 2010 cyclone in Haiti 345:http:// news.bbc.co.uk/2/hi/africa/7925509.stm[cited 25 October 2011].6Lampman J. A crusade after all? Plans of come Christian to evangelize as they offer aid pose dilemma for Iraqi reconstruction. Chris Sci Monitor. April 17, 2003. Available from:http://www.csmonitor. com/2003/0417/p14s01-lire.html[cited 25 October 2011].7. All these situations had two main themes: an accusation of hidden agendas (i.e. a lack of transparency), and inadequacy of agreed mechanisms to ensure their accountability that led to erratic responses such as expulsion of INGOs from Sudan, arrest of volunteers in Haiti and fast-track regulatory changes in Sri Lanka.

An analysis of the current milieu also reveals why there is room for alleging lack of transparency. Firstly, there is an absence of internationally accepted instruments or mechanisms to check the credentials of INGOs. This is particularly important because INGOs are increasingly undertaking sensitive functions and roles. The INGOs active in Sudan undertook a range of activities from the least controversial areas such as provision of health care and humanitarian assistance, to the more sensitive areas of promoting human rights. This enables INGOs to interact with people from diverse settings and ability to influence communities in client states. As a result, it is relatively easy to be accused of 'interference' in national politics, cultures or ideologies. On the contrary, this wide range of activities also gives opportunities for unscrupulous INGOs to pursue hidden agendas other than pure altruism, as shown in the example on faith-based NGOs. These agendas could include political, social or commercial objectives (e.g. spreading the ideology of a free market), and aid for profit 234.

Secondly, there are almost opaque, secretive and close links between some of the INGOs and their donors. This situation is mainly a result of INGOs' dependency on external funding for their survival and growth. In reality, they negotiate with the donors on utilisation of funds and are accountable to the latter. The details of these negotiations and agreements are rarely made public, and remain unknown to host governments and 'client' communities where projects are conducted. As a result of this combination of factors, it is reasonable to suspect that some of the work programmes of INGOs are directly or indirectly driven by the agendas of global funding organisations, philanthropists and donors.

As for the alleged lack of accountability of INGOs, the main reason appears to be their ascendency in power. Over the years, they have gained influence, power and financial resources that often outweigh individual developing states, especially those with weak regulatory structures. It is said that 'a small handful *(of them)*, while working in some of the most dangerous and impoverished places on earth, wield enormous influence – setting aid agendas, shaping policy, and changing the way the world does development' 8Bronstein P, 2008. The List: The World's most powerful development NGOs. Foreign Policy. July 1, 2008. Available from:http://www.foreignpolicy.com/story/cms.php?story_id=4364][cited 25 October 2011].. A recent example is the renewed emphasis given by large philanthropic groups to control specific diseases such as malaria, HIV/AIDS and tuberculosis, which may have distorted health priorities in developing countries. These initiatives are criticised for promoting a selective form of primary health care and for promoting internal brain drain (from the public sector health system to the NGO sector), thus depleting already under-staffed health systems 9from:http://www.medicinasocial.info/index.php/socialmedicine/article/viewFile/193/352[cited 25 October 2011].10. This power to influence global and national health policies is derived from their large resource base of INGOs and philanthropists (e.g. Bill and Melinda Gates Foundation distributed US$ 2 billion in grants in 2006) that often exceeds the budgets of smaller nations, and their recognition by institutions such as the UN where some of INGOS have 'independent' observer status in statutory institutions, e.g. Economic, Social and Cultural Council of the UN [ECOSOC] 11 Available from:http://csonet.org/content/documents/E2010INF4.pdf[cited 25 October 2011].. By way of these memberships, some INGOs provide reports on the conduct of nation-states, and these encounters are known to be acrimonious. There is also the possibility of bias in the perspectives of INGOs because of approximately 3,000 of them in the ECOSOC's consultative category, about two-thirds are from North America and Europe, which constitutes less than a fifth of the global population. Despite this obvious asymmetry of power between INGOs and host states, there are no universally accepted guidelines or rules of engagement between host states and INGOs.

What can be done to stem this erosion of trust of INGOs? The author of this article proposes three main strategies and corresponding policy instruments to tackle the issues of relative lack of transparency and accountability, thereby improving the situation from global and national levels. It also delineates a potential role for a UN organisation such as the WHO.

Strategies to tackle root causes

There are at least three ways to tackle the root causes described in the previous section. These are 1 lack of transparency to be tackled by improving access to information of INGOs 2 weak accountability of INGOs to be countered by, developing a template of fair legal instruments, rules of engagement, and 3 procedures for the interactions between INGOs and host states.

IMPROVING ACCESS TO INFORMATION

Increasing access to information on INGOs could be achieved by establishing a Global Register of INGOs. The large number of INGOs, estimated in 2,000, to be around 26,000 makes this a truly global task, because a single nation or a grouping cannot keep track of the fast proliferating INGOs 12.

A Global Register of INGOs

The idea behind a Global Register is to collate and have accessible information on the INGOs. Relevant information includes, their goals, objectives, relationship to principal donors or faiths, portfolio of work and areas of expertise, previous work and their outcomes, sources of funds, annual summary budget (at local and international level), number of employees, areas of humanitarian assistance, approvals by other host states to provide humanitarian assistance and any situations where they were denied access to a country. The records of previous work should include an outline of the project, summary budgets, clients and donors and complying with time lines. An important aspect is a clear statement of the donors and the basic agreement made with the donors about specific projects. Expenditures should, perhaps, include the proportion spent on the project *per se* in contrast to the administrative costs (that includes consultation fees). The required information will improve transparency of the dealings of INGOs and should be updated at regular intervals. One may have to provide a hyperlink to the respective INGO website to give more elaborate information.

Entry into the Global Registry will require a process of validation. The process used by ECOSOC to award consultative status will provide a template 11 Available from:http://csonet.org/content/documents/E2010INF4.pdf[cited 25 October 2011].. One criterion could be that the INGO be a signatory to an acceptable code of conduct (e.g. the Code of Conduct of the International Red Cross and Red Crescent Movement). Second criterion could be to present supporting documentation from the countries where the INGO is already registered, funding sources and strategies for sustainability. Initially being in the register could be voluntary, and those wishing to work across national borders should be encouraged to be included. The register should be accessible globally via the Internet.

An example of a register in the UN system is the one by ECOSOC that has basic information of 3,187 NGOs that have links with the UN 11 Available from:http://csonet.org/content/documents/E2010INF4.pdf[cited 25 October 2011].. The information in this register is limited to activities of the NGO in relation to the UN. A more informative register is the one maintained by the Charity Commissioner's Office in the UK 13Charity Commissioners for England and Wales. Register of Charities. Available from:http://www.charity-commission.gov.uk/showcharity/registerof charities/registerhomepage.aspx?&=&[cited 25 October 2011].. The Office maintains a register of charities (almost 189,000), their governing documents and accounts (of those who earn more than 10,000 sterling pounds), all of which are accessible to the public. The register gives specific aspects of each registered charity (e.g. main activities, countries they work in, number of employees and annual turnover of funds, etc.). There are other examples of registers that have been developed to increase transparency and to facilitate access of information such as the clinical trials register of the US government 14. It lists more than 65,000 entries from 161 countries, with information about a trial's purpose, that may participate, locations and phone numbers for more details. Entry to the register requires approval 'by a human subject review board (or equivalent) and conform to the regulations of the appropriate national health authorities'. The registry is a public document and gives information to potential recruits as well as investigators.

Hosting the Register can be contentious, and the process will require dedicated funding and human resources. A UN-based institution such as the WHO or the UNDP or the ECOSOC could establish the register. The WHO that has some expertise in health ethics may be better placed to take the initiative in this endeavour. They could begin by hosting a register of INGOs working in the area of health. This experience could be used to widen scope where other INGOs are also progressively included. Such a mechanism of registering is not alien to the WHO that has a template for certification of institutions such as drug manufactures 15 Available from:http://www.who.int/medicines/areas/quality_safety/regulation_legis

lation/certification/guidelines/en/index.html[cited 25 October 2011].. The Global Register could also improve the quality of INGOs working in host states. In addition to being an authoritative source of information, host states could regulate that INGOs should be in the Register prior to working in the country.

The contents of the Register should also be available as a printed manual that could be used by state officials during negotiations. The Register could also include information in a tabulated form and updated at intervals, may be yearly.

A complaints procedure

To improve the process of accountability and transparency, there could be a special official or an ombudsman within the UN to arbitrate on serious conflicts in relation to entries in the Register. This is analogous to the office of the Independent Expert on Human Rights and International Solidarity, established in 2005 under the Human Rights Council. At times of conflict, the ombudsmen could solicit for information from relevant sources, directly observe the functioning of the INGOs by making country visits and evaluate the performance of INGOs using published reports.

Although this is not a foolproof system, a Global Register on the lines described above is a step in the right direction to reduce asymmetry of information and improve transparency of INGOs. This will enhance the credibility and trust on INGOs and facilitate the implementation of their humanitarian agendas.

FAIR LEGAL INSTRUMENTS, CODES OF CONDUCT AND RULES OF ENGAGEMENT

Most developed countries have regulatory instruments that enable the states to monitor and facilitate the work of the voluntary sector. In contrast, developing countries often have neither sophisticated regulatory instruments nor legislations to facilitate and regulate the voluntary sector. A recent example was the situation that arose after the December 2004 tsunami in Sri Lanka. In the aftermath, there were almost 2,000 new NGOs working on tsunami relief, as a result of an influx of foreign NGOs and newly established local ones. The government had to take several measures to control this chaotic situation (e.g. to require all NGOs to register their activities, in some instances obtain the Defence Ministry clearance, new procedures to grant visas and adoption of procedures to facilitate customs clearance) 7. This lack of clear legislations to meet diverse challenges during humanitarian emergencies leads governments to formulate ill-conceived measures. To meet this challenge and improve accountability of

INGOs, a generic template of a fair legal instrument ought to be developed. This will facilitate legitimate work within host countries, and although adding to bureaucracy it will prevent exploitation of its vulnerable citizens. The WHO could draw on its technical expertise to formulate such legal instruments, as has been done in other situations: setting 'ground rules for contracting practices' in the health sector and legislation to control tobacco 15 Available from:http://www.who.int/medicines/areas/quality_safety/regulation_legislation/certification/guidelines/en/index.html[cited 25 October 2011].16. Ideally, these legislations should be formulates by consensus within the international community, and enable INGOs to be aware of their potential and limitations for work in different countries. An illustrative example is the Charities Act of 2006 in England and Wales that defines the parameters of charity work by stating that 'an essential requirement of all charities is that they operate for the public benefit and independently of government or commercial interests' 13Charity Commissioners for England and Wales. Register of Charities. Available from:http://www.charity-commission.gov.uk/showcharity/registerofcharities/registerhomepage.aspx?&=&[cited 25 October 2011].. The Commissioner facilitates the work of the voluntary sector by releasing guidelines on good practice, releasing useful information (e.g. details of relevant legislations) via the Internet and by conducting training programmes. As part of their regulatory role, they review the accounts of charities and pay visits to observe the conduct of the charity organisations.

By their very nature, the voluntary sectors tend to be loosely knit and prefer a considerable degree of autonomy in their work. Thus, self-regulation is probably the most favoured strategy that would help them to harmonise the altruistic intentions with other constraints they experience. Therefore, another strategy is to develop, or improve existing codes to a globally accepted Code of Conduct 1017. There are a number of codes such as that of Red Cross, with varying degrees of success and after 10 years of its existence, by 2004 the Red Cross's Code had only 300 signatories 1017.

The Code could reiterate some of the aspects of the Global Register, taking into account the conditions stipulated in the generic regulatory template, and the 'rules of engagement' described below. For example, the Code could include a statement that INGOs should provide basic information as regards to their goals, objectives, work plans, funding sources to their client communities and make the agreements with donors accessible to clients and governments. Acceptance of the conditions of the Code could be a prerequisite for entry to the Global Register.

PROCEDURES FOR INTERACTIONS

The third option is to develop clear rules of engagement between INGOs and client states that promote fair procedures 18. These procedures for interactions should be institutionalised within the regulatory frameworks of host countries and in the Codes of Conduct of NGOs. They should be adhered to when INGOs wish to begin work in a host country. This will also increase transparency of transactions and prevent or soften conflicts.

An example of a fair procedural process is outlined below:

- *Initial public consultation:* This focuses on type of humanitarian assistance required by a nation-state and to establish 'ground rules'. A process of public consultation will enable to identify the broad needs of the communities, and the process could be facilitated by the government or local administration of a country. The 'ground rules' would focus on how to avoid conflicts in some of the areas: criteria to select areas for assistance, mix of services to be provided, fair selection of INGOs to provide assistance, espousing particular political, sociocultural or religious opinions. Other areas that could be discussed include ensuring equity of access to services, sustainability of interventions and evaluation of the performance of the INGOs. This will be a healthy exchange of ideas, and the different stakeholders will be able to know each other more closely. In contrast, the current situation in most countries is for the INGOs to obtain permission from a government department or authority to commence work in the country. The target community for humanitarian assistance is rarely consulted or made aware of the work or the projects of INGOs.

- *Process of decision making:* Decisions are made on overcoming the contentious issues listed above (and any others). These decisions ought to be based on reasons and principles that are explicitly stated. There should also be an inbuilt method to appeal against any decisions, for example, the appointment of an independent ombudsman who could arbitrate and make a final decision.

- *Publicity for decisions:* Publicity ought to be given to the decisions via official documents, media releases aimed especially at the client country.

- *Constant review*: A mechanism is in place in the country's regulatory system and within INGOs to review the policies regularly during the period when it is working and after completion of the project.

- *Enforcement:* There are mechanisms within the INGOs and the country's regulatory system to ensure that the above conditions are met. For example, INGOs are accountable to their Trustees or Board of Governors, donors and to the client country, if they default on their work plan. Some of the larger projects may even warrant an insurance policy, to cover against sudden unexpected disruption from the agreement.

Some may criticise these procedures as unnecessary and too bureaucratic. However, INGOs, donors and international organisations have clearly laid down extensive procedures for tenders and procurements for projects. If so, there is no reason as to why a similarly extensive document cannot be developed to explicitly state the ground rules for engagement between INGOs and client states. It is also necessary to enhance the capacities of states to negotiate with INGOs about the fair procedures described in the previous section. This objective can be achieved by producing manuals that describe the procedures and by conducting training programmes for state officials and civil society groups. The manuals ought to be available in print form as well as in the web.

CONCLUSION

Despite conducting difficult and essential humanitarian tasks, there is a sense of increasing mistrust of INGOs. The author proposes several related strategies and policy instruments that may help to tackle and reverse this situation. If preventive measures are not introduced at a global level, the trust between communities, countries and INGOs will gradually erode. This would eventually compromise the long-term provision of health care, humanitarian assistance, developmental aid and promotion of human rights by INGOs.

CONFLICT OF INTEREST AND FUNDING

The author has not received any funding or benefits from industry or elsewhere to conduct this study.

REFERENCES

1. Palmer N, Strong L, Wali A, Sondorp. Contracting out health services in fragile states. BMJ. 2006; 332: 718–21.
2. Gilson L, Sen PD, Mohammed S, Mujinja P. The potential of health sector nongovernmental organizations: policy options. Health Policy Plan. 1994; 9: 14–24.
3. Anonymous. Editorial: growth of aid and the decline of humanitarianism. Lancet. 2010; 375: 253.

4. Fisher WF. Doing good? The politics and antipolitics of NGO practices. Annu Rev Anthropol. 1997; 26: 439–64.

5. BBC mobile News. 2009. UN pleads with Sudan over ban. 5 March 2009. Available from: http://news.bbc.co.uk/2/hi/africa /7925509.stm [cited 25 October 2011].

6. Lampman J. A crusade after all? Plans of come Christian to evangelize as they offer aid pose dilemma for Iraqi reconstruction. Chris Sci Monitor. April 17, 2003. Available from: http:// www.csmonitor.com/2003/0417/p14s01-lire.html [cited 25 October 2011].

7. Jayasinghe S. Faith based NGOs and health care in poor countries: a preliminary exploration of ethical issues. J Med Ethics. 2007; 33: 623–26.

8. Bronstein P, 2008. The List: The World's most powerful development NGOs. Foreign Policy. July 1, 2008. Available from: http://www.foreignpolicy.com/story/cms.php?story_id=436 4] [cited 25 October 2011].

9. Katz A. New Global Health. A reversal of logic, history and principles. Soc Med. 2008; 3: 1–3. Available from: http://www. medicinasocial.info/index.php/socialmedicine/article/viewFile/19 3/352 [cited 25 October 2011].

10. Pfeiffer J, Johnson W, Fort M, Shakow A, Hagopian A, Gloyd S, *et al.*. Strengthening health systems in poor countries: a code of conduct for nongovernmental organizations. Am J Public Health. 2008; 98: 1234–40.

11. United Nations Department of Economic and Social Affairs. 2011. The NGO Branch. Available from: http://csonet.org /content/documents/E2010INF4.pdf [cited 25 October 2011].

12. Ferris E. Faith-based and secular humanitarian organizations. Int Rev Red Cross. 2005; 87: 312–25.

13. Charity Commissioners for England and Wales. Register of Charities. Available from: http://www.charity-commission.gov.uk /showcharity/registerofcharities/registerhomepage.aspx?&=& [cit ed 25 October 2011].

14. Hirsch L. Trial registration and results disclosure: impact of US legislation on sponsors investigators, and medical journal editors. Curr Med Res Opin. 2008; 24: 1683–9.

15. World Health Organization. Guidelines on the implementation of the WHO certification scheme on the quality of pharmaceutical products moving in international commerce. Available from: http://www.who.int/medicines/areas/quality_safety/regula

tion_legislation/certification/guidelines/en/index.html [cited 25 October 2011].

16. Kadai A, Sall FL, Andriantsara G, Perrot J. The benefits of setting the ground rules and regulating contracting practices. Bull World Health Organ. 2006; 84: 897–902.

17. Hilhorst D. Dead letter or living document? Ten years of the Code of Conduct for disaster relief. Disasters. 2005; 29: 351–69.

18. Beauchamp TL, Childress JF. Principles of biomedical ethics6th ed. Oxford University Press. Oxford, 2001

3

HOW DID THE MEDIA REPORT ON THE GREAT EAST JAPAN EARTHQUAKE? OBJECTIVITY AND EMOTIONALITY SEEKING IN JAPANESE MEDIA COVERAGE

Yukiko Uchida[1]*, Chie Kanagawa[2], Ako Takenishi[3], Akira Harada[2], Kiyotake Okawa[4], Hiromi Yabuno[2]

[1] Kokoro Research Center, Kyoto University, Kyoto City, Kyoto, Japan,

[2] Faculty of Management, Otemon Gakukun University, Ibaraki City, Osaka, Japan,

[3] Hyogo University of Teacher Education, Kato City, Hyogo, Japan,

[4] Faculty of Liberal Arts, Teikyo University, Hachioji City, Tokyo, Japan

ABSTRACT

The Great East Japan Earthquake was a tragic event requiring critical media involvement. Since the media played an important role in conveying factual information, journalists expressed feeling that it was difficult to guarantee the objectivity of their coverage. As media coverage constructs a socio-culturally shared reality among its audience, an examination of the objectivity and emotionality of the contents of the news coverage is needed. In Study 1, we conducted an exploratory content analysis of TV and newspaper coverage from the six month period following the March 11, 2011 disaster, finding that the news media generally reported neutral and objective factual information about the event, with emotionality shown only in the commentary. In order to examine how media coverage was constructed and evaluated by journalists, in Study 2 we conducted an online survey of 115 journalists working for mass media organizations. We found that that the journalists' orientations tended to be more objective than emotional, which is consistent with the findings of Study 1. However, their evaluations of the objectivity of the published articles were low, especially for the coverage of the nuclear power plant accident, which was an accident of an unprecedented nature. The negative emotions that journalists experienced during their investigations negatively affected subsequent evaluations of the objectivity of their reporting.

INTRODUCTION

"Reporting on the tsunami-afflicted area was a difficult experience. As a journalist, I had to report a very sad story, but I also think I had to be more objective."

"I tried to be fair in my reporting on the Fukushima nuclear power plant accident, but it was difficult to fully understand what happened and what it meant."

Socio-cultural constructions of "objectivity"

These are personal quotes from journalists who covered the Great East Japan Earthquake in 2011. Most of the journalists expressed feeling that covering this event was much more difficult than their previous experiences as journalists, particularly with regards to "how to guarantee the objectivity of coverage" and "how to manage their own strong negative emotions when covering the disaster." Once their stories were published, even if the writers had ambiguous feelings about the objectivity of the piece, readers might understand their reporting as a description of "objective facts". On the other hand, readers might also expect media reports to contain not only objective information, but also emotional information of the type that can strongly affect understandings of the event.

The perception that the world and its events are a "shared reality" is held not only by individuals, but is also institutionalized in everyday practices and public artifacts such as media coverage (see [1–2]). Media accounts are powerful socio-cultural artifacts that both reflect and foster common socio-cultural understandings [1]. This means that the media does not only present objective facts, but also communicates cultural and personal attitudes, values and emotions [1]. Just as Morling and Lamouex [2] approached media coverage as a "cultural product"—a manifestation of psychological tendencies—we need to consider the psychological aspects of the coverage.

News coverage is a dynamically constructed phenomenon that reflects the audience's points of view (what they would like to know) and the journalists' points of view (what they would like to report), and both of them are comprised of socio-cultural factors (what is important in a given socio-cultural context or situation) [1]. Most research on the media has been conducted using a macro-level approach that emphasizes socio-cultural factors, but from a current sociological and social psychological perspective, examining individual journalists' emotions or perceptions about the media coverage could help reveal how news is constructed (i.e., [1, 3]).

Disaster and the media: Seeking to be objective

In particular, the media focuses on large-scale events and the responses of the audience to both positive events (e.g., the Olympic Games [1]) and negative events (e.g., natural disasters). For such major events, "information needs" are greatly amplified [4–5]. Therefore, an analysis of mass communication about natural disasters is important (e.g., [6]).

The Great East Japan Earthquake was a critical event that attracted international media coverage, partially due to the shocking footage of the tsunami and the disastrous accident at the Fukushima Daiichi nuclear power plant. The media coverage of the earthquake had a psychological impact on people, including those in areas not directly affected by the disaster [7]. Owing to the enormity of the disaster, it was too difficult for individuals to obtain the "accurate and reliable" information that was necessary to regulate their behaviors (e.g., escaping or helping) and emotions (e.g., anxiety) in an atmosphere of increasing anxiety and decreasing trust in government institutions (see [8]). Especially during the first year, people in Japan were struggling to obtain reliable information about the effects of radiation that would help them make decisions about travel and food choices, and also about tsunami victims in the Tohoku area that would help them understand the extent of damage, what kind of help was needed and the victims' expected levels of resilience (see [9]).

Usually individuals seek information from both the mass media and social networking services (SNSs). During the disaster period, mass media outlets, such as TV and newspapers, played a primary role in providing emergency alert information and risk communication (e.g., [10]), especially for those who could not or do not access SNS services, such as the elderly. Thus, the mass media had a considerable responsibility during the disaster because it plays a key role in risk management [11].

An analysis of media coverage of national emergencies provides an opportunity to understand the process of socio-cultural meaning-making during risk situations (see [12]). Three years after the March 11th triple disaster, the Japanese public still holds mixed opinions about the evacuation of people from the area surrounding the Fukushima Daiichi nuclear plant, as well as the use of nuclear power in Japan as a whole. Such ambivalence is partly due to the "mixed" information that was delivered by the media during this unprecedented situation.

Objectivity vs. Emotionality in Japanese Culture

We should look not only at the role of the media in risk situations, but also at the socio-cultural orientations found in the media within Japanese contexts. Previous research has suggested that there are sizable cross-cultural differences in how the media portrays events and at what point in the event timeline they begin coverage [13].

One of the features of the Japanese media is emotionality (see [1]). Emotionality in Japan is related to the "culture of sympathy" [14], a bonding tool that is used to achieve interdependence between people. Sharing emotional states with others is perceived as important to understanding others [1]. Markus et al. [1] analyzed Olympic media coverage and found that, compared with American media coverage, the Japanese media depicted more emotional "tearjerkers" detailing the hardships that athletes had overcome. Thus, we expected that during the disaster period, attention might have been given not only to objectivity, but also to the emotionality of the shared experience of sadness or anger.

Present Study

Our purpose in this study was to ascertain the level of objectivity and emotionality in the media coverage of this national disaster in Japan. Objectivity-seeking might be one important factor in journalism, but in the socio-cultural context of Japan, emotionality might also be present. If so, which element were journalists emphasizing: objectivity or emotionality? And how were these two types of orientations (objectivity and emotionality) related to each other?

In Study 1, we conducted an exploratory analysis of the content of media coverage from one TV news program (NHK) and two Japanese newspapers with nationwide circulation that were published during the six month period immediately following the disaster (from March 11th to September 30th, 2011). Study 1 was an exploratory study, but we had two viewpoints for analysis. First, we examined whether the Japanese media would attempt to seek a balanced emotional valence (seeking neutrality) to attain objectivity, even in such negative and chaotic circumstances; thus, we investigated how often neutral facts were reported (Analysis 1: A1). In addition, we examined how the media coverage portrayed objective and emotional information and whether "factual reports" or "commentaries about the facts" contained either objective or emotional information (Analysis 2: A2).

In Study 2, we conducted a survey of journalists asking about their strategies for seeking objectivity and how they evaluate objectivity and emotionality; our focus was on their psychological processes, particularly the journalists' orientations toward the objectivity and emotionality of their reporting. We predicted that journalists working in a Japanese socio-cultural context seek to report both objectivity and emotionality (H1), but evaluate the objectivity of articles written in chaotic conditions as not meeting their expected standards (H2). We also focused on the negative emotions they experienced during their journalistic investigations and the effects that they subsequently had on how they evaluated the objectivity of their reporting (H3).

In these two studies, we tried to identify how the news broadcasts and articles contained objective factual information and emotional reactions, and how the psychological processes of journalists affected the creation of the reports and their evaluations of the news broadcasts and articles.

STUDY 1

Method

We collected, coded and analyzed nationwide coverage of the Great East Japan Earthquake from one television channel and two newspapers dating from the period of March to September 2011. We chose the program "News Watch 9" (aired weekdays, from 9 to 10pm) on the channel "NHK," which had a large audience share (16.8% during April 2011), the second highest for the month after the earthquake. The highest-ranking program was "News 7" (17.9%) on NHK (aired weekdays, from 7 to 7:30pm), but because this program was shorter and had the same content, we selected "News Watch 9." We also collected print coverage from the "*Asahi*" and "*Yomiuri*" newspapers since they ranked first and second for nationwide circulation. We only analyzed "news" articles, excluding longer arguments and interpretative reports in order to establish equivalence with the TV program. During the initial period after March 11th, the news was not reported on the regular News Watch 9 program, but was reported around the clock in continual coverage; we therefore analyzed this coverage (broadcast by NHK) at the same time as News Watch 9 (from 9 to 10pm).

The first segment of coverage that we looked at was from March 12 to 31, the month following the earthquake; the second was from the month of

April, the second month after the earthquake; the third segment was from May to June; and the fourth was from August to September. Within each segment, we only analyzed news that was broadcast or published on Mondays, Wednesdays and Fridays in order to avoid overlap, and also because of the time-saving for doing a large volume of content analysis.

To develop an inductive coding scheme, three Japanese adults who were unaware of the purpose of the study watched selections from television news programs (excluding News Watch 9). The coders were asked to catalogue and categorize all descriptions or analyses of the earthquake and nuclear accident as either factual reports or commentaries. A discussion of the topics of coverage generated by the coders yielded (1) seven conceptually distinct topics of coverage: the government, the electric company and nuclear power plant, other business enterprises, the tsunami-afflicted Tohoku area in general, other areas of Japan, areas outside of Japan, and people assisting in aid efforts, such as rescue or volunteer workers; (2) five categories of commentators: victims, specialists, journalists, aid workers/rescue personnel and government people and (3) three valences: positive, negative and neutral. Coding categories are shown in Table 1 and Table 2. Ten Japanese coders independently coded each sentence of the video segments and newspaper articles (following [1]), judging whether each sentence mentioned one or more topics included in the coding scheme and noting the topics of coverage mentioned in each case. For example, if the TV reporters said, "The tsunami victims are suffering so much. The electric company has not yet solved the nuclear power plant problem," we coded a score of 1 for both "tsunami victims" and "the electric company and nuclear power plant." During the practice session (for which we used ten episodes of News Watch 9 which were not included in the analysis), coders were trained to share their understandings of the coding scheme. The coding results showed a good rate of consistency (78%–91%). Twenty percent of the coverage was coded by at least two people.

Coding Categories

First, each sentence was categorized as either a "factual report" or a "commentary on reported facts." If a sentence was categorized as the former, the coder selected the topic of the factual report. The valence of the reported fact (positive, neutral or negative) was also coded. If a sentence was categorized as a comment on reported facts, we coded the commentator (victim, specialist, journalist, aid worker / rescue personnel, or government person) and valence (positive, negative or neutral).

Table 1. Coding categories and prevalence in TV program contents (percentage).

Factual report				
		Valence		
Topics	Positive	Neutral	Negative	Total
Government	0.0	2.6	0.8	3.4
Electronic company/Nuclear power plant	0.0	5.8	6.1	11.9
Other business enterprises	0.1	0.7	0.3	1.1
Tsunami-afflicted Tohoku area	0.4	11.0	12.4	23.8
Other areas in Japan	0.1	1.9	0.8	2.8
Outside of Japan	0.2	1.3	0.4	1.9
Aid workers/rescue personnel	0.1	2.8	0.8	3.7
Other categories	0.0	1.5	1.0	2.5
Total	0.9	27.6	22.6	51.1
Commentary on reported fact				
		Valence		
Topics	Positive	Neutral	Negative	Total
Victims	1.8	3.7	7.7	13.2
Specialists	0.3	6.3	3.2	9.8
Journalists	1.0	5.9	7.4	14.3
Aid workers/rescue personnel	0.4	0.9	1.1	2.4
Government-related people	0.0	0.1	0.1	0.2
Others	0.2	0.3	0.4	0.9
Total	3.7	17.2	19.9	40.8

Table 2. Coding categories and prevalence in newspaper contents (percentage).

Factual report				
		Valence		
Topics	Positive	Neutral	Negative	Total
Government	0.1	8.2	2.1	10.4
Electronic company/Nuclear power plant	0.0	6.2	5.1	11.3
Other business enterprises	0.1	4.0	2.2	6.3
Tsunami-afflicted Tohoku area	0.6	15.0	14.6	30.2
Other areas in Japan	0.0	1.9	1.2	3.1
Outside of Japan	0.4	2.5	0.8	3.7
Aid worker	0.3	4.0	0.6	4.9
Other categories	0.1	0.8	0.3	1.2
Total	1.6	42.6	26.9	71.1
Commentary on reported facts				
		Valence		
Topics	Positive	Neutral	Negative	Total
Victims	0.9	4.7	4.5	10.1
Specialists	0.1	2.0	1.2	3.3
Journalists	0.0	1.4	1.4	2.9
Aid workers/rescue personnel	0.2	0.8	0.3	1.3
Government-related people	0.0	0.8	0.5	0.2
Others	0.2	0.4	0.2	1.8
Total	1.4	10.1	8.1	19.6

RESULTS

Tables 1 and 2 show how frequently each topic was coded in the media coverage.

Factual Reports.

We analyzed the two types of media (TV and newspaper) separately (Table 1 shows the results from TV coverage and Table 2 shows the results from newspapers). Factual reports made up 51.1% of the news on TV programs; of this, 22.6% was made up of negative factual information and 27.6% was made up of neutral factual information, a considerable amount even under such adverse circumstances. Regarding topics, coverage on the tsunami-afflicted Tohoku area and the electric company contained both negative factual reports (12.4% and 6.1% of all content, respectively) and neutral factual reports (11.0% and 5.8% of all content, respectively). Reports on the government had more neutral (2.6% of all content) than negative news (0.8%).

Factual reports made up 71.1% of newspaper articles, a higher rate than in the TV coverage. Furthermore, a large percentage of the content was made up of neutral factual reports (42.6% of all descriptions) and a smaller percentage was negative (26.9%). Neutral information was more likely to be reported across all topics of coverage.

Commentaries.

In the TV programs, commentaries made up 40.8% of all content. A majority of the commentaries were delivered by journalists (14.3%), followed by victims (13.2%) and specialists (e.g., nuclear scientists, 9.8%). In the TV programs, 19.9% of the commentaries were negative and 17.2% were neutral. Thus, the rate of negativity was higher than the rate of neutrality for commentaries as opposed to factual reports. Journalists (e.g., newscasters), victims and aid workers/rescue personnel gave more negative than neutral commentaries. On the other hand, specialists and government officials gave more neutral than negative commentaries.

With regard to newspapers, 19.6% of all content was comprised of commentaries. One reason for such a low percentage may have been that commentaries in newspapers tended to appear in argumentative essays and longer articles that were excluded from the study because they were not news reports, while the TV coverage included brief commentaries alongside factual reports. Most commentaries in newspapers were by victims (10.1% of all content), followed by specialists (3.3%) and journalists (2.9%). In newspapers, 8.1% of commentaries were negative and 10.1% were neutral. Thus, there were fewer negative commentaries in newspapers than in the TV programs.

Discussion

The analysis revealed that the media coverage of the Great East Japan Earthquake sought to maintain objectivity by conveying neutral information in considerably chaotic circumstances, especially in the newspaper articles (A1). Inconsistent information, such as presenting neutral factual reports alongside negative commentaries, was also conveyed (A2). However, such negative commentaries appeared more often in TV programs than in newspaper articles. This might be because we excluded "commentary" articles—which would likely include emotional comments—from our analysis of newspapers; thus only TV programs showed informational inconsistency in containing both factual reports and commentaries. However, it could be argued that the TV programs contained both factual reports and commentaries within the same story, rather than separately, as in the newspaper articles. In fact, such a co-occurrence of neutral and emotional information in the same report could have affected audiences' perceptions of the reports [15].

Even within the adverse conditions surrounding the events of March 11th, media coverage included neutral information for both the nuclear accident and the tsunami-afflicted areas. As such, it is important to investigate whether this was due to the journalists' attempts to maintain objectivity. Study 2 was designed to clarify this point. In Study 2 we selected two topics (the nuclear accident and the tsunami-afflicted Tohoku area) about which reports were shown to be more factually-oriented than those regarding other topics.

STUDY 2

In Study 1, we found that the media coverage of the Great East Japan Earthquake was mostly neutral. Since the news was produced by journalists, we attempted to examine the extent to which journalists explicitly expressed an orientation towards either objectivity or emotionality, as well as the intentionality behind their news coverage, e.g., emphasizing or omitting content. Additionally, we were interested in their evaluations of the objectivity and emotionality of competing coverage. In the content analysis, the coverage of the nuclear power plant accident and the tsunami-afflicted Tohoku area had similar patterns of valence. Therefore, we predicted that journalists generally seek to be objective as part of their work, as opposed to seeking emotionality (H1), as shown in Study 1's finding that the objectivity of the media coverage was similar for both the nuclear accident and tsunami-afflicted areas. However, the characteristics of coverage on the nuclear accident and the tsunami-afflicted areas were different. Whereas people might require objective information about the former to make critical decisions [4], in the latter case emotional information about the tsunami-afflicted Tohoku area might be conveyed in order to elicit an emotional response in people living in non-afflicted areas (e.g., increasing sympathy to incite aid) in the Japanese socio-cultural context (see [7]). Thus we predicted that there would be an interaction effect wherein orientations towards objectivity would be greater for coverage of the nuclear power plant than for coverage of the tsunami-afflicted Tohoku area.

In addition, we predicted that, particularly with regard to the nuclear accident, journalists' evaluations of objectivity would judge it as falling short of their expected standards (H2), since the objective information that the public required would be complicated by the nature of the accident, which was the first of its kind in both complexity and scale.

Furthermore, journalists might experience negative emotions (including trauma) during their investigative work (see [16]), and such emotional reactions might be related to their evaluations of the objectivity of their articles (H3).

Method

The survey study was approved by the Kokoro Research Center at Kyoto University following the Japanese Psychological Association guidelines. We made an online web survey (using "surveymonkey") so that anonymous participants could easily access and complete the questionnaire. The URL of the survey website was announced and participants were provided written informed consent agreements to participate in this study. They provided consent by completing the survey (the consent button was a required field on the web survey). This procedure was approved by each news organization (e.g., newspaper company) that agreed to recruit potential participants.

Participants.

First, the authors sent the link of the online survey to journalists we personally knew and asked them to complete the online questionnaire and/or to send the survey link to their colleagues. We also asked five mass media organizations (including TV broadcasting companies and newspaper-related organizations) to participate in this study, and three of them agreed to recruit participants by sending details of the survey to journalists belonging to their organization. In total, we asked 44 individuals and three organizations to respond to or distribute the web-based survey link to journalists. The participants of this study were 115 Japanese journalists (55 male, 13 female, 47 uncategorized), who ranged in age from 23 to 70 years (the majority were in their 30s) and worked at broadcasting companies, newspaper publishing companies, or news service agencies.

They completed the survey between March and April 2012 (a year after the earthquake). Of the 115 participants, we used 98 who reported on either the nuclear power plant, the tsunami-afflicted Tohoku area, or both for the main analysis. A total of 62 participants (53.9%) covered both the nuclear power plant accident and the tsunami-afflicted Tohoku area, 17 participants (14.8%) reported only on the nuclear accident, and 19 (16.5%) on only the tsunami-afflicted Tohoku area.

We asked them to report what type of organization they worked for (TV or newspaper) but 42.6% did not answer this question. Thus we were unable to do a comparison of responses based on the media type.

Survey.

The questionnaire consisted of four parts: (1) the journalists' investigative activities and their evaluation of their coverage of the nuclear power plant accident, (2) their activities and their evaluation of their coverage of the tsunami-afflicted Tohoku area, (3) their emotions during their investigative work and (4) their attitudes toward journalism in general and a free description of the earthquake coverage and the media in general. We first asked whether they were engaged in covering (writing/reporting on) the nuclear accident and the tsunami-afflicted Tohoku area, and those who answered "yes" completed part 1, part 2, or both (if applicable), and part 3. All participants completed part 4.

Orientation.

For items in parts 1 and 2—which were scored on a 5-point Likert scale ranging from 1 (not at all) to 5 (very much)—we asked about their orientations toward objectivity (2 items) and audience emotion (4 items) for each topic of coverage (the nuclear power plant accident and the tsunami-afflicted Tohoku area). Items for orientation toward objectivity were "try to maintain a balance when introducing commentaries" and "avoid having only positive or negative information in coverage." Since the correlations between these two items were sufficiently high (.52 and. 62 for nuclear power plant and the tsunami-afflicted Tohoku area coverage, respectively), we calculated the average scores of the two items. Orientation towards audience emotion (orientation toward emotionality) questions were "try to elicit joy or hope", "try to show the tragedy of the event", "try to elicit crisis awareness" and "try to reduce anxiety." Cronbach's alpha coefficients were. 61 and. 64 for the nuclear accident and the tsunami-afflicted Tohoku area, respectively, and we calculated the mean scores.

Evaluation.

We asked participants the extent to which their coverage reflected (1) objective facts, (2) personal opinions, (3) the opinions of the organization they belonged to, (4) specialists' opinions and (5) victims' opinions, using a 4-point scale (1 = not at all, 2 = somewhat, 3 = considerably, 4 = almost entirely), for both types of coverage (the nuclear power plant accident and the tsunami-afflicted Tohoku area). We calculated the average scores for both types of coverage since they were highly correlated, and the result was no different than when they were examined separately in the pre-analysis.

A second 4-point objectivity evaluation scale (1 = not at all, 2 = not very much, 3 = somewhat, 4 = very much) measured the objectivity of the coverage (3 items). The items were "to what extent did the broadcast coverage you were involved in adhere to the facts", "to what extent was the coverage more objective than emotional" and "to what extent did the coverage reflect the real situations you experienced during your investigative work?" Since this scale had only three items, the Cronbach's alpha coefficient for each topic of coverage was relatively low (.55 and. 50 for the nuclear power plant and the tsunami-afflicted Tohoku area coverage, respectively) but we calculated the mean scores for each topic of coverage since preliminary analysis showed that the pattern of the results was similar when we did same analysis with each item.

We also asked participants whether their organizations preferred to cover certain topics, for which possible answers were "yes", "it is likely", "no" and "I don't know."

Emotion.

Participants rated the intensity of the emotions they experienced from 1 (did not feel at all) to 5 (felt very intensely) for both negative and positive emotions. A factor analysis revealed three factors: positive emotions (pride, hope, joy, respect, friendliness; α =. 77), negative emotions (resentment, anger, pity, desperation, hopelessness, anxiety, sadness; α =. 87) and guilt-related emotions specific to this situation (indebtedness, guilt, feelings of restraint toward the interviewee, loneliness, pity; α =. 86). We calculated the mean scores for each domain of emotion.

Perception of the Japanese Media as Having an Emotional Presentation Style.

We asked participants about their general attitudes toward the "emotionality" of media coverage in Japan (6 items, 1 = completely disagree, 5 = completely agree). The items were "in general, I think the majority of news coverage in Japan caters to the audience's preferences", "generally speaking, audiences prefer stories that are sad or are about overcoming hardship over happy stories", "in general, news that relates the emotional aspects of a situation is important in coverage", "someone's story of hardship is preferred over someone's story of honor as a topic of news coverage", "for disaster coverage, the media tends to convey more negative emotional material such as misery or hardship" and "most disaster coverage is constructed using a story where someone has overcome some form of hardship." The Cronbach's alpha coefficient of these items was. 76. We calculated the mean scores.

Free Description.

At the end of the survey, we asked participants to freely describe their emotions or thoughts about their investigative activities and the emotions they experienced during their work reporting on the earthquake.

Results

Post-earthquake Investigative Coverage Activities.

Of those covering the nuclear accident, the majority of their investigative work was conducted in Fukushima, followed by Tokyo. The 98 journalists who reported on either the nuclear power plant, the tsunami-afflicted Tohoku area, or both were the most likely to interact with disaster victims or local government officials in the affected areas, followed by risk managers from the government, Tokyo Electric Power Company (TEPCO) and the Fukushima Daiichi nuclear power plant. For the tsunami-afflicted Tohoku area, investigative work was primarily conducted in Miyagi, which was severely damaged by the tsunami (26.1% went there to cover the nuclear accident in Fukushima and 49.5% went there to cover the tsunami-afflicted area), followed by Fukushima (48.9% went there to cover the nuclear accident and 22.2% went there to cover the tsunami-afflicted area) and Iwate (19.6% went there to cover the nuclear accident and 39.5% went there to cover the tsunami-afflicted area). The greatest number of interviewees for the nuclear accident were local government officials in the afflicted areas (45.7%) and disaster victims (41.3%), followed by officials from the Japanese government (30.4%) and TEPCO, which owned the Fukushima Daiichi nuclear power plant (27.2%). The greatest number of interviewees in the tsunami afflicted areas were disaster victims (61.7%) and local government officials in the afflicted areas (54.3%), followed by aid workers (46.9%). The most frequently stated reason (37.1%) for why they conducted interviews in the tsunami-afflicted Tohoku area was "both because of their own personal desire and also at the request of the organization they work for."

Orientation and Comparison of the Coverage of the Nuclear Power Plant and the Tsunami-afflicted Tohoku Area.

Overall, the orientation toward objectivity was above the mid-point for both topics of coverage (*ts* > 5.6, *ps* <. 001, *rs* >.57). The mean scores of orientation toward objectivity in the coverage of the nuclear power plant and the tsunami-afflicted Tohoku area were 3.77 (*SD* = 0.98) and 3.53 (*SD* = 0.77), respectively. The correlation between these scores was significant (*r* =. 35, *p* <. 01); therefore, journalists who were objectively oriented tried to be somewhat consistent in their attitudes towards both topics of coverage. An orientation towards emotionality was above the mid-point for both topics of coverage (*ts* > 3.91, *ps* <. 001, *rs* >. 41). The mean score for emotionality orientation for the nuclear power plant coverage was 3.34 (*SD* = 0.76), and was 3.41 (*SD* = 0.77) for the tsunami-afflicted Tohoku area coverage. The correlation between these scores was significant (*r* =. 63, *p* <. 001), implying that those who displayed an orientation toward emotionality tried to be consistent in their attitudes for both topics of coverage. A 2 (topic of coverage: nuclear power plant vs. the tsunami-afflicted Tohoku area) × 2 (orientation: objectivity vs. emotionality) x 3 (gender: male, female, unknown) mixed ANOVA for journalists who answered orientation questions for both topics of coverage revealed a main effect of orientation ($F(1, 52) = 8.00$, $p <. 01$, partial $\eta^2 =. 13$); specifically, journalists were more likely to be oriented towards objectivity than towards emotionality. A significant interaction effect was found, indicating that the difference between an objective and an emotional orientation was larger for the coverage of the nuclear power plant than for the coverage of the tsunami-afflicted Tohoku area ($F(1,52) = 4.64$, $p <. 04$, partial $\eta^2 =. 08$; Fig 1). There was no gender difference.

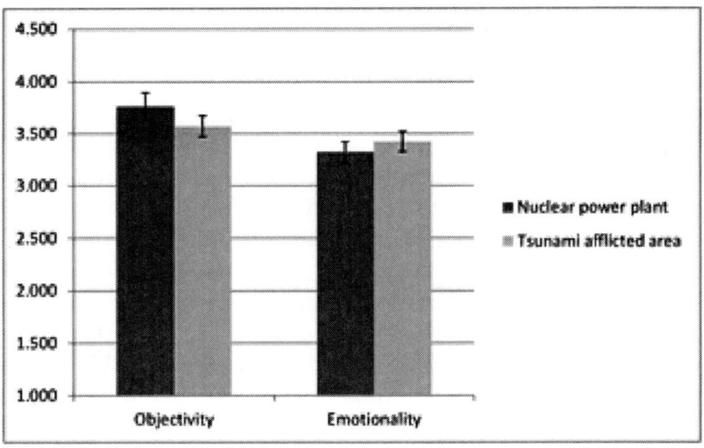

Figure 1. Journalists' orientations toward objectivity and emotionality in the coverage of the nuclear power plant accident and the tsunami-afflicted Tohoku area.

Furthermore, an orientation toward objectivity and emotionality were both positively correlated with coverage of the tsunami-afflicted Tohoku areas (r =. 29, p <.02), but this was not the case for coverage of the nuclear plant accident (r = -.19, p <.11). This result suggests that for topics for which journalists were more likely to express emotionality, their perceptions of objectivity and emotionality were not separated. However, for topics for which they sought objectivity more strongly, they felt objectivity to be independent of emotionality.

Evaluation.

Participants evaluated the coverage as predominantly reflecting objective facts (M = 3.29, SD = 0.58), followed by victims' opinions (M = 2.84, SD = 0.66), specialists' opinions (M = 2.39, SD = 0.60), personal opinions (M = 2.20, SD = 060) and the opinions of the organizations to which they belonged (M = 1.39, SD = 0.59). All differences between categories were significant (F (4, 31) = 27.52, p<.001, partial η^2 =. 78), except for the differences between journalists' personal opinions and the opinions of their organizations. Thus, their evaluations of the broadcast or published coverage suggest that, from their perspective, their coverage was more likely to reflect reality and less likely to be influenced by "pressure" from their news organizations.

As predicted, evaluations about objectivity were higher for the coverage of the tsunami-afflicted Tohoku area (M = 3.08, SD = 0.55) than for coverage of the nuclear accident (M = 2.96, SD = 0.63). A within-subjects t-test for participants who reported on both topics of coverage was significant (t(53) = 2.19, p <. 04, r =. 29): that is, journalists were more confident about the objectivity of the coverage of the tsunami-afflicted Tohoku area than they were about the coverage of the nuclear accident. Specifically, 35% of the participants evaluated the published and broadcast coverage of the nuclear accident as being incapable of adhering to the facts. This implies that they felt they could not fully comprehend the scope of the accident because the facts were too complicated to obtain all the information necessary for completely objective coverage.

A correlation analysis was conducted to investigate the extent to which participants' orientations toward objectivity and emotionality were related to their evaluations of news coverage and their perceptions of the Japanese media. Results revealed that both orientations (objectivity and emotionality) for coverage of the tsunami-afflicted Tohoku area were positively correlated with responses stating that the coverage reflected facts (r =. 27 and. 29, ps <. 03) and participants' evaluations of the objectivity of the coverage of the tsunami-afflicted Tohoku area (r =. 41, p <. 001 and r =. 29, p <. 02). Thus, journalists believed that depicting the reality of the situation accurately was related to both an orientation toward objectivity and emotionality when covering the tsunami-afflicted Tohoku area. However, the results for the coverage of the nuclear accident were mixed. We found that having an orientation toward emotionality was positively correlated with the inclusion of victims' opinions in coverage ($r = .40, p < .03$) and a perception of the Japanese media as using emotionality in their stories ($r = .24, p < .07$) when covering the nuclear accident; this suggests that emotionality was associated with the journalists' perspectives on the Japanese media's emotionality and was affected by victim opinions. Furthermore, evaluations of objectivity for the nuclear accident coverage were not significantly correlated with accurately reflecting reality or with having an orientation toward objectivity when covering the accident ($rs < .08$, ns). Thus, in coverage of the nuclear accident, journalists' attitudes toward objectivity were not related to their evaluations of the objectivity of the news coverage, suggesting that they experienced ambivalence and waning confidence in the nuclear coverage.

With regard to whether journalists believed their organizations preferred particular topics, 29.6% answered "yes" and 10.4% answered "it is likely:" thus, in total, 40% believed that there was a preference for topics. Only 3.5% answered "no," 15.7% answered "I don't know," and 40.9% did not answer the question. These results suggest that a preference for particular content existed to some extent, and that journalists were aware of this preference.

Emotion.

Journalists were more likely to feel negative emotions ($M = 3.73, SD = 0.92$), followed by guilt-related emotions ($M = 2.91, SD = 1.15$), and less likely to feel positive emotions ($M = 2.61, SD = 0.89$). The differences between each valence were significant ($F(2,142) = 31.50, p < .0001$, partial $\eta^2 = .31$); a post hoc test indicated that negative emotions were felt more intensely than were other types. Among negative emotions, sadness was felt most intensely ($M = 4.4$). This pattern did not differ between those who were involved in the coverage of the nuclear power plant and those who were not, or between those who were involved in the coverage of the tsunami-afflicted Tohoku area and those who were not. Negative and guilt-related emotions were positively correlated with journalists' evaluations of their own coverage as reflecting their personal opinion ($r = .30, p < .02$ and $r = .20, p < .09$, respectively); furthermore, both types of emotion were negatively correlated with their evaluations of their own coverage as reflecting the facts ($r = -.20, p < .11$ and $r = -.36, p < .002$), evaluations of objectivity for coverage of the nuclear accident ($r = -35$ and $-.38$, $ps < .005$) and evaluations of objectivity for coverage of the tsunami-afflicted Tohoku area ($r = -35$ and $-.46$, $ps < .004$, respectively). We could not identify a causal relationship; however, the journalists' experiences of negative or guilt-related emotions during their fieldwork may have influenced their opinions and coverage, leading to an overall reduction of objectivity in their reporting.

Regression Analysis for the Evaluation of Objectivity.

To examine what was predictive of an evaluation of objectivity for the coverage, we performed a regression analysis on the analysis of objectivity for the coverage of both the nuclear power plant accident and the tsunami-afflicted Tohoku area. The dependent variables were guilt-related emotion (since it had a stronger correlation coefficient to objectivity evaluation than the other two emotions), orientation toward objectivity and emotionality (see Table 3). For the coverage of the nuclear accident, the evaluation of objectivity was negatively related with guilt-related emotions (β = -.37, p <. 004). For the coverage of the tsunami-afflicted Tohoku area, an evaluation of objectivity was negatively related to guilt-related emotions (β = -.38, p <. 001) and positively related to an orientation toward objectivity (β =. 25, p <. 03). Again, we could not identify a causal relationship; however, journalists' guilt may have reduced the objectivity of their coverage or, conversely, lowered objectivity may have resulted in increased guilt.

Table 3. Regression analysis for the evaluation of objectivity of the broadcast and published news reports.

	Target article: Nuclear power plant accident			Target article: Tsunami-afflicted area		
	β	t	p	β	t	p
Guilt-related emotion	-.37	-3.01	.004	-.38	-3.46	.001
Objectivity orientation	.10	0.79	n.s.	.25	2.22	.03
Emotionality orientation	.10	0.81	n.s.	.18	1.60	.114.
R^2	.19			.32		

Free Description.

Forty-one participants (36% of the 115 participants) provided free-format descriptions. Participants expressed resentment about the nuclear power plant accident (9.8% of those who provided a free description), difficulty to understand the facts of the situation (7.32%), and a feeling of responsibility for the decreasing trustworthiness of the media, such as the spreading of harmful rumors about Fukushima (14.6%). As for the tsunami-afflicted Tohoku area, they expressed having low confidence in the accuracy of coverage (22.0%), feelings of helplessness in trying to help the victims (12.2%), a sense of responsibility to continue reporting on the tsunami-afflicted area (17.1%) and ambivalence toward the objectivity of their coverage (14.6%). In addition, 7.31% of those who wrote a free description reported experiencing PTSD (see [15]) and described their own experience as victims.

Discussion

Study 2 suggests that the journalists' were more likely to be objectively-oriented rather than emotionally-orientated to the nuclear power plant accident and the tsunami-afflicted Tohoku area (H1).

While journalists' attitudes toward objectivity were not related to their evaluation of the objectivity of the coverage of the nuclear accident, they were related for the coverage of tsunami-afflicted area. An objectivity orientation might have increased their evaluation of articles about the tsunami-afflicted area, but this was not the case for coverage of the nuclear accident, suggesting that the accident was too difficult to be objective about, even if the journalist tried to be.

Interestingly, for the coverage of the tsunami-afflicted area, orientations toward objectivity and emotionality were positively correlated. Thus, for Japanese journalists, the concept of emotionality does not conflict with objectivity when they feel they have allowances to write emotionally evocative articles. This might reflect a Japanese socio-cultural context in journalism that requires both objective facts and emotional comments to evoke sympathy [1]. However, this pattern was not found in the nuclear power plant coverage, where journalists felt a strong orientation toward objectivity. For this type of coverage, orientations towards objectivity and emotionality were fairly negatively correlated (though this effect was not significant).

Participants' evaluations of objectivity were higher for the coverage of the tsunami-afflicted Tohoku area than for coverage of the nuclear accident. This suggests that the journalists lacked confidence in dealing with such a novel and large-scale accident (H2). They also noticed that the content that was preferred by the media organizations changed with time. They experienced strong feelings of guilt as a result of their investigative work, which may have resulted in decreased objectivity in their reporting (H3). In particular, guilt-related emotions reduced their evaluation of the objectivity of the articles, both for the nuclear power plant accident and tsunami-afflicted area.

Thus, in line with our hypotheses, journalists sought objectivity, but in circumstances such as those present in the aftermath of the Great East Japan Earthquake, they evaluated their objectivity as not sufficiently meeting their expectations, especially for coverage of the nuclear power plant accident,.

GENERAL DISCUSSION

As we presumed that the media plays an important role in constructing socio-culturally shared realities, we analyzed media coverage during the aftermath of the massive earthquake in Japan and investigated how such realities were shown to the audience and constructed by journalists. Thus, we need to consider the psychological aspects of the coverage, as such coverage is not just a macro-level phenomenon, but is constructed through micro-level phenomena by journalists under the influence of psychological functions (e.g., motivation, emotion and cognition).

Through an analysis of media coverage and a survey of journalists, we found that the content of the coverage consisted of neutral factual reports, even in the rather chaotic situation that existed during the first six months after the March 11th triple earthquake-tsunami-nuclear disaster. We examined how the journalists evaluated the objectivity and emotionality of their work in Study 2 and found that journalists sought to maintain objectivity, as shown in the broadcast reports and published articles that we examined in Study 1.

Though the broadcast coverage contained neutral information, the journalists' attitudes toward the reporting were somewhat ambivalent, especially with regard to the nuclear accident. For the coverage of tsunami-afflicted area, they simultaneously sought both objectivity and emotionality, which might be the default attitude in Japanese socio-cultural constructions. In contrast, for the coverage of the nuclear power plant accident, they felt a stronger orientation towards objectivity than emotionality, and those two orientations showed a fairly negative correlation. Furthermore, the journalists felt less confident about the objectivity of their reporting on the nuclear power plant accident, especially where they felt guilt-related emotions. Study 1 suggested that although the broadcast reports and published articles were fairly neutral, the journalists were not fully satisfied with their objectivity.

Actually, Niwa and Fujita [9] have suggested that from a journalist's perspective, the Great East Japan Earthquake was distinct in the extent, complexity and enormity of the disaster, which was beyond comparison due to the simultaneity of the earthquake, tsunami and nuclear accident. Therefore, journalists were unsure of how to report on this multi-faceted event ([4–5]). In particular, this kind of nuclear accident was a first for Japan and it was difficult for even science journalists to obtain concrete objective information. As a result of this journalistic bewilderment, lay people felt strong distrust toward the media, politicians, and even nuclear power experts ([17]). Some might have suspected these experts of having connections with the nuclear plant company (TEPCO) that were leading them to express positive attitudes to protect TEPCO's image. Future research should investigate whether these phenomena are observable only in Japan, or if they are widely shared across cultures after disasters. As previous research has suggested ([13] [1]), a comparison of the media coverage of the Great East Japan Earthquake by agencies in Japan and other countries (e.g., *The New York Times* and BBC News) may contribute to an understanding of the cultural differences and similarities in the coverage of a specific tragic event. Indeed, a previous study has suggested that the disaster was treated as major news both in the US and Japan (but not in some other countries), although the content and communication style differed [18].

Our findings are limited by the fact that our analysis only looked at media coverage from a six-month period and examined news from only one TV program. An analysis covering a longer span of time and involving several programs would improve generalizability. In a follow-up study, how the media conveyed information related to the Great East Japan Earthquake after an extended period could also be examined. In Study 2, we were unable to compare responses from the TV and newspaper journalists because many participants did not answer the questions about their respective organizations; thus, future studies that made such comparisons could yield more robust results.

Media analyses from a sociological perspective sometimes treat the media as "collective" phenomena; however, content is created by individual journalists and reflects their orientation and emotional states. As such, media coverage is not just a collective or macro phenomenon, but is also comprised of individual psychological factors.

ACKNOWLEDGMENTS

We would like to express our appreciation to Yasuo Suehiro, Manami Ichikawa, Yuji Ogihara, Yasunori Okada and Yuri Yano for assisting in the content analysis for this study and to Ken Suzuki for his advice on the survey study. We also thank Pamela Taylor for providing comments for the draft of this paper.

AUTHOR CONTRIBUTIONS

Conceived and designed the experiments: YU CK AT AH KO HY. Performed the experiments: YU CK AT AH KO HY. Analyzed the data: YU CK AT AH. Contributed reagents/materials/analysis tools: YU CK AT AH KO HY. Wrote the paper: YU CK AT.

REFERENCES

1. Markus HR, Uchida Y, Omoregie H, Townsend SS, Kitayama S. Going for the gold: Models of agency in Japanese and American contexts. Psychol Sci. 2006; 17: 103–112.

2. Morling B, Lamoreaux M. Measuring culture outside the head: A meta-analysis of individualism–collectivism in cultural products. Pers Soc Psychol Rev. 2008; 12: 199–221.

3. Dickinson R. Accomplishing journalism: towards a revived sociology of a media occupation. Cultur Sociol, 2007; 1: 189–208.

4. Erigawa, S. Disaster coverage and television. A Paper presented at the 39thBehaviometric Society of Japan. 2011.

5. Tanihara, K. Huge disasters and TV coverage. [Kyodai shinsai to TV houdou. Tumaduki nagara susunda fukugo-saigai tokuban]. Journalism, 2011; 6.

6. Quarantelli, EL. The social science study of disasters and mass Communications; 1987. Preliminary Paper #116, Disaster Research Center, University of Delaware.

7. Uchida Y, Takahashi Y, Kawahara K. Changes in hedonic and eudaimonic well-being after a severe nationwide disaster: The case of the Great East Japan Earthquake. J Happiness Stud. 2014; 15: 207–221.

8. Hommerich C. Trust and subjective well-being after the Great East Japan Earthquake, tsunami and nuclear meltdown: Preliminary results. Int J Jpn Sociol. 2012; 21: 46–64.

9. Niwa Y, Fujita M. Trembling media: TV, radio, and the Great East Japan Earthquake. [Media ga furueta: TV, radio and higashi nihon daishinsai]. The University of Tokyo Press. Tokyo, Japan; 2013.

10. .Nomura Research Institute. Survey research on media exposure during the Great East Japan Earthquake.; 2011. Available: http://www.nri.com/jp/news/2011/110329.html.

11. Ueno, N. Harmful rumors on food and risk communication. [Shokuhin no fuhyo higai to risk communication]. A paper presented at the 22th Japan Society for Science Policy and Research Management. 2007.

12. Koshiro E. The Hanshin Awaji Earthquake and the merits and demerits of mass communication. [Hanshin Awaji daishinsai to masskomi houdou no kouzai: Kishatachi no mita daishinsai]. Akashi Shoten, Hyogo, Japan; 1997.

13. Morris MW, Peng K. Culture and cause: American and Chinese attributions for social and physical events. J Pers Soc Psychol. 1994; 67: 949–971.

14. Uchida Y, Kitayama S. Development and validation of a sympathy scale. Japanese Journal of Psychology. 2001; 72: 275–282. pmid:11797327

15. Yabuno H. Effect of emotional comment in the risk management TV programs to audiences' perception. Otemon Business Management Review. 2013; 19: 281–307.

16. Hatanaka M, Matsui Y, Ando K, Inoue K, Fukuoka Y, Koshiro E, et al.Traumatic stress in Japanese broadcast journalists. J Trauma Stress. 2010; 23: 173–177.

17. Yamanaka S. We need a straightforward examination of how the reconstruction is being reported. [Fukko houdou ni motomerareru uwasuberisenu jimichi na kensho]. 2011; Journalism, 6.

18. Quarantelli, EL, Wenger, DE. A cross-societal comparison of disaster news reporting in Japan and the United States. 1990; Preliminary Paper #146, Disaster Research Center, University of Delaware.

4

TWEETING SUPERTYPHOON HAIYAN: EVOLVING FUNCTIONS OF TWITTER DURING AND AFTER A DISASTER EVENT

Clarissa C. David[1], Jonathan Corpus Ong[2], Erika Fille T. Legara[3]

[1] Graduate Studies, College of Mass Communication, University of the Philippines, Quezon City, Philippines,

[2] Department of Media and Communication, University of Leicester, Leicester, United Kingdom,

[3] Complex Systems Group, Computing Science Department, Institute of High Performance Computing, A*STAR, Singapore, Singapore

ABSTRACT

When disaster events capture global attention users of Twitter form transient interest communities that disseminate information and other messages online. This paper examines content related to Typhoon Haiyan (locally known as Yolanda) as it hit the Philippines and triggered international humanitarian response and media attention. It reveals how Twitter conversations about disasters evolve over time, showing an issue attention cycle on a social media platform. The paper examines different functions of Twitter and the information hubs that drive and sustain conversation about the event. Content analysis shows that the majority of tweets contain information about the typhoon or its damage, and disaster relief activities. There are differences in types of content between the most retweeted messages and posts that are original tweets. Original tweets are more likely to come from ordinary users, who are more likely to tweet emotions, messages of support, and political content compared with official sources and key information hubs that include news organizations, aid organization, and celebrities. Original tweets reveal use of the site beyond information to relief coordination and response.

INTRODUCTION

The social network microblogging site Twitter has played an increasingly important role in communication during disasters, both on the side of the public and of institutions involved in disaster relief and response. In parallel, the literature on functions of Twitter during disasters is growing, with different disciplines examining unique aspects of its use in hazardous events. Research shows that it is most heavily used as a platform to disseminate information quickly through a population, to a lesser extent as a source of information from people who are witnesses to an event, and as a way for the public to contribute to efforts in generating awareness through retweeting of relevant information [1–5]. As our knowledge continues to develop about how Twitter is used during emergencies, and how its purposes can be expanded, users continue to innovate on its functions before, during, and after a disaster.

This paper contributes to current knowledge by showing how the content of Twitter during and after a global humanitarian event evolves over time, from a channel of information dissemination about a storm and its impacts, to a venue for mobilizing relief and response on a global scale, to a place to where emotions are shared. Content analyzed Twitter messages related to Haiyan, over the course of 20 days, suggest that the issue attention cycle [6] on Twitter for this global humanitarian crisis began to wean after 9 or 10 days. Unlike much of the existing work in this area we analyzed retweeted messages and non-retweeted messages separately, allowing for a differentiated view of the site's functions for those who compose original posts (most likely ordinary people) and those that are widely shared across the network, which often are from official sources and key information hubs. This way results are not heavily skewed toward the types of messages that are most often shared, and the voices of ordinary Twitter users who are not often retweeted are not drowned out in the analysis. Results indicate that there are meaningful differences in the content and sources of tweets that are the most-retweeted, and the ones that emanate from the broader audience. While there has been interest in the use of Twitter during crises [7, 8], this paper contributes to this growing body of work by focusing on how attention cycles operate in social media platforms and identifies the voices and messages that drive attention and conversation.

Twitter data were collected the day before supertyphoon Haiyan (locally known as Yolanda) and for 18 days afterwards. Haiyan was a trending topic on Twitter for over two weeks, with activity coming from many countries. This was the strongest typhoon to ever make landfall in recorded history [9, 10], severely damaging areas of different countries in Southeast Asia. It directly hit the middle of the Philippine archipelago, which is comprised of a group of islands, decimating the city of Tacloban in Leyte province and flattening many other municipalities along its path. While both local and international relief efforts were quickly mobilized from outside the province, it took several days for help to reach the affected areas. For over a week little was known about the extent of the damage, the situation on the ground, where survivors were, and how many were killed (government figures report over 6,000 people died in Tacloban, but thousands more remain missing one year after Haiyan hit). Delayed access to the site also perhaps lengthened the attention cycle on social media and traditional media, as information about damage in Tacloban was slow to reach the press because of difficulties in reaching affected areas. The international media were on site as soon as transportation systems allowed, broadcasting to the world images of devastation, stories of loss, and as days passed with no help arriving, criticisms against the national government's efforts rose.

Twitter's functions during disaster events

While Twitter was not originally conceived for use in emergency response situations and disaster events, the public and institutions are increasingly turning to it for gathering and disseminating information [11]. The growing empirical work on Twitter's functions in relation to disasters shows that it is a valuable channel of information for both official institutional sources such as government agencies and news outfits, and witnesses on the ground close to the event who are able to post updates as texts and photos. Its use has been studied in relation to the 2011 Tohoku earthquake [12] the Red River Valley flood threat [4], the Pakistan floods [1], the Waldo Canyon wildfires [13] the Australian floods [14] and several others. Twitter contains features that are particularly useful for disaster reporting and monitoring: real-time posting, short-burst message style (140 characters), default public settings when posting, multimedia capacities, hyperlinking, presentation of posts in reverse chronological order, and easy retweeting or forwarding of messages to followers and the public Twitter space.

Informal networks on social media are used for different purposes, including information transmission, emotional expressions, activity reporting, media content sharing, and collective sensemaking [11, 15, 16]. During emergencies Twitter functions as a backchannel source of information [17], a means of rapid information dissemination [8], a venue for information sourcing to enhance situational awareness [18], and as a channel for sharing opinions and experiences [19, 20]. There may be other functions as yet understudied, following Palen et al's [4] observation that Twitter and other social media serve various functions depending on the type of user and type of event.

A number of studies have closely examined various aspects of Twitter's use as an information source and channel for dissemination during disasters. In addition to being a place to find and share information, people also use it to share personal experiences, crack jokes, express concern, and ask questions [19]. Information sharing is done often through retweeting of links, with a larger portion of links coming from news websites rather than official government sources [21, 22, 23]. For many studies of Twitter messages during disasters, the main finding is that over half are information-related and contain links to websites (e.g. Refs. [24] and [19]). The platform functions largely as a broadcasting medium during emergency events and other non-routine situations [24].

In response to its institutional use as a broadcasting medium, people or "audiences" use the site to actively seek out information—a more common behavior than starting an online conversation or other similar forms of interactive strategies [25]. Publics are drawn to the site by active information seeking because in crisis situations, affected populations seek out explanations to reduce uncertainty. Information "hubs" [26, 27] tend to be official sources with announcements and situation updates, dominating the most retweeted messages and reaching the widest audiences. A content analysis of Twitter messages posted by international organizations involved in the response after Haiti's earthquake revealed evolving use of the medium over time [28] from that of information dissemination, to expressions of support, to fundraising. The earthquake was a trending topic on Twitter for several weeks, throughout breaking news, fundraising, organizing of events, and updates on response on the ground [29].

Engaging through Twitter as a response to disasters and crisis situations is motivated by a felt "need to contribute, and by doing so, (being) better able to cope with the enormity of the situation" [17] (p.5). A study of people who tweeted about Haiti found that their reasons included connecting with others for a common cause, promoting relief efforts, and personalizing their own activities in response to the disaster [30]. From an organization's point of view, nonprofits and media institutions craft messages on Twitter to motivate citizen response [31]. This in turn generates greater interest in taking action like donating money or contributing to relief efforts.

In light of these previous findings, we coded for many different types of content using the Twitter posts during and after Haiyan. These include information about the typhoon and its damage, posts about disaster relief as reported from the ground, reports of different disaster relief efforts from those who are initiating them, posts of emotional response (e.g. "afraid of Haiyan"), supportive messages (e.g. "sending prayers for Tacloban"), and posts about politics. This will allow for a detailed view of the make-up of Twitter posts overall throughout the issue cycle of Haiyan, and changes across the days in terms of content.

Global interest in disasters

The impact of Haiyan was hardest on a handful of islands in the Philippines, but the interest in the typhoon, the damage it created, and the recovery of hardest hit towns like Tacloban, was international in scale. A day after the Philippine President Aquino declared a "State of Calamity" and formally accepted international assistance on 11 November 2013, the United Nations declared a Level 3 humanitarian response and triggered relief operations from international governments and NGOs [32]. Countries like Japan, the US, Australia, and the UK pledged billions of dollars in aid funds and sent valuable disaster experts and military personnel in disaster response. Humanitarian agencies descended on the small city with emergency supplies, bringing their own transportation, communication, and fuel. Closely following the responders were international media such as CNN, NBC and other television networks in the US, the BBC of the UK, the wires, and many others from different countries. Sentiments on Twitter came from around the globe, with messages conveying support, emotion, and sharing of efforts to contribute to the relief operations. This was an event that held the attention of many people in many countries, similarly with other global humanitarian crises like the Haiti earthquake, the Japan tsunami, and the Pakistan floods.

Global interest in local crises may be more common in the age of online social networks. Following the predictions of Castell [26], information flows in the digital world now reflect structures of networks organized around communication hubs and nodes. Communication hubs function as main exchangers; coordinating elements in the network while nodes become the bases for locally initiated activities (p. 443). Content can be generated by any person or organization, and shared to or by any entity on the network. This communication structure, enabled by Twitter, allows local citizens to broadcast worldwide and allows the world to respond. During Haiyan, information flows with such patterns was evident for many days. Photos of hard-hit areas were being tweeted by relief workers on the ground, and then shared across the world. The global public posted messages of support and in some cases, used the platform to coordinate response.

The 2010 Haiti earthquake, in many ways, brought into global focus the capacities of Twitter for disaster outreach and fundraising [31]. Scholars have pointed out how humanitarian agencies recognized the significance of Twitter for aid mobilization in the context of Haiti [33, 34]. One organization successfully designed a communication protocol to have mobile SMS systems and Twitter messages work together to make donations to Haiti relief efforts convenient. The NGO ARC, used a 5-digit number to text if a person wants to donate, and then used Twitter to publicize the mechanism for donating in a fixed $10 amount [35]. In eight days $305 Million was raised [28, 36]. As humanitarian agencies continue to develop innovative social media approaches to fundraising and response, they will become a greater presence in Twitter traffic during and after disasters.

Murthy and Longwell's [1] examination of the uses of Twitter during flooding in Pakistan suggests that there is a global/local divide in perceived legitimacy of information. While most links shared by Twitter users emanated from traditional media with social media trailing far behind, social media sources were more often linked to, among those tweeting from Pakistan. Moreover, messages from Pakistani sources were conferred more authority status during the floods, a manner of communication from sites of disasters that were previously unavailable in events of global interest. Social networking sites are now members of the larger media ecosystem that operates during disasters of global implications; they have become an important part of the communication system used to inform organizations and citizens [37].

In a communication environment where online social networks, no matter how transient, provide an "always on" firehose of news and information from many places to many places, certain types of events like disasters will find its way more easily to global consciousness. When information sources are as diverse as they are on Twitter, the source becomes an important heuristic in sorting out good information from bad. Official information sources like governments and news organizations would be the entities with the widest reach and following [22, 38] as their status confers credibility onto information tweeted. Language matters as well, primarily as an indicator of where the source is located and who their main audience is. Local-language tweets (local to the country of the disaster event) may have different content from English-language tweets intended for a global audience. Local users may produce and seek out particular content from their media, especially for those in the disaster zone. In contrast, English-language tweets may be written with a global audience in mind and express solidarity through more general language.

The evolution of content, dominant sources, and volume of Twitter traffic post-disaster is reflective of an issue cycle for similar events on the social network site. Communities that form are informal and loosely knit together, those who are part of the Haiyan community are held together by a series of hashtag terms. Most of these connections disappear eventually several days following an event. It is posited that this issue cycle, the one that will be found for Haiyan, would be similar with what one would find for any large-impact disaster event that finds a global audience.

Gaps in the literature and research questions

The growing literature on Twitter use during disasters paint a consistent picture of its value and function as an expeditious way of disseminating information. Information often emanate from official sources, mostly news organizations. Many of these studies however, do not examine changes of tweeted content over time, although there are those that offer observations of overall declines in information sharing as days pass. Since retweets comprise a large portion of overall Twitter traffic during disasters, this means that keeping the retweets and original posts together will obscure non-informational types of content that regular citizens may be posting. The analysis in this paper separates these two categories of messages and compares patterns between them.

We expect that by coding for other message content that are not purely information, namely posts about: disaster relief, emotion, support, personal experience, and political commentary, a more detailed understanding of the various functions of Twitter during such events can be discussed. To illuminate whether and how content evolves over time and the potential alternate forms of content that are posted, we ask:

RQ1: How do volume and content of Twitter messages about a disaster evolve over time?

RQ2: Are there differences in message content between the most widely shared messages and original posts on Twitter?

Following research on the news issue attention cycle (e.g. Refs. [6] and [39]), a longitudinal analysis of the rates of increase and decrease of various types of messages about Haiyan on Twitter should provide valuable information on parallel issue attention cycles in relation to global disasters. Coding for other types of content like emotions and supportive messages may reveal differing patterns from informational posts, when examined through the days post-disaster.

To provide a more nuanced understanding of the network's behavior regarding reception and sharing of certain types of messages, features of the most retweeted messages were analyzed for content and source to determine characteristics of the most retweeted messages.

RQ3: Which types of content are most shared? What types of messages and sources act as the most effective communication hubs on Twitter during disasters?

METHOD

Tweets were collected using a Twitter API at the "Spritzer" level between November 7 and 27, 2013. This means that 1% of all tweets posted are made available by Twitter to the API for collection. The tweets were filtered to include messages that contain the following keywords: BagyoPH, RescuePH, FloodPH, TracingPH, ReliefPH, TyphoonHaiyan, HaiyanPH, HaiyanPH, Haiyan Typhoon, Typhoon Haiyan, Haiyan, TyphoonPH, Mindanao, Visayas, Samar, Leyte. These include both the international and local name of the typhoon, names of places in the Philippines that were hit, common hashtag words for the typhoon, and official hashtags used by the Philippine government over Twitter. In addition to the message tweeted, the data included user location for a subsample, Twitter handle, time zone of the user, hashtags, time the tweet was posted, whether the tweet is a reply to a message, and whether a tweet is a retweet. All Twitter data collected for this study are publicly available and can be collected by anyone in the same manner as it was collected here. The data collection was conducted in compliance with the terms and conditions stipulated by the site. The fields included Twitter usernames alone which are publicly viewable, and dates of the post, data collected did not include any identifying information or geolocation tags. There are no data protection committees in the Philippines that may be consulted, but data collected were not shared with anybody outside of the authors and research assistants named in this paper.

During large natural disaster events (e.g. Queensland floods, Haiti earthquake) much of the circulating information are retweets from media and other official sources. These predominate the universe of tweets and are often the focus of many published studies since the contents of retweeted messages are considered the most influential. This research focuses as well on the content of unique messages being tweeted, to provide greater visibility in the data toward individuals that post thoughts and information, the "public" as it were. Thus, the dataset were first filtered of retweets, this was done in an automated manner that removes all messages beginning with "RT." The most retweeted messages were analyzed separately. After the automated filtering, which excluded a large proportion of the total Twitter data (70%), two undergraduate students manually scanned the dataset to delete duplicates that did not have RT tags, messages that were not in English or Filipino, and messages that were not related to Haiyan. These deletions comprised 35% of the dataset without RTs. The process yielded a dataset that reflects original comments by different sources and represents 19.5% of the original set of tweets from the Twitter feed API collection (n = 536,363). From the cleaned dataset, a random sample of 1,000 tweets was drawn per day, resulting in a final sample size of 20,000 (S1 File for full data availability statement).

Two graduate students coded the sample for a number of variables that indicate the content of tweets. Krippendorff's kappa was calculated for each variable to test for reliability, with each round of reliability testing done with a sample of 500 tweets from the full dataset minus retweets. Acceptable reliability levels according to De Swert [40] are .80 and above, with a minimum of .67 for exceptional circumstances. The majority of coded variables reached the .80 acceptable threshold (S1 Table) with a few exceptions. Variables with reliability coefficients between .67 and .79 had low incidence rates and were therefore very sensitive to each disagreement. The table reports percent agreement and incidence for these variables.

The coding scheme was designed so that all content variables could overlap; no restrictions were placed for mutual exclusivity. That is, a single tweet could contain typhoon information, emotional expressions, and a comment about climate change and would then be coded for each of the three. In making decisions, they were instructed to read the body of the text as well as all the words with hashtags (#). Some tweets would have content-relevant words in hashtags, for instance a tweet with #heartbroken or #sad would be coded under negative emotion.

The most retweeted messages were coded in an identical manner. For each day of data collection, data were ranked according to the number of times a message was retweeted. The top 100 most retweeted messages for each day were compiled and coded using the same coding scheme and by the same coders. Sources of the most retweeted messages were also coded into categories that included news media, Philippine government sources, international aid organizations, and media celebrities.

Measures

Appendix A contains all content variables coded, their definitions, subcategories, examples, and reliability coefficients. Two background variables were coded, language and source. Since the research team has the capability to comprehend the top 2 languages used in the dataset during Haiyan, these were tagged for purposes of comparative analysis of content by language. These languages were Filipino or Tagalog and Cebuano (and closely related dialects). Source was coded in a centralized manner, a list of all unique Twitter handles was generated and a graduate student did research-based determinations of whether the handles belonged to private individuals, entertainment media celebrities, heads of institutions (e.g. Pontifex as head of Catholic Church), politicians, aid organizations, and local or international media.

The remaining content variables fall under the following general categories: information, expressions of support, emotion, disaster relief and aid, and political expressions. Each category has a number of subcategory variables defined and described below:

Information.

These tweets contain information about the typhoon, its impact, and where to help with monetary donations. Although solicitation of information does not happen often, these were coded as well. There are a number of subcategories of information coded, to allow for disaggregation in the analyses when there is an interest in specific types of information. *Typhoon information* is tweets containing information about the weather phenomenon of Haiyan itself, including trajectory, strength, time of landfall or place of likely impact. *Class suspension* was coded separately; these are simple announcements about suspension of school and work as a result of the typhoon and its damage. *Damage information* are messages that describe the extent and type of damage, number of deaths, places hit, or scale of the impact. *Fundraising information* are shared details about drives to raise money to send to victims of the storm. *Requests for information* include queries about current situation or specifics like whether an area was hit, whether a street is flooded, or whether electricity has been restored.

Disaster relief.

In the aftermath of the typhoon institutions and individuals undertook massive relief and recovery efforts. Tweets that were about disaster relief were coded in several subcategories. *Personal relief* are activities of any relief effort a tweeter has provided to the affected populations. These include monetary and nonmonetary aid. *Relief of others* is those that report efforts of other people and institutions. *Relief coordination* is messages that contain actionable information pertaining to the provision of aid. For example, tweets that say what a community needs, or where one can go to volunteer, or messages containing logistical information reporting on the status of aid distribution. *Specific calls for help* contain specific information like place where help is needed and what kind of help is needed (e.g. please send water to Guian, people are in dire need of help).

Foreign response.

Many tweets report on the pledges of support from countries and international aid agencies, even individuals in places outside the Philippines. These were coded into a separate category and include news about monetary or nonmonetary assistance provided by any entity that is not based in the Philippines. Foreign response may overlap with disaster relief, and in those cases the tweets would be coded positively for both. The distinction would reveal when the event reached and sustained international attention.

Personal information.

Messages that contain personal reports and questions were tagged. These include messages that ask for information to *help finding people* (e.g. looking for any news about my sister, was Alangalan Leyte badly hit?), specific *local information about impact* or status of the storm (e.g. please send help to Bantigue Leyte, there are people there dying of hunger), reports of direct *personal loss* of people or material possessions (e.g. our house in Tacloban is completely gone). Personal information is separated out as its own category to try to distinguish tweets from those who were directly affected or witnesses, from those that are general information from institutions such as government and media.

Emotions.

The literature on use of Twitter suggests one of its main functions is for users to tell others how they feel. Emotions were coded into three broad categories: *negative*, positive, and *expressions of gratitude (thanks*). Messages of thanks were pervasive over some days, and thus, were coded separately from other forms of positive emotions, however in the end positive emotions were not reliably coded. Since there are only few instances of positive emotion tweets, the reliability tests were extremely sensitive to even the slightest disagreement. However, since we were coding for negative emotions it would be inappropriate to not code for positive ones. Results for positive emotions should be interpreted with caution. Negative emotional statements included expressions of shock, sadness, grief, and anger among others. Expressions of positive emotions included having hope, feeling inspired.

Expressions of support.

Haiyan was a global phenomenon both as a weather disturbance and after it hit Tacloban, as a humanitarian crisis. We coded for messages that expressed *calls for safety* (e.g. stay safe everyone in the Philippines!), and *prayers* (e.g. praying for everybody in the path of the supertyphoon). A separate category on other *supportive messages* was coded but did not achieve reliability (.57) and are thus, excluded in the analyses.

Politics.

Discussions and news about politics and government were common in the days after the storm hit, related to relief and recovery operations. These were primarily criticisms related to the slowness of response, to statements made by public officials, and news and commentary about fights between political factions (local and national government). Positive and negative messages were coded in separate categories to capture valence.

The data were examined longitudinally to reflect changes in functions over time. Simple descriptive summative statistics are used to provide an overall picture of the types of messages that are posted related to Haiyan. By-day distributions of variables are presented to examine longitudinal patterns. By-group and by-day differences presented are statistically significant, a result that is more readily attained since the sample size is large.

RESULTS

The first research question is about how volume and content of Twitter messages about a disaster evolve over time. Fig 1 shows the number of tweets collected by day through the API, since these are a fixed percentage, randomly selected sets of tweets from the collected data, it is assumed that the volume changes per day in the sample reflect volume changes per day among all collected tweets. Tweets about Haiyan started off November 7 with low frequency, shooting up to 5 times its volume the on November 8; the day the storm hit Tacloban at 5 in the morning. While the storm was happening and the day it made landfall, there was little information coming out of the hardest hit areas. Towns were isolated from any communication and transportation for close to 48 hours, reflected in a slight dip in tweet volume following November 8. Tweets increased again starting November 11, peaking on 12th. Tweets during these days were about the scale of the damage, the press had arrived on site and descriptions, photos, and videos were being circulated to the public. The rate of decline in tweet volume was equally steep in the following two days. Thus, from this example the issue attention cycle peters off after about 17 days.

The vast majority of tweets were retweets, a manner for individual citizens to share information they see on the platform. The solid line in Fig 1 illustrates volume after all retweets are excluded, showing a much flatter line, although an increase in original content posting is also evident following the same dates as the line including retweets. Differences in patterns of overall Twitter traffic and posts that exclude retweets reflect the platform's use as an effective dissemination channel. Through communication hubs and social networks, information can be retweeted any number of times.

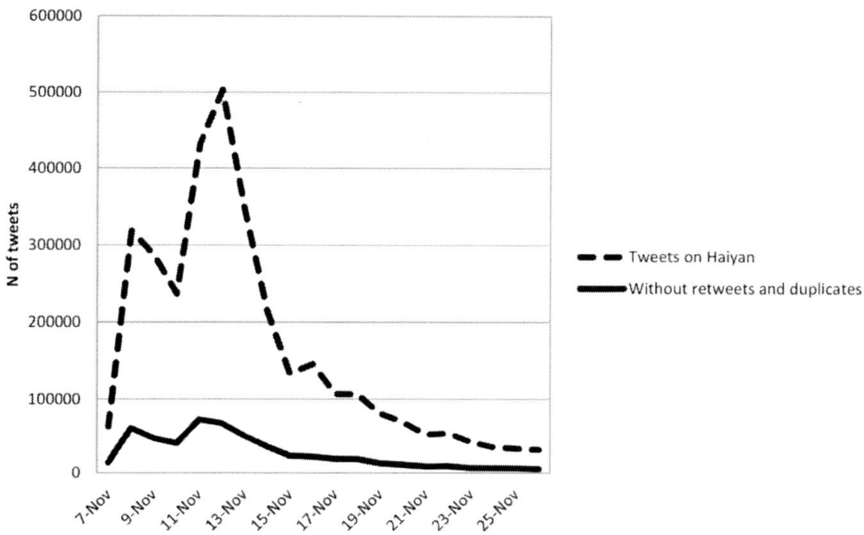

Figure1. Number of tweets by day.

Much of the available literature on Twitter posts during disasters find that the majority of content being posted is information, by a large margin, with other forms of posts lagging far behind in frequency. The second research question asks whether there are differences in message content between the most widely-shared messages and those that are original posts. Fig 2 shows general content category distributions for both the most retweeted messages and messages without retweets. While 59% of the most retweeted messages contain information about the typhoon, a smaller portion (43%) of the general Twitter messages contains information. Still, the overall pattern is that information about the typhoon and about disaster relief dominates Twitter. We argue that the vast majority of original posts are from ordinary citizens or the general public. Results show that these tend to contain more messages with emotions, personal information, and commentary about politics, although these do not occur frequently. Among the original tweets, 10% of messages have content about emotions, compared to a smaller 4% among the most retweeted messages. Personal information in general does not get tweeted often, however given the scale of Twitter [41], even small proportions could be consequential. There are more instances of personal information tweets from original posts compared to the retweeted messages.

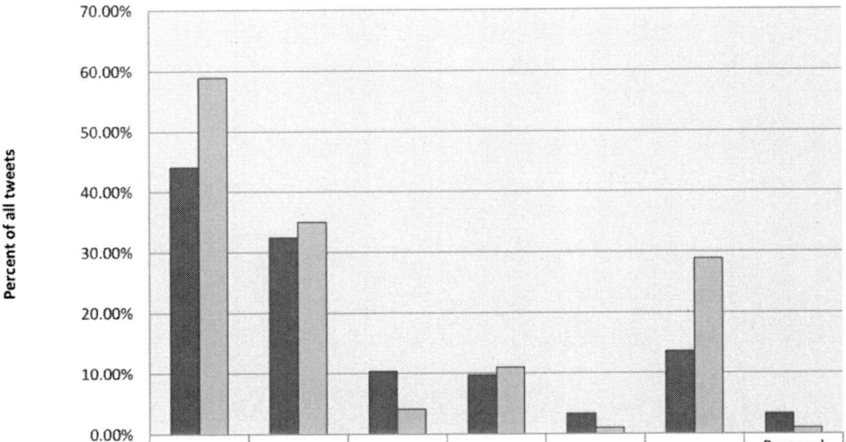

	Information	Disaster Relief	Emotion	Support	Politics	Foreign Response	Personal Information
No Retweets	44.10%	32.40%	10.30%	9.70%	3.30%	13.60%	3.30%
Most Retweeted	58.90%	35.00%	4.10%	11.00%	1.00%	28.80%	1.00%

Figure 2. Content of tweets.

Of note is a dearth of messages related to politics. According to an international comparative study by Pew Research Center [42], while social media enjoys relatively high use rates in the Philippines, its use for posting content related to politics is low compared to other developing countries. This is reflected in the content coding done here, where political posts comprised very little of the total Twitter traffic on Haiyan. This could be specific to the country however, and it would be interesting to do further cross-country comparisons of Twitter use during global humanitarian crises to determine if the lack of political discourse post-disaster varies by location.

Over the course of several days, tweets with informational content about the typhoon and its damage declines sharply for both retweets and non-retweeted messages (Fig 3). These are replaced by messages with information about disaster relief and foreign response (which often also contain information about relief; 34% of disaster relief messages are about foreign response). As a proportion of total tweets these two categories comprise the vast majority of posts. Emotions are shared across all the days for tweets of the general public, peaking at 16.8% of tweets the day the storm hit, with the lowest values at 5% at 20 days post-typhoon. For retweets, emotions do not comprise a substantive proportion of messages, hovering around 3% for the days around the typhoon, and then peaking 8 days after at 10%.

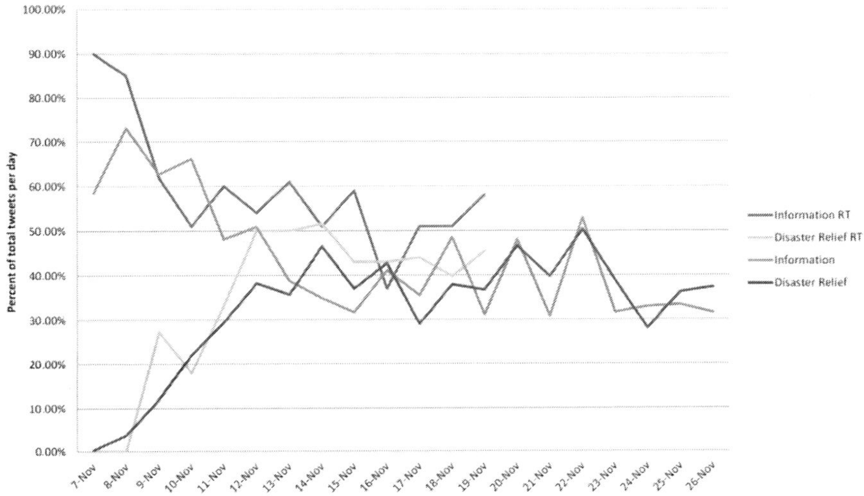

Figure 3. Tweets of information and disaster relief.

Informational tweets among the general public are comprised of 18% information about the typhoon, 8% about fund drives, 4% questions asking for information, and the vast majority, 75% information about the damage and impact of the typhoon (categories are not mutually exclusive). The volume of informational tweets decreases over time but always stays above other forms of content in terms of proportion of total tweets.

Of interest are tweets about disaster relief, as these have not been examined as a separate category in existing research on the functions of Twitter during disasters. Of the total sample of tweets from the general public that were classified under disaster relief, 12% reported on personal acts of disaster relief, 67% reported on the relief activities of others, 8% were solicitations of specific kinds of help (e,g. water needed in Guian, Samar. It's been 3 days), and 54% are coordinative in nature (e.g. @abscbnnews: find your family in #Haiyanph-hit areas using the #kapamilyafinder: http://t.co/9oxy6trvkt (click "find"; @reliefphcom please add abs-cbn legaspi to the list of drop-off points in albay. #reliefph #rescueph; pia-ndrrmc: doe has 147 generator sets waiting to be transported to leyte, eastern samar, roxas capiz). Twitter, therefore, not only acts as a channel to disseminate information about the typhoon and the disaster relief activities that go on, it also is used as a platform to coordinate and mobilize relief efforts, to share personal stories helping, and to share information about help being extended by others.

Retweets are mostly information messages for more than a week after the typhoon, comprising 85% and 90% the day of the typhoon and the day before it, respectively (Fig 4). These are messages with news about the intensity and size of the storm, its trajectory, and where it will make landfall. There are large increases in news about the foreign humanitarian response to those affected, starting at 15% only 2 days after, and rising to 53% of the most retweeted messages one week after. Disaster relief messages that circulate among the most retweeted messages are usually about large fundraising campaigns, these began in earnest the day immediately after the storm, the day that information about the size of its damage started appearing on the news. By November 12, 50% of the most retweeted messages were about disaster relief, staying at around that level until the end of data gathering.

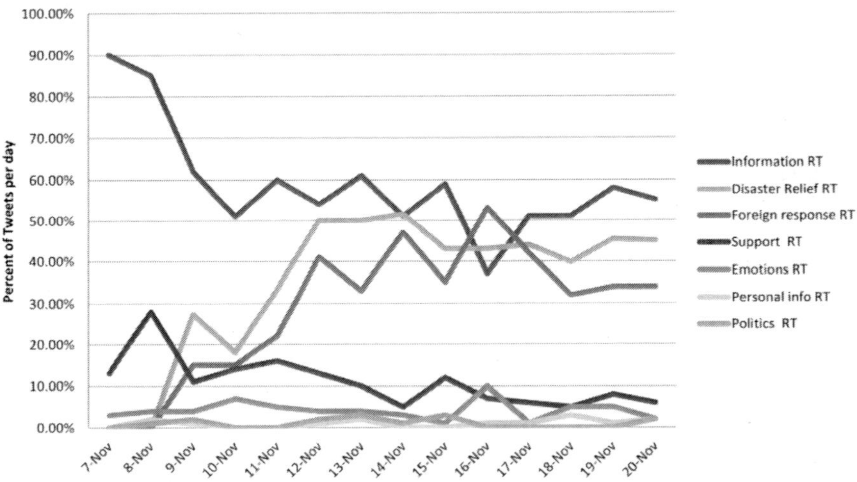

Figure 4. Content categories by day, retweets.

There are slight by-language differences in the overall distribution of content types tweeted by the general public. Filipino language tweets, which comprises 11% of the sample (English 87%), have higher rates of messages with emotions, support, politics, and information (Table 1). English language tweets have higher rates of messages about disaster relief and foreign response. Local-language tweets represent sentiments of people who are closer to the site of the disaster and therefore are either directly or indirectly affected, as opposed to the rest of the world on Twitter who are spectators to the event as it unfolds. The international community responded through disaster relief, and this is evident in the higher proportion of disaster relief messages in English.

Table 1. Content of non-retweeted messages by language (percent).

	Filipino	English
Information	53	42.5
Disaster Relief	22.9	31.9
Foreign Response	5.9	13.2
Personal Information	8.3	2.8
Emotions	18.5	9.3
Support	13.8	10.2
Politics	5.8	2.7

The most retweeted messages are often from news sources, media celebrities, and aid organizations involved in disaster relief. Fig 5 shows the progression of how different sources of tweets dominate in different stages of the issue cycle. Interestingly, while we coded for Philippine government agencies and key officials, these were not substantive sources of popular information on Twitter. In the initial days when circulating messages are comprised mostly of information about the storm and the extent of damage, local news sources played an important part in circulating critical safety messages. Their influence over the network began to decline as soon as news about the scale of the damage became public, international news organizations started covering it as a global event. Foreign news sources had more retweeted messages than local news sources two days after the storm and continued for a week. Local news became more prominent again beyond November 16, when local news outfits carried a story about the Empire State Building having been lit up as a tribute to those killed by Haiyan. The most influential communication hubs are clearly celebrities, most of whom are non-Filipino celebrities. Table 2 lists the top most retweeted messages each day, and for most days the top are from celebrities Harry Styles, Liam Payne, and Alicia Keyes. The current Pope Francis, head of a state and a religious institution, we argue, has celebrity status given his high visibility in international media. Celebrities clearly have an inordinate amount of influence over circulating information on the network, particularly during disasters when they are active in publicizing fundraising efforts. Aid organization are also a prominent source of the most retweeted messages, these are mostly fundraising drives and are aided in turn by the activities of interested celebrities.

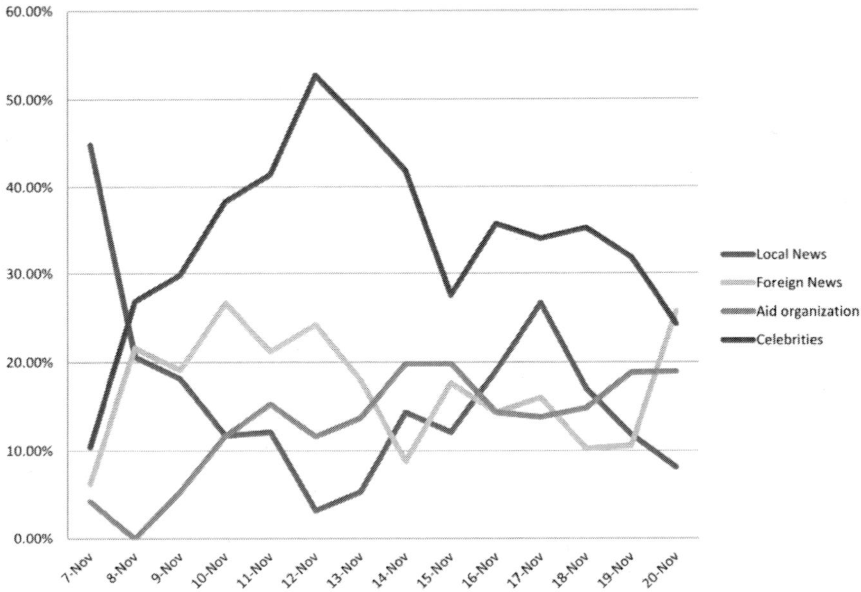

Figure 5. Sources of most retweeted messages, by day.

Table 2. Most retweeted messages, top for a sample of days.

Day	Tweet	N of RT
7	@makatiinfo: dear students: instead of praying for class suspension, pray for the safety of those who are in the direct path of	976
9	@pontifex: i ask all of you to join me in prayer for the victims of typhoon haiyan / Haiyan especially those in the beloved is	13768
11	@aliciakeys: to the people of the philippines my heart is with you #praye	3413
13	@harry_styles: millions in the philippines need clean water & shelter now. @oxfamgb is there: donate to their #haiyan appeal! h	27187
14	@harry_styles: millions in the philippines need clean water & shelter now. @oxfamgb is there: donate to their #haiyan appeal! h	5580
16	@empirestatebldg: 2nite & tmrw night, our lights shine in the color of the #philippines flag 2 raise awareness of the #haiyan t	6410
17	@harry_styles: millions in the philippines need clean water & shelter now. @oxfamgb is there: donate to their #haiyan appeal! h	1639
19	@real_liam_payne: contribute to #haiyan relief efforts. donate to the @redcross via itunes at http://t.co/	8063
20	@real_liam_payne: contribute to #haiyan relief efforts. donate to the @redcross via itunes at http://t.co/	5578

To answer research question 3, even more so than news organizations, media celebrities act as the most effective communication hubs for disseminating across the network, if we define effectiveness as being able to enable the widest dissemination. Fig 6 shows the average number of retweets by source among the most retweeted messages, clearly indicating a large advantage of foreign (non-Filipino) celebrities over all other sources. Interestingly, non-news media sources are the second most-retweeted sources, these are often social media-centric Twitter accounts like Instagram or television brands like National Geographic and the Ellen DeGeneres Show.

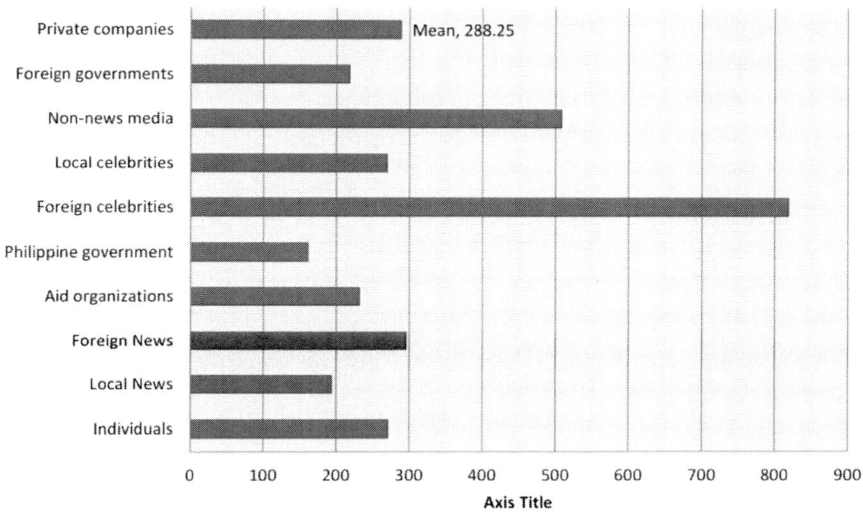

Figure 6. Average number of retweets by source.

DISCUSSION AND CONCLUSIONS

This research sought to provide an over-time examination of the various functions of Twitter, reflected by the types of messages that are posted, how these message types gain dominance and then decline in frequency, the main communication or information hubs in the network and how their posts differ from those of the general Twitter public. By examining these throughout a 20-day period between the day before Haiyan, a predicted weather event, to the days when rescue and relief were in full force, we hope to show a more nuanced picture of the issue attention cycle on the Twitter network. This is shown in the context of a global weather event that turned into a humanitarian crisis, since it hit a developing nation. As the biggest storm in recorded history hit the Philippine island of Leyte, killing more than 6,000 people with a 20-foot storm surge, Twitter users posted information, retweeted, and engaged actively in the relief effort.

Consistent with findings of studies that examine social media use during disasters, posts related to Haiyan were comprised mostly of retweeted informational content [8, 43]. About 80% of the total traffic in the 20-day span were retweets of messages from media sources, celebrities, and Philippine government agencies. As a proportion of tweets, retweets comprised the largest portion of messages on the day the storm hit, and 5 days afterward. When news stories become available, users take it upon themselves to retweet throughout their network. The steep curve of information dissemination on Twitter suggests that users are not just relying on the site for news but also have a sense of engagement, enough to retweet stories that are of interest. Changes in volume of retweets indicate the public and news' engagement with the issue, which declined sharply on the 5th day and then slows even more over the next few days. This, we propose, is a typical news issue cycle on Twitter, and with similar studies of other global disaster events may be reflected in other instances. An event's presence on the site may not be as extended for disasters that do not have international attention, as much of this attention was sustained by disaster relief efforts by organizations that are not in the Philippines.

Without the retweets in the dataset, the content analysis reveals that original tweets coming from ordinary people are of only a slightly different character in terms of content type distribution. Ordinary people are more likely to tweet emotional expressions, reports about disaster relief efforts, and personal information. While the differences do not appear large compared to the retweets, and the proportions are at or below 10%, the massive scale of Twitter's traffic [41] means those even low proportions could translate to tens of thousands of messages. These types of messages have not been examined thoroughly in the literature, possibly because retweeted messages usually are included in sample codings, drowning out alternative types of messages being posted by the regular users. The exception is Chew and Eysenbach [19], but their study is in the context of a global pandemic and its interest is more in Twitter's use as an alternative source of statistical information for a disease's spread. In the case of global disaster events such as Haiyan, which evolves into a humanitarian crisis, the types of posts from ordinary people and their changes over time indicate Twitter's functionality as a space to express solidarity and work through emotions. Significantly, it is also a space where people share information and activities about disaster relief done by those outside of the Philippines. Such information sharing and locally organized fundraising and volunteering carry great potential for government and humanitarian agencies to widen their pool of potential volunteers and donors.

The role that Twitter plays as a functional communication tool for disaster preparedness, emergency response, crisis communication, and relief provision continues to grow as institutions and individuals innovate on the various ways it can be used to deploy and gather information. Disaster relief messages comprised a substantial portion of both the retweets and general public messages. The retweeted messages are mostly announcements and retweets of celebrities that publicize fundraising drives of aid organizations. However other tweets that are not among the most retweeted contain actionable coordinative information. These include things like calls for volunteers to a specific location to help with packing goods for delivery to affected sites, calls for volunteers with cars to drive relocated individuals to places where they can stay, and lists of supplies needed in specific locations. These are important logistical coordinative functions that may spur greater involvement among those who are active on the Twitter platform. Beyond the functionality for publicity during fundraising activities, Twitter may also effectively improve upon disaster response and relief delivery from volunteers and aid groups insofar as it brings together into conversation engaged and interested actors. Twitter amplifies voice, creating a potentially wider audience, greater mobilization efforts, and greater attention from the aid community at large as disaster events capture global attention more easily now than before. Nevertheless, we recognize that it is important to also assess the impact of Twitter in relation to how affected people themselves accessed and used Twitter and benefited from any campaigns organized through the platform. Research on affected communities' own uses of social media suggest a disconnect between global initiatives (which we identify here as having many potential benefits for fundraising and aid mobilization) with experiences on the ground [44].

The evolution of posted content moves from a predominance of information about the typhoon to disaster relief messages and reactions and stories about foreign response. The news cycle, media sources writing stories about the storm and its aftermath, sustains attention at a high level for several days. This signals the relevance of official information sources in providing the original content that generates interest in the network, as it is retweeted at scale, attention spreads throughout different countries bringing the event to international importance. This high level of attention, indicated by the volume of retweets in the early days, creates a community of followers of hashtags about Haiyan which in turn serves as the main audience for all other non-informational posts that follow in the days of response and relief. As members of the Twitter public contribute to relief efforts in various ways (e.g. donating, joining events, attending concerts, volunteering services, being directly involved in aid), they post about their own and others' efforts, extending issue interest in the network and potentially creating a sense among followers of the hashtags that a large public is directly involved, which may in turn create a perceived social normative pressure to contribute [45].

Celebrities had a central role in acting as information hubs and key entities in the network that would increase attention and then sustain it through time. Specifically, Harry Styles and Liam Payne, members of a musical group called One Direction with a large international fan base, showed up in the results as being central information hubs for disaster relief drives. There are many other celebrities that appear among the top sources of retweeted messages, highlighting the importance of information hubs in creating wide networks of followers for issues. Even the Twitter fan pages of celebrities often appear as top sources of retweeted content on certain days. The scale of this effect is large, and a systematic empirical network analysis of the size and speed of information diffusion from celebrities is in order to clarify exactly the depth and breadth of this influence.

This research is limited by some key constraints. First, the spritzer level access to Twitter data and the opacity of the selection of tweets the platform supplies limits the ability of many studies like this to show the real scale of attention and content diversity. However, this does not threaten the validity of the distributions and relationships examined here. Second, the content analysis can only be done for English language and Filipino language tweets, excluding many messages that were posted in other foreign languages that are a substantive portion of the international attention. Third, the sheer volume of even sampled content made coding of sources difficult to complete, as information is not available for every Twitter account that was sampled. This limited our ability to draw inferences about the relationship between content types and sources for the non-retweeted messages.

Use of Twitter during and after disaster events spans a variety of functions including information dissemination, disaster relief and response coordination, fundraising, and emotional expression. The distribution of content in the network evolves in the days following a disaster event, particularly one that becomes a global humanitarian issue as what happened in Haiyan. Various sources play important roles as information hubs that either generate original content, or in the case of celebrities, amplify the reach of messages to new publics that would otherwise be less engaged and aware. The issue attention cycle on Twitter, taking into account key sources and hubs, and the evolution of content, provides important information for strategic communication. Crisis communicators from government can apply what is learned here to widen the audience base for messages. Aid organizations doing fundraising drives should connect with effective amplifiers of messages such as entertainment celebrities to improve collections. Smaller microvolunteer networks in local areas can use it to broadcast needs and coordinate effective response.

News outlets can use Twitter accounts to sustain attention on the issue by continued postings of new information constantly, even if the information base changes from details about the event to details about the response. It would be of empirical and theoretical interest for future research to examine whether the issue attention cycle on Twitter is different from that of other media outlets, or even for that matter, from Facebook.

Unfortunately, global weather events that lead to humanitarian crises are a constant threat and will continue to happen periodically. Efficient and targeted use of available communication channels such as social media networks can make a real difference in preparing communities for disasters, and transforming response and relief into larger and more effective efforts.

ACKNOWLEDGMENTS

The authors are grateful for the research assistance of Karen Varona, Ana Desamparado, Lina Luisa Vergara, Arno Borrero, Pamela Combinido, and Aina Lopez.

AUTHOR CONTRIBUTIONS

Conceived and designed the experiments: CCD EL. Performed the experiments: EL. Analyzed the data: CCD EL. Wrote the paper: CCD JO. Conceptualized the narrative: JO. Collected the data: EL.

REFERENCES

1. Murthy D, Longwell SA. Twitter and Disasters: The Uses of Twitter during the 2010 Pakistan Floods. Information, Communication, & Society. 2013; 16(6):837–855.
2. Kongthon A, Haruechaiyasak C, Pailai J, Kongyoung S. The Role of Twitter during a Natural Disaster: Case Study of 2011 Thai Flood. In: Proceedings of PICMET '12: Technology Management for Emerging Technologies; 2012. p. 2227–2232.
3. Lotan G, Graeff E, Ananny M, Gaffney D, Pearce I, Boyd D. The Revolutions were Tweeted: Information Flows during the 2011 Tunisian and Egyptian Revolutions. International Journal of Communication. 2011; 5:1375–1405.
4. Palen L, Starbird K, Vieweg S, Hughes A. Twitter-based Information Distribution During the 2009 Red River Valley Flood Threat. Bulletin of the American Society for Information Science and Technology. 2010; 36(5):13–17.
5. Guy M, Earle P, Ostrum C, Gruchalla K, Horvath S. Integration and Dissemination of Citizen Reported and Seismically Derived Earthquake Information via Social Network Technologies. In:

Lecture Notes in Computer Science Series: Advances in Intelligent Data Analysis IX; 2010: 6065. p. 42–53.

6. Downs A. Up and Down with Ecology—the "Issue-attention Cycle". Public Interest, 1972; 28:38–50.

7. Moddock J, Starbrd K, Al-Hassani H, Sandoval D, Orand M, Mason R. Characterizing Online Rumoring Behavior Using Multi-Dimensional Sigantures. In: CSWC '15 Proceedings of the 18th ACM Conference on Compute Supported Cooperative Work and Social Computing; 2015. p. 228–241.

8. Starbird K, Palen L. Pass it on? Retweeting in Mass Emergency. In: Proceedings of the 7th International ISCRAM Conference, Seattle, WA; 2010.

9. Fischetti M. Was Typhoon Haiyan a Record Storm? Scientific American. 27 Nov 2013. Available: http://blogs.scientificamerican .com /observations/was-typhoon-haiyan-a-record-storm/

10. BBC News. Typhoon Haiyan Death Toll Rises over 5,000. 22 Nov 2013. Available: http://www.bbc.com/news/world-asia-25051606

11. Spiro E, Butts C. When Bad Things Happen to Good People: Online Communication Dynamics During Natural Hazard Events. In: Proceedings of Annual Meeting of the American Sociological Association; 2013. Available: http://citation.allacademic. com/meta/p650462_index.html

12. Doan S, Ho Vo B, Collier N. An Analysis of Twitter Messages in the 2011 Tohoku Earthquake. In: Lecture Notes of the Institute for Computer Sciences, Social Informatics and Telecommunications Engineering, V; 2011: 91. p. 58–66.

13. Sutton J, Spiro E, Johnson B, Fitzhugh S, Gibson B, Butts C. Warning Tweets: Serial Transmission of Messages during the Warning Phase of a Disaster Event. Information, Communication, & Society. 2014; 17(6):765–787.

14. Cheong F, Cheong C. Social Media Data Mining: A Social Network Analysis of Tweets During the 2010–2011 Australian Floods. In: Proceedings of the 2011 PACIS; 2011. Available: http://aisel. aisnet.org/pacis2011/46/

15. Humphreys L, Gill P, Krishnamurthy B. Twitter: A Content Analysis of Personal Information. Information, Communication & Society. 2014; 17(7):843–857. doi: 10.1080/1369118X.2013.848917.

16. Lansdall-Welfare T, Vasileios L, Cristianini N. Nowcasting the Mood of the Nation. Significance. 2012; 9:26–28.

17. Sutton J, Palen L, Shklovski I. Backchannels on the Front Lines: Emergent Uses of Social Media in the 2007 Southern California Wildfires. Crisis. 2008; i.

18. Vieweg S, Hughes Al, Starbird K, Palen L. Microblogging During Two Natural Hazards Events: What Twitter May Contribute to Situational Awareness. In: Proceedings of the 28th International Conference on Human Factors in Computing Systems; 2010.

19. Chew C, Eysenbach G. Pandemics in the Age of Twitter: Content Analysis of Tweets during the 2009 H1N1 Outbreak. PLoS ONE. 2010; 5(11).

20. Heverin T, Zach L. Microblogging for Crisis Communication: Examination of Twitter Use in Response to a 2009 Violent Crisis in the Seattle-Tacoma, Washington Area. In: Proceedings of the 7th International ISCRAM Conference, Seattle, WA; 2010.

21. Bongwon S, Lichan H, Peter P, Chi E. Want to be Retweeted? Large Scale Analytics on Factors Impacting Retweet in Twitter Network. In: Proceedings of the IEEE International Conference on Social Computing and IEEE International Conference on Privacy, Security, Risk and Trust; 2010. p. 177–184. 10.1109/SocialCom.2010.33

22. Stieglitz S, Dang-Xuan L. Emotions and Information Diffusion in Social Media—Sentiment of Microblogs and Sharing Behavior. Journal of Management Information Systems. 2013; 29(4): 217–247.

23. Zarrella D. Science of Retweets. 2009. Available from: http://danzarrella.com/the-science-of-retweets-report.html.

24. Hughes A, Palen L. Twitter Adoption and Use in Mass Convergence and Emergency Events. In: Proceedings of the 6th international ISCRAM Conference, Gotherberg, Sweden; 2009.

25. Merrifield N, Panechar M. Uncertainty Reduction Strategies via Twitter: The 2011 wildfire threat to Los Alamos National Laboratory. In: Proceedings from AEJMC Annual Conference; 2012.

26. Castells M. The Rise of the Network Society: The Information Age. 2nd ed. Oxford: Blackwell; 2000.

27. Gesualdi M. Global Networks, Social Media, and the Iceland Ash Cloud: A Crisis Communication Case. Presented at the International Communication Association Conference. 2012.

28. Ellenberger N, Katz J, Gurman T. Tweets Reaching the Global Community During Disasters: Organizational Use of Twitter Surrounding the Haiti Earthquake. In: Annual meeting of the International Communication Association, Sheraton Phoenix

Downtown, Phoenix; 2012. Available from: http://citation.allacademic.com/meta/p554032_index.html

29. Smith, A. Haiti Donations: $1.3 Billion. Money. 9 Jul 2010. Available: http://money.cnn.com/2010/07/09/news/international/haiti_donation/

30. Smith B. Socially Distributing Public relations: Twitter, Haiti, and Interactivity in Social Media. Public Relations Review. 2010; 36(4):329–335.

31. Muralidharan S, Rasmussen L, Patterson D, Shin Jae-Hwa. Hope for Haiti: An Analysis of Facebook and Twitter Usages During the Earthquake Relief Efforts. Public Relations Review. 2011; 37:175–177.

32. Buchanan-Smith M, Ong JC, Routley S. Who's Listening? Accountability to Affected People in the Haiyan Response. Plan International. 2015. Available: http://www.alnap.org/resource/20632.

33. Frank T. Social Media Play Part in Haiti's Recovery Efforts. USA Today. 1 Feb 2010. Available: http://usatoday30.usatoday.com/tech/news/2010-02-01-haiti-monitor-social-media_N.htm

34. Rossman J. Social Media Plays Star Role in Haiti Relief Efforts, for Better or Worse. Dallas Morning News. 30 Jan 2010. Available: http://www.dallasnews.com/business/technology/20100130-Social-media-plays-star-role-in-1582.ece

35. Manjoo F. Online Giving, One Person at a time. New York Times. 10 Nov 2010.

36. Ellis B. Haiti Donations Exceed $305 Million. Money. 21 Jan 2010. Available: http://money.cnn.com/2010/01/21/news/international /haiti_donations/?section=money_latest.

37. Hanna R, Rohm A, Crittenden VL. We're All Connected: The Power of the Social Media Ecosystem. Business Horizons. 2011; 54:265–273.

38. Suh B, Hong L, Pirolli P, Chi EH. Want to be Retweeted? Large Scale Analytics on Factors Impacting Retweet in Twitter Network. In: IEEE Second international Conference; 2010. p. 177–184.

39. Shih T, Wijaya R, Brossard D. 2008. Media Coverage of Public Health Epidemics: Linking Framing and Issue Attention Cycle Toward an Integrated Theory of Print News Coverage of Epidemics. Mass Communication & Society. 2008; 11(2):141–160.

40. De Swert K. Calculating Inter-coder Reliability in Media Content Analysis using Krippendorff's Alpha. 2012. Available from: http://www.polcomm.org/wp-content/uploads/ICR01022012.pdf

41. Wike R, Oates R. Emerging Nations Embrace Internet, Mobile Technology. Pew Research Center. 2014: 1–42. Available from: http://www.pewglobal.org/files/2014/02/Pew-Research-Center-Global-Attitudes-Project-Technology-Report-FINAL-February-13-20146.pdf.

42. Bruns A, Burgess J, Crawford K, Shaw F. #qldfloods and @QPSMedia: Crisis Communication on Twitter in the 2011 South East Queensland Floods. 2012. Brisbane: ARC Centre of Excellence for Creative Industries and Innovation.

43. Madianou M, Longboan L, Ong JC. Finding a Voice through Humanitarian Technologies? Communication and Participation in Disaster Recovery. International Journal of Communication. 2015; 15(9):3020–3038.

44. Martin JA. Closing Gaps in International Knowledge and Participation: News Attention, Online Expression, and the 2010 Haiti Earthquake. Mass Communication and Society. 2013; 16:417–440.

45. Schultz PW, Nolan JM, Cialdini RB, Goldstein NJ, Griskevicius V. The Constructive, Destructive, and Reconstructive Power of Social Norms. Psychological Science. 2007;18(5):429–434.

5

RISING TIDES OR RISING STARS?: DYNAMICS OF SHARED ATTENTION ON TWITTER DURING MEDIA EVENTS

Yu-Ru Lin[1], Brian Keegan[2], Drew Margolin[3], David Lazer[2,4]

[1] School of Information Sciences, University of Pittsburgh, Pittsburgh, Pennsylvania, United States of America,

[2] College of Social Sciences and Humanities, Northeastern University, Boston, Massachusetts, United States of America,

[3] Department of Communication, Cornell University, Ithaca, New York, United States of America,

[4] College of Computer and Information Science, Northeastern University, Boston, Massachusetts, United States of America

ABSTRACT

"Media events" generate conditions of shared attention as many users simultaneously tune in with the dual screens of broadcast and social media to view and participate. We examine how collective patterns of user behavior under conditions of shared attention are distinct from other "bursts" of activity like breaking news events. Using 290 million tweets from a panel of 193,532 politically active Twitter users, we compare features of their behavior during eight major events during the 2012 U.S. presidential election to examine how patterns of social media use change during these media events compared to "typical" time and whether these changes are attributable to shifts in the behavior of the population as a whole or shifts from particular segments such as elites. Compared to baseline time periods, our findings reveal that media events not only generate large volumes of tweets, but they are also associated with (1) substantial declines in interpersonal communication, (2) more highly concentrated attention by replying to and retweeting particular users, and (3) elite users predominantly benefiting from this attention. These findings empirically demonstrate how bursts of activity on Twitter during media events significantly alter underlying social processes of interpersonal communication and social interaction. Because the behavior of large populations within socio-technical systems can change so dramatically, our findings suggest the need for further research about how social media responses to media events can be used to support collective sensemaking, to promote informed deliberation, and to remain resilient in the face of misinformation.

INTRODUCTION

Social media has transformed the media landscape by providing individuals with the technical capability to compete with mass media in disseminating informati-on, setting agendas, and framing conversations [1], [2]. By providing a technological solution to the costs of directing, aggregating, and disseminating discourse, social media might contribute to political deliberations that are more participatory, support larger exchanges of better information, and promote greater mobilization of political action [3]. Among many uses, tweet streams can both detect breaking news and share information about breaking news events [4]–[6], augment community members' and first responders' awareness of unfolding disasters [7]–[9], and disseminate political speech to both mobilize protests and criticize opposition to established regimes [10]–[12]. Twitter potentially supports more deliberative political participation by facilitating collective sensemaking of fast-paced but ambiguous information, broadening participation in and awareness of policy discussions, and a subjecting messages containing misinformation to greater scrutiny. In many ways, Twitter and other social media offer the promise of advancing collective deliberation toward philosophical ideals in which all individuals are free both to contribute to collective discourse and to directly challenge one another in a public forum [13].

Despite the promise offered by what social media makes technically possible, there is the matter of the socio-technical systems that emerge and evolve around these capabilities. Firstly, there is the question of whether people actually use the affordances of the medium. For example, do Twitter users take advantage of its opportunity for direct public interaction to discuss important issues? Research examining online citizen communication has examined the extent to which messages are deliberative and whether users selectively expose themselves to ideologically polarized messages that insulate them from deliberation [14]–[17]. The openness of social media also makes these discussions vulnerable to misinformation, partisanship, interest groups, activists, and political indifference that undermine offline deliberation [18], [19]. Second, and often overlooked, is the way behavior of and within these systems responds to different conditions and stimuli. Despite growing interest in characterizing the content or behavior on social media [20]–[26], empirical analyses often proceed from the assumption that individual motivations to participate and the behavior of the system are generic and relatively constant [27]. Such an assumption presents communication technologies in an unrealistically deterministic light and disguises the ways that observed changes in social media systems can reveal more general mechanisms of social behavior.

In this paper, we examine how behavior on social media systematically shifts in response to one such condition, the *shared attention to media events*. Our findings reveal that communication behaviors can change significantly under conditions of shared attention both in terms of how individuals produce content and how they attend to it. The primary outcomes of this change are a simultaneous increase in general productivity alongside a general decrease in the diversity of attendance. That is, more people speak, but listening is increasingly focused only on elite speakers. These findings thus suggest that when social media's potential to democratize discourse is technically greatest — when a large number of people are simultaneously connected in virtual space — individual motivations, social norms, and algorithmic prioritization of some tweets over others inhibit its ability to do so.

Background

Twitter plays an increasingly important role in fostering simultaneous communication around planned events such as political debates [28], sporting events [29], television shows [30], [31], and other large-scale social gatherings [32]. For example, television producers increasingly invite viewers to use a "second screen" so they can "dual screen" and share their reactions to program's content with an audience that is both watching the program and attending to related Twitter streams [33]. Audience members can then see others' responses and interact with each other in real time around their shared interests [34], [35]. Rather than being distractions, the use of textual interactions while attending to video content can bolster the strength of social relationships, even among strangers [36].

Media events can be differentiated from other types of events that encourage dual screening, such as breaking news or viral memes. Unlike breaking news, media events are scheduled in advance and become highly scripted and ceremonial occasions that displace other events and create a collective awareness of its boundaries and content [37]. In particular, media events create conditions in which the audience on social media is simultaneously an audience for traditional media. Interaction is thus about more than the content of the performance or the possibility of social interaction but rather the shared awareness of experiencing the event with others. These broad, collective recognition of media events also potentially undermine the ability for audience members to fragment and selectively expose themselves to polarized media messages [38]–[41].

The simultaneous media use during media events create a social condition we call *shared attention*. We define shared attention as a temporary state in which the individual members of an audience for an event are mutually aware of each other's attention to the event. As we explain below, conditions of shared attention should have important consequences for individuals' dispositions to interact via social media both in terms of how they *produce* and *attend* to messages. In particular, larger potential audiences, altered norms, and high levels of shared understanding can all contribute to shifts in the ways in which users produce content, such as by composing tweets, as well as attend to content by retweeting or replying to the tweets produced by others.

Our approach

In this study, we use a computational focus group technique [28] to analyze the communicative behavior of Twitter users across varying levels of shared attention during the 2012 U.S. presidential campaign. U.S. presidential campaigns provide natural variations in shared attention. These campaigns generate news and disseminate messages on a daily basis, yet the campaign season includes several planned media events, such as the national party conventions and the candidate debates, that draw national attention both in TV viewership and social media participation [42]. The debates in particular represent high levels of shared attention as they disrupt normal patterns of broadcast television programming and attract large audiences of pundits, partisans, and undecided voters [43]. Social media participation is high during these events with users enthusiastically improvising humorous content [44] and there is some evidence that Twitter use can influence vote choice [45]. Furthermore, the Pew Research Center estimated 11% of the audience for these presidential debates engaged in “dual screening” [46].

Examining how users behave during these media events and comparing it with how they communicate outside of these events permits us to address two research questions. At an individual level, do Twitter users produce and attend to content differently in the context of a media event as compared to their behavior in the context of unexpected news events or normal time? At a collective level, do these individual differences in production and attention alter the collective structure of the conversation during such events?

There are several reasons to expect the shared attention will influence behavior at both the individual and collective levels. Conditions of shared attention are both infrequent and temporary, but this rarity also makes them compelling social experiences that could alter both individual communication behavior as well as the collective structure of audience responses.

Concentrated audiences.

The potential audience for a given user's content enlarges enormously under conditions of shared attention. Typically, tweets labeled with a hashtag may only be viewed by a few dozen people [47], but under shared attention conditions there may be an audience of thousands that attend to a hashtag for a single topic. However, competition for this larger supply of attention will be more intense. For example, in normal times, tweets on a particular topic are likely to appear on the screens of the small number of people who are paying attention to a particular hashtag at that time, but may stay visible in their feed for several minutes. During a media event about this topic, a tweet would go to a large number of people but be quickly replaced by tweets from others in a matter of seconds.

New norms.

The uncertain unfolding of the event in real time may also encourage the temporary adoption of new norms regarding the timing of communication [34]. For example, the nature of shared attention may encourage synchronicity in which messages are meant to be immediately read with an understanding that their relevance will quickly fade [48]. Users may also perform other identities or appropriate other affordances of the communication in medium under the conditions of shared attention. For example, Twitter users may shift practices from broadcasting others' tweets to generating their own tweets or engaging in more interpersonal conversations using mentions and replies. Individuals may share particularly informative, funny, or touching messages to communicate to others that they have seen it and are also members in the event [49].

Shared understandings.

The mutual awareness of the content of the media event can create a common ground for discussion [50]. During media events, individuals can freely construct messages without justifying or explaining their context because they hold common understandings that reduce the need to coordinate content and process [51]. For example, the event relevance of concepts like "Big Bird," "binders," and "bayonets" would be difficult to surmise in general, but for viewers of the 2012 U.S. Presidential debates they clearly refer to statements made by the candidates during the media event. Sharing this implicit understanding, individuals can converse without needing to re-explain the context. This common ground may also impose more discipline on the way messages are constructed, as false claims can be easily checked or refuted by a large audience [52], [53].

To examine the extent to which shared attention to media events changes individual and collective communication behaviors, we observed the behavior of approximately 200,000 Twitter users by collecting more than 290 million tweets during eight events, including six media events and two breaking news events, related to U.S. politics that occurred between late August and mid-October 2012. Media events like the national political conventions and presidential debates are compared to a baseline (activity in four normal days preceding each of the four presidential debates) and breaking news events, including the Obama administration's response to the Benghazi attacks and Governor Romney's "47%" statement. We examine the changes in communication patterns, connectivity and concentration, and user responsiveness under the different levels of shared attention imposed by these events.

We focus on two particular behaviors throughout: retweeting and replies. While these practices can be used and interpreted differently across contexts [34], [47], we argue they capture important behaviors in how users signal attention and equality. We treat retweeting as a hierarchical direction of attention, as users draw attention to a message sent by a third user, implicitly asserting the authority of that user for expressing something that others ought to read. By contrast, we view replies as an egalitarian form of production, in which users attempt to alert specific others to their own messages, implicitly asserting an equality of standing where individuals mutually attend to one another's contributions. Because retweeting and replies signal distinct motivations to either allocate followers' attention or demand attention from another user (respectively), each may undergo distinctive changes under the conditions of shared attention to media events.

Our findings indicate that shared attention to media events is associated with two broad effects which we call "rising tides" and "rising stars." We borrow the term "rising tides" from the aphorism "a rising tide lifts all boats". In "rising tides" the individual behaviors and collective structure of communication increase, but the distributions of users' production of and attention to information remains similar. It is also possible, however, for average behavior to change due to shifts concentrated in a minority of users. We term this outcome a "rising star" in which the individual behaviors and collective structure of communication shifts in such a way that occurs disproportionately for some users, generally to their benefit. Our results show that the increased attention to social media engendered by media events tends toward the latter effect of "rising stars" by disproportionately concentrating attention to elite users' content.

MATERIALS AND METHODS

Research design

We identified six real world events in which high levels of shared attention were present. Such conditions are difficult to create in the laboratory where it is generally infeasible to enlist or manipulate large scale audiences [54]. Identifying such conditions and appropriate controls is difficult in real-world settings as well. Most media events have relatively unique content. Thus, any effect observed to be correlated with the media event would also likely be correlated with the topic of the event. Without a "control for topic," inferences attributing association to shared attention would be specious [48].

To assess the impact of this variation in shared attention we identified eight events related to the 2012 U.S. Presidential campaign that occurred over the approximately six-week period of time between late August and mid-October 2012. Six media events were identified during this time: the Republican National Convention (RNC) from August 27 through August 30 ("CONV 1"), the Democratic National Convention (DNC) from September 4 through 6 ("CONV 2"), three debates on October 3 ("DEB 1"), 16 ("DEB 3"), and 22 ("DEB 4") involving the presidential candidates, and single vice presidential debate on October 11 ("DEB 2"). We contrast these media events with two news events that occurred in the same span of time: the terrorist attack on the American consulate in Benghazi that killed Ambassador J. Christopher Stevens on September 11 ("NEWS 1") and the release on September 18 of a video in which Mitt Romney argues "47 percent" of Americans are "dependent upon government" ("NEWS 2"). Both of these news events were major stories that dominated media attention for several days.

To provide a baseline, we included activity during the four days before each of the debates when there were no media or news events of similar magnitude (denoted as "PRE"). We term these observation periods "null events." Although tweet volumes vary regularly throughout the week [55], these null events fell on different days of the week during each of their 96-hour windows reducing the systematic bias of these events. In general, users' behavior during the "typical" time preceding the debate events might have been impacted by the excitements of expected debates and other campaign events, leading to a conservative comparison of changing behavior. This conservative comparison is more appropriate because it ensures that the change we measure is not a result of long-term behavioral drift. Together, these twelve observation periods (four debates, two conventions, two news events, and four "typical" timeframes representing four null events) make up a continuum of varying shared attention: (1) "typical" periods when shared attention is at its baseline level for Twitter as a whole (2) news events that should exhibit low levels of media event-driven behavioral changes since these have diffuse audiences and low mutual awareness of audience members, (3) the national political conventions that should exhibit medium levels of media event-driven changes since partisans selectively expose themselves to the conventions reflecting their political beliefs, and finally (4) the debates that should exhibit the highest levels of media event-driven change as their live and ceremonial nature drive intense shared interest. The array of these observations provides us with natural variation in our independent variable – shared attention.

Data extraction

Our design requires tracking behavioral change across multiple treatments, thus random sampling from the "garden hose" is inappropriate. We identified a specific sub-population of politically-engaged Twitter users and created a large "computational focus group" [28] to track their collective behavior over time as a panel as follows. If a user tweeted using a hashtag like "#debate" or mentioned one of the candidates' Twitter accounts during any of the four presidential debates and their tweet appeared in the Twitter "garden hose" streaming API [56], the user was selected into our user pool. Next, we collected the complete tweeting history for these users going back to mid-August using Twitter's REST API [57]. Because these queries are expensive owing to rate limits, we prioritized users who tweeted during more of the debates. Thus users who tweeted during all four debates are more likely to be represented in the sample than users who tweeted during only one of the debates. We wrote Python scripts to constantly request the users' past tweets through the "GET statuses/user_timeline" call. Since this method can only return up to 3200 of a user's most recent tweets, over the data collection period (from August to November, 2013), we used parallel processes to request data for each sampled user at least once per week and ensured their tweeting history over the data collection period is complete. The resulting corpus has 290,119,348 tweets from 193,532 unique users including elites such as politicians, journalists, and pundits as well as non-elite partisans and aspiring comedians. Subject to Twitter's Terms of Usage, part of this dataset (the ID numbers for the tweets used in this study) can be shared for replication.

For each of the eight events, we examined tweets made during a 48– to 96–hour window covering the event itself and its aftermath. Within these windows, we examined tweet volumes and identified the hour containing the peak level of cumulative activity. Descriptive statistics for the time of the window, unique users, tweets, retweets, mentions, and hashtags observed in each of the 12 observations (8 events and 4 baseline *null events*) are summarized in Table 1. An "event relevance ratio" is also calculated to validate the differences between events. This ratio is the fraction of tweets during each of the events that containing the names (*e.g.*, "Obama" or "Romney"), candidates' twitter handles (*e.g.*, "barackobama" or "mittromney"), or any of the the events (*e.g.*, "DNC", "RNC", "debate", "benghazi", "47 percent", etc.) at the peak time. The event relevance ratio captures the extent to which attention in our observed population is focused on the event topics. The event relevance ratio ranges from 0.08 (PRE) to 0.16 (NEWS), 0.50 (CONV), and to 0.63 (DEB), corroborating our assumption that there is more shared attention to the media events, and to the debates in particular. In the remainder of the paper, we sort these different levels of shared attention into distinct and non-overlapping categories of PRE, NEWS, CONV, or DEB. All tweets within each category's time window is given the same shared attention level label and no tweets have more than one label.

Table 1. Summary of datasets.

	PRE	NEWS	CONV	DEB
description	Pre-debate baseline	Benghazi attack, 47% controversy	Republican Nat'l Conv. Democratic Nat'l Conv.	Presidential debates
time	4 days before each debate (20:00–20:00 EDT)	2-day news cycle (14:00–14:00 EDT)	3 days (08:00–14:00 EDT)	4 hours (20:00–02:00 EDT)
duration	96 hours × 4	48 hours × 2	66 hours × 2	6 hours × 4
peak tweet volume	441,168	131,636	296,138	1,591,513
peak unique users	58,823	30,684	38,864	114,663
event relevance ratio	0.08	0.16	0.50	0.63
shared attention	none	low	medium	high

In Figure S1 in File S1, we provide detailed plots for the distributions of tweet volumes for the hours preceding and following the one-hour window we analyzed.

Measure of concentration

We measure the level of degree concentration in these Lorenz curves using the Gini coefficient. It is defined as the ratio of the area that lies between the line of equality (the line at 45 degrees) and the Lorenz curve over the total area under the line of equality. The Gini coefficient for a set of users or tweets with degrees y_i ($i = 1,\ldots,n$) and probability function $f(y_i)$ is given by: $G = 1 - \frac{\sum_{i=1}^{n} f(y_i)(S_{i-1}+S_i)}{S_n}$, where $S_i = \sum_{j=1}^{i} f(y_j)y_j$ and $S_0 = 0$. The Gini coefficient is a measure for identifying preferential patterns in general, as opposed to measures such as power-law exponent which can only apply to networks following power-law distribution.

RESULTS

We analyze the changes in communication patterns across four levels of shared attention: very low (an arbitrary baseline period), low (political news events), medium (national political conventions) and high (presidential debates). First, we compare the differences in activity levels across event types by analyzing differences in individual activity rates at each level of shared attention. Next, we examine the distributions of this activity to understand whether activity differences are broadly adopted by all users or concentrated around a few users. Finally, we analyze the relationship between a user's pre-existing audience size and their position in these activity networks to determine whether skews in the activity distribution are arbitrary or reflect pre-event status.

Changes in communication activity

Figure 1 plots the changes in communication volumes for each of the four levels of shared attention. Tweet volumes do not appear to vary significantly across the first three levels of shared attention (Figure 1(a)). The tweet volumes for the debates are much larger partly due to our sampling scheme, which focused on those active during the debates (see **Materials and Methods**). The rate of hashtag use nearly doubles during media events over the non-media event rate (Figure 1(b)). Because hashtags are an *ad hoc* way to create a sub-community focused topic by affiliating a tweet with a label [34], [58], the rise of this behavior during media events suggests users are broadcasting diffuse interests in topics.

Twitter activity volume change in different events. Diamond shapes indicate the mean value of each category (PRE: pre-debate baseline; NEWS: Benghazi attack and 47% controversy; CONV: Republican and Democratic Natl Conv; DEB: presidential debates). (a) The tweet volumes at the peak hour in the 12 events (including 4 null events). (b) The ratio of tweets with at least one hashtag to the total tweets at the peak hour. (c) The ratio of tweets replying to users to the total tweets at the peak hour. (d) The ratio of retweets to the total tweets at the peak hour. The results show an increase in topical communication (hashtag ratio) and a decrease in interpersonal communication (reply ratio) during the media events over the typical and news events.

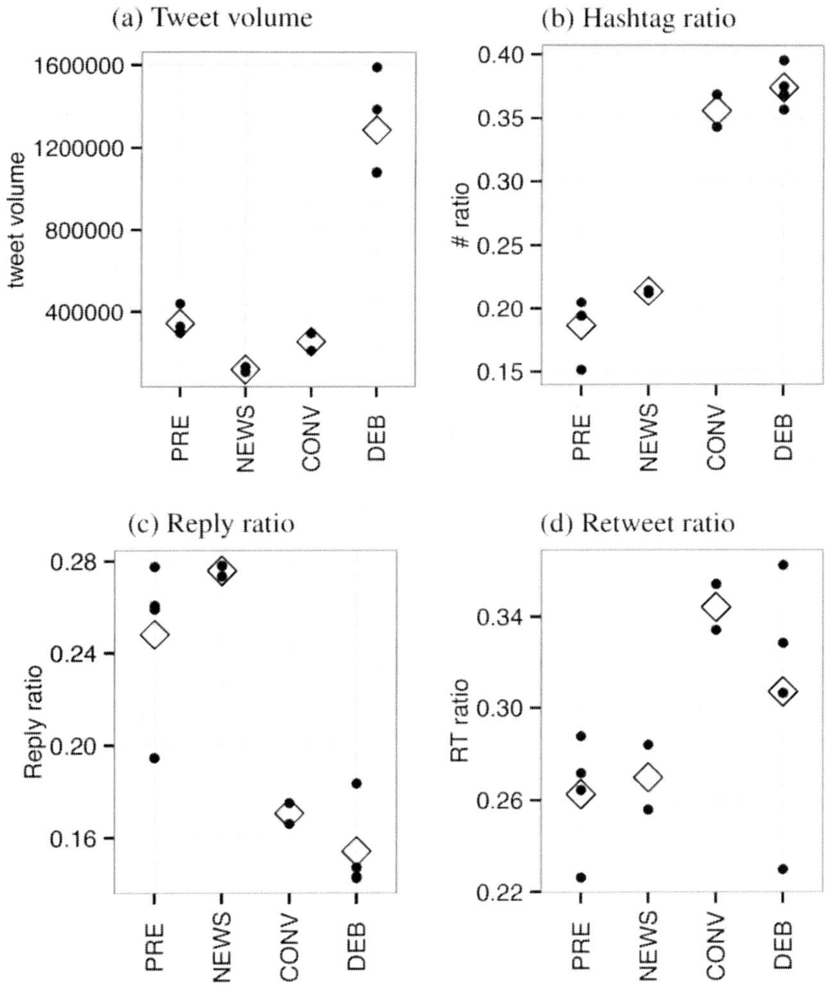

Figure 1. Changes in communication activity.

The fraction of tweets that were replies to one or more users (Figure 1(c)) declines substantially during media events like the debates. This 40% decline in directed communication suggests media events may not only dominate attention, but they also change social media behavior to become less interpersonal and more declarative. At the same time, imitation and re-broadcasting of particular messages appears to increase under shared attention. The ratio of tweets that include any mentions of users in the tweet exhibits similar decline pattern (see Figure S2 in File S1). The retweet ratio during the conventions and debates is substantially greater than under the lower attention conditions, though the mean is greater during the conventions than the debates (Figure 1(d)). Taken together, the results show shared attention is correlated with an increase in topical communication and a decrease in interpersonal communication, suggesting that the shared content of the media event plays a role in organizing the discourse. The increased rate of retweets also suggests that social and psychological processes such as competition for attention or fear of public embarrassment may lead to greater conformity in communication, as individuals are more inclined to repeat what others say than to invent their own messages.

Changes in distribution

The previous section demonstrated significant changes in the aggregate behavior of the users, however it is unclear whether these differences are driven by broad changes across many users ("rising tides") or shifts in the activity of a few ("rising stars"). We construct networks of users replying to users (user-to-user) and tweets being retweeted by users (user-to-tweet). Using Lorenz curves, we plot the cumulative distribution of activity in the system for each of the four types of events (see **Supporting Information** for details about activity networks). A Lorenz curve shows for the bottom $x\%$ of users or tweets, the percentage $y\%$ of the activity they generated. More equally-distributed activity is indicated by a linear diagonal while more highly concentrated activity will be more parabolic. A pattern of "rising tides" will be indicated by distributions that are similar to the typical pre-debate events while a pattern of "rising stars" will be indicated by activity during the DEB and CONV events becoming significantly concentrated as compared to the PRE and NEWS events.

Figure 2 plots the out- and in-degree Lorenz curves for the activity networks of replies and retweets. The out-degree distribution represents individual user level decisions — the kinds of tweets (replies, retweets) each user produced without considering the other users to whom they referred. The out-degree distributions in the activity networks show significant similarities across the four event types. In each case, the level of concentration is fairly high: a few users are responsible for most of the replies to other users (Figure 2(a)) and retweets of users' content (Figure 2(b)). However, the differences in the out-degree distributions between these event types is negligible suggesting that content production follows a pattern of "rising tides" in which concentration remains unaltered. Specifically, the aggregate shifts presented in Figure 1 are the result of changes in behavior by users across the board.

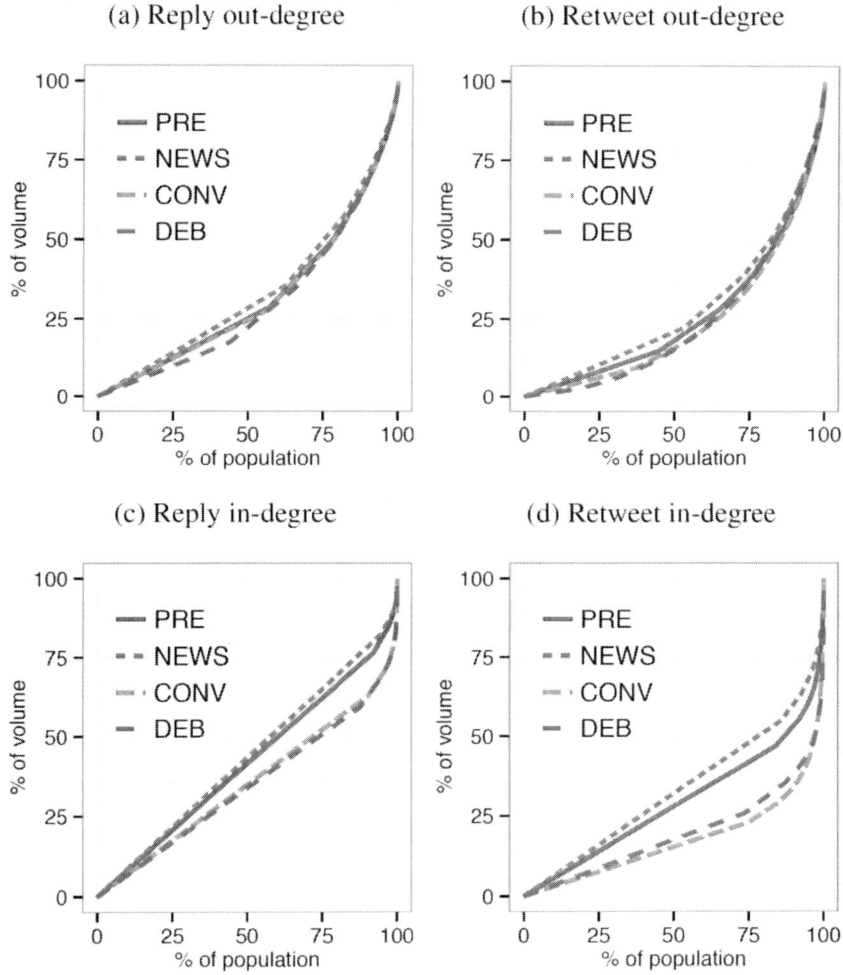

Figure 2. Lorentz curves for cumulative degree distributions of activity.

(a,c) The out- and in-degree Lorenz curves for the networks of replies. (b,d) The out- and in-degree Lorenz curves for the networks of retweets (RT). Increasing equality converges toward diagonal line from the origin to the upper-right and increasing inequality converges toward a hyperbola rising to 100% of volume at the 100th percentile. The out-degrees of activity networks (a,b) show significant similarities across the four event types and comparatively high levels of concentrated activity. The in-degrees show more substantial differences between event types. The convention and debate media events drove increased concentration of reply activity (c) around top users as compared to pre-events and news events. In retweet network (d), the top 25% of users' tweets accounted for approximately 75% of all retweet activity, indicating users' behavior under conditions of shared attention become increasingly concentrated around elites rather than increasingly distributed across many users. (PRE: pre-debate baseline; NEWS: Benghazi attack and 47% controversy; CONV: Republican and Democratic Natl Conv; DEB: presidential debates).

However, the in-degree distribution curves show significant differences between event types. The in-degree distribution represents collective behavior of all other users' activities within our sample directed at a single user or tweet — the kinds of individuals that everyone was paying attention to while paying attention to the event. During periods of low shared attention (baseline and news event), in-degree distributions are fairly flat with only slight leaning toward a very few "stars." But under conditions of greater shared attention (conventions and debates), the curves bend substantially. Replies are increasingly directed toward a group of approximately 10% of users and away from the bottom 75% of users (Figure 2(c)). We use a two-sample Kolmogorov-Smirnov statistic to test the magnitude and significance of the differences between the baseline and media event distributions. The in-degree distributions for retweet activity (Figure 2(d)) for the conventions and debates show the largest differences from the pre-debate baseline (see Table S1 in File S1 for the statistics of differences). The top 25% of users' tweets account for approximately 75% of all retweet activity under the shared attention conditions, with a much smaller portion being devoted to the other users. In comparison, during the pre-debate and news events, the same amount (75%) of all retweet activity are produced from the top 43% and 50% of users' tweets, respectively. The changes in these distributions for events with higher levels of shared attention suggests that "rising stars" prevail in the attention to content: the concentration of replies and retweets increased despite the increase in retweets and the decrease in replies.

Rising tides or rising stars?

The preceding analyses suggested the presence of "rising tides" in the production of content as well as the presence of "rising stars" in the attention to content under conditions of shared attention. To compare these effects more directly, we examine the relationship between individuals' connective activity and the concentration of these connections within the networks generated by user activity. Figure 3 plots the average degree of activity in each network against its concentration as measured by the Gini coefficient of its distribution for both replies and retweets (see **Materials and Methods**). Individual-level effects during media events should be reflected in the increased average degree as users increase the extent to which they issue social tweets, increasing the chances that any particular individual is retweeted or replied to and thus increasing connectivity in the graph (-axis). Alternatively, system-level changes during media events should be reflected in the increased Gini coefficient as users concentrate their activity around fewer users or tweets (y-axis).

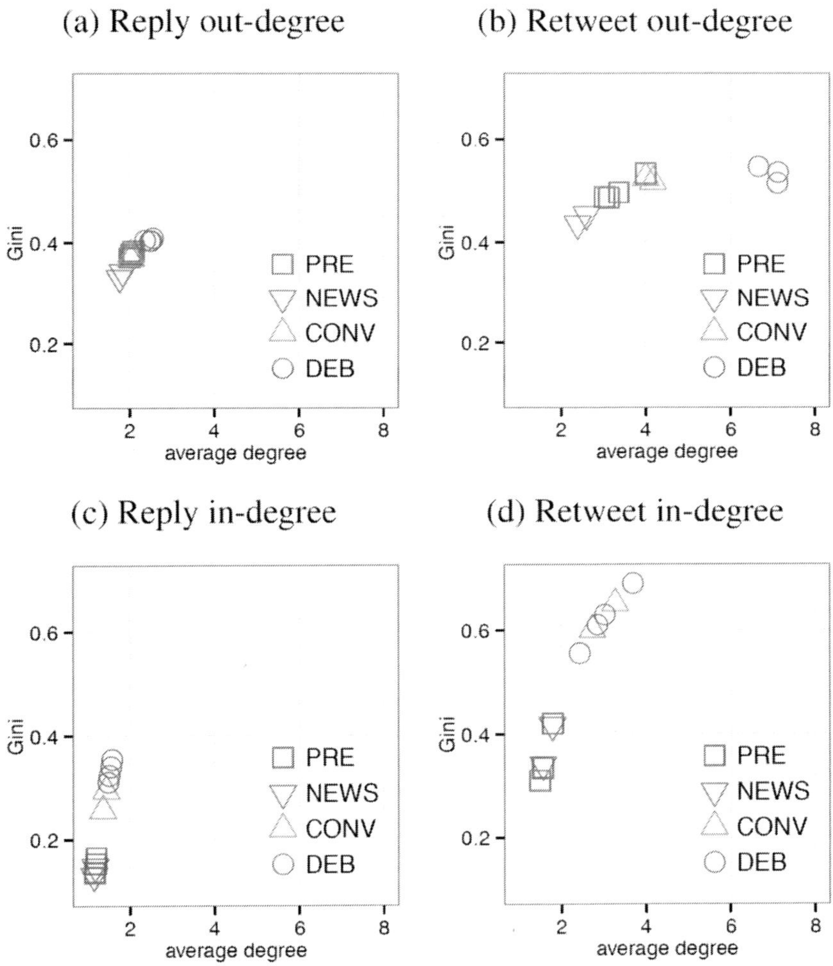

Figure 3. Connectivity-concentration state spaces.

(a,c) The out- and in-degree statistics of user-to-user reply network. (b,d) The out- and in-degree statistics of user-to-user retweet network. For each of the twelve observed events, the Gini coefficient (y-axis) measures the level of concentration of the network's degree distribution, and a lower Gini coefficient indicates a more equal distribution; the average degree of the network (x-axis) measures average activity of everyone for the event. Across activity types, the in-degrees show consistent patterns of increasing centralization (Gini coefficient) but limited increases in average connectivity degree (average degree) in response to media events while the out-degrees show patterns of increasing degree rather than concentration in response to media events, suggesting that while users across the system become more active during media events, this additional activity predominately benefits a handful of users and tweets. (PRE: pre-debate baseline; NEWS: Benghazi attack and 47% controversy; CONV: Republican and Democratic Natl Conv; DEB: presidential debates).

The phase space can be partitioned into four quadrants: networks in which the users are evenly but poorly connected would cluster around the lower-left, networks with poor connectivity but high levels of centralization would cluster in the upper-left, networks with an even distribution of highly connected nodes would cluster in the lower-right, and networks with highly connected but nevertheless highly concentrated activity would cluster in the upper-right. "Rising tides" will manifest with horizontal movement indicating increases in connectivity without changes in concentration. "Rising stars" will manifest with vertical movement indicating stable connectivity accompanied by an increase in concentration.

As described above, out-degree behavior reflects users' production of tweets. In the user-to-user reply network (Figure 3(a)), the out-degree behavior shows little difference between the events. Though reply rates differ across events (Figure 1), the number of users to whom our sampled users reply appears to increase only slightly for the debates, and the concentration also grows only slightly. In the user-to-user retweet network (Figure 3(b)), the out-degree corresponds to the number of other unique users a user retweets. There is a substantial shift in the out-degree of these networks as the average user retweets between 6–8 individuals during the debates, approximately 4 individuals during the conventions, and less than 4 in the other conditions. This is again evidence of a "rising tide." Under conditions of shared attention, then, we observe changes in overall activity across users changes (increases in average out-degree) without a substantial change in the concentration of this activity (stable Gini coefficients). Thus, from the median user's perspective, there are more users producing more tweets from more people.

As with Figure 2, the in-degree plots show a very different pattern as users attend to others' tweets. In the user-to-user reply network (Figure 3(c)), the in-degree corresponds to the number of other unique users who reply to a given user. Events characterized by higher levels of shared attention have slighter higher average reply in-degrees, but the concentration approximately doubles from 0.15 to 0.30. This suggests that although the number of users who are replied to on average does not change significantly, the replies that are issued skew heavily toward a few individuals. In the user-to-user retweet network (Figure 3(d)), the in-degree corresponds to the number of unique users retweeting a given user. The in-degree shows a similar pattern for events with high levels of shared attention having more users retweeting them on average (from 2 to 3), but these retweets becoming highly concentrated around specific users.

The connectivity and concentration in other types of activity networks, such as mentions, exhibit similar patterns (see Figures S3 and S4 in File S1). Across these activity types, the out-degrees show consistent patterns of increasing connectivity and limited changes in concentration while the in-degrees show the opposite pattern of marginal growth in connectivity with substantial increases of concentration. In other words, the production of information during media events exhibits patterns of "rising tides," but the attention to this information by other users leads to "rising stars." This is not a paradox, but rather a fundamental shift in the nature of the conversation throughout the audience: users of all stripes attend to more users and content than they do typically, but this audience focuses their collection attention on fewer users than is typical. Thus, conditions of shared attention result in a profound homogenization of information intake even as there is greater diversity in what is shared.

Changes in user responsiveness

The prior sections examined behavioral changes by aggregating all users irrespective of their historical pattern of Twitter use or their position in the Twitter network. These analyses revealed a tendency for Twitter users engaging with media events to participate more actively across the board but to attend more closely to a few users. Yet while this attention is more centered on rising stars, it is unclear who these rising stars are. Are rising stars selected seemingly at random from the tide of users flooding into the system, or are users with existing advantages more likely to seize the benefits of shared attention to media events?

We explore the types of users who contribute to and benefit from these shifts in information production and attention. We segment users into three classes based upon their audience size: "elites" are in the 90th percentile for number of followers (≥ 1805), "rookies" are in the 10th percentile for number of followers (≤ 88), and "typicals" are the middle 80%. Based on this segmentation, Figure 4 plots the distributions for several of the activity types related to the concepts analyzed above, focusing on the average increase of degrees during debates compared with the typical events. We measure the difference between each user's average degree across the four debates and the same user's average degree across the four baseline events.

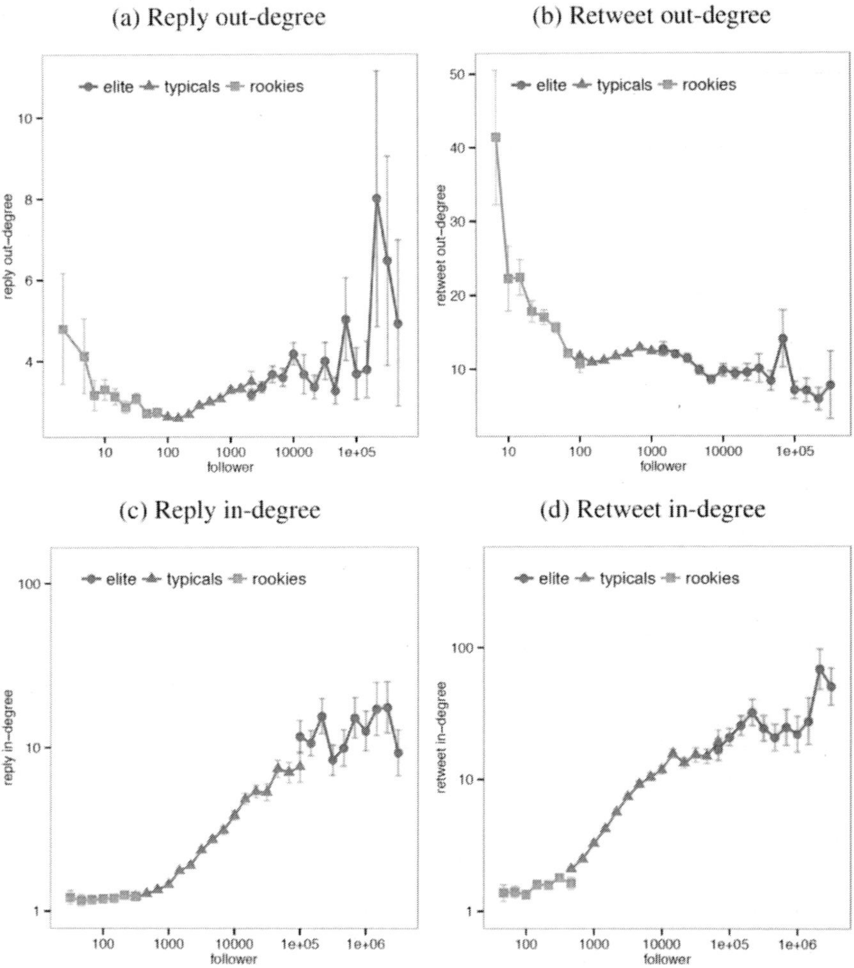

Figure 4. Responsiveness of users during debates.

The average increase of the in- and out-degrees for the reply and retweet network during debates compared with the typical events. The x-axis are logarithmic bins for all users with k followers and the y-axis measures change of in- or out-degree for all users with k followers. (a) Elites and rookies engage in more interpersonal communication than typicals. (b) Elites retweeted less frequently than other types of users. (c) Elites are largest target of users' replies. (d) Elites have their content retweeted more than other users. In all plots, the x-axis plots the number of followers on a log-scale. The y-axes are in linear scale in (a,b) and log-scale in (c,d).

Although overall levels of interpersonal communication (as measured by replies) decreased in Figure 1, there were significant differences between user classes during the media event. In Figure 4(a), elites and rookies both tended to reply to more users than typical users during the debates. This non-monotonic pattern is interesting as it suggests normative and strategic dimension for interpersonal communication during media events. Rookies may fail to realize that most users (the typicals) are not attending to interpersonal relationships during media events and vainly attempt to engage them in conversation. On the other hand, elites may use these events to cultivate strategic relationships by engaging other elites they know to be active and engaged as well as performing for the rest of their audience. In Figure 4(b), rookies show a significantly higher frequency of retweeting content while elites rarely retweet content. The difference in these propensities is revealing as it suggests highly strategic behavior on the part of elites being selective in whom to award attention.

While there is interesting behavioral variation on the production-side of the shared attention equation, the story of who benefits from this attention is unambiguous: elites. In Figure 4(c), elites are much more likely to be replied to by other users while rookies are effectively ignored relative to their usual rate for garnering attention. In Figure 4(d), elites are much more likely to be retweeted while rookies' content, as before, is eschewed during this period of heightened attention.

As shown in Table 2, for example, the most re-tweeted user during each of the first three debates (first two presidential plus vice-presidential) was comedian/pundit Bill Maher. Barack Obama himself was also in the top 5 during these debates, which also featured conservative commentator Sean Hannity and conservative comedian Dennis Miller. Despite the potential for conditions of shared attention to provide a coherent and egalitarian space for discussion and creativity, users with largest audiences nevertheless become the focus of attention. Furthermore, these tweets have substantial variation in their deliberative intent with many containing irreverent and humorous content rather than assertions intended to motivate political action or re-evaluate policy preferences. These findings provide additional evidence that the dynamic of information production and attention for media events within this population is better described by "rising stars" than "rising tides".

These findings are consistent with prior research [27], but in light of our previous findings suggest novel dynamics within the collective conversation. First, the variations in behavior across users of different pre-existing status suggests that typicals and elites are aware of the dynamics of shared attention in a manner that rookies are not. Comedian Demetri Martin, the 4th most retweeted user during the final debate, appropriately stated "I am live tweeting the debate. This tweet is about it but not directly." Martin's tweet highlights both how conditions of shared attention alter norms for information dissemination as well as his privileged position as a media personality with a large audience. Examining Figure 4 column-wise,

Table 2. Most retweeted users and their tweets across four debates.

Event	Most re-tweeted tweets
DEB 1	@billmaher: "Its Obama's anniversary - he's got to deliver twice tonight!"
	@BIGBIRD: "WTF Mitt Romney...:("
	@BarackObama: "Watch live: President Obama discusses his specific plans to keep us moving forward in the first presidential debate. http://t.co/3JJ2Yhlt"
	@DennisDMZ: "Jim Lehrer...be a mensch and get out of the way...These are big boys, you are Snooki."
	@Obama2012: "Jim Lehrer: "What are the major differences between the two of you about how you would go about creating new jobs?""
DEB 2	@billmaher: "Debate must be about to start, Chris Mathews breathing into paper bag"
	@BarackObama: "Watch live: @JoeBiden lays out the Obama-Biden plan to keep us moving forward. http://t.co/tK4y3oZR #ReadyForJoe"
	@seanhannity: "Biden is going to be "Talking Point Joe" all night #VPDebate"
	@KarlRove: "Ala 2004, are those packs on Raddatz's back a way for ABC higher ups to feed her questions? Just kidding. #debate"
	@TruthTeam2012: "The President is determined to find those responsible for the attack in Libya and to bring them to justice."
DEB 3	@billmaher: "100 people around stage - Mitt sees more than that at his breakfast table"
	@BarackObama: "Watch live: President Obama lays out his specific plan to keep growing the economy in tonight's presidential debate. http://t.co/BsVgAWvQ"
	@seanhannity: "Middle class crushed last 4 years... #PresidentialDebate2012"
	@TruthTeam2012: "Romneys 12 million jobs claim? 4 Pinocchios: http://t.co/uR4eLlek"
	@DickMorrisTweet: "#debates and there is nothing else holding Obama up. So all Mitt needs to do is be good as he was in the last debate. Obama's performance"
DEB 4	@YABOYMITT: "GAME TIME BITCHES! THEY SEE ME ROLLLLIIINNN THEY HATTTIINNN #YABOYMITT"
	@tyleroakley: "Watching and live-tweeting throughout the Presidential #Debates: http://t.co/rOtOOU8u RT if you're watching with me!:]"
	@realjohngreen: "(I'll mostly be retweeting other people's debate jokes, but occasionally I will sound my barbaric yawp over the rooftops, etc.)"
	@DemetriMartin: "I am live tweeting the debate. This tweet is about it but not directly."
	@GlobalGrind: "President Obama's leadership has made America stronger, safer, and more secure than we were 4 years ago. #StrongerWithObama"

rookies reach out interpersonally via replies but do not receive proportionate responses. By contrast, typical users appear to "know their place" as they appear to recognize that attention is scarce and others are unlikely to respond. Interestingly, elites actually increase their rate of reply, perhaps in an attempt to initiate dialogue with other elites or in awareness that they have moved to the center of attention. Elites also appear to guard their status, indicated by their restraint in retweeting others at a time when both rookies and typicals increase retweeting behavior, suggesting a reluctance to "anoint" others as worthy of attention through retweeting their content. The rising tide of retweets is supplied by the other users, in particular, rookies. Here rookie retweets may be used as safe ways to express ideas by using the words of others to stand in for their own voices, a phenomenon that might be expected given the intensity of shared attention from a large audience. These dynamics suggest that under shared attention, conversations self-organize into a contemporary two-step flow [59], reminiscent of the format used in broadcast media where elites are appointed to have a conversation among themselves while others receive their wisdom by watching from home [60].

DISCUSSION

Previous work examining the dynamics of socio-technical systems like Twitter relied upon the assumption that the behavior of users within these systems are self-similar and stable across changing social contexts. Our findings however complicate this assumption by demonstrating large populations of users change their individual and collective patterns of producing and attending to information under conditions of shared attention to media events. At the individual user level, information sharing behaviors, like using hashtags or retweeting, increased during media events, while interpersonal communication behaviors, like replies, decreased. This lends support to the idea that the condition of shared attention created by media events serves to make individuals more group focused and less involved with their normal social foci.

At the collective level, we examined whether these media events created "rising tides" that changed the behavior similarly across the system or if these events created "rising stars" that reinforced the attention and audience for already elite users. While there were increases in both the overall production of and attention to content by users in our population, shared attention clearly rewarded some users over others. References to users or tweets through retweets or replies became significantly more centralized during media events without correspondingly large changes in the average behavior of users. Crucially, the beneficiaries of this newfound attention were not distributed throughout users with different numbers of followers, but concentrated among users with the largest pre-existing audiences.

Despite the potential for social media to create larger public squares with more diverse voices speaking, occasions for large-scale shared attention such as media events appear to undermine this deliberative potential by replacing existing interpersonal social dynamics with increased collective attention to existing "stars". The particular socio-technical mechanisms that drive the behavioral changes we have identified remain unclear. On one hand, temporary social norms of exuberant information sharing and psychological processes of sensemaking may be the primary factors in these individual and collective behavioral changes. For example, the uncertainty of live events may predispose users to seek information from authorities and their expert sensemaking processes rather than from their peers. On the other hand, the algorithmic infrastructure of Twitter's technical systems could also privilege certain tweets and practices. For example, Twitter announced in September 2013 that it would allow "verified" accounts (users whose identities have been declared to be authentic by Twitter) to filter replies, mentions and, retweets to only include messages and notifications from other verified accounts [61]. Although our analysis pre-dates the implementation of this feature, it nevertheless points to both the demand from elite users to manage the connections they attend to as well as the technical capability for Twitter to privilege some users' messages over others.

These behavioral changes during shared attention to media events also have implications for ensuring the resilience of socio-technical systems for political communication in the face of misinformation. The engaging nature of these events can potentially make audience members less critical of incoming information as well as complicate the ability for users to establish the credibility of tweets and their authors [62]–[64]. Combined with our findings about concentrated attention to elite voices and diminished use of interpersonal communication, these factors could combine to create ideal conditions for rumor persistence, belief polarization, and the dissemination of misinformation that can (intentionally or unintentionally) undermine deliberation. However, the attention given to elite users during media events may provide opportunities for good-faith actors to limit the spread of misinformation by using content-based strategies of issuing repeated retractions, emphasizing facts instead of repeating myths, giving pre-exposure warnings about the likelihood of future information, offering simple rebuttals to complex myths, and fostering norms of strong skepticism [65].

Our analyses have several limitations that are opportunities for future work. Our data included only eight major events across a relatively brief six-week period of time on topics related to politics, limiting the generalizability of these findings to other domains. Future work might explore whether similar patterns are found in other types of media events such as sports (*e.g.*, Super Bowl) and awards ceremonies (*e.g.*, Academy Awards) or across longer spans of time such as an entire political campaign. Despite the size of user cohort whose behavior we analyzed and our intent to capture the behavior of politically-engaged users, the sampling strategy we employed potentially oversampled active users during the debates. Alternative sampling strategies might uncover weaker or different social dynamics. A variety of more advanced metrics and features such as waiting times between tweets and assortative degree mixing could be used to analyze social dynamics of elite users attending to other elites' content. The content and motivation of these tweets was also not analyzed for sentiment, discursive intent, or user background that could be revealed by participant interviews, topic modeling, or content analysis.

By considering not only changes in the overall level of activity, but changes in the structure of the networks of users and tweets, we identified the influence of several processes operating at micro- and macro-levels. Our findings demonstrate that changes in the aggregate levels of activity during media events are driven more by "rising stars" as elite users become the focus of collective attention rather than being driven by "rising tides" as users distribute their attention more broadly to new and diverse voices. Social media like Twitter are not only sites for political communication among politicians and their supporters, they are increasingly becoming spaces for otherwise segmented audiences to come together in a third space to participate in consequential events.

ACKNOWLEDGMENTS

We gratefully acknowledge the support of the Lazer Lab at Northeastern University. We also thank Alan Mislove, Deborah Keegan, members of the Cooperation reading group at the Berkman Center for Internet and Society, and many others.

AUTHOR CONTRIBUTIONS

Conceived and designed the experiments: YRL BK DM DL. Analyzed the data: YRL. Contributed reagents/materials/analysis tools: YRL. Wrote the paper: YRL BK DM DL.

REFERENCES

1. Bennett WL, Iyengar S (2008) A new era of minimal effects? the changing foundations of political communication. Journal of Communication 58: 707–731.
2. Rainie L, Wellman B (2012) Networked: The new social operating system. The MIT Press.
3. Farrell H (2012) The consequences of the internet for politics. Annual Review of Political Science 15: 35–52.
4. Sakaki T, Okazaki M, Matsuo Y (2010) Earthquake shakes Twitter users: Real-time event detection by social sensors. In: Proceedings of the 19th International Conference on World Wide Web. New York, NY, USA: ACM, WWW '10, pp. 851–860.
5. Weng J, Lee BS (2011) Event detection in Twitter. In: Proceedings of the AAAI International Conference on Weblogs and Social Media. AAAI, ICWSM'11, pp. 401–408.
6. Hu M, Liu S, Wei F, Wu Y, Stasko J, et al.. (2012) Breaking news on Twitter. In: Proceedings of the SIGCHI Conference on Human Factors in Computing Systems. New York, NY, USA: ACM, CHI '12, pp. 2751–2754.
7. Hughes AL, Palen L (2009) Twitter adoption and use in mass convergence and emergency events. International Journal of Emergency Management 6: 248–260.
8. Vieweg S, Hughes AL, Starbird K, Palen L (2010) Microblogging during two natural hazards events: What Twitter may contribute to situational awareness. In: Proceedings of the SIGCHI Conference on

Human Factors in Computing Systems. New York, NY, USA: ACM, CHI '10, pp. 1079–1088.

9. Starbird K, Palen L, Hughes AL, Vieweg S (2010) Chatter on the red: What hazards threat reveals about the social life of microblogged information. In: Proceedings of the 2010 ACM Conference on Computer Supported CooperativeWork. New York, NY, USA: ACM, CSCW '10, pp. 241–250. doi:10.1145/1718918. 1718965

10. Conover M, Ratkiewicz J, Francisco M, Gonçalves B, Menczer F, et al.. (2011) Political polarization on Twitter. In: Proceedings of the AAAI International Conference on Weblogs and Social Media. AAAI, ICWSM'11, pp. 89–96.

11. Tufekci Z, Wilson C (2012) Social media and the decision to participate in political protest: Observations from Tahrir Square. Journal of Communication 62: 363–379.

12. Aday S, Farrell H, Freelon D, Lynch M, Sides J, et al. (2013) Watching from afar: Media consumption patterns around the Arab Spring. American Behavioral Scientist 57: 899919.

13. Habermas J (1985) The theory of communicative action: Volume 2: Lifeword and system: A critique of functionalist reason, volume 2. Beacon Press.

14. Wright S, Street J (2007) Democracy, deliberation and design: the case of online discussion forums. New Media & Society 9: 849–869.

15. Freelon D (2013) Discourse architecture, ideology, and democratic norms in online political discussion. New Media & Society: 1461444813513259.

16. Coleman S, Moss G (2012) Under construction: the field of online deliberation research. Journal of Information Technology & Politics 9: 1–15.

17. Wright S (2012) Politics as usual? revolution, normalization and a new agenda for online deliberation. New Media & Society 14: 244–261.

18. Margolis M, Resnick D (2000) Politics As Usual. Thousand Oaks, CA, USA: Sage Publications, Inc.

19. Morozov E (2011) The Net Delusion: The Dark Side of Internet Freedom. Cambridge, MA, USA: Perseus Books.

20. Wu F, Huberman B (2007) Novelty and collective attention. Proc National Academy of Sciences 104: 1759917601.

21. Crane R, Sornette D (2008) Robust dynamic classes revealed by measuring the response function of a social system. Proc of the National Academy of Sciences 105: 1564915653.

22. Lerman K, Ghosh R (2010) Information contagion: An empirical study of the spread of news on Digg and Twitter social networks. In: Proceedings of the AAAI International Conference on Weblogs and Social Media. AAAI, ICWSM'10, pp. 90–97.

23. Weng L, Flammini A, Vespignani A, Menczer F (2012) Competition among memes in a world with limited attention. Scientific Reports 2..

24. Yang L, Sun T, Zhang M, Mei Q (2012) We know what @you #tag: Does the dual role affect hashtag adoption? In: Proceedings of the 21st International Conference on World Wide Web. New York, NY, USA: ACM, WWW '12, pp. 261–270.

25. Counts S, Fisher K (2011) Taking it all in? visual attention in microblog consumption. In: Proceedings of the AAAI International Conference on Weblogs and Social Media. AAAI, ICWSM'11, pp. 97–104.

26. Hodas N, Lerman K (2012) How visibility and divided attention constrain social contagion: 249–257.

27. Romero DM, Meeder B, Kleinberg J (2011) Differences in the mechanics of information diffusion across topics: Idioms, political hashtags, and complex contagion on Twitter. In: Proceedings of the 20th International Conference on World Wide Web. New York, NY, USA: ACM, WWW '11, pp. 695–704.

28. Lin YR, Margolin D, Keegan B, Lazer D (2013) Voices of victory: A computational focus group framework for tracking opinion shift in real time. In: Proceedings of the 22Nd International Conference onWorldWide Web. Republic and Canton of Geneva, Switzerland: International World Wide Web Conferences Steering Committee, WWW '13, pp. 737–748.

29. Nichols J, Mahmud J, Drews C (2012) Summarizing sporting events using Twitter. In: Proceedings of the 2012 ACM International Conference on Intelligent User Interfaces. New York, NY, USA: ACM, IUI '12, pp. 189–198.

30. Ciulla F, Mocanu D, Baronchelli A, Gonçalves B, Perra N, et al. (2012) Beating the news using social media: the case study of American Idol. EPJ Data Science 1: 1–11.

31. McPherson K, Huotari K, Cheng FYS, Humphrey D, Cheshire C, et al.. (2012) Glitter: A mixed-methods study of Twitter use during Glee broadcasts. In: Proceedings of the ACM 2012 Conference on Computer Supported Cooperative Work Companion. New York, NY, USA: ACM, CSCW '12, pp. 167–170.

32. Becker H, Iter D, Naaman M, Gravano L (2012) Identifying content for planned events across social media sites. In: Proceedings of the Fifth ACM International Conference on Web Search and Data Mining. New York, NY, USA: ACM, WSDM '12, pp. 533–542.

33. Sharma A (1 June 2013) TV networks play to 'second screen'. The Wall Street Journal.

34. Boyd D, Golder S, Lotan G (2010) Tweet, tweet, retweet: Conversational aspects of retweeting on Twitter. In: Proceedings of the 43rd Hawaii International Conference on System Sciences. HICSS-43, pp. 1–10.

35. Shamma DA, Kennedy L, Churchill EF (2009) Tweet the debates: Understanding community annotation of uncollected sources. In: Proceedings of the First SIGMM Workshop on Social Media. New York, NY, USA: ACM, WSM '09, pp. 3–10.

36. Weisz JD, Kiesler S, Zhang H, Ren Y, Kraut RE, et al.. (2007) Watching together: Integrating text chat with video. In: Proceedings of the SIGCHI Conference on Human Factors in Computing Systems. New York, NY, USA: ACM, CHI '07, pp. 877–886.

37. Dayan D, Katz E (1992) Media events: The live broadcasting of history. Harvard University Press.

38. Webster JG, Ksiazek TB (2012) The dynamics of audience fragmentation: Public attention in an age of digital media. Journal of Communication 62: 39–56.

39. Messing S,Westwood SJ (2012) Selective exposure in the age of social media: Endorsements trump partisan source affliation when selecting news online. Communication Research.

40. Prior M (2013) Media and political polarization. Annual Review of Political Science 16: 101–127.

41. 41.Flaxman S, Goel S, Rao JM (2013) Ideological segregation and the effects of social media on news consumption.

42. Massanari AL, Howard PN (2011) Information technologies and omnivorous news diets over three U.S. presidential elections. Journal of Information Technology & Politics 8: 177–198.

43. Schroeder A (2008) Presidential debates: fifty years of high-risk TV. Columbia University Press.

44. Driscoll K, Ananny M, Bar F, Guth K, Kazemzadeh A, et al.. (2013) Big bird, binders, and bayonets: Humor and live-tweeting during the 2012 U.S. presidential debates. Selected Papers of Internet Research 3.

45. Maruyama MT, Robertson SP, Douglas SK, Semaan BC, Faucett HA (2014) Hybrid media consumption: How tweeting during a televised political debate influences the vote decision. In: Proceedings of the 17th ACM Conference on Computer Supported Cooperative Work & Social Computing. New York, NY, USA: ACM, CSCW '14, pp. 1422–1432.

46. (2012) One-in-ten "Dual-Screened" the presidential debate. Technical report, Pew Research Center for the People and Press. Available: http://www.people-press.org/files/legacy-pdf/10-11-12%20Debate%20Media%20Release.pdf. Accessed 2013 October 22.

47. Marwick AE, Boyd D (2010) I tweet honestly, I tweet passionately: Twitter users, context collapse, and the imagined audience. New Media & Society 13: 114–133.

48. Lin YR, Margolin D, Keegan B, Baronchelli A, Lazer D (2013) #Bigbirds never die: Understanding social dynamics of emergent hashtag. In: Proceedings of the AAAI International Conference on Weblogs and Social Media. ICWSM'11, pp. 370–379.

49. Gilbert E (2012) Designing social translucence over social networks. In: Proceedings of the SIGCHI Conference on Human Factors in Computing Systems. New York, NY, USA: ACM, CHI '12, pp. 2731–2740.

50. Fussell SR, Krauss RM (1989) The effects of intended audience on message production and comprehension: Reference in a common ground framework. Journal of Experimental Social Psychology 25: 203–219.

51. Clark HH, Brennan SE (1991) Grounding in communication. In: Resnick LjB, Levine JM, Teasley SD, editors, Perspectives on socially shared cognition.

52. Garrett RK (2011) Troubling consequences of online political rumoring. Human Communication Research 37: 255–274.

53. Tripathy RM, Bagchi A, Mehta S (2010) A study of rumor control strategies on social networks. In: Proceedings of the 19th ACM International Conference on Information and Knowledge Management. New York, NY, USA: ACM, CIKM '10, pp. 1817–1820.

54. 54.Campbell DT, Stanley JC, Gage NL (1963) Experimental and quasi-experimental designs for research. Houghton Miffin Boston. Available: http://moodle.technion.ac.il/pluginfile.php/219643/mod_resource/content/0/Campbell_and_Stanley_1963.pdf. Accessed 2013 November 2.

55. Golder SA, Macy MW (2011) Diurnal and seasonal mood vary with work, sleep, and daylength across diverse cultures. Science 333: 18781881.

56. Twitter (2012) The Streaming APIs. Available: https://dev.twitter.com/docs/streaming-apis. Accessed 2013 October 22.

57. Twitter (2012) REST API v1.1 Resources. Available: https://dev.twitter.com/docs/api/1.1. Accessed 2013 October 22.

58. Wang YC, Kraut R (2012) Twitter and the development of an audience: Those who stay on topic thrive! In: Proceedings of the SIGCHI Conference on Human Factors in Computing Systems. New York, NY, USA: ACM, CHI '12, pp. 1515–1518.

59. Katz E, Lazarsfeld PF (1955) Personal influence: The part played by people in the flow of mass communications. The Free Press.

60. McCombs ME, Shaw DL (1972) The agenda-setting function of mass media. Public Opinion Quarterly 36: 176–187.

61. Gutman E (2013). Filtering mentions. Available: https://blog.twitter.com/2013/ filtering-mentions. Accessed 2013 October 22.

62. Schmierbach M, Oeldorf-Hirsch A (2012) A little bird told me, so I didn't believe it: Twitter, credibility, and issue perceptions. Communication Quarterly 60: 317–337.

63. Kang B, O'Donovan J, Höllerer T (2012) Modeling topic specific credibility on twitter. In: Proceedings of the 2012 ACM International Conference on Intelligent User Interfaces. New York, NY, USA: ACM, IUI '12, pp. 179–188.

64. Morris MR, Counts S, Roseway A, Hoff A, Schwarz J (2012) Tweeting is believing?: Understanding microblog credibility perceptions. In: Proceedings of the ACM 2012 Conference on Computer Supported Cooperative Work. New York, NY, USA: ACM, CSCW '12, pp. 441–450.

65. Lewandowsky S, Ecker UKH, Seifert CM, Schwarz N, Cook J (2012) Misinformation and its correction: Continued influence and successful debiasing. Psychological Science in the Public Interest 13: 106–131.

6

THE RELATIONSHIP BETWEEN MEDIA CONSUMPTION AND HEALTH-RELATED ANXIETIES AFTER THE FUKUSHIMA DAIICHI NUCLEAR DISASTER

Amina Sugimoto[1], Shuhei Nomura[1], Masaharu Tsubokura[2], Tomoko Matsumura[2], Kaori Muto[3], Mikiko Sato[3], Stuart Gilmour[1]

[1]Department of Global Health Policy, Graduate School of Medicine, The University of Tokyo, Bunkyo-ku, Tokyo, Japan,

[2] Division of Social Communication System for Advanced Clinical Research, The Institute of Medical Science, The University of Tokyo, Minato-ku, Tokyo, Japan,

[3] Department of Public Policy, The Institute of Medical Science, The University of Tokyo, Minato-ku, Tokyo, Japan

ABSTRACT

Background

The Fukushima Daiichi nuclear disaster caused a global panic by a release of harmful radionuclides. In a disaster setting, misusage of contemporary media sources available today can lead to disseminated incorrect information and panic. The study aims to build a scale which examines associations between media and individual anxieties, and to propose effective media usages for future disaster management.

Methods

The University of Tokyo collaborated with the Fukushima local government to conduct a radiation-health-seminar for a total of 1560 residents, at 12 different locations in Fukushima. A 13 item questionnaire collected once before and after a radiation-seminar was used on factor analysis to develop sub-scales for multiple regression models, to determine relationships between the sub-scales and media type consumed. A paired t–test was used to examine any changes in sub-scale of pre- and post-seminar scores.

Results

Three sub-scales were revealed and were associated with different media types: was with rumors, while concern for the future was positively associated with regional-newspapers and negatively with national-newspapers. Anxiety about social-disruption was associated with radio. The seminar had a significant effect on anxiety reduction for all the three sub-scales.

Conclusion

Different media types were associated with various heightened concerns, and that a radiation seminar was helpful to reduce anxieties in the post-disaster setting. By tailoring post-disaster messages via specific media types, i.e., radio, it may be possible to effectively convey important information, as well as to calm fears about particular elements of post-disaster recovery and to combat rumors.

INTRODUCTION

Significant radiation-release events are rare and can cause elevated health risks over a wide area. The consequences of such events can include large scale evacuations, health testing, risk assessment and closure of businesses such as farms and fisheries, leading to social disruption on a wide scale and a significant level of social insecurity and fear amongst affected citizens [1]. Modern disaster settings can receive significant media coverage from a wide range of contemporary media sources [2], enabling people to obtain information of varying quality about the health and social consequences of such an event. This media coverage can be available to those directly affected by the radiation-release events, and offer risks and opportunities in disaster management in modern settings [3]. Unreliable or alarmist media coverage may lead to dissemination of incorrect information, panic and misconceptions about both disaster response and the health consequences of the accident; however, authoritative or highly trusted media sources may provide an ideal avenue for disaster responders to disseminate important public health and safety messages [4]. Therefore, understanding the relationship between collective anxiety over the impact of radiation on individuals and society and various types of mass media may serve those responsible for planning or implementing disaster responses [5]. This is especially important because lay understanding of radiation risk can vary widely from the understanding of experts responding to a disaster [6], and media reporting of radiation risk has been heavily criticized for both its poor scientific basis and alarmism [7], [8]

The Great East Japan Earthquake and subsequent nuclear reactor shutdown at Fukushima created just such a radiation-release incident. Though much information about the events of the reactor shutdown and subsequent radiation release remains unclear [9], the progress of the disaster and its consequences for local residents have been well documented [10], and included: evacuation of some residents near the nuclear plant; movement restrictions on other residents; cessation of local agricultural and outdoor laboring activities; and closure of local food suppliers. Coupled with the evacuation of residents affected by the tsunami, the disaster affected a large area and left many local residents uncertain about the risks to their own health, the security of their immediate area and the long-term impact on their health, fertility, work opportunities and future plans.

In order to help the local residents come to terms with their situation, the University of Tokyo, in collaboration with the Fukushima local government, offered radiation risk seminars to residents of the affected areas concurrently with health assessments, which included administration of a questionnaire covering basic health and social concerns, as well as media consumption information. The aim of this study is to understand the anxieties felt by the residents, and to explore the relationship between the dimensions of anxiety and types of mass media used by residents to obtain information about radiation risks. This information may be useful in planning post-disaster media responses and identifying the best channels through which information should be disseminated.

METHODS

Subjects and questionnaire survey

From June 20th to July 19th 2011, a total of 1560 residents of Soma city, Fukushima Prefecture, participated in radiation information seminars at 12 different locations, including the city hall, hospitals and schools. Information about the seminars was publically disseminated at local schools and the city hall. All participants were recruited through voluntary participation. As part of the radiation seminar, participants were administered a questionnaire both before and after the seminar, to assess their level of concern regarding the effect of radiation on health and the extent of change due to the seminar. As part of the questionnaire, information on media consumption was also collected. Because the questionnaire was not administered as a health assessment tool, but as an evaluation tool for the seminars, no health or mental well-being questions were asked. The questionnaire contained the following three major components:

1. Demographic information: This included age, sex, educational background, occupation, personal and family history of cancer, residential area, and living status (e.g., number of child relatives).

2. Media consumption information: Asked on arrival at the seminar, this section provided questions concerning frequency and types of mass media used to obtain information about the nuclear disaster. Respondents were asked to indicate the weekly frequency with which they used the following media: TV news, TV tabloid shows, national newspapers, regional newspapers, radio news, radio tabloid shows, internet news, internet personal websites, rumors and notice boards. Frequency was rated as: "do not use", "use once a week", "use a few times a week", and "use more than once a day."

3. Information on anxiety about radiation risks: The questionnaire contained 14 items addressing fears about radiation and health, future social and economic prospects, and the current social and physical circumstances in which respondents lived. All but one question was measured on a five-point Likert scale, from *not concerned at all* (1 point) to *very concerned* (5 points). One of the questions (question 14) was open-ended. The participants answered these questions twice: once on arrival at the seminar, and again upon completion of the seminar.

In a few cases, people aged below 16 and over 70 completed the questionnaire. These responses were excluded from the data set, because of suspicion that people in these age groups might be rephrasing their answers to describe their opinions on family member's worries or concerns. Age was categorized into three groups: younger than 35, between 35 and 50, and older than 50. Educational background was categorized into three groups: middle/high school, college, and university and above. Similarly, occupation was categorized into five groups: outdoor, medical/educational/technological, housewife, unemployed and other. Area where the residents live was categorized in to three groups: mountain, seaside, and urban.

Approval for the study was granted by the ethics committees at the Institute of Medical Science, the University of Tokyo, and written informed consent was obtained from all the participants prior to commencement of the seminar.

Statistical analysis

After excluding one open-ended question, all 13 Likert-scale questions about radiation-related anxiety were converted into a scale to measure radiation concerns suitable for analysis by media-usage. Sub-scales amongst the 13 questions were identified by analyzing all pre-seminar responses using factor analysis with a principal component factor extraction method and varimax rotation. The cut-off point for selecting factors was at the point of inflection of the scree plot. Accepted sub-scales were then assembled using two methods: naïve construction in which the individual variables were summed together to construct scale values, and weighted construction, in which the scales were composed as scores from the rotated factors. Post-seminar scales were also generated using the same method applied to the post-seminar questions. All subscales are referred to as factors in this study.

Cronbach's Alpha was used as an internal reliability test. External reliability of the questionnaire was evaluated to measure the extent to which distributions of scores of the pre- and post-seminar questionnaires were similar, using a test-retest analysis on the difference between pre- and post-seminar scores for all individuals. For this analysis the naïve factors were used, as the weighted factors have mean zero both before and after the seminar, by design. Because the radiation seminar was expected to change subject's responses, a mean change score of less than zero was expected in this analysis. However, seminar served to contaminate test-retest analysis, so test-retest validity cannot be definitively established in this study. For this reason, the scale developed, though expected to be appropriate for the regression analysis presented here, should not be considered a valid or reliable measure of anxiety or radiation-related health concerns without further research. The relationship between each factor and key demographic and media use variables was explored using one-way analysis of variance (ANOVA). Variables shown to be statistically significant ($p<0.05$) were then analyzed using a multiple regression model. Backwards stepwise model selection was used for model building and residual analysis was used to check the validity of the regression model. These models were conducted on the weighted factor scores, so that outcome variables used in each of the regressions were not correlated with each other. The possible confounders of age, sex and area were retained in the models regardless of their significance. Since almost all respondents used TV news as a common information source, it was excluded from the modeling processes. A separate regression analysis was conducted for each factor identified by factor analysis.

RESULTS

Of the 1560 seminar participants, 1298 (83%) gave consent to participate in the health survey. There were 1277 valid responses (completion of demographic items), giving a final response rate of 79%. Response rates at individual sites varied between 50 to 89%. After excluding the very young and old, 969 observations (62%) remained in the data set.

Table 1 summarizes the demographic characteristics of the study sample. The rate of missing responses was lower than 10% for all questions. Over 70% of the participants were female, the majority were aged above 50 (64%), and 63% had their last education in either middle or high school. About half of the participants (46%) had a personal or family history of cancer. A few people were living alone (9%). It also shows the proportion of respondents who use media more than once a week by media type. Over 95% answered to having used TV news as a common media source. All the media types, except for radio tabloid shows, internet news and internet personal websites, were used by more than 50% of people as a common information source.

Factor analysis was conducted on the anxiety section of the questionnaire. After excluding those who did not fill in all 13 items from the data set, 87% of the 969 participants were eligible for this analysis.

Application of the scree plot criterion resulted in a three factor solution explaining 95% of the variance. Table 2 shows the loadings of each variable on the three factors generated from the factor analysis; the highest loading for each variable is indicated in bold. A variable was considered associated with a factor if its loading was above 0.4, and assigned to the highest-loaded factor where a conflict occurred. Three clear dimensions of radiation-related concern were identified: *radiation/health fears* (questions 1–5 and 9), *fears for the future* (question 6–8), and *fears about social disruption* (question 10–13).

Table 1. Respondent demographics and media consumption.

Variable	Respondents	Frequency (%)
Age		
Under 35	1014	115 (11)
Between 35 to 49		246 (24)
Over 49		653 (64)
Sex		
Male	1011	277 (27)
Female		734 (73)
Education		
Middle/High school	982	615 (63)
College		216 (22)
University and above		151 (15)
Occupation		
Outdoor	939	98 (9.96)
Medical/Education/Tech		184 (18.70)
Housewife		270 (27.44)
Unemployed		161 (16.36)
Other		271 (27.54)
Cancer History (personal or family)		
No	965	519 (54)
Yes		446 (46.22)
Living status*		
Alone	1014	89 (9)
With partner		702 (69)
With parents		366 (36)
With children		592 (58)
With grandchild		140 (14)
Total number of media types used		
0–3 types	1014	124 (12)
4–6 types		435 (43)
7–8 types		455 (45)
Area		
Mountain	1014	211 (21)
Seaside		233 (23)
Urban		570 (56)
Age		Mean/sd
Female	1014	52.82/12.57
Male		52.40/12.64
Combined		52.55/12.61
Media type		
TV news		968 (95)
TV tabloid shows		713 (70)
National newspapers		631 (62)
Regional newspapers		778 (77)
Radio news		531 (52)
Radio tabloid shows		319 (31)
Internet news		393 (39)
Internet personal websites		143 (14)
Rumors		670 (66)
Notice board		668 (66)

*Multiple answers possible for this question.

Table 2. Factor loadings for pre-seminar variables.

Variables	Factor 1	Factor 2	Factor 3
Own health	0.55	0.27	0.29
Family health	0.59	0.20	0.34
Food safety	0.84	0.21	0.20
Water safety	0.81	0.25	0.20
Danger of being exposed to radiation in daily life	0.64	0.32	0.32
Effect on employment	0.30	0.77	0.16
Infertility	0.29	0.56	0.08
Effect on income	0.18	0.77	0.19
Radiation dose in the neighboring area	0.61	0.26	0.44
State response	0.42	0.25	0.44
How long this will last?	0.36	0.07	0.53
Future evacuation order	0.35	0.27	0.57
Media information	0.38	0.27	0.62

Cronbach's Alpha was calculated at 0.91 for factor 1, 0.82 for factor 2, and 0.78 for factor 3, indicating good internal reliability. Post-seminar scales were also generated using the same method applied to the post-seminar questions, and produced exactly the same set of factors with very similar numerical details. Correlation between pre- and post-seminar scores for the naïve summed factors ranged from 0.60 (factor 1) to 0.74 (factor 3), and all three factors showed a statistically significant decrease from pre- to post-seminar testing (paired T-test p-value<0.0001 in all cases). For all three factors, more than 80% of respondents' post-seminar scores were equal to or lower than their pre-seminar scores, suggesting a consistent downward shift in measures of anxiety that is likely to be due to the effect of the seminars themselves rather than a consistent bias in the testing mechanism, though this effect cannot be ruled out.

Multiple regression results for the relationship between the three factors and key demographic variables and media types are shown in Table 3 (factor 1), Table 4 (factor 2) and Table 5 (factor 3). The only type of media associated with radiation/health fears was "rumors." Fears for the future (factor 2) were associated with national and regional newspapers, with

Table 3. Multiple regression model of factor one against the media variables.

Variables	Coefficient (95% CI)	Standard Error	T statistic	P value
Intercept	−0.66 (−0.86 to −0.47)	0.10	−6.62	<0.001
Experimental variables:				
Rumors				
Do not use	Ref			
Use	0.22 (0.09 to 0.35)	0.07	3.35	<0.001
Confounders:				
Age				
Under 35	0.24 (0.05 to 0.43)	0.10	2.51	0.01
Between 35 to 49	0.22 (0.07 to 0.36)	0.07	2.96	0.003
Over 49	Ref			
Sex				
Female	0.30 (0.17 to 0.44)	0.07	4.49	<0.001
Male	Ref			
Cancer History				
Yes	0.08 (−0.05 to 0.20)	0.06	1.21	0.2
No	Ref			
Area				
Mountain	0.30 (0.12 to 0.48)	0.09	3.31	<0.001
Downtown	0.14 (−0.01 to 0.28)	0.07	1.82	0.07
Seaside	Ref			
Living status				
Living with grandchild	0.30 (0.12 to 0.49)	0.09	3.17	0.002
Not living with grandchild	Ref			

Table 4. Multiple regression model of factor two against the media variables.

Variables	Coefficient (95% CI)	Standard Error	T statistic	P value
Intercept	−0.62 (−0.87 to −0.37)	0.13	−4.91	<0.001
Experimental variables:				
National newspapers				
Do not use	Ref			
Use	−0.14 (−0.26 to −0.01)	0.06	−2.17	0.03
Regional newspapers				
Do not use	Ref			
Use	0.18 (0.04 to 0.32)	0.07	2.46	0.01
Confounders:				
Age				
Under 35	0.13 (−0.06 to 0.31)	0.10	1.33	0.2
Between 35 to 49	0.11 (−0.03 to 0.26)	0.07	1.53	0.1
Over 49	Ref			
Sex				
Male	0.00 (−0.14 to 0.15)	0.08	0.06	1.0
Female	Ref			
Education				
Middle/High school	0.31 (0.13 to 0.49)	0.09	3.43	<0.001
College	0.17 (−0.02 to 0.39)	0.10	1.82	0.07
University and above	Ref			
Occupation				
Outdoor	0.59 (0.35 to 0.83)	0.12	4.76	<0.001
Medical/Education/Tech	0.28 (0.02 to 0.39)	0.09	2.18	0.03
Housewife	Ref			
Housewife	Ref			
Unemployed	0.08 (−0.12 to 0.28)	0.10	0.79	0.4
Other	0.19 (0.02 to 0.35)	0.08	2.19	0.03
Living status				
Living with children	0.14 (0.01 to 0.27)	0.06	2.17	0.03
Not living with children	Ref			
Area				
Mountain	0.02 (−0.13 to 0.17)	0.08	0.26	0.8
Seaside	0.07 (−0.07 to 0.21)	0.07	0.95	0.3
Downtown	Ref			

Table 5. Multiple regression model of factor three against the media variable.

Variables	Coefficient (95% CI)	Standard Error	T statistic	P value
Intercept	−0.14 (−0.34 to 0.06)	0.10	−1.37	0.2
Experimental variables:				
Radio				
Do not use	Ref			
Use	0.16 (0.05 to 0.27)	0.05	2.96	0.003
Confounders:				
Age				
Under 35	−0.12 (−0.29 to 0.06)	0.09	−1.33	0.2
Between 35 to 49	−0.18 (−0.34 to −0.02)	0.08	−2.15	0.03
Over 49	Ref			
Sex				
Female	0.30 (0.19 to 0.42)	0.06	5.14	<0.001
Male	Ref			
Area				
Mountain	0.03 (−0.10 to 0.17)	0.07	0.48	0.6
Seaside	0.02 (−0.11 to 0.15)	0.07	0.29	0.8
Downtown	Ref			

regular use of national newspapers associated with a reduced level of fear on this factor, while use of regional newspapers was associated with heightened fears. Fears about social disruption were only associated with radio news.

DISCUSSION

This study aimed to examine associations between mass media consumption and health-related anxiety after a radiation-release accident. The exploratory factor analysis on both pre- and post-seminar questions led to a meaningful three factor solution which showed strong internal reliability and some evidence of test-retest validity.

Analysis of factor 1 showed that those who use rumors as a source of radiation information were more worried about the radiation effects on health than those who do not, while the multiple regression model of factor 2 suggests that users of national newspapers were less worried about prospects for future, and those who use regional newspapers more worried about their future prospects. This may be because regional papers present less authoritative information about radiation risks and government actions than national newspapers, which contain clearer lines of communication with government officials over current/prospective countermeasures against radiation. A strong correlation was also found between fears about social disruption (factor 3) and use of radio news, but this may reflect the nature of disaster planning in Japan: possession of a radio is considered a key element of an individual disaster preparation plan [11], and it could be that those more worried about social disruption due to disasters are more likely to both own and use a radio as part of their disaster planning.

This study's most serious limitation can be attributed to the nature of the seminars. Our ability to test the external (test-retest) reliability of the questionnaire was constrained by the effect of the health seminars: these were designed to influence participant's radiation fears, and due to this a simple change in mean might be expected from the seminars. However, because the effectiveness of the seminar was assessed simultaneously with the test-retest validity of the questionnaire itself, it is impossible to say whether the change in level observed in pre- and post-seminar scores reflects a true effect of the seminars or a consistent bias in the second administration of the questionnaire. It is unlikely; however, that poor test-retest reliability would be associated with a consistent reduction in statistically significant levels of anxiety across the three factors: the most likely effect of test-retest errors is to create a non-differential bias, with post-seminar scores distributed randomly relative to the pre-test scores. Given such an assumption, the magnitude, significance and consistent distribution of changes in the three factors between pre- and post-seminar assessments suggests that the changes in level observed were likely to be due to the seminar itself rather than validity problems in the questionnaire.

A second limitation is that the findings of the study represent only an aging and female-majority population in rural settings. In an urban setting, levels of concern over the three factors and the availability to mass media types listed on this study may be different.

Selection bias also limited the findings of the study. Seminar attendance was voluntary, and the participants may already have higher levels of radiation concerns than would be expected in a random sample of residents of the area.

Despite these limitations, this study may be useful for those planning or implementing a response to a radiation disaster of uncertain duration, harm and scale, giving insights into the relationship between radiation concerns and media consumption patterns. In the immediate post-disaster setting, as emergency response efforts begin, those disseminating information about the government response and the immediate and long-term health risks, should consider carefully the media to be used. This study shows that television of all kinds is a ubiquitous medium for the dissemination of information, and an ideal way to distribute basic health and safety information after a radiation release. Both television and internet usage do not show any particular pattern of association with particular concerns. However, efforts should be made to combat rumors, by which means erroneous information about the health effects may be transmitted. In addition, disaster responders should consider the role of regional newspapers, which may be harder to target and overlooked in favor of national newspapers that may have a closer relationship to government and health departments, and easier lines of communication. In this study, those with higher levels of concern about the future were more likely to read regional newspapers, suggesting that these newspapers may offer an avenue by which disaster responders can calm fears about the future more readily. This study also shows that fears about social disruption are related to use of a radio, and suggest that messages targeted to radio broadcasting may help to reduce such concerns.

Although the effectiveness of radiation health seminars could not be assessed directly through this study, due to the simultaneous assessment of seminar effect and test-retest validity, the evidence from the survey is suggestive of an effect of such seminars in reducing attendants' concerns about all dimensions of the disaster. Early and comprehensive provision of such seminars, in conjunction with assessments of individual radiation exposure risks, may be useful in both reducing anxiety, establishing trust at a local community level, and identifying those who are most concerned about the disaster's effects and the best means of delivering information to them.

Finally, this study found no strong evidence that social media were associated with heightened or reduced fears or concerns. This is surprising given the well-publicized role of social networking sites such as Twitter and Facebook in disaster response [12], [13]. However, the age of the sample and relatively low useage of such media (about 15%) suggests that this population's media preferences are not reflective of other, younger populations [14], and more research is needed before definitive conclusions can be drawn about the value of social networking sites as methods of information dissemination after a disaster.

This study found that there was a significant association between some types of media use and concerns about health and public order after the disaster. Media messages can be tailored to different audiences and delivery methods by disaster response planners to maximize the impact of messages being delivered, to reduce anxiety, and to improve their ability to deliver correct, accurate and timely information in a post-disaster setting. Radiation health seminars may also provide a useful forum both for delivering health-related information and for assessing the best methods for disseminating post-disaster messages. Disaster planners should be aware that media consumption patterns are not homogeneous and attention to their heterogeneity may make post-disaster information dissemination more effective and responsive to public health needs.

ACKNOWLEDGMENTS

The research project would not have been possible without the support of many people. Especially we would like to express our sincere gratitude to Mr.Yasuo Miyazawa (President of the SEISA group), Dr.Hidekiyo Tachiya (The mayor of Soma city, Fukushima) and Prof. Masahiro Kami (Professor of Division of Social Communication System for Advanced Clinical Research, The Institute of Medical Science, The University of Tokyo) who were abundantly helpful and offered invaluable assistance, support and guidance in providing a health check for the residents in Fukushima.

AUTHOR CONTRIBUTIONS

Conceived and designed the experiments: AS MT KM MS. Performed the experiments: AS SN MT TM. Analyzed the data: AS SN MT SG. Contributed reagents/materials/analysis tools: SG KM MT. Wrote the paper: AS.

REFERENCES

1. Bromet EJ (2011) Lessons learned from radiation disasters. World Psychiatry 10: 83–84.
2. American Red Cross (2011) Social Media in Disasters and Emergencies. American Red Cross.
3. 3.Raphael B, Ma H (2011) Mass catastrophe and disaster psychiatry. Molecular Psychiatry 16: 247–251.
4. Barnes MD, Hanson CL, Novilla LM, Meacham AT, McIntyre E, et al. (2008) Analysis of media agenda setting during and after Hurricane Katrina: implications for emergency preparedness, disaster response, and disaster policy. American Journal of Public Health 98: 604–610.
5. Drottz-Sjoberg BM, Persson L (1993) Public reaction to radiation: fear, anxiety, or phobia? Health Physics 64: 223–231.
6. Slovic P (1996) Perception of risk from radiation. Radiation Protection Dosimetry 68: 165–180.
7. Friedman SM, Gorney CM, Egolf BP (1987) Reporting on Radiation - a Content-Analysis of Chernobyl Coverage. Journal of Communication 37: 58–67.
8. Brewin TB (1994) Chernobyl and the Media. British Medical Journal 309: 208–209.

9. Taira T, Hatoyama Y (2011) Nationalize the Fukushima Daiichi atomic plant. Nature 480: 313–314.

10. .Smith J (2011) A long shadow over Fukushima. Nature 472: 7.

11. Kanayama T (2007) Community Ties and Revitalization: The Role of Community Radio in Japan. Tokyo: Keio University.

12. Shklovski I, Palen L, Sutton J (2008) Finding community through information and communication technology in disaster response.

13. Hosaka T (2011) Tohoku disaster sparks innovative social media responses. The Japan Times online. Tokyo, Japan.

14. Vance K, Howe W, Dellavalle RP (2009) Social Internet Sites as a Source of Public Health Information. Dermatologic Clinics 27: 133.

7

TWITTER IN THE CROSS FIRE—THE USE OF SOCIAL MEDIA IN THE WESTGATE MALL TERROR ATTACK IN KENYA

Tomer Simon[1,2,3], Avishay Goldberg[4], Limor Aharonson-Daniel[1,2], Dmitry Leykin[1,2,5], Bruria Adini[1,2]

[1] Department of Emergency Medicine, Recanati School for Community Health Professions, Faculty of Health Sciences, Ben-Gurion University of the Negev, Beer Sheba, Israel,

[2] PREPARED Center for Emergency Response Research, Ben-Gurion University of the Negev, Beer Sheba, Israel,

[3] Ready.org.il – Emergency readiness and preparedness in Israel, Givatayim, Israel,

[4]Department of Health Systems Management, Faculty of Health Sciences, Ben-Gurion University of the Negev, Beer Sheba, Israel,

[5] Department of Psychology, Tel Hai Academic College, Kiryat Shmona, Israel

ABSTRACT

On September 2013 an attack on the Westgate mall in Kenya led to a four day siege, resulting in 67 fatalities and 175 wounded. During the crisis, Twitter became a crucial channel of communication between the government, emergency responders and the public, facilitating the emergency management of the event. The objectives of this paper are to present the main activities, use patterns and lessons learned from the use of the social media in the crisis. Using TwitterMate, a system developed to collect, store and analyze tweets, the main hashtags generated by the crowd and specific Twitter accounts of individuals, emergency responders and NGOs, were followed throughout the four day siege. A total of 67,849 tweets were collected and analyzed. Four main categories of hashtags were identified: geographical locations, terror attack, social support and organizations. The abundance of Twitter accounts providing official information made it difficult to synchronize and follow the flow of information. Many organizations posted simultaneously, by their manager and by the organization itself. Creating situational awareness was facilitated by information tweeted by the public. Threat assessment was updated through the information posted on social media. Security breaches led to the relay of sensitive data. At times, misinformation was only corrected after two days. Social media offer an accessible, widely available means for a bi-directional flow of information between the public and the authorities. In the crisis, all emergency responders used and leveraged social media networks for communicating both with the public and among themselves. A standard operating procedure should be developed to enable multiple responders to monitor, synchronize and integrate their social media feeds during emergencies. This will lead to better utilization and optimization of social media resources during crises, providing clear guidelines for communications and a hierarchy for dispersing information to the public and among responding organizations.

INTRODUCTION

In recent years, the social media, and especially Twitter, have emerged as important, near real-time communication channels and technologies during emergency response. Social media consist of tools that enable open and online exchange of information through conversation, interaction and exchange of user generated content [1], [2]. These tools constantly produce vast amounts of data, both relevant and irrelevant. Researchers state that emergency managers should utilize filtering and pattern recognition algorithms on the data streams, in order to access important and meaningful information in real-time, facilitate an immediate response, and understand events as they unfold [3], [2]. Twitter has been shown to provide faster updates in developing emergencies in comparison to traditional media channels [4]. Social media, as opposed to traditional information and communications technologies, manage the content of the conversation or interaction as an artifact in the online environment (post or tweet) [5].

A recent study showed that Kenya is the second most active country in Africa on Twitter, surpassed only by South Africa [6]. Compared to the global average age of Twitter users, which is 39, 60% of Africa's users are 21 to 29, and 57% use Twitter from their mobile phones. Kenya's president, Uhuru Kenyatta, is the fourth most followed African leader [7].

The use of social media in emergencies, specifically Twitter and Facebook, is growing. The different social media channels have become an integral tool in the response of official authorities and the general public to emergency situations [2], [3], [8]. The continuous rise in Twitter and Facebook use during routine times and in emergencies indicates their potential contribution towards creation of situational awareness and status reports, tasks that have proven challenging in mass casualty incidents [4].

Sentiment analysis (also called subjectivity analysis or opinion mining) has been defined as the task of finding the opinions of authors about specific organizations [9]. It has been used extensively to gain insight into people's opinions, sentiments, evaluations, attitudes, and emotions from written language [10]. Nagy & Stamberger [11] noted that microblogs are an opportunity to search for critical information such as sentiments, and later use such information to rapidly detect the sentiment of the crowd towards crises or disasters. Kryvasheyeu, Chen, Moro, Hentenryck & Cebrian [12] studied sentiment analysis in over 50 million Twitter messages posted before, during and after Hurricane Sandy. They concluded that analyzing sentiments from Twitter (along with other metrics), may enable the use of "sentiment sensing" to detect and locate disasters. Previous studies have suggested that emergency dispatches and communications centers should convey information authoritatively and without emotion, even though they work in emotionally-charged environments, handling calls from victims, families of casualties and relaying information to and from field emergency personnel [13], [14]. Therefore we expect that the emotional orientation of communications dispatched by the operation centers will be less negative than the organizations' managers communicating from the scene.

In September 2013, an attack on the Westgate shopping mall in Kenya led to a four day siege, resulting in 67 fatalities and about 175 wounded. Around noon on September 21, an unknown number of armed terrorists entered the Westgate shopping mall in Nairobi, Kenya and took control. During the following days, the Kenyan security forces tried to retake the mall using ground and air forces. Kenyan emergency authorities managing the crisis established a perimeter surrounding the mall and provided support and medical treatment to the injured and their families. The Al-Shabaab militant group took responsibility for the attack through one of their Twitter accounts.

The Kenya Westgate Mall attack provides a unique opportunity to assess and understand how emergency organizations utilize social media to improve their responses to the event through content and activity analysis. This research aims to address three main hypotheses:

- Sentiment of emergency dispatches/EOC (Emergency Operations Center) tweets will be more positive than the sentiment of tweets made by the managers in the field.
- Use of social media during urban terror attacks leads to breaches of security.
- Emergency managers new to Twitter will use it as a basic, one-way, communications channel.

This case study offers two significant contributions. The first is a unique opportunity to study an event that took place in Africa, an understudied region in the field of social media. The second is the limited geographic nature of this event (which occurred in a defined set of buildings), enabling an understanding of the contribution of social media in an ongoing emergency. Currently, there is not enough evidence for best practice when incorporating social media in emergency response. In this study we make progress in understanding crisis communication patterns mediated by social media. Learning lessons from this event concerning the use of social media to create situational awareness can facilitate the creation of standard operating procedures for first responders that will encompass information sharing, control and command operations, and risk communication.

MATERIALS AND METHODS

The Research Tools

The Kenya Westgate mall attack began on September 21, 2013 and lasted four days until September 24, 2013. Between September 21 and September 25, 2013, structured monitoring, collection, storing and analysis of Twitter information was carried out.

Data collection was performed using TwitterMate, a self-developed system specifically intended to collect tweets from Twitter. TwitterMate's architecture includes four main components- 1. A graphical user interface (GUI) where a user can define the basic Twitter search according to one or more usernames, hashtags and specific tweet IDs. TwitterMate can also collect the followers of specific Twitter users. Through the username search, TwitterMate is able to extract all tweets made by a specific Twitter account. The searches cover Twitter Search, REST and Stream APIs to collect tweets, and can run in an automatic or manual mode. 2, An Excel-based data store where all tweets are saved. Tweets are saved according their search parameters in different tabs, and are broken into 11 different information classifications. 3. A generic built-in API section that can operate and consume any natural language processing REST API calls i.e., Alchemy API. The API calls can be run on a specific tab in the Excel to analyze tweets. 4. In the Excel, further text analysis is conducted using a series of macros and formulas to extract hashtags and user accounts from the messages and clean tweets, running them through NLP analysis. The use of TwitterMate during a number of time intervals, as presented in Table 1, facilitated the collection of 67,849 tweets, based on the relevant hashtags and accounts of managers/organizations involved in the response to the event. Although TwitterMate collects tweets in all languages, only tweets in English, communicated by the emergency organizations were analyzed in this study, constituting 99.99% of all tweets made by the emergency organization accounts.

Table 1. TwitterMate tweets collection time intervals.

Date	Collection Time Interval
21/9/2013	13:39–18:44
22/9/2013	05:12–19:02
23/9/2013	05:07–15:01
24/9/2013	06:07–22:00
25/9/2013	05:56–09:51

As mentioned, TwitterMate has a built-in feature utilizing Alchemy API (http://www.alchemyapi.com/), a collection of natural language processing tools which provides multiple targeting options for sentiment analysis, including document-level, entity-level, and keyword-level directional, relational and user-specified sentiment analysis. In the present work, we used document-level (tweet level) sentiment analysis. Each tweet received a sentiment score: −1 (negative sentiment), 0 (neutral) and 1 (positive sentiment), and a general classification of polarity (negative, neutral or positive). Alchemy API has previously been used for sentiment analysis tasks in different contexts, including tourism [15], consumer behavior [16], education [17], [18], online technical support [19] and more. Alchemy API application on data extracted from Twitter has been documented as well [20]. Meehan et al. [15] examined the performance of a sentiment analysis classifier and reached 86.01% accuracy level (ACC). ACC represents the proportion of true results (true positives and true negatives) in the population. In the present study we randomly selected 15% of the total tweets and manually labeled them into three categories (negative, positive and neutral sentiment). We randomly selected 50% of managers' tweets, and 10% of organizations' tweets (total 299 tweets) and manually labeled them into sentiment categories: negative, positive and neutral. Overall, there was moderate agreement (61.5%) between two MA level researchers in labeling the tweets. A test set was created from the agreed upon tweets. Alchemy API sentiment analysis classification and our manual labeling were next entered into a confusion matrix to estimate true positives (manually classified as true, and classifier indicated true), false positives (manually classified as false, and classifier indicated true), false negatives (manually classified as true, and classifier indicated false) and true negatives (manually classified as false, and classifier indicated false). The ACC that was obtained was not satisfactory (61.27%) and it was found that both precision (i.e., proportion of true positives out of all true positives and false positives) and recall (i.e., sensitivity or the true positives out of all positives) were low for neutrality classification. After excluding all tweets that were classified neutral by Alchemy API (23%), we re-examined the performance of the classification on negative vs. positive values only (n=87). This time we obtained acceptable ACC of 86.2%, with precision values of 90.48% and 84.85% for negative and positive (respectively), and recall values of 65.52% and 96.55% for negative and positive classifications (respectively). For our analysis, we used the sentiment score values (ranging from −1 to 1) for each tweet received, enabling us to incorporate more continues measure of sentiment. In addition, we used a binary measure of sentiment (negative vs. positive).

Twitter enables users to add a direct reference to a user in their tweets by inserting the user's account name (@username); i.e., a 'mention' [21] into the text. A mention can also be created by retweeting ("RT") another person's message, and this user account is automatically inserted into the new message. When a person or organization is mentioned in a tweet, a notification is sent directly to their inbox. The Facebook pages of the governmental authorities, which can be publicly accessed, were analyzed in order to understand the differences in the use of various social media tools during emergencies and their effect on the public. For the sentiment analysis task, we first pre-processed the tweets by cleaning punctuation characters and other symbols frequently found in twitter, including: , : ; ? ( ) { } [ ] @ # $ & * + ~ % and |. We also removed extra white spaces, converted website addresses (e.g. https://*) to URL, and converted @username to AT_USER. Finally, we removed stop words as they usually have little meaning. Such preprocessing is common and standard procedure in sentiment analysis [20], [22].

Study Design

The event's hashtags, as well as specific users' and/or organizations' accounts were followed using TwitterMate. The collection process was initiated on September 21, based on the hashtag "#westgate". Hashtag identification was based on content analysis and Excel formulas that extracted from each tweet any hashtag mentioned within it. The identified hashtags were then inserted manually into TwitterMate in order to integrate them in the automatic collection process. Two main hashtags (#WestGate and #WestGateAttack) and all governmental accounts and emergency organizations' accounts that participated in the response were followed and collected continually during the crisis, between September 21 and September 25. The participants followed were representatives of the Kenyan government and emergency authorities, and are thus considered formal and valid agents of Kenya's administration. Accordingly, tweets published by these organizations were considered as valuable and with impact on the population. We used the collected data to understand the progression and use of Twitter by the emergency authorities and to identify lessons learned. Using Statistical Package for the Social Sciences (SPSS), 19 we conducted a chi-squared test on the sentiment scores of the emergency authorities and their managers.

RESULTS

The collection was made during the hours of the day as it required manual interventions as new hashtags were created. All tweets made by the accounts mentioned in Table 2 from September 21 to September 25 were collected regardless of the time the collection process took place, as Twitter allows the collection of all tweets made by a specific account using its API.

Sentiment Analysis

In order to avoid bias we used the AlchemyAPI to analyze only original tweets communicated by emergency organizations and their managers, while disregarding re-tweets.

The difference in sentiment average score between managers and organizations was statistically significant, as observed in an independent samples t-test, $t\,(2004)=1.76$, $p<0.05$ (one-tailed), $d'=0.12$. Managers' average sentiment ($M=.04$, $SD=0.17$) was more positive than organizations' average sentiment ($M=.01$, $SD=0.18$). However, using a two-sided chi-squared statistical test we found no difference in sentiment expression between managers and organizations, although descriptively, organizations had more negative classifications of their tweets (46.5% vs. 40.4%), while managers had more positive classifications of their tweets (59.6%). Therefore, the initial hypothesis that sentiments of emergency dispatches/EOC's tweets would be more positive than the sentiments of tweets communicated from on-site by the managers was refuted.

Table 2. Extent of tweets, retweets and mentions during the Westgate mall attack.

User Name	Description	Twitter Join Date	Total # of Tweets	% (n) of RT's	% (n) of Mentions (excluding RT's)	% (n) of Tweets with Hashtags
@UKenyatta	President of The Republic of Kenya	26/8/2010	17	0% (0)	0% (0)	0% (0)
@WilliamsRuto	Deputy President of Kenya	12/7/2011	6	0% (0)	0% (0)	0% (0)
@PSCU_Digital	Home of Presidential and Government News	15/7/2013	228	25% (58)	54% (123)	78% (179)
@CabinetOfficeKE	Kenya's Cabinet Affairs Office in the Presidency	30/5/2013	78	95% (74)	0% (0)	24% (19)
@InteriorKE	Kenya's Ministry of Interior and Coordination of National Government	14/7/2013	1,523	49% (753)	26% (404)	32% (484)
@NDOCKenya	The Kenya National Disaster Operation Centre	28/4/2011	558	29% (163)	49% (274)	31% (172)
@joelenku	Cabinet Secretary - Interior and Co-ordination of National Government Kenya	4/9/2013	45	55% (25)	18% (8)	20% (9)
@F_Kimemia	Head of Civil Service and Secretary to the Cabinet of Kenya	31/5/2013	143	45% (65)	22% (32)	19% (28)
@IGKimaiyo	Inspector General of National Police Service, Kenya	24/6/2013	365	72% (264)	11% (40)	20% (75)
@KDFInfo	Kenya Defense Forces	13/9/2013	28	0% (0)	0% (0)	0% (0)
@MajorEChirchir	Kenya Military Spokesman	27/10/2011	35	28% (10)	46% (16)	6% (2)
@PoliceKE	Kenya Police	12/9/2013	569	54% (309)	21% (121)	24% (136)
@Abbas_Gullet	Secretary General of Kenya Red Cross	24/10/2011	18	55% (10)	22% (4)	55% (10)
@KenyaRedCross	Kenya Red Cross	30/4/2010	189	11% (22)	42% (79)	72% (136)
@AmbulanceKenya	St. John Ambulances	Not Available	81	34% (28)	18% (15)	62% (50)
@HSM_PR, @HSM_PRESOFFICE2, @hsmpress_	Al-Shabaab Terrorist Organization	Not available	258	1.5% (4)	6% (15)	89% (231)

Figure 1 presents a comparison of average sentiment scores of the managers communicating from the field. As can be seen, all managers' sentiment scores were positive (>0), except for tweets communicated by deputy president of Kenya William Ruto (n=6) which were all analyzed as having a negative sentiment score.

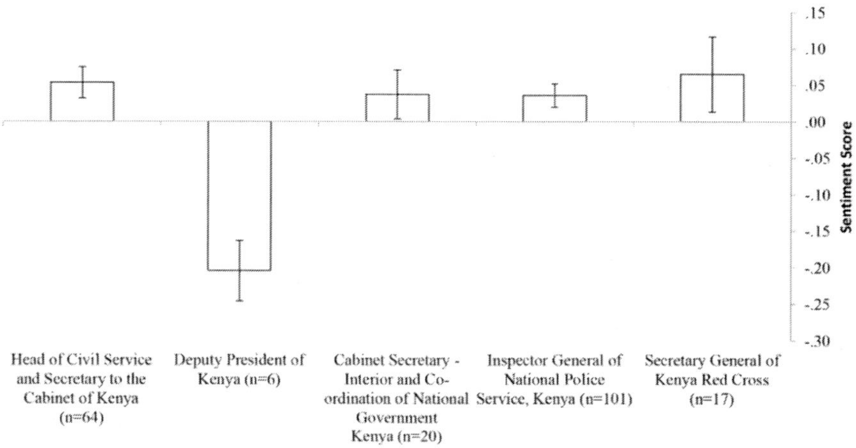

Figure 1. Average sentiment score of tweets made by the managers. For each account the number of tweets analyzed is provided (n).

Figure 2 presents the average sentiment score of the emergency authorities responding to the event or coordinating the response to it. The average sentiments of the Ministry of the Interior as well as those of the PSCU Kenya Digital were positive compared to the average sentiment scores of the other emergency responders, which were negative.

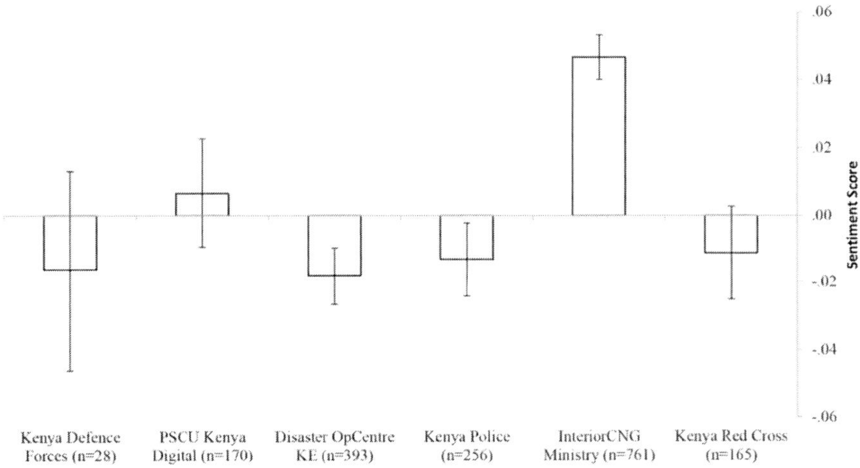

Figure 2. Average sentiment score of tweets made by the organizations. For each account the number of tweets analyzed is provided (n).

Hashtags

Through content analysis, four categories of hashtags used during the crisis were identified, referring to: 1) geographical locations – e.g., #WestGate, #WestGateMall, #Kenya, #Nairobi. These hashtags existed and were used on Twitter prior to the attack; 2) terror/violent attacks– e.g., #WestGateAttack, #WestGateSiege, #WestGateMallAttack and #WestGateShootout. Kenyan government officials, organizations and first responders used #WestGateAttack only; 3) social support, resilience and cohesiveness– e.g., #WeAreOne and #UnitedWeStand. The latter, though used by the public was absent from all official tweets; and, 4) organizations – e.g., #RedCross and #AlShabaab.

During the first days of the attack, numerous complaints were posted on Twitter stating that there were too many hashtags for the event or alternatively posting a list of hashtags, such as "One incident, many hashtags" or "So many different hashtags for today's tragedy #Westgate #WestgateMall #WestagateAttack #WestgateShootOut #WestGateMallShootOut". Different variations were used inconsistently and interchangeably by the public, the media, and NGOs. On September 24 the PSCU Kenya Digital tweeted that all of the social media managers had held a synchronization meeting- "This morning we held a WhatsApp meeting with all bloggers running the @InteriorKE @PoliceKE @kdfinfo @NDOCKenya our voice is #WithOneAccord", following which all responders consistently used the #WithOneAccord hashtag.

Moreover, while the fourth category of hashtags was present in many tweets, government officials preferred to use the "@" handle to mention the different organizations and individuals in their messages, as shown in Table 3.

Table 3. Government officials use of "@" in their tweets.

Official Account	# of Tweets	# of Tweets with "@"	Total %
Inspector General of the Kenya Police (@IGKimaiyo)	365	304	83.28%
Secretary of the Cabinet (@f_kimemia)	129	94	72.86%
Secretary of the Interior (@joelenku)	45	33	73.33%

Mentions

Mentioning was frequently used by government officials and responding organizations as presented in Table 2. Both public and official users directly mentioned other official accounts during the entire crisis.

Use of Twitter and Facebook

During this crisis, Twitter seems to have been the dominant social media platform used by the public and responding organizations. Though limited in scope, Facebook too was used. For example, the Kenya Police started posting on Twitter on September 21, but posted for the first time on its Facebook wall only on September 23, following an announcement on Twitter that included their Facebook page address [23]. Furthermore, the Kenya Police tweeted 569 times on Twitter during the entire crisis, while posting only ten times on Facebook. The Kenya Police had 20,267 followers on Twitter but only 2,506 fans ('likes') on Facebook. The same messages that were posted on Twitter were published on Facebook, keeping the hashtags while removing the mentions. Kenya's Ministry of Interior used its Twitter accounts 1,533 times while not posting a single message on their Facebook page.

Participants

As an integral component of responding to the crisis, a number of governmental officials, organizations, first responders, and NGOs tweeted information concerning the event. The different organizations are presented in Table 2. The table also presents the date the Twitter account of the person/organization was created. The creation date of the Twitter account was extracted using the Twopcharts website (http://twopcharts.com/howlongontwitter). Eight of the accounts were created between May and September 2013, two of which (Kenya Police and Kenya Military) joined Twitter less than ten days prior to the attack.

In most organizations, communications were transmitted simultaneously by both the manager of the organization and the organization itself (see Table 4). Frequently, the managers of emergency organizations/ministries posted from the scene of the event, while coordinating the response, whereas the organization published more extensive information to the general public. For example, this was well displayed by the Ministry of Interior (@InteriorKE) and its minister Joseph Ole Lenku (@JoeLenku) communicating from the scene near the Westgate mall. Furthermore, both the Kenya Police and the Ministry of Interior tweeted throughout the event that official communications would be posted through their respective managers' Twitter accounts.

Table 4. Organizations or managers of organizations that tweeted during the Westgate mall attack.

Organization	Manager
Kenya Police (@PoliceKE)	Inspector General of National Police Service, Kenya (@IGKimayio)
Ministry of Interior (@InteriorKE)	Cabinet Secretary - Interior and Co-ordination of National Government Kenya (@JoeLenku)
Home of Presidential and Government News (@PSCU_Digital)	President of The Republic of Kenya (@UKenyatta)
Kenya Red Cross (@KenyaRedCross)	Secretary General of Kenya Red Cross (@Abbas_Gullet)
Cabinet Affairs Office in the Presidency (@CabinetOfficeKE)	Head of Civil Service and Secretary to the Cabinet of Kenya (@F_Kimemia)
Kenya Defense Forces (@KFDInfo)	Kenya Military Spokesman (@MajorEChirchir)

The abundance of Twitter accounts providing official information regarding the event made it difficult to synchronize and follow the flow of information. For example, on September 22, the Kenya Police stated "For systematic flow of information on the operation at West Gate please follow @kdfinfo @InteriorKE @PoliceKE @IGkimaiyo @joelenku", which was retweeted 108 times. On September 23, the Ministry of Interior requested the Kenyan Military to follow them back on Twitter [24].

On the previous night, starting at 10:10 PM all government organizations started using the #WithOneAccord hashtag, initiated by the PSCU Kenya Digital account. On the following morning, September 24th, The PSCU Kenya Digital held a WhatsApp synchronization meeting with all of the social media managers in charge of the governmental Twitter and Facebook accounts [25]. Following the meeting, government organizations started using the #WithOneAccord hashtag consistently.

One first responder organization that participated in the response phase and which was referred to in other organizations' tweets was the Red Cross ambulance services (@EMS_Kenya). Prior to the attack, their account had been active on Twitter.

Figure 3 shows the number of tweets made by 12 Twitter accounts of government officials, organizations and NGOs during the four days of the crisis. The Kenyan Ministry of Interior tweeted between twice to five times more than other organizations, probably because it was the ministry in charge of coordination and response. The rise in the number of tweets made by the PSCU Kenya Digital, the official communications channel of the Kenyan government, can be explained by the efforts made to synchronize and align the response and messages to the public.

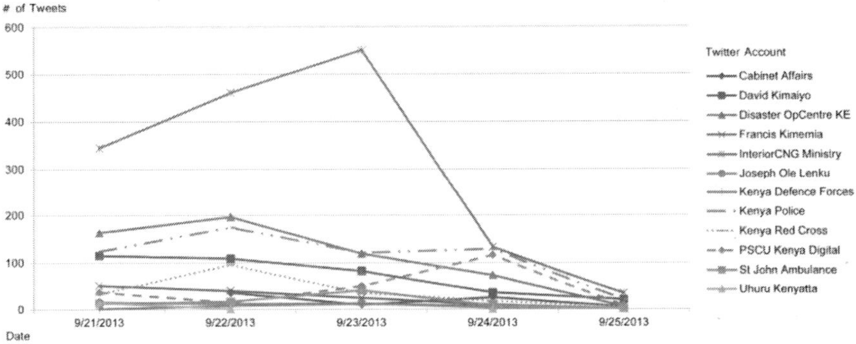

Figure 3. Number of tweets per day made by Twitter accounts of managers and organizations.

Public

The general public was active on Twitter throughout the crisis. This activity can be classified into six main categories, 1) producing information concerning the event, 2) sharing and consolidating information, 3) expressing emotional and social support for individuals, communities or responders affected by the crisis 4) sharing concerns about privacy and security issues regarding social media, 5) requesting or offering to volunteer, and 6) criticizing the government and its security services.

Terrorist organization

The Al-Shabaab organization twitted 258 times between September 21 and September 25. They claimed responsibility for the attack on the Westgate mall through Twitter. The Al-Shabbab used a number of accounts to try to avoid being caught by Twitter, but often had to change accounts as Twitter suspended them for breaching their terms of use. We followed three different accounts that were active on different dates "@hsmpress_" (21–

22/9), "@HSM_PRESOFFICE2" (22–23/9) and "@HSM_PR" (24–25/9). The Al-Shabaab tweeted from the "@hsmpress_" account regarding their suspension on September 22 – "Alshabab has suffered another great casualty: Twitter account loss!".

Situational awareness updates by the first responders and government officials

Using their Twitter accounts, all government organizations and officials provided the public and other responding organizations with situational awareness updates. These updates included five classifications of information, including 1) risk communication and public warnings – e.g., Kenyan Police tweeted an hour after the attack: "The public should stay away from West Gate and its environs and we ask the media to refrain from any unnecessary comments." The Kenya military tweeted: "Report any suspicious looking individuals or activities to the nearest security organizations of the Govt". 2) Status updates about the armed response towards controlling the mall – e.g., the Kenya Police tweeted: "We have taken control of the ground floor and we urge you to be patient", or the Kenya military, which communicated that: "KDF has dominated all floors of Westgate Mall building. Troops are now concentrating on clearing the building". 3) Information hubs for other organizations and officials. Table 2 shows the percentage of retweets made by these accounts. 4) Communications and rumor control – e.g., the PSCU Kenya Digital tweeted: "Let us avoid unreliable sources in our Media and Social Media coverage of the Security Operation currently underway - Do not speculate.", or the Minister of Interior that posted: "I urge Kenyans online to be responsible when you share information, it's better to share nothing and save a life." 5) Reassurances, condolences and verbal reinforcements to the public and responding organizations– e.g., the Kenyan military tweeted on the second day: "All efforts are underway to bring this matter to a speedy conclusion"; the Minister of Interior tweeted: "I would like to reiterate that our security forces are fully in charge of the situation."; and Secretary of the Cabinet tweeted: "My heartfelt condolences to the families and friends of those who perished in the heinous crime."

By the public

The public contributed to the situational awareness by tweeting information regarding the developments as they experienced them from the surroundings of the Westgate mall. Some even shared tweets with photos taken from the scene.

Two-way communication and engagement

All responding organizations used Twitter to communicate and notify other organizations during the crisis. This was done by adding a mention to a tweet with a "cc" before it (as in emails), i.e., a tweet sent out by the Ministry of Interior: "Give way to ambulances making their way to #WestgateMall cc @NDOCKenya". This tweet was sent out to the general public, but it also notified the Kenyan Disaster Operation Center by mentioning it, which retweeted it approximately two hours later. Almost an hour and a half after the attack began, the Minister of Interior arrived at the scene and tweeted: "I am at the scene and urge the public to be calm, give support to @IGkimaiyo and @PoliceKE and we will resolve this quickly. cc @InteriorKE". It was retweeted by the Ministry of Interior less than a minute later.

The government organizations and officials were reading tweets that mentioned their names. In some cases they retweeted the original message, as the Police Inspector General retweeted: "RT @CitizenTVNews: Inspector General of Police David Kimaiyo via his twitter account @IGkimaiyo says the Westgate mall is currently surroun...". The hypothesis that emergency organizations and managers new to Twitter would use it as a basic, one-way, communications channel was refuted. No differences were found in the use patterns of Twitter between new versus more experienced users.

Crowdsourcing

We identified two ways emergency authorities requested assistance from the public during the crisis: 1) a direct call for information – e.g., the Inspector General of the police requested information regarding potential hostages "Kindly share information of the families who have been shopping and have not been traced. " 2) Requesting the public to retweet their messages or share information on Facebook, e.g., the Kenya police tweeted "Forensic probe is underway. We urge the public to stay away for their own safety. Pls RT."

Threat assessment

At the beginning of the crisis, the responding organizations and the public did not understand the nature of the event. Stemming from the initial tweets, the police perceived that robbers rather than terrorists were attacking the mall. The Ministry of Interior tweeted approximately 30 minutes after the attack: "We've managed to evacuate some people to safety as @PoliceKE pursues the thugs". Fifteen minutes later, they tweeted: "The IGP @IGkimaiyo is heading to the scene of crime to assess the situation. He'll also give a statement." Approximately three hours after the attack began, Reuters tweeted that there was a possibility that terrorists might be perpetrating the attack.

Operational security and censorship

Both the responding organizations and the public were wary about operational security. Many bystanders and journalists on site tweeted and broadcast their operations in real time. One bystander tweeted "why is this our media showing us the cops sneaking in??." The Kenyan military tweeted "We urge all Kenyans to be cautious on what is being communicated on social media.", and the PSCU Digital Kenya tweeted "We are appealing to Media to avoid showing photos of our @kdfinfo soldiers. Kindly, Only tweet what you are absolutely sure about #Westgate." In one instance the Kenya Police asked a Twitter user to delete a message that contained pictures of military helicopters preparing to launch an attack on the mall [26]. On the second day of the crisis, the Kenyan Disaster Operation Center tweeted to a news channel asking that they remove a story "@CapitalFM_kenya Please take that story down. It is misleading and bound to confuse." Eight minutes later they tweeted "Once again we request media houses to exercise caution in airing/publishing stories on operations at Westgate which are still sensitive." These requests to the media and the public continued throughout the entire crisis. The Ministry of the Interior tweeted on the morning of the second day to a specific user "kindly keep such thoughts or DM them. The enemy is somewhere watching" (DM refers to a private direct message on Twitter). The hypothesis that the use of social media during urban terror attacks leads to breaches of security was confirmed.

On the third day of the crisis, the police published a direct threat of prosecution to those sharing 'repugnant' information on Twitter - "Those who have shared content that is repugnant to our sense of nationhood be warned that you will be found and charged."

Misinformation

During the first day of the attack, two unique tweets were posted, claiming to show pictures of the attackers. These messages were retweeted 106 times, 81 of them within 30 minutes. We found that these pictures were not of the attackers but rather of the Kenyan armed forces. The photos were removed after approximately two days.

Geo-location information

Tweets can include the coordinates of the location the tweet was sent from. While government organizations and officials' accounts did not include geo-location information, 0.9% of tweets collected from the public included geo-location information. Out of all the accounts listed in Table 2, geo-location information was identified in only two tweets of Deputy President Ruto, placing him directly next to the Westgate mall.

The location of the managers was deduced based on the tweets' text or geo-location information. Although they did not include their own location they did include location based information in the text of the messages, whether with clearly identifiable information or with a location reference. One example of a tweet with a clear location can be found in a tweet by the Kenyan Disaster Operation Center 20 minutes after the attack had begun "Mwanzi Road between Peponi Rd and Ring Road Parklands is CLOSED TO ALL TRAFFIC." The Ministry of Interior tweeted a message that included location based information by referring to an identifiable place "Roads adjacent to the #WestGateMall have been cordoned off, PLEASE use alternative route."

Verified Twitter accounts

On the third day of the attack, Twitter contacted the Kenyan government so that they could verify their accounts used to publish information on the Westgate attack. PSCU Kenya Digital first tweeted about it "@twitter has shared its support by contacting @PSCU_Digital to verify Government accounts-we have started with those communicating #WestGate." In the following three hours, most accounts of the Kenyan government organizations and officials, including the Kenya Red Cross, were verified.

Prior to the verification process, the governmental organizations had to inform the public as to which accounts were sharing verified information, as tweeted by the Kenya Police on the second day "We urge all Kenyans to wait for official information from @InteriorKE @IGkimaiyo @joelenku @StateHouseKenya."

DISCUSSION

Our findings show that Twitter served as an integral tool for emergency management in Kenya; all emergency related organizations and officials had accounts and actively communicated through them during the crisis, both with the public and among themselves. The use of Twitter in Kenya is not restricted to emergency situations alone but rather characterizes routine activities throughout the year. Merchant et al. [27] have presented the advantages of integrating social media into routine activities of emergency organizations.

The response to the attack was managed and coordinated by the Kenyan Police, supported by other first responders including the Red Cross ambulance service, EMS, and the fire brigade. The Kenyan military arrived on the first day to support and enhance the response, and the Kenyan National Disaster Operations Center oversaw the entire operation.

As presented in previous emergencies by different governments worldwide, the Kenyan government and ministers widely adopted the use of the social media during the terror attack and leveraged it in order to better understand the situation in real time, communicate with the public and improve their safety [2], [28]. The responding organizations often used two voices to communicate, both through the account of the organization and through the account of its manager.

Service providers, and especially public officials, emergency responders and spokespersons [13], are expected to manage their feelings while working with the public (control their "emotional labor") and even "suppress their own feelings in order to show desirable work-related emotions" [29]. As described by Guy et al. [13] emergency responders are trained to "keep their emotions in check" and provide compassionate and emphatic service to those in need during emergencies, even though the surroundings may be chaotic and intense. Aligned with these expectations, we found that managers of the responding authorities tended to be more positive in their communications with the public. The initial hypothesis that emergency dispatch operators, working in a more disconnected environment than their on-site managers, would present more positive sentiment was refuted. Their communications tended to be more negative than those of their managers. This finding contrasts with former studies recommending that emergency dispatches and communications centers minimize the use of emotion during their communication with the public despite their emotionally charged work environment [13], [14]. However, emergency managers and public officials using positive language in their communications with the public during a crisis contributed to increased trust and credibility. The high engagement of the managers on Twitter throughout the crisis can be explained by the fact that they were considered more "approachable" by the public as they used positive language in their messages. In his paper, Seeger [30] showed that spokespersons using compassion and empathy in their communications enhanced their credibility and legitimacy in the eyes of the public, who would also respond more favorably during the crisis, Twitter's 140 characters limitation made managers write simple messages, which were more easily understood by the general public and could be repeated. This is consistent with the findings of Wray et al. [31], indicating that messages in emergencies should use basic and positive language throughout the crisis to provide clear information. During this crisis senior managers and government officials communicated from the scene also providing eyewitness accounts, which we think enhanced their public image and credibility. Messages from high ranking officials, or experts, are perceived by the public as credible sources of information, as presented by Reynolds et al. [32].

In this study, we found 15 different Twitter accounts disseminating and communicating messages, which caused information overload and synchronization problems. Bharosa, et al. [33] showed that information sharing between organizations during emergency response is one the biggest challenges. This may indicate that although Twitter has been implemented as a formal communication channel and organizations are proficient users, a standard operating procedure for its synchronization and use during emergency situations has not yet been formulated and formalized.

Official responders and organizations were not prepared to manage Twitter communications 24/7 during the crisis, and had long breaks during the night, sometimes for up to 10 hours. It was also apparent that some organizations did not know, or were unaware of the Twitter accounts of other responding organizations, creating gaps between the ministry and the military. In one case we found that the Ministry of Interior was unaware of the Kenyan Military's Twitter account, although it was active from the first day of the crisis. Most probably, this resulted from the Military tweeting messages without any hashtag or mentions, causing them to be visible only to their direct followers.

The rapid rise in information available on Twitter within minutes after the initiation of the attack may be explained by two main factors: Twitter is highly used in Kenya and thus serves as a popular platform for sharing information [6], and the time and place of the terror attack, a central shopping mall in the capital, on a weekend, when it was crowded and active. During the crisis, individuals strived to connect with their communities and country, and the social media facilitated this quick and broad bonding. Furthermore, Twitter enabled the public to get the information in almost real-time and with very easy access as the crisis developed. This strengthens the use patterns identified in previous studies regarding the use of social media by the public in emergencies [34], [35], [8].

Throughout the crisis civilians, reporters, and responding organizations, as well as the terrorists, shared information on Twitter about the status of the response. From the tweets it was clear that many media personnel were present in the vicinity of the mall, as were numerous bystanders. During emergencies it is common to access situational awareness updates from the responding organizations, the media and the general public on Twitter [36], [37]. In the present attack, reporters and bystanders shared information, both textual and visual, in almost real-time, with no control and with minimal official monitoring and censorship, regarding the status and location of the forces. This kind of information may endanger the lives of the responders, and might have contributed to the prolonged siege, as the terrorists received live information detailing the armed response against them and were able to use this information to enhance their response. A study on the 2008 Mumbai terror attack suggests that "unregulated real time Twitter postings can contribute to increase the level of situation awareness for terrorist groups to make their attack decision" [38]. This indeed is a major concern that should be considered in future events. It presents a challenge, as censorship and regulation are alien to the nature of social media.

From this crisis we can learn that the 'traditional' two-way communications channel view of Twitter was used with a more extensive approach, as a cross-hierarchy, inter- and intra-organizational tool for communications and coordination of the response. All responding entities and their managers, whether ministers, managers or commanders, used it to communicate with the public, with their own organization and with other responding organizations. This indicates that the organizations have the support of their management to implement and use Twitter, but nevertheless, a standard operating procedure (SOP) is crucially needed for effective implementation in emergencies. The SOP should delineate ways to synchronize communication between official first responders and emergency organizations, such as the WhatsApp synchronization meeting that was conducted during the Kenyan terror attack. This online meeting included all bloggers managing the social media accounts of the government organizations, emphasizing the fact that the social media managers are not employees of the government. The SOP should also relate to the challenge of continuous communication during crises. The fact that during the night there was a pause in Twitter updates to the public, sometimes for up to ten hours, suggests that only one person operated the social media account, lacking replacements or organized shifts. Kenya's Police Twitter operator reported this in one of his tweets referring the public to other official accounts for updates – "After almost 36 hours without sleep, I'm off duty at Visa Oshwal Center. Please follow @kpsya @interiorke @policeke @kdfinfo.via @kangai" [39]. Kavanaugh et al. [2] stated that a government organization that wants to employ a social media tool for crisis communications must first define the policies, as well as outline what information should be shared and through which channels. As we found, the Kenya government operates at least three social media networks (Twitter, Facebook and WhatsApp), with unclear strategy as to what information should be published on which network and time frames. Latonero & Shklovski [40] recommended incorporating a public information officer, or technology evangelists in the organization.

Publishing situational awareness updates through social media during emergencies is a common practice for numerous participants [37]. Although emergency organizations were highly active on Twitter during the attack, they provided only minimal and general situational awareness updates to the public. More specific situational updates were published on Twitter by the public and journalists as they witnessed and reported it, while emergency organizations continuously published their dissatisfaction with this practice. We found that during routine times these same organizations published situational updates through Twitter. This contrast probably led to confusion of the population. The need to clearly define expectations of both the authorities and the public, as well as direct policies of utilization of the social media in response to emergencies, reinforces the need to develop an SOP that will provide tools and guidelines for when, how and what can be made public during emergencies. Furthermore, such an SOP could suggest ways for emergency managers in the field to coordinate their messages and status among themselves and with the emergency operation centers. Twitter and other social media could be used to support public and open communications, but could also convey private messages that are not accessible or visible to unwanted parties. This method of operation can serve to reduce the need for information coordination meetings, increasing managers' exposure to data from the field as well as freeing valuable time that could be dedicated to putting more focus on managing the crisis.

During the first day of the attack, many civilians published photos of what they thought were the attackers. Some of these photos were retweeted by hundreds, not knowing that they were incorrect. The same photos were published by news agencies, such as the New York Times, describing them as "plainclothes officers" [41]. Publishing misinformation may occur during emergencies, especially during the initial phases of the response when the situation is unclear and characterized by speculation. While analyzing the tweets we found that these images were often deleted by the users, most probably because they realized their mistake. This indicates that social media can be 'self-regulating' to filter and refute misinformation, and even rumors, as described by Mendoza et al. [42]. We did not find the Kenyan authorities publishing corrections to disinformation or to rumors during the crisis.

The Kenyan officials and organizations tried to direct the public to their accounts for access to verified and reliable information, but this was not necessarily implemented. This reflects two main challenges of using social media in emergencies: Anyone can open an account on social media sites and publish information [27], and during emergency situations people are exposed to large amounts of information that might contain inaccuracies [43]. Twitter, and other social media sites, understand the need to verify the accounts of official emergency authorities, and Twitter has recently released a new tool to allow sending verified emergency notifications, called Twitter Alerts, directly to users' phones [44].

CONCLUSIONS

Social media offer an accessible, widely available means for bi-directional flow of information between the public and the authorities in charge of public safety. Their use is growing across geographies, cultures, languages and organizations. This manuscript portrays the use of social media by the various participants in an unexpected event, and focuses mainly on use by emergency organizations. Emergency management almost always entails the response of multiple organizations and NGOs; in this crisis, all of these used and leveraged social media networks, not solely for communicating with the public, but also among themselves, frequently using two different Twitter accounts (for managers and for organizations), and for both public and private communications. Twitter offers emergency entities a communications platform that is ubiquitous and does not have interoperability issues, like other communication systems. This event showed that such a scenario may cause synchronization and coordination problems affecting response, and may waste valuable resources. Lessons learned from this event should contribute to the development of an SOP that will allow multiple responders to monitor, synchronize and integrate their social media feeds during emergencies. This will lead to better utilization and optimization of social media resources during crises, providing clear guidelines for communications and a hierarchy for dispersing information to the public and responding organizations during emergency situations. We recommend that future research analyze the differences between routine and emergency utilization of the social media by emergency organizations.

Limitations of the present study include the current state of sentiment analysis of crisis communication. Unfortunately, there is still a lack of studies analyzing emotional valence of micro-blog information during emergencies [12], and more work is needed to adapt sentiment analysis to emergency situations. During emergency situations some communications behavior, as seen in the present study, include words like "terrorists", or "attack", which are part of the emergency event (e.g., the Westgate mall attack). These terms should be analyzed as neutral words as they are informative pieces of information and do not necessarily reflect an opinion or an attitude of the communicator.

TwitterMate or similar instruments can become a tool that will help to manage and coordinate emergency events. Governments as well as emergency organizations should consider the availability of social media tools when they define their policies, and outline information they wish to share, and through what channels. Regulating the information provided by the public is yet another challenge that can possibly be better achieved through education rather than through regulation.

AUTHOR CONTRIBUTIONS

Conceived and designed the experiments: TS. Performed the experiments: TS DL. Analyzed the data: TS DL. Contributed reagents/materials/analysis tools: TS. Wrote the paper: TS. Contributed with the interpretation of data:

BA AG LAD. Reviewed the manuscript, revised it and approved its final version: BA AG LAD.

REFERENCES

1. Huang CM, Chan E, Hyder AA (2010) Web 2.0 and Internet Social Networking: A New tool for Disaster Management? - Lessons from Taiwan. BMC Med Inf Decis Making
2. Kavanaugh A, Fox EA, Sheetz S, Yang S, Li LT, et al.. (2011) Social Media Use by Government: from the routine to the critical. Paper presented at: Proceedings of the 12th Annual International Digital Government Research Conference: Digital Government Innovation in Challenging Times
3. Abbasi A, Hossain L, Hamra J, Owen C (2010) Social Networks Perspective of Firefighters' Adaptive Behaviour and Coordination among them. Paper presented at: ACM International Conference on Cyber, Physical and Social Computing.
4. Cassa CA, Chunara R, Mandl K, Brownstein JS (2013) Twitter as a Sentinel in Emergency Situations: Lessons from the Boston Marathon Explosions. PLOS Currents 2 (5)
5. Yates D, Paquette S (2011) Emergency knowledge management and social media technologies: A case study of the 2010 Haitian earthquake. International Journal of Information Management 6–13.
6. Portland Communications (January 2012) How Africa Tweets. Portland Communications Available: http://www.portland-communications.com/wp-content/uploads/2013/05/Twitter_in_Africa_PPT.pdf. Accessed 2013 Sep 24.
7. Twiplomacy (July 2013) Kenya. Twiplomacy Available: http://twiplomacy.com/info/africa/kenya/. Accessed 2013 Sep 24.
8. Bird D, Ling M, Haynes K (2012) Flooding Facebook – the use of social media during the Queensland and Victorian floods. The Australian Journal of Emergency Management 27 (1) 27–33.
9. Feldman R (2013) Techniques and applications for sentiment analysis. Communications of the ACM 56 (4) 82–89.
10. Liu B (2012) Sentiment analysis and opinion mining. Synthesis Lectures on Human Language Technologies 5 (1) 1–167.
11. Nagy A, Valley CMS, Stamberger J (2012) Crowd sentiment detection during disasters and crises. Paper presented at: Proceedings of the 9th International ISCRAM Conference.

12. Kryvasheyeu Y, Chen H, Moro E, Van Hentenryck P, Cebrian M (2014) Performance of Social Network Sensors During Hurricane. CoRR

13. Guy ME, Newman MA, Ganapati NE (2013) Managing emotions while managing crises. International Journal of Emergency Services 6–20.

14. Tracy SJ, Tracy K (1998) Emotion labor at 911: A case study and theoretical critique. Journal of Applied Communication Research 26 (4) 390–411.

15. Meehan K, Lunney T, Curran K, McCaughey A (2013) Context-aware intelligent recommendation system for tourism. Paper presented at: In Pervasive Computing and Communications Workshops (PERCOM Workshops), 2013 IEEE International Conference on.

16. Saritha SK, Devshriroy D (2013) Semantic Orientation of Sentiment Analysis on Social Media. International Journal of Computers & Technology 11 (4) 2401–2409.

17. Adamopoulos P (2013) What Makes a Great MOOC? An Interdisciplinary Analysis of Student Retention in Online Courses. Paper presented at: Proceedings of the 34th International Conference on Information Systems

18. Ciancarini P, Di Iorio A, Nuzzolese AG, Peroni S, Vitali F (2013) Semantic Annotation of Scholarly Documents and Citations. Paper presented at: XIIIth International Conference of the Italian Association for Artificial Intelligence

19. Kononenko O, Dietrich D, Sharma R, Holmes R (2012) Automatically locating relevant programming help online. Paper presented at: 2012 IEEE Symposium on Visual Languages and Human-Centric Computing (VL/HCC)

20. Saif H, He Y, Alani H (2012) Semantic sentiment analysis of twitter. Paper presented at: 11th International Semantic Web Conference

21. What are @replies and mentions? Twitter Available: https://support.twitter.com/articles/14023-what-are-replies-and-mentions. Accessed 2013 Sep 27.

22. Pak A, Paroubek P (2010) Twitter as a Corpus for Sentiment Analysis and Opinion Mining. Paper presented at: Proceedings of the Seventh International Conference on Language Resources and Evaluation (LREC)

23. Kenya Police (2013) Kenya Police. Twitter Available: https://twitter.com/PoliceKE/status/382031875117948928. Accessed 2013 Sep 26.

24. Kenya Ministry of Interior (2013) Kenya Ministry of Interior. Twitter Available: https://twitter.com/InteriorKE/status/381960772420923392. Accessed 2013 Sep 26.

25. PSCU Kenya Digital (2013) PSCU Kenya Digital. Twitter Available: https://twitter.com/PSCU_Digital/status/382440642657267712. Accessed 2013 Sep 26.

26. owden D (2013) Daniel Howden. Twitter Available: https://twitter.com/howden_africa/status/381800712193052672. Accessed 2013 Sep 26.

27. 27.Merchant RM, Elmer , Lurie N (2011) Integrating Social Media into Emergency-Preparedness Efforts. NEJM 289–291.

28. Cameron MA, Power R, Robinson B, Yin J (2012) Emergency Situation Awareness from Twitter for Crisis Management. Paper presented at: 21st international conference companion on World Wide Web

29. Mastracci SH, Guy ME, Newman MA (2011) Emotional Labor and Crisis Response: Working on the Razor's Edge: M.E.Sharpe.

30. Seeger MW (2006) Best practices in crisis communication: An expert panel process. Journal of Applied Communication Research 34 (3) 232–244.

31. Wray RJ, Becker SM, Henderson N, Glik D, Jupka K, et al. (2008) Communicating With the Public About Emerging Health Threats: Lessons From the Pre-Event Message Development Project. American Journal of Public Health 2214–2222.

32. Reynolds B, Seeger MW (2005) Crisis and Emergency Risk Communication as an Integrative Model. Journal of Health Communication 43–55.

33. Bharosa N, Lee J, Janssen M (2010) Challenges and obstacles in sharing and coordinating information during multi-agency disaster response: Propositions from field exercises. Journal of Information Systems Frontiers 49–65.

34. Lerman K, Ghosh R (2010) Information Contagion: An Empirical Study of the Spread of News on Digg and Twitter Social Networks. Paper presented at: Proceedings of the Fourth International AAAI Conference on Weblogs and Social Media

35. Taylor M, Wells G, Howell G, Raphael B (2012) The role of social media as psychological first aid as a support to community resilience building. The Australian Journal of Emergency Management 27 (1) 20–26.

36. Vieweg S, Hughes AL, Starbird K, Palen L (2010) Microblogging during two natural hazards events: what twitter may contribute to situational awareness. Paper presented at: Proceedings of the 28th international conference on Human factors in computing systems

37. Qu Y, Huang C, Zhang P (2010) Microblogging after a Major Disaster in China: A Case Study of the 2010 Yushu Earthquake. Paper presented at: Proceedings of the ACM 2011 conference on Computer supported cooperative work

38. Oh O, Agrawal M, Rao HR (2011) Information control and terrorism: Tracking the Mumbai terrorist attack through twitter. Information Systems Frontiers 33–43.

39. 39.Kenya Police (2013) Kenya Police. Twitter Available: https://twitter.com/PoliceKE/status/382177721125978112. Accessed 2013 Sep 26.

40. Latonero M, Shklovski I (2011) Emergency Management, Twitter, and Social Media Evangelism. International Journal of Information Systems for Crisis Response and Management 3 (4) 1–16.

41. 41.The New York Times (2013) Attack on a Kenyan Mall. The New York Times Available: http://www.nytimes.com/slideshow/2013/09/21/world/africa/20130922_NAIROBI2_337-1.html. Accessed 2013 Sep 26.

42. Mendoza M, Poblete B, Castillo C (2010) Twitter Under Crisis: Can we trust what we RT? Paper presented at: Proceedings of the First Workshop on Social Media Analytics

43. Lu Y, Yang D (2010) Information exchange in virtual communities under extreme disaster conditions. Decision Support Systems 529–538.

44. Pena G (2013) Twitter Alerts: Critical information when you need it most. Twitter Blog Available: https://blog.twitter.com/2013/twitter-alerts-critical-information-when-you-need-it-most. Accessed 2013 Sep 26.

8

AVAILABILITY AND DIVERSITY OF TRAINING PROGRAMS FOR RESPONDERS TO INTERNATIONAL DISASTERS AND COMPLEX HUMANITARIAN EMERGENCIES

Gabrielle A. Jacquet

Chioma C. Obi, [...], and Jamil D. Bayram

ABSTRACT

Introduction: Volunteers and members of relief organizations increasingly seek formal training prior to international field deployment. This paper identifies training programs for personnel responding to international disasters and complex humanitarian emergencies, and provides concise information – if available- regarding the founding organization, year established, location, cost, duration of training, participants targeted, and the content of each program. Methods: An environmental scan was conducted through a combination of a peer-reviewed literature search and an open Internet search for the training programs. Literature search engines included EMBASE, Cochrane, Scopus, PubMed, Web of Science databases using the search terms "international," "disaster," "complex humanitarian emergencies," "training," and "humanitarian response". Both searches were conducted between January 2, 2013 and September 12, 2013. Results: 14 peer-reviewed articles mentioned or described eight training programs, while open Internet search revealed 13 additional programs. In total, twenty-one training programs were identified as currently available for responders to international disasters and CHE. Each of the programs identified has different goals and objectives, duration, expenses, targeted trainees and modules. Each of the programs identified has different goals and objectives, duration, expenses, targeted trainees and modules. Seven programs (33%) are free of charge and four programs (19%) focus on the mental aspects of disasters. The mean duration for each training program is 5 to 7 days. Fourteen of the trainings are conducted in multiple locations (66%), two in Cuba (9%) and two in Australia (9%). The cost-reported in US dollars- ranges from $100 to $2,400 with a mean cost of $480 and a median cost of $135. Most of the programs are open to the public, but some are only available by invitation only, such as the International Mobilization Preparation for Action (IMPACT) and the United Nations Humanitarian Civil-Military Coordination (UN-CMCoord) Field Course. Conclusions: A variety of training programs are available for responders to disasters and complex humanitarian emergencies. These programs vary in their objectives, audiences, modules, geographical locations, eligibility and financial cost. This paper presents an overview of available programs and serves as a resource for potential responders interested in capacity-building training prior to deployment.

Keywords: complex humanitarian emergencies, disaster, pre-deployment, preparedness, training programs

INTRODUCTION

The competence of responders to international disasters is one of the cornerstones for successful program interventions. Hence, building capacity for responders before deployment is an investment to their organizations.[1, 2]International relief efforts depend heavily on volunteers when responding to international disasters, and volunteers look for structured training programs as an opportunity to build their capacity and to be better prepared.[3] The total percentage of volunteer responders working with non-governmental organizations (NGO) in response to international disasters and complex humanitarian emergencies is not well documented in the literature. Adequately trained responders not only provide better service, but also present a smaller risk for organizations and a higher level of operational efficiency.

When responding to international disasters, most health care professionals face austere environments with limited resources. Some volunteers are organized in advance and have been trained and directed to respond through government programs (e.g., Disaster Medical Assistance Teams [DMAT], Medical Reserve Corps [MRC]) and private sector efforts (e.g., American Red Cross, Orthopedic Trauma Association Mass Casualty Teams [OTAMCT]).[4, 5, 6] There are also "spontaneous volunteers" who show up ready to help but lack organization, identification, credentials, and, ultimately, utility. Rather than assisting in the emergency efforts, the presence of many uncoordinated volunteers can actually impede effective emergency responses and create a liability to organizations and to themselves.[2] The most vulnerable responders are novice spontaneous volunteers who lack the experience going on their own instead of through an organization. They may find themselves in situations that require heightened security awareness, cultural sensitivity, and behavioral mental health skills. The better prepared a volunteer is to fill his or her role, the smaller the chance of unintended harm. Volunteers need to know not only what they should do but also what they should not do. As part of this strategy, organizations should make available volunteer position descriptions, a code of conduct, and appropriate training courses and exercises.[7]

In addition, some volunteers need specialized training in caring for pediatric patients or patients who are suffering from mental health issues. Children are often the worse victims of disasters, with the under-5 mortality rate approaching 13% in a typical 5-year war.[8, 9] They require specialized medical care as well as intense psychological support.[10]

The exact number of responders to international disaster and Complex Humanitarian Emergencies (CHEs) is not well documented in the literature, nor is the percentage that have received formal structured training before actual response. Many organizations do not formally train their own personnel before deployment, let alone volunteers.[11] This is perhaps the case because identification and characterization of various structured training programs and opportunities available to responders to international disasters is lacking. The objective of this manuscript was to identify and compile a list of the various structured training programs available for responders to international disasters and complex humanitarian emergencies, highlighting their diverse scopes and characteristics.

METHODS

An environmental scan was conducted through a peer-reviewed literature search of PubMed, Scopus, EMBASE, Web of Science, Cochrane databases, and an open Internet search for training program websites. The landscape literature search was conducted by combining the search terms "international," "disaster," "complex humanitarian emergencies," "training," and "humanitarian response." All searches were conducted from January2,

2013 to September 12, 2013. Initially, 681 citations were retrieved from the above named search engines. Screening by titles narrowed the focus to 165 articles and a further screening by abstract led to 40 articles, of which a full text review revealed 14 articles that contained information regarding training programs for responders to international disasters and CHE.[8, 11, 12, 13, 14, 15, 16, 17, 18, 19, 20, 21, 22]

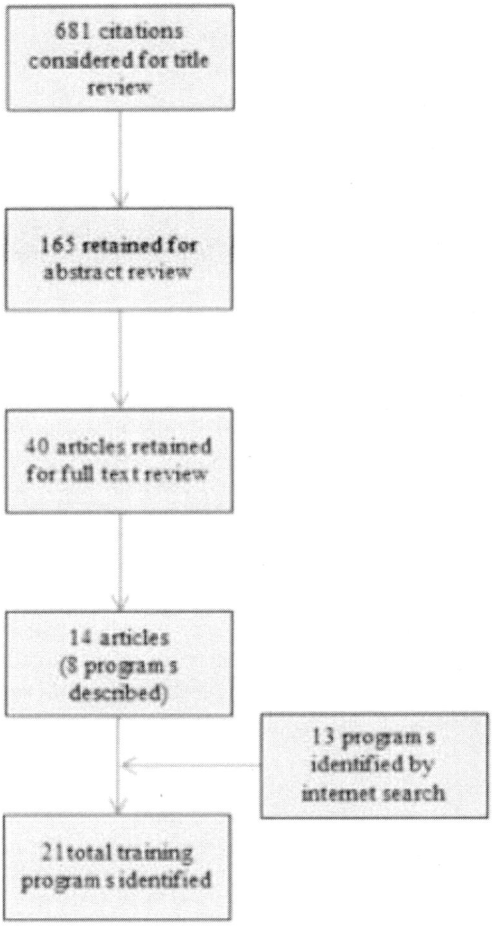

Figire 1 Program Identification Method

RESULTS

A total of 14 peer-reviewed articles mentioned or described eight training programs, while open Internet search revealed 13 additional programs. In total, twenty-one training programs were identified as currently available for responders to international disasters and CHE.

Each of the programs identified has different goals and objectives, duration, expenses, targeted trainees and modules. Seven programs (33%) are free of charge and four programs (19%) focus on the mental aspects of disasters. The mean duration for each training program is 5 to 7 days. Fourteen of the trainings are conducted in multiple locations (66%), two in Cuba (9%) and two in Australia (9%). The cost-reported in US dollars- ranges from $100 to $2,400 with a mean cost of $480 and a median cost of $135. Most of the programs are open to the public, but some are only available by invitation, such as the International Mobilization Preparation for Action (IMPACT) and the United Nations Humanitarian Civil-Military Coordination (UN-CMCoord) Field Course. The target audience for IMPACT should satisfy three conditions: 1) have met the established criteria (technical competency in an international emergency response context in one of the "core functions", "field experience", and available for four-week voluntary deployment), 2) successfully completed screening interviews, and 3) completed World of Red Cross (WORC) training program.[23] UN-CMCoord Field course participants should satisfy the following five conditions: 1) completed the UN-CMCoord course, 2) have a minimum of five year experience with civil-military coordination in the humanitarian assistance, 3) fluency in oral and written English; 4) fluency in other UN language and 5) currently performing a task that require interaction with the Military.[24]

Table 1 displays the twenty-one structured training programs (in alphabetical order), along with the organizer, location(s), cost, duration, and year established.

Table 1 abbreviations:

ADPC= Asian Disaster Preparedness Center; CDAC= Capacity Development across Cultures; CDHRTP= Canadian Disaster and Humanitarian Response Training Program; CHART= Combined Humanitarian Assistance Response Training; CHR= Contingency Henry Reeve Program; CIHC =Center for International Humanitarian Cooperation DMTC= Disaster Management Training course; DMHP= Disaster Mental Health Program by the American Red Cross. ELAM Escuela Latino Americana de Ciencias Médicas (in Spanish; in English Latin American Medical School); FEMA= Federal Emergency Management Agency; HELP= Humanitarian Emergencies for Large Populations; IHAT= International Humanitarian Action Training; IHPT= International Humanitarian; Protection Training; IDM= Integrated Disaster Management Program; IMPACT= International Mobilization and Preparation for ACTion; ICISF= International Critical Incident Stress Foundation; ICRC= International Committee of the Red Cross; IDHA= International Diploma in Humanitarian Assistance; IFRC= International Federation of Red Cross and Red Crescent Societies; ICTC=In country training course; IHE= International Health Exchange programs; IRC= International Rescue Committee; MIHA=Masters in International Humanitarian Action; MHCE=Mental Health in Complex Emergencies; NI=No information; OCHA= United Nations Office for the Coordination of humanitarian Affairs; PHCE= Public Health Complex Emergencies ROC= Recovery Orientation Course, SIU= Symbiosis International University TAP= Training assistance program; UN-CMCoord= Humanitarian Civil-Military Coordination WE Inc.= World Education, Inc. WORC= World of Red Cross; Yr. Est.= year established.

Table 1: Training Programs

Name	Organizer	Type of Participants	Location	Cost (USD)	Duration	Year Established
ADPC	NI	Government officials responsible for disaster management plan and policy; personnel involved in defense forces and emergency services	Thailand	$2,275-3,175	2 weeks	1986
CDAC	Australia Red Cross	Red Cross staff, volunteers; anyone interested in building international capacity	Australia	$650-920	2 days	NI
CDHRTP	University of Toronto Koffler Scientific Reserve	Anyone interested in humanitarian work	Canada	$2,080	2 weeks	NI
CHART	ICRC	Civilian and military disaster planners	Multiple	NI	5 days	1993
CHR	Cuba	Not reported	Cuba	Free	Rolling	2005
DHMP	American Red Cross, FEMA	Professionals from diverse mental health backgrounds	Multiple	$500	2 days	1990
DMTC	Rainbow Center for International Child Health	Health care professionals and physicians	Multiple	Free	5 days	1996
ELAM	Cuba	Anyone interested in disaster preparedness	Cuba	Free	6 years	1999

HELP	ICRC	Medical and public health professionals, environmental health engineers, and epidemiologists	Multiple	$1,800	2-3 weeks	1986
IDM	Indian Government	Undergraduate and post-graduate students in Symbiosis International University (SIU), India	SIU India	Free	18 months	2005
IHAT/IHPT	Australia Red Cross	Humanitarian aid workers, program officers/coordinators, caseworkers, policy officers or others working with people affected by disaster	Australia	$650-850	3 days	NI
IHE	RedR	Health workers and any professional groups who wish to work in emergency relief	Multiple	$600-2,500	5-7 days	1980
IMPACT	IFRC	By invitation only	Multiple	Free	2 weeks	NI
MIHA, IDHA, ICTC, DMTC, MHCE	CHIC	Members of international relief organizations and humanitarian workers	Multiple	$1,000-5,000	1,2,4 weeks	1992
PHCE	IRC & WE Inc.	NGO staff who are responsible for making decisions that affect the health of refugees, internally displaced persons, and those affected by CHE: District Medical Officers and other Ministry of Health staff working in regions affected	Multiple	$2,400	2 weeks	NI

ROC	Medair	Mandated for prospective Medair employees but open to the public	Europe & Asia	$750	7 days	NI
TAP	ICRC	Civilian and military disaster planners	Multiple	NI	2-4 days	1980
UN-CMCoord Course and Field Course	OCHA	Governmental and non-governmental organizations, aid agencies, civil protection units, military and civil defense organizations, UN agencies and other intergovernmental bodies, the Red Cross, and Red Crescent Movement	Multiple	Free	2-7 days	1998
Various training programs	Salvation Army	Spiritual care officers, disaster workers trained in critical incident stress debriefing, chaplains, and mental health professionals	Multiple	$135-$350	4-8 hours to 3 days	2004
Various training programs	ICISF	People working in the following fields: crisis intervention, disaster response, education, emergency services, employee assistance, healthcare, homeland security, human resources, mental health, military, spiritual care, transportation, and traumatic stress	Multiple	$100-$700	2-3 days per course	1989
WORC	IFRC	Red Cross and Red Crescent staff, volunteers, government authorities, donors, media, schools, and interested public	Multiple	Free	1 week	NI

Below are descriptions of the objectives, target audience, course size, and training content of the twenty structured training programs listed in the table above. Information is listed alphabetically and depends on its availability from the various sources queried.

Asian Disaster Preparedness Center (ADPC) [21]: The objective is to develop participants' skills with the aim that they should gain a solid grasp of disaster management processes and be able to address key implementation issues in disaster. Typical participants include government officials responsible for disaster management plan and policy; and personnel involved in defense forces and emergency services. There is a maximum of 30 participants per course. The main topics include disaster preparedness planning and disaster risk reduction.[25]

Capacity Development Across Cultures (CDAC): The objectives include developing skills for building relationships, understanding capacity, and working collaboratively with partners and colleagues to achieve capacity development outcomes. The participants are Red Cross staff, volunteers, and anyone interested in building capacity internationally. There is no course size restriction.[26] The main topics are not delineated in details.

Canadian Disaster and Humanitarian Response Training Program (CDHRTP): The objectives include developing capacity for essentials during a humanitarian response, managing acute issues in complex disasters, and learning research skills. This course also places participants in a three-day simulation complex humanitarian emergency to train their capacity building and problem solving skills. The participants are anyone interested in humanitarian work. There is no course size restriction listed. Topics include gender based violence, leadership, human rights, monitoring and evaluation, and, refugee protection.[27]

Combined Humanitarian Assistance Response Training (CHART) [11, 28]: The objective is to develop civilian and military response to humanitarian crises in a more efficient manner. It is designed to provide responders with the tools and knowledge to work effectively in rapidly evolving situations. Participants are civilian and military disaster planners, and the maximum number of participants admitted per course is sixty. The main subjects include the complex environment, security, logistics, nutrition, public health, international standards, responder readiness, planning, peacekeeping issues, and international humanitarian law.[29]

Contingency Henry Reeve Program (CHR): The objective is to develop responders who can aid in saving lives, especially in remote areas. The training program focuses on delivering primary care in disasters and epidemics. The type of participants is not documented. There are no restrictions to number of participants. The main topics includes disaster medicine courses for all types of emergencies.[30]

Disaster Mental Health Program (DMHP): The objective is to develop resilience among responders by ameliorating acute post disaster stress responses among Red Cross workers and the disaster victims they serve. Participants are comprised of professionals from diverse mental health backgrounds. The number of participants and course titles are not delineated.[31]

Disaster Management Training Course (DMTC): The specific objectives are to develop participant understanding as to why children are among the most vulnerable populations in disasters and to identify the most important problems and priorities. The program targets health care professionals and physicians as participants. There is no restriction to the number of participants. Lecture topics included epidemiological assessment, triage during disasters, and malnutrition.

Escuela Latino Americana de Ciencias Médicas (ELAM) [14]: The objective is for participants to develop skills necessary for disaster response. The program has a strong clinical component. Participants worldwide are welcome if they have an interest in disaster preparedness. There are no restrictions to the number of participants. The main topics include disaster medicine courses for all types of emergencies.[30]

Humanitarian Emergencies for Large Populations (HELP) [11, 12, 16, 32]: This course is a multicultural and multidisciplinary learning experience created to enhance professionalism within humanitarian assistance programs in the setting of disasters and CHE. Participants are medical and public health professionals, environmental health engineers, and epidemiologists. Twenty-five to thirty participants are admitted per course. The main topics include public health activities, communicable diseases, epidemiology, international humanitarian law (IHL), security, humanitarian principles, and ethics.[33]

Integrated Disaster Management (IDM): The objectives are to ensure and develop awareness of the nature, type, and management of disasters, design disaster management plans as well as hands-on training in handling medical and non-medical emergencies. The participants are undergraduate and post-graduate students in Symbiosis International University (SIU), India. The number of participants and main topics were not outlined.[15]

International Humanitarian Action Training (IHAT)/ International Humanitarian Protection Training (IHPT). IHAT: The objective is to develop and equip individuals and organizations with the knowledge needed to respond effectively and implement recovery after disasters. It is open to current and aspiring aid workers, volunteers, and those interested in international emergency response. There are no restrictions to the number of participants per course.[26]The main topics were not listed. **IHPT:** The objective is to develop understanding and competencies for protection into humanitarian action (Sphere 2011) in four key areas: child protection, gender-based violence (GBV), sexual exploitation and abuse (SEA), and other human rights abuses. Participants are humanitarian aid workers, program officers/coordinators, caseworkers, policy officers or others working with people affected by disaster. There are no restrictions to the number of participants per course. The IHAT course is a pre-requisite to this course.[34] The main topics include gender-based violence (GBV) and child protection among others.

International Health Exchange programs (IHE): The objective is for aid workers around the world to develop the latest skills to ensure the quality and effectiveness of humanitarian programs. The participants are health workers and any professional groups who wish to work in emergency relief. There are no restrictions to number of participants per course. The main topics include humanitarian essentials, security, and technical training.[35]

International Mobilization and Preparation for ACTion (IMPACT) [19]: The objective is to provide additional training to participants by taking an in-depth look at the roles of the ICRC, the Federation, and National Societies in times of disaster and conflict. Another objective is to provide contextual and capacity building skills for relief and development activities. Participation is by invitation only and limited to 20 applicants. Interested parties who meet the established criteria, successfully complete screening interviews, reference checks, and WORC? may be invited to participate in the course. The course covers practical subjects such as dealing with stress, security, and cross-cultural awareness.[23]

Masters in International Humanitarian Action (MIHA & OTHER PROGRAMS): Center for International Humanitarian Cooperation (CHIC) offers several humanitarian training programs. The objective is for humanitarian workers and members of international relief agencies to perform more effectively in conflict and post-conflict areas. The CHIC designs training courses tailored to organizations or geographical location. Participants are members of international relief organizations and humanitarian workers. There are no restrictions to the number of participants per course. Main topics include mental health issues, disaster management, and negotiation techniques.[36]

Public Health Complex Emergencies (PHCE) [12]: The objectives are to develop and sharpen practical problem-based skills in an interactive group setting and to help participants become well-informed decision-makers and managers of public health policy in complex emergencies. Participants are non-governmental organization (NGO) staff who are responsible for making decisions that affect the health of refugees, internally displaced persons, and those affected by CHE. Other participants include District Medical Officers and other Ministry of Health staff working in regions affected by complex emergencies. There are no restrictions to the number of participants per course. The main topics include context of emergencies, reproductive health, epidemiology psychosocial health, communicable disease weapons, violence and trauma, and environmental health protection and security and nutrition coordination.[37]

Recovery Orientation Course (ROC): The ROC uses an intensive experiential teaching approach to develop a hands-on experience for working in the humanitarian sector. It is mandated for prospective Medair employees but open to the public. There are no restrictions to the number of participants. The main topics include an overview of Medair and understanding humanitarian aid, others and self. The cost of the course is dependent on the participant's experience with relief work.[38]

Training Assistance Program (TAP) [19]: This training program is similar to the CHART program. The difference is that the host organization helps with the designing of the curriculum and develops a draft agenda based on the training objectives and target audience.[32] The main topics are similar to CHART, and the class size is not outlined.

United Nations Humanitarian Civil-Military Coordination (UN-CMCoord) Course and Field Course [32]: The objective of these courses is to equip humanitarian and military personnel with the skills and knowledge necessary to communicate and effectively interact with each other. Participants include governmental and non-governmental organizations, aid agencies, civil protection units, military and civil defense organizations, UN agencies and other intergovernmental bodies, the Red Cross, and Red Crescent Movement. The maximum numbers of participants for the course and field course are twenty and twenty-eight, respectively. The main topics include the roles of military and humanitarian actors in emergencies and complex emergencies. Participation in the field course is by invitation only. The prerequisites are the UN-CMCoord course and a minimum of five years of experience in civil-military coordination.[24]

Various programs by The Salvation Army: The goal of The Salvation Army's disaster training program is for individuals to develop the skills needed to serve during times of crises particularly in the field of mental health. Participants include spiritual care officers, disaster workers trained in critical incident stress debriefing, chaplains, and mental health professionals. There are no restrictions to the number of participants per course. The main topics include foundations of emotional and spiritual care, disaster food services, disaster social services, and incident command systems.[39]

Various programs organized by International Critical Incident Stress Foundation (ICISF): These programs currently offer over 40 different courses selections at conferences and trainings held around the United States. The objective is to develop the skills for handling critical incident stress and mental health issues. Participants include people working in the following fields: crisis intervention, disaster response, education, emergency services, employee assistance, healthcare, homeland security, human resources, mental health, military, spiritual care, transportation, and traumatic stress.The main topics are group crisis intervention, compassion fatigue, emotional, spiritual and psychological first aid.[40]

World of Red Cross (WORC): This online general orientation program introduces the main elements of the Red Cross Red Crescent Movement. The objective is to educate participants on the history and principles of the Red Cross Red Crescent Movement, in order to improve understanding and commitment to the mandate and culture. The course is open to all Red Cross Red Crescent staff, volunteers, government authorities, donors, the media, schools, and the interested public. There are no restrictions to the number of participants per course. The main topics include the origin and history of the Red Cross. This course is one of the three prerequisite for the IMPACT program.[23]

DISCUSSION

A successful and efficient response to international disasters and complex humanitarian emergencies depends on the capacity, skills, and prior training those responders have already acquired. As the number of complex humanitarian emergencies and disasters increase, one of the challenges facing responding organizations is to maintain well-trained volunteers and employees. There is an increasing demand for skilled health providers, public health professionals, and field program administrators; this requires a cadre of trainees with both general and specific capacities.[11]

The SPHERE standards were created in 1997 to define a set of universal minimum standards in core areas of humanitarian assistance.[41] This project was a collaborative effort by many agencies to produce standards that relate to disaster assistance in: 1) water supply and sanitation; 2) nutrition and food aid; 3) shelter and site planning; and 4) health services.[42] Despite the definition of the SPHERE guidelines, many organizations do not train their personnel in the applications of these guidelines.[11]

Due to the various objectives of the programs along with the various expectations and interests of the trainees, there is no single training program that is universally accepted as the ideal. The main language used for these trainings is English, but the HELP courses are taught in multiple languages. Regionalized trainings conducted in other languages such as French, Arabic, or Spanish may reduce the burden to find interpreters or obtain visas. This would reduce costs and improve logistics for participants.

The list provided in this paper offers a general description of the various training programs offered worldwide. This will help potential responders – volunteers or non-volunteers- to identify training opportunities that will build their capacities in the specific areas they are responsible for. This will allow them to consider the financial, linguistic, and logistical characteristics. With evolving technology, the responders of the future may not be limited to attending in-person training programs, but have access to virtual environment experiences. However, this modality of training is still infantile for training programs geared towards international disasters and CHE and requires a large amount of financial and technical resources. For the foreseeable future, in-person training programs remain indispensable, and they continue to grow in number, scope, breadth, location and targeted audience

The vast majority of these programs target volunteers and are known worldwide for being offered by large, reputable, and established international organizations; however many more specialized trainings exist as well. NGOs typically do staff training targeted for specific roles in the field, however these training courses are seldom published in peer-reviewed journals and may not even appear on the websites of the NGOs who offer them. A centralized database of all training programs would be beneficial.

Limitations

There is a paucity of peer-reviewed literature with substantial information on structured training programs for responders to international disasters and CHE. Twelve articles on specific training programs were published in peer-reviewed journals. However, it is important to note that the literature search was not conducted in a systematic fashion due to resource constraints. There is no single web-based resource that is comprehensive, robust, and well known enough that potential responders can consider. In addition to the programs reported and analyzed in this report, there are many other smaller programs with different foci.

Additionally, there is no published literature on the recommended consensus-based recommendations for competencies or curricula. Future work could include surveying participants on their experiences in each program.

CONCLUSIONS

Training programs available for responders to international disasters and CHE vary in their objectives, target audiences, modules, geographical locations, and financial cost. Currently, there is no resource that centralizes the descriptions of humanitarian response training programs. This paper presents an overview of available programs and serves as a resource for potential responders and organizations interested in capacity-building training prior to an international disaster response or complex humanitarian emergency.

BIOGRAPHIES

Director of Global Health, Assistant Residency Program Director

Associate Director, Office of Critical Event Preparedness and Response (CEPAR) *Assistant Professor, School of Medicine- Department of Emergency Medicine Bloomberg School of Public Health- Department of International Health

FUNDING STATEMENT

This study had no external funding. The authors have declared that no competing interests exist.

CONTRIBUTOR INFORMATION

Gabrielle A. Jacquet, Department of Emergency Medicine, Boston University School of Medicine, Boston, Massachusetts, USA; Center for Global Health and Development, Boston University, Boston, Massachusetts, USA.

Chioma C. Obi, Department of International Health, Johns Hopkins Bloomberg School of Public Health, Baltimore, Maryland, USA.

Mary P. Chang, Department of Emergency Medicine, Johns Hopkins University School of Medicine, Baltimore, Maryland, USA.

Jamil D. Bayram, Johns Hopkins University, Baltimore, Maryland, USA; Johns Hopkins Office of Critical Event Preparedness and Response, Baltimore, Maryland, USA; Center for Refugee and Disaster Response, Bloomberg School of Public Health, Johns Hopkins University, Baltimore, Maryland, USA.

REFERENCES

1. Cranmer HH, Biddinger PD. Typhoon Haiyan and the Professionalization of Disaster Response. N Engl J Med. 2014 Feb 19. PubMed PMID:24552286.
2. Van Hoving DJ, Wallis LA, Docrat F, De Vries S. Haiti disaster tourism--a medical shame. Prehosp Disaster Med. 2010 May-Jun;25(3):201-2. PubMed PMID:20586008.
3. Sherraden MS, Lough B, McBride AM. Effects of International Volunteering and Service: Individual and Institutional Predictors. Voluntas 2008;19:395-421.
4. Born CT, DeLong WG Jr. Organizing the orthopaedic trauma association mass casualty response team. Clin Orthop Relat Res. 2004 May;(422):114-6. PubMed PMID:15187842.
5. Forgione T, Owens PJ, Lopes JP, Briggs SM. New horizons for OR nurses--lessons learned from the World Trade Center attack. AORN J. 2003 Aug;78(2):240-5. PubMed PMID:12940424.
6. MRC Units. Accessed 27 October, 2013.

7. Promising practices toolkit for volunteer code of conduct. Accessed 27 October, 2013.

8. Olness K, Sinha M, Herran M, Cheren M, Pairojkul S. Training of health care professionals on the special needs of children in the management of disasters: experience in Asia, Africa, and Latin America. Ambul Pediatr. 2005 Jul-Aug;5(4):244-8. PubMed PMID:16026191.

9. Health in emergencies. Accessed 27 October 2013.

10. Special Issues of Children and Families in Humanitarian Emergencies. Accessed 27 October 2013.

11. Moresky RT, Eliades MJ, Bhimani MA, Bunney EB, VanRooyen MJ. Preparing international relief workers for health care in the field: an evaluation of organizational practices. Prehosp Disaster Med. 2001 Oct-Dec;16(4):257-62. PubMed PMID:12090207.

12. Bayram J, Rosborough S, Bartels S, Lis J, VanRooyen MJ, Kapur GB, Anderson PD. Core curricular elements for fellowship training in international emergency medicine. Acad Emerg Med. 2010 Jul;17(7):748-57. PubMed PMID:20653590.

13. Benedek DM, Ritchie EC. "Just-in-time" mental health training and surveillance for the Project HOPE mission. Mil Med. 2006 Oct;171(10 Suppl 1):63-5. PubMed PMID:17447627.

14. Mas Bermejo P. Preparation and response in case of natural disasters: Cuban programs and experience. J Public Health Policy. 2006;27(1):13-21. PubMed PMID:16681185.

15. Deshpande V. Disaster management as part of curriculum for undergraduate and postgraduate courses: The Symbiosis model. Indian J Occup Environ Med. 2011 Sep;15(3):97-9. PubMed PMID:22412285.

16. Dhillon PS. Health emergencies in large populations: a disaster medicine learning experience. Am J Disaster Med. 2011 May-Jun;6(3):137-41. PubMed PMID:21870662.

17. Everly GS, Hamilton SE, Tyiska CG, Ellers K. Mental health response to disaster: Consensus recommendations: Early Psychological Intervention Subcommittee (EPI), National Volunteer Organizations Active in Disaster (NVOAD). Aggression and violent behavior 2008;13:407-12.

18. Hamilton SE. Volunteers in disaster response: The American Red Cross. Journal of aggression, maltreatment & trauma 2005; 10: 621-32.

19. Kutcher S, Chehil S, Roberts T. An integrated program to train local health care providers to meet post-disaster mental health needs. Rev Panam Salud Publica. 2005 Oct-Nov;18(4-5):338-45. PubMed PMID:16354431.

20. O'Dempsey T. Fair training a new direction in humanitarian assistance. Progress in Development Studies 2009; 9:81-6.

21. Rego A, Mehta S. Opportunities and challenges in risk resilient recovery. World Hosp Health Serv. 2005;41(4):33-5. PubMed PMID:16512061.

22. Stevens I. Public oriented risk communication in the new risk society. 2009.

23. International Mobilization and Preparation for ACTION (IMPACT). (Accessed October 27, 2013, 2013, at http://www.redcross.org/images/MEDIA_CustomProductCatalog/m4540098_ISD_IMPACT.pdf.)

24. United Nations Humanitarian Civil-Military Coordination(UN). Accessed 27 October 2013.

25. Training/Relief Web. 2013. Accessed 27 October 2013.

26. Training Courses/Australian Red Cross: The Power of Humanity. Accessed 27 October 2013.

27. CANADIAN Disaster and Humanitarian Response Training Program. Accessed 19 March 2014.

28. Guide to Nongovernmental Organizations for the Military. A primer for the military about private, voluntary, and nongovernmental organizations operating in humanitarian emergencies globally. 2009. Accessed 19 March 2014.

29. Combined Humanitarian Assistance Response Training (CHART-Courses) Accessed 27 October 2013.

30. Newhouse E. Contending with Natural Disasters. 2011.

31. North CS, BCD A, Dingman RL, Hong BA. The American Red Cross disaster mental health services: Development of a cooperative, single function, multidisciplinary service model. Journal of behavioral health services & research 2000; 27: 314-20.

32. Center for Excellence in Disaster Management and Humanitarian Assistance. (Accessed 27 October, 2013, at http://en.wikipedia.org/wiki/Center_for_Excellence_in_Disaster_Management_and_Humanitarian_Assistance.)

33. Humanitarian assistance training: Health Emergencies in Large Populations. Accessed 27 October 2013.

34. International Humanitarian Protection Training/Australian. Accessed 27 October 2013.

35. International Health Exchange (IHE). Accessed 27 October 2013.

36. The Center for International Humanitarian Cooperation (CIHC). Accessed 27 October 2013.

37. Short Courses on Public Health in Complex Emergencies. Accessed 27 October 2013.

38. Curriculum-Medair. Accessed 27 October 2013.

39. The Salvation Army Emergency Disaster Services-Training. Accessed 27 October 2013.

40. Education and training-International Critical Incident. Accessed 27 October 2013.

41. Psychosocial support. Accessed 27 October 2013.

42. Beyond the sphere standards/ Migration & displacement/ Agenda. 2013. Accessed 27 October 2013.

9

INFORMATION DISSEMINATION ANALYSIS OF DIFFERENT MEDIA TOWARDS THE APPLICATION FOR DISASTER PRE-WARNING

Nan Zhang, Hong Huang*, Boni Su, Jinlong Zhao, Bo Zhang

Institute of Public Safety Research, Department of Engineering Physics, Tsinghua University, Beijing, China

ABSTRACT

Knowing the information dissemination mechanisms of different media and having an efficient information dissemination plan for disaster pre-warning plays a very important role in reducing losses and ensuring the safety of human beings. In this paper we established models of information dissemination for six typical information media, including short message service (SMS), microblogs, news portals, cell phones, television, and oral communication. Then, the information dissemination capability of each medium concerning individuals of different ages, genders, and residential areas was simulated, and the dissemination characteristics were studied. Finally, radar graphs were used to illustrate comprehensive assessments of the six media; these graphs show directly the information dissemination characteristics of all media. The models and the results are essential for improving the efficiency of information dissemination for the purpose of disaster pre-warning and for formulating emergency plans which help to reduce the possibility of injuries, deaths and other losses in a disaster.

INTRODUCTION

Natural and man-made disasters seriously threaten human life and property. A more reliable and efficient pre-warning information dissemination system could improve public emergency responses, and enable people to evacuate and take protective measures before and during a disaster [1]. In the Indian Coast, for example, more than one hundred people could be saved because a scientist, using his cell phone, managed to warn about an imminent serious tsunami caused by an 8.7 magnitude earthquake [2]. Moreover, victims easily survived in an effective and efficient way if they have more detailed information [3]. Therefore, the research on information dissemination is of great theoretical and practical value. This paper focuses on information dissemination relating to disaster pre-warning; it does not concern itself with research subjects such as economic-geographic development [4].

Information media can be divided into social and traditional media. Social media including short messages, microblogs, and news portals, because of their high impact and coverage ratio made possible by developments in information technology [5]–[6], are becoming increasingly popular and therefore critical tools of information dissemination [7]. For instance, they can enhance the decision-making process since more data is provided than it is the case with traditional media [8]. However, some traditional media, including cell phones, television, and oral communication, also play important roles in information dissemination. In some serious disaster cases, when all electronic networks are paralyzed, traditional media such as oral communication, albeit slower, can still be employed [9].

The different characteristics of each information dissemination medium have been studied in different fields. Sattler found that an effective message could be issued by a credible source and transmitted in a quick and stable way through warning message transmission by cell phone and e-mail [10]. Wei analyzed the optimal combination of television broadcasting sequences which ensured the best information dissemination to television viewers [11]. Whittaker researched information management of emails and found habits of email users in information management [12].

Furthermore, there are some studies that looked at information dissemination media in disasters and emergencies. Odeny found that short message services could improve the attendance at post-operative clinic visits after adult male circumcision for HIV prevention [13]. Zhang established that different information media, including cell phones, television and emails, have different information dissemination characteristics in disaster's pre-warning [14]. Shim used wireless TV to improve disaster management and to provide communications for respondents during a natural or man-made disaster [15]. Katada created a simulation model and built a general-purpose system for the efficient study of the dissemination of information concerning disasters and scenarios of information transmission [16]. Zhang used sound trucks to transmit information in an optimal path in the case of network paralysis caused by a serious disaster [17].

Analysis of recent studies reveals that most works focus on a single medium, but neglect detailed comparisons of different media. However, in actual situations, a single information medium cannot ensure the dissemination of large amounts of information. Therefore, each medium should be analyzed and compared to other media to improve overall efficiency of information dissemination.

In this study, information dissemination models of six information media, including short message service (SMS), microblogs, news portals, cell phones, television, and oral communication were developed and the information dissemination characteristics were studied and compared. The capabilities and mechanisms of these information dissemination media were also studied concerning people of different ages, genders and residential areas. The developed models were applied to the city of Beijing. Based on the simulation and effectiveness analysis of all information media, optimized plans and suggestions were put forward to improve the effectiveness of information dissemination during emergencies. The results of this research are useful in the development of a comprehensive information dissemination system to transmit emergency information in an effective way.

METHOD

In this study we use the following evaluation indices to compare the different information dissemination characteristics: total coverage of information reception, the time it takes for half of the population to believe the information, frequency of media usage and time, the degree of trust, total cost, and delay time. Among these indices, the degree of trust and frequency of media usage and time can be directly obtained through questionnaires and the total cost can be obtained from the internet: Taobao (the most famous electronic mall in China; URL: www.taobao.com). Another three indices need to be calculated by the computational simulation based on information dissemination models. The models are established considering special information dissemination characteristics such as dissemination mechanisms and individual preference for different media. Some required parameters in the models such as average forwarding times were also collected by questionnaires which were distributed on site. The simulation allows the calculation of the total coverage of information reception, the time it takes for half of the population to believe the information and the delay time. All the parameters mentioned above are obtained from questionnaires and the internet. Different information dissemination models are described below:

1 Basic parameters in information dissemination

1.1 Brief introduction of basic parameters.

In the information dissemination process effective information dissemination probability and delay time are two important factors. Effective information dissemination probability expresses the probability of a recipient receiving and believing the information after a message is distributed from an information source. Delay time is the time difference between information reception by media and by recipients.

Effective information dissemination probability and delay time are related to service usage and the degree of trust which reflects the probability that people believe the media. For service usage, media usage frequency, media coverage ratio, and forwarding number are thought to be three important components. To obtain the above data, a questionnaire is considered to be a useful tool.

1.2 Questionnaires.

In this study 370 questionnaires were filled out (350 of them were available) in May and June, 2013. In the period of disaster pre-warning, individual differences are very obvious in information acquisition and dissemination. The questionnaires include six multiple-choice questions and twenty-nine fill-in questions. We collected the following data: age, gender, educational background, vocation, media usage number (N_{use}) and times per day (T_{use}), information forwarding number (n_{fw}) and probability (p_{fw}), and the degree of trust of each of the six information media. All respondents were between the ages of 10 and 80. About half of questionnaires derived from urban areas while the rest were filled out in rural areas.

The questionnaires allowed a detailed analysis of the degree of trust and service usage for short messages, microblogs, news portals, cell phones, television and oral communication. The data are presented in Table.1

Table 1. Comparison of the degree of trust and service condition of six media.

	The degree of trust (%)	Media coverage (%)	Usage frequency (times/day) or (minutes/day)	Average forwarding number (persons)
SMS	41.3	97.2	>10 times	11.8
Microblog	48.3	66.5	7.5 times	132
News portal	57.7	85.0	84.5 min	0
Cell phone	43.3	99.0	>10 times	9.7
Television	79.0	91.7	99.9 min	0
Oral	38.91	100.0		3.9

The degree of trust in an information medium reflects its importance, and is crucial in information dissemination [18]. The questionnaires suggest that television, news portals, and microblogs have the three highest degrees of trust (79.0%, 57.7%, and 48.3% respectively); they are followed by cell phones (43.3%), short messages (41.3%) and oral communication (38.91%). Television and news portals have the highest degrees of trust among the six media because these two media are managed by the government.

Media coverage ratio determines whether the media could be used in information dissemination for pre-warning of a disaster. Oral communication, cell phones, and short messages as the top three (100%, 99%, and 97% respectively) had the top three coverage ratios; reflecting our dependence on these media in our daily lives. Microblogs rank at the bottom of the six media types (66%) which is due to personal preference. The analysis of the data on media coverage ratios reveals that the usage coverage is very high although the degree of trust of some media is low.

The frequency of media usage is an important factor, reflects the popularity of the respective medium, and determines the difficulty of information acquisition. Oral communication is the most frequently used medium in our daily lives. Cell phone and short messaging forms of communication come second as they are used more than 10 times per day. Television and news portals as mass media have lower usage numbers but longer watching times. Microblogs are very popular as well (7.5 usage times per day).

Forwarding number indicates the speed of information dissemination from person to person. Strong forwarding capability could lead to rapid information acquisition [19]. Microblogs had the highest average forwarding number (132); followed by short messaging (11.8), cell phone (9.7) and oral communication (3.9). However, television and news portals are one way media transmitting information from a public organization to a wide audience, and cannot be used for forwarding information person to person.

The detailed results of effective information dissemination probability and delay time are introduced and calculated below.

2 Model Establishment

The models of six typical information media including short messages, microblogs, news portals, cell phones, television and oral communication could be divided into three types. The first type was based on person to person without geographical limitation, including short messages and cell phones, the initial stage of which may present an exponential growth in recipients. The second type was based on person to person with geographical limitation such as oral communication where information can be disseminated only within a limited distance. In addition, television and news portals can transmit information from a mass media to person with a logarithmic growth in recipients which were defined as the third type. In order to establish the information dissemination model of the media, we assigned three statuses to the people who are facing the disaster: "ignorance", "receiver", and "believer". "Ignorance" is assigned to people who have not received information about the disaster; "receiver" refers to people who get the information but do not believe it; "believer" designates people who have received the information and believed it.

In this study the information dissemination models of microblogs, oral communication and television were taken as the representative media to analyze. The effective information dissemination probability and delay time of each information medium were obtained through process analysis and data calculation.

2.1 Microblog.

Due to fast speed and convenient operation in information dissemination, microblogs have become increasingly popular in recent years. Fig. 1 shows the information dissemination process of a microblog and the probability of a person being assigned to the status of ignorance, receiver or believer. In Fig. 1 $P_{1(b)}$ expresses the probability of microblog users using a microblog per minute, and n_{blog} is the average usage number of microblog users (16 hours are the effective time per day). $P_{2(b)}$ is the probability of ignorant users receiving information and N_{use} is the number of people using a microblog. $N_{sp(b)}$ is the number of spreaders $N_{sp(b)}=N_{bel(b)}*P_{fw(b)}$, $N_{bel(b)}$ is the number of information believers and $n_{fw(b)}$ is the average number of microblog fans (The parameter n_{blog}, $N_{use(b)}$, $n_{fw(b)}$ and $p_{fw(b)}$ can be directly obtained from questionnaires). $P_{3(b)}$ is the probability of that those people who received information believe the same; it is related to the degree of trust of the microblog and received information numbers in the time interval ($n_{rec(b)}$ can be obtained by computational simulation). The detailed simulation process is listed below:

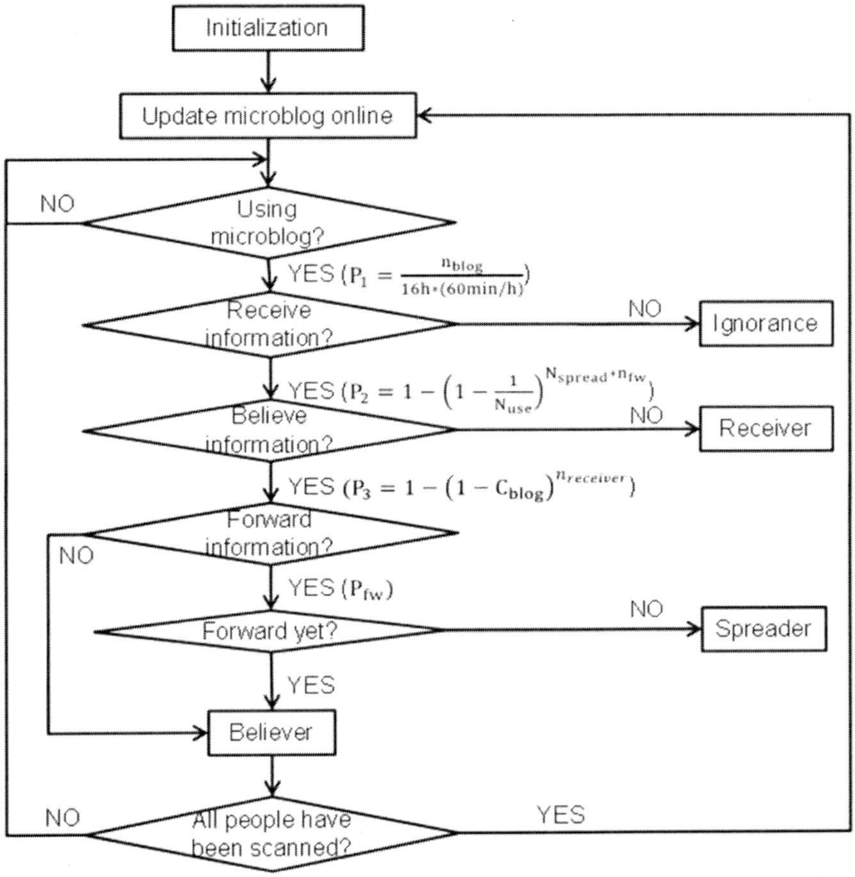

Figure 1. Microblog information dissemination process.

1. Set all the parameters which are obtained from questionnaires to target people and create 5 initiative believers which are regarded as the information sources forwarding the information through microblog.

2. Search for the target people who have qualification to forward microblogs in this step. These target people should follow four conditions:

   a. The person is using microblog at this step

   b. The person is the information believer

   c. The person wants to forward the microblog

   d. The person hasn't forward the microblog yet

1. Update all the microblog online users.
2. The microblog user i checks the blog.

With the increase of received information number and the degree of trust, the probability will also rise. $P_{fw(b)}$ is the average forwarding probability from believers to spreaders.

Based on Fig. 1, the effective information dissemination probability P_{blog} is expressed by Equation 1.

$$P_{blog} = P_{1(b)} \cdot P_{2(b)} \cdot P_{3(b)} = \frac{n_{blog}}{16 \cdot 60\,\text{min}} (1-(1-\frac{1}{N_{use(b)}})^{N_{sp(b)} \cdot n_{fw(b)}}) \cdot (1-(1-C_{blog})^{n_{rec(b)}}) \quad (1)$$

Fig. 2 shows the calculation of delay time of a microblog T_{blog}. Users are hypothesized not to check microblogs at night (midnight to 8 a.m.). Based on the usage number of microblogs per day, people check microblogs n times between 8 a.m. to midnight with the same interval $\frac{16}{n+1}$. In Fig. 2 period 1 is the checking time and period 2 is the rest time without checking microblogs.

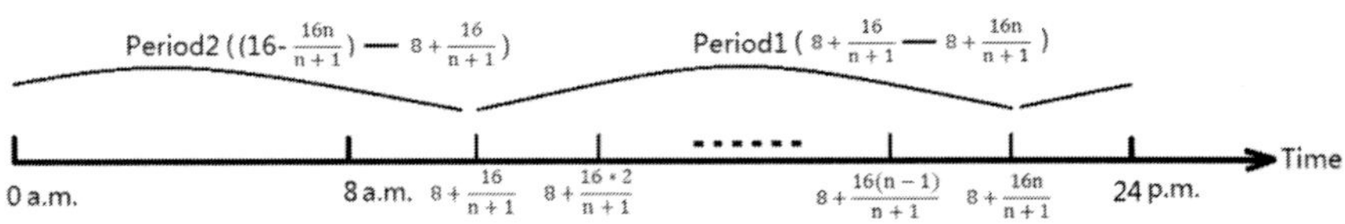

Figure 2. Microblog delay time calculation.

a. Microblog (received information at period 1)

$$T_{1,blog}(t_1, t_2) = P_{1,blog} \int_{t_1}^{t_2} f_{1,blog}(t) \cdot p_{1,blog}(dt) \quad (2)$$

Here $T_{1,blog}$ is the total delay time, $P_{1,blog}$ denotes the proportion of period 1 to 24 hours; $f_{1,blog}$ is the function of delay time; $P_{1,blog}$ represents the time weight of dt.

$$T_{1,blog}(n) = \frac{\frac{16}{n+1}(n-1)}{24} \int_0^{\frac{16}{n+1}} (\frac{16}{n+1} - t) \cdot \frac{dt}{\frac{16}{n+1}} = \frac{2(n-1)}{3(n+1)} \cdot \frac{1}{2} \cdot (\frac{16}{(n+1)}) = \frac{16(n-1)^2}{3(n+1)^2} \quad (3)$$

1.

a. Microblog (received information at period 2)

$$T_{2,blog}(t_3,t_4)=P_{2,blog}\int_{t_3}^{t_4} f_{2,blog}(t)\cdot p_{2,blog}(dt) \tag{4}$$

where $T_{2,blog}$ is the total delay time, $P_{1,blog}$ is the proportion of period 2 to 24 hours; f2,blog shows the function of delay time; $P_{2,blog}(dt)$ expresses the time weight of dt

$$\begin{aligned} T_{2,blog}(n) &= \frac{n+5}{3(n+1)}\int_0^{8+2\cdot\frac{16}{n+1}}\left(8+2\cdot\frac{16}{n+1}-t\right)\cdot\frac{dt}{8+2\cdot\frac{16}{n+1}} \\ &= \frac{4(n+5)^2}{3(n+1)^2} \end{aligned} \tag{5}$$

$$\begin{aligned} T_{blog}(n) &= T_{1,blog}(n)+T_{2,blog}(n) \\ &= \frac{16(n-1)}{3(n+1)^2}+\frac{4(n+5)^2}{3(n+1)^2} \\ &= \frac{4((n+7)^2-28)}{3(n+1)^2} \end{aligned} \tag{6}$$

$$T_{blog}(n)=\begin{cases} \frac{12}{n} & n<1 \\ \frac{4((n+7)^2-28)}{3(n+1)^2} & n\geq 1 \end{cases} \tag{7}$$

If the usage frequency is less than 1 ($n<1$), i.e., the microblog user will not check the microblog every day, the average delay time is easy to calculate. Equation 7 is the comprehensive calculation of average delay time of microblog T_{blog} where n is the usage number of the microblogs per day.

Effective information dissemination probability can be obtained through the same analysis since the information dissemination models of short messaging and cell phones are very similar to that of a microblog. The delay time for short messaging was directly obtained through questionnaires. The delay time of cell phones was acquired by conducting 150 calling experiments covering different situations, including answering the phone, busy line, powering off, and hanging up. The models for cell phones and short messages are given in the Appendix A and B of Appendix S1 respectively (information dissemination characteristics curves are shown in Fig. S1 and Fig. S2).

2.2 Oral communication.

Oral communication is a very universal and flexible information dissemination form. However, the distance over which information can be transmitted is very limited. Because of this limitation, population density is the most important influencing factor in information dissemination. Beijing's population density decreases from the center to the periphery in concentric circles. Fig. 3 illustrates this population distribution pattern by dividing Beijing into 16 annular regions. In the urban areas depicted by the center annular region, the population density is 23000 persons/km^2, while the outermost annular region has a population density of just 200 persons/km^2 (All data were taken from the 2010 Beijing census.). In addition, the speed of information dissemination will decrease as the distance from the central area increases.

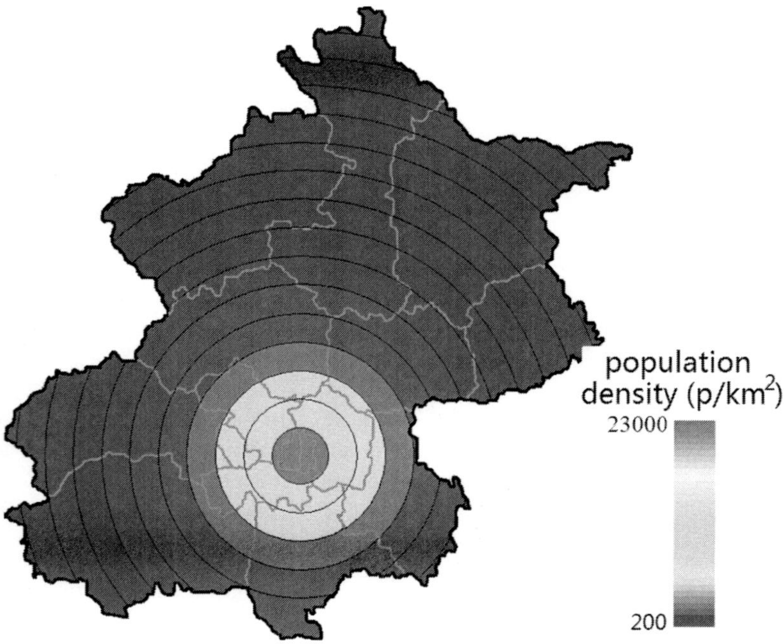

Figure 3. The approximate population distribution map of Beijing.

An over 100 times difference in population density among different areas leads to an obvious difference in information dissemination speed between urban areas and rural areas. Considering that the positioning of information sources will strongly influence information dissemination, the Monte Carlo method was used to simulate the information dissemination process. It was calculated that the information believers would notify on average 3.87 target people within a range of 90 m. seventy-nine percent of target people would be notified within the distance of 30 m, 14.6% in the range between 30–60 m, and 6.4% within a greater distance [20]. Therefore, the simulation grid was set to be 30 m*30 m and the Beijing area was divided into more than 20 million grids. The dissemination distance and the number of notified people were then obtained. The information dissemination time in one grid was set to one minute, i.e., all people in this grid can obtain within one minute any information disseminated by sources located in the same grid. The effective information dissemination probability, which is the product of probability of information reception, degree of trust, and average delay time, can be obtained through computational calculation.

2.3 Television.

Television is a mass medium with strong influence and high degree of trust that transmits information from medium to person using images and sound. In this study the television-watching period was divided into 8 phases with 3 hour intervals. Fig. 4 shows the television watching time at different time periods based, on questionnaires. The average time of TV watching peaked at 73 minutes after 6 p.m. which indicates that the majority of people choose to watch TV in the evening. This means that television may be a very good choice for disaster information dissemination during the evening.

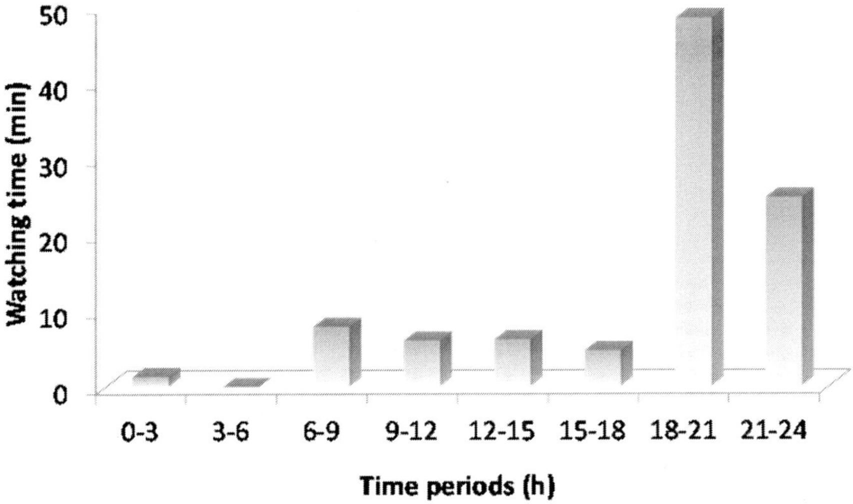

Figure 4. Television watching time distribution.

Fig. 5 shows the information dissemination process of TV. The information is assumed to be broadcast once every hour. Among the processes, $P_{1,TV}$ is the ratio of watching TV in each time period. $P_{2,TV}$ expresses the probability of a TV watcher getting the information from a TV station. A person should get the information at least once during a 60 minute period. $P_{2,TV}$ is therefore a piecewise function related to the duration of watching time t_i. Finally, the probability that television viewers believe the information $P_{3,TV}$ is calculated through the degree of trust of TV (C_{TV}) and receiving times of information n ($T_{use(i)} \leq 60,\ n = \frac{T_{use}(i)}{60};\ T_{use}(i) > 60,\ n = \left\lceil \frac{T_{use}(i)}{60} \right\rceil$). In summary, the effective information dissemination probability P, is calculated by Equation 8.

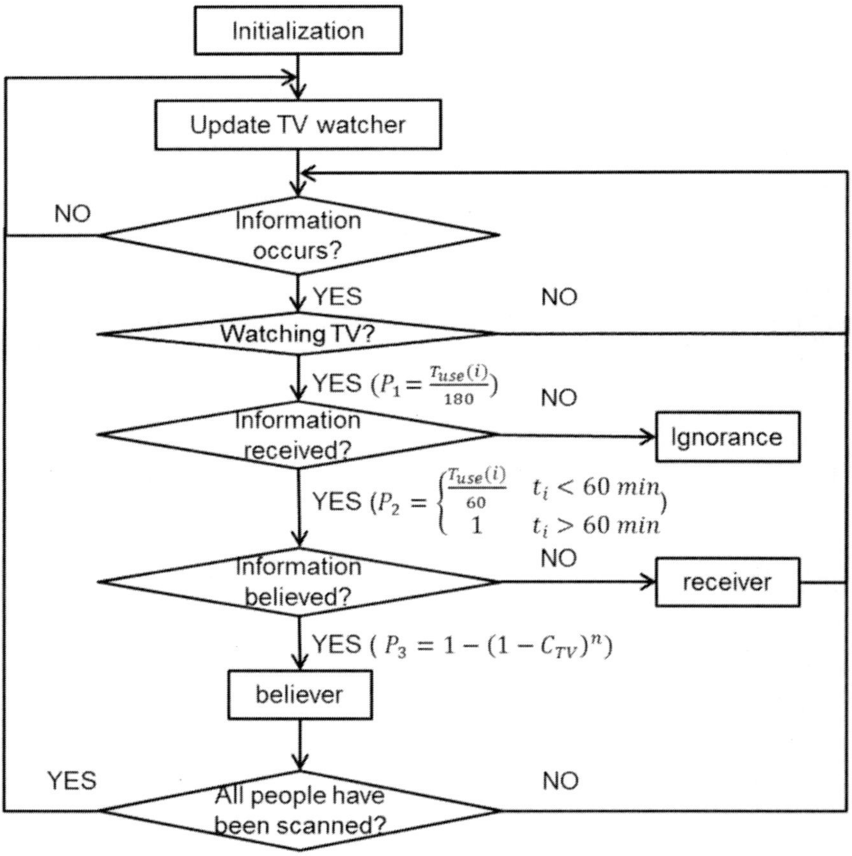

Figure 5. Television information dissemination process.

$$P_{TV}=P_{1,TV}\cdot P_{2,TV}\cdot P_{3,TV}$$

$$=\begin{cases}\frac{T_{use}(i)}{180}\cdot\frac{T_{use}(i)}{60}\cdot(1-(1-C_{TV})^{n}) & t_i<60\,\text{min}\\ \frac{T_{use}(i)}{180}\cdot(1-(1-C_{TV})^{n}) & t_i>60\,\text{min}\end{cases} \qquad \textbf{(8)}$$

In contrast to a microblog, watching television is a continuous activity. In Fig. 6, the pink color expresses the continuing watching time periods. For example, t1 shows that the watcher watched TV t1 minutes between midnight and 3 a.m. When an information source is broadcast during period 1, the average delay time is calculated based on Equation 9.

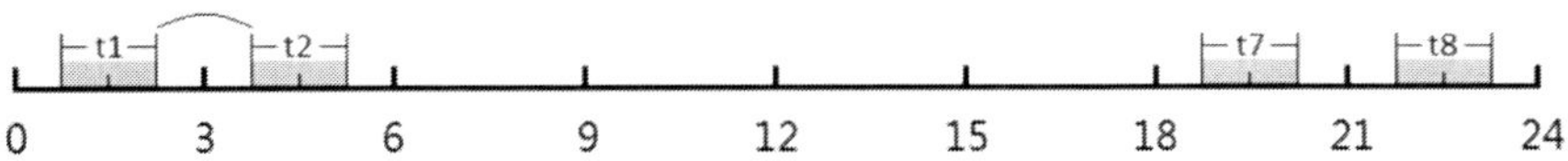

Figure 6. Television delay time calculation.

$$T_{1,TV}(t_1,t_2)=P_{1,TV}\int_{t_1}^{t_2} f_{1,TV}(t)\cdot p_{1,TV}(dt)$$

$$=\frac{3-\frac{t_1}{2}-\frac{t_2}{2}}{24}\int_{1.5+\frac{t_1}{2}}^{4.5-\frac{t_2}{2}}(4.5-\frac{t_2}{2}-t)(\frac{dt}{3-\frac{t_1}{2}-\frac{t_2}{2}}) \qquad \textbf{(9)}$$

where $T_{1,TV}$ expresses the delay time; $P_{1,TV}$ denotes the proportion of a 24 hour period; $f_{1,TV}(x)$ is a function of delay time; $P_{1,TV}(dt)$ represents the time weight of dt. The comprehensive function is calculated by Equation 10 considering different delay times from period 1 to period 8.

$$T_{TV}=$$

$$\frac{1}{48}\left[\sum_{i=2}^{8}\left(\frac{t(n-1)}{2}+\frac{t(n)}{2}-3\right)^{2}+\left(\frac{t_1}{2}+\frac{t_8}{2}-3\right)^{2}\right] \qquad \textbf{(10)}$$

The television model could also be used to simulate the dissemination of information by a news portal because the information dissemination mechanism of a news portal is similar to that of television. The model of a news portal is given in the Appendix C in Appendix S1 (the information dissemination characteristics curve is shown in Fig. S3).

RESULTS

1. Capability analysis of information dissemination

Simulations were performed concerning all the models mentioned above; and different curves were drawn to judge their capability to disseminate information, taking into account typical influencing factors such as age, gender, and residential area. In this study the information dissemination capability is reflected by the number of information believers within a fixed time period. Since the majority of children and elders acquire information from their families, the sample size of this population is small. Thus, we have set the age range from 16 to 55. According to census data [21], there are about 25 million people in Beijing. Using all the data from the simulations, detailed results of information dissemination are analyzed below:

Information media 1: short messages.

Fig. 7 shows the information dissemination of short messaging with different influencing factors. The curves indicate that short messages can be sent very rapidly. Statistical data analysis reveals that the information dissemination of SMS accords with equation 11.

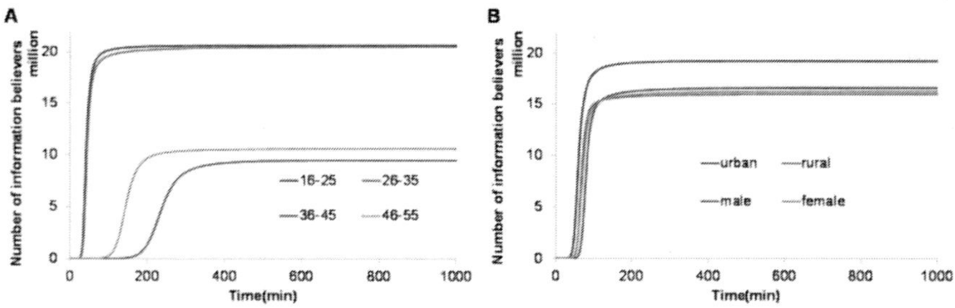

Figure 7. Temporal change of the information believers' number in different groups: short message service.

(A) age. (B) gender and residential area.

$$N_{SMS}(t) = \frac{1}{6.11 \times 10^{-8} + 0.0002609 \times e^{-t/7.663}} \quad \textbf{(11)}$$

where t is the time for information dissemination and $N_{SMS}(t)$ is the total number of information believers. This curve follow the logistic distribution which R^2=0.9963.

Fig. 7 (A) discloses that the capability of disseminating information of the younger group (16–35) is much greater than that of the middle-aged group (36–55). The delay time and usage time are two key factors that explain the difference between various age groups. According to Fig. 7 (B), about 18 million people will receive and believe the information within five hours of information dissemination in the urban area. Fig. 7 (B) also illustrates that the efficiency of information dissemination via short message relies more on the distribution of residential while the impact of gender can be ignored. It can be concluded that increasing short message usage frequency and usage time of people living in rural areas would greatly improve total information dissemination efficiency.

Information media 2: microblogs.

Fig. 8 demonstrates the information dissemination of a microblog which obeys logarithmic growth. Information source can be transmitted in a short time because there are many microblog fans. Furthermore, the number of people who believe information just reaches about 11 million because of a low degree of trust and low usage. In Fig. 8 (A) we see that the information dissemination effectiveness is low in the group aged 36–55. In contrast, the younger group shows a strong capability in information dissemination. Fig. 8 (B) illustrates that the capability of information dissemination in the urban and female groups is stronger than that in the rural and male group.

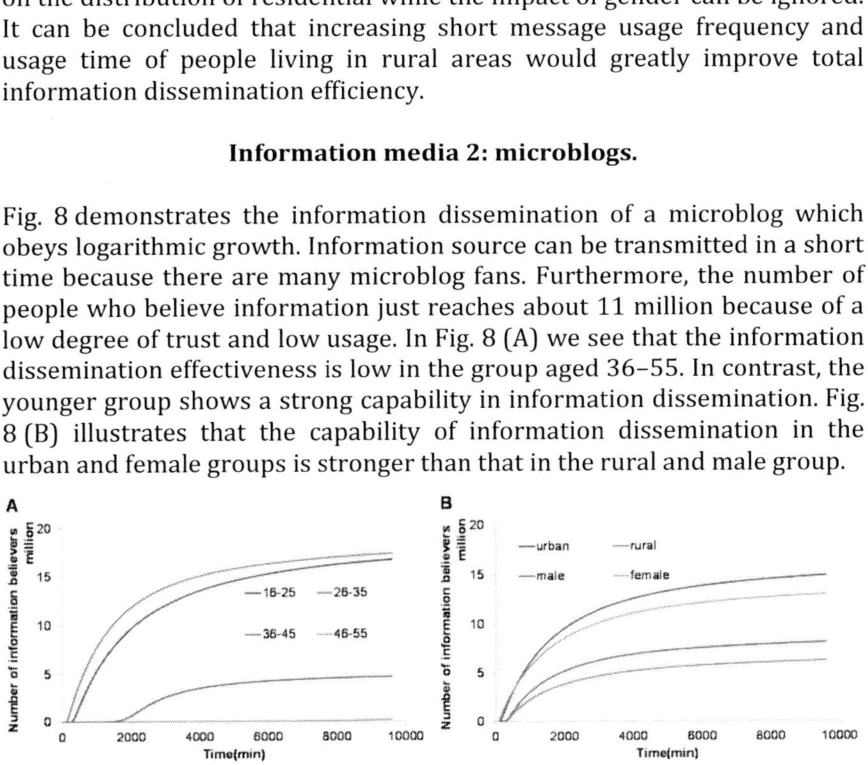

Figure 8. Temporal change of the information believers' number in different groups: microblog.

(A) age. (B) gender and residential area.

Information media 3: cell phone.

Cell phones are the most common information dissemination media used in our daily lives. Fig. 9 reveals that the information dissemination curves of cell phones also fit a logistic distribution with a slow initial dissemination speed. According to our statistical data analysis, the information dissemination of cell phone accords with equation 12.

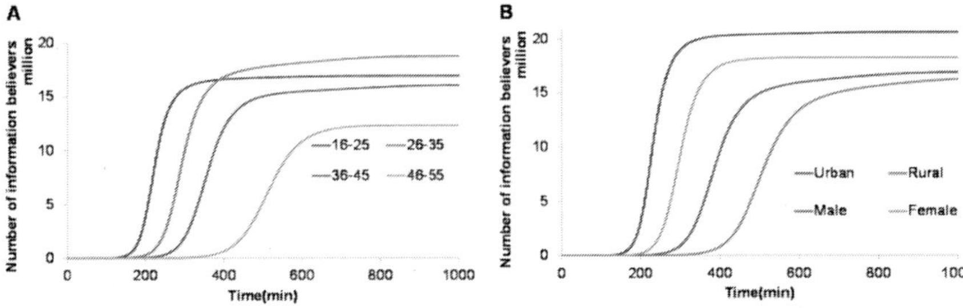

Figure 9. Temporal change of the information believers' number in different groups: cell phone.

(A) age. (B) gender and residential area.

$$N_{phone}(t) = \frac{1}{6.075 \times 10^{-8} + 0.001548 \times e^{-t/34.06}} \quad \textbf{(12)}$$

where t is the time for information dissemination and $N_{phone}(t)$ is the total number of information believers. This curve follow the logistic distribution which R^2=0.9987.

Fig. 9 shows that more than 10 million people can be informed via cell phone communication within 6 hours after the curves abruptly became flat due to busy lines and powering off of cell phones. Fig. 9 (A) demonstrates that cell phone usage by young people (16–35) is obviously higher than that of middle-aged people (36–55). Fig. 9 (B) shows that after about 16 hours the final value reached 16.8 million, while the rest 8.2 million people had not changed into information believers because of the low degree of trust in cell phones and the usage ratio of rural areas. The unusual continuous increase should be attributed to the long communication time periods via cell phones (about three hours). It also can be seen that females have a higher capability of information dissemination by cell phone than males. In addition, inhabitants in urban areas use cell phones frequently, which means this medium has a better information dissemination capability there than in rural areas immediately before a disaster situation.

Information media 4: Oral communication.

Fig. 10 shows that an increase in the degree of trust and forwarding number results in an increase of both the growth rate and the final number of information believers. The curves were drawn under different conditions, including different residential areas, forwarding people numbers, and degrees of trust. However, because of the geographical limitation of information dissemination via oral communication, continued increase of forwarding numbers did not result in a significant improvement. A comparison of the black to the brown line shows that, consistent with the law of population density distribution, the speed of information dissemination in urban areas is much higher than in rural areas. Considering that the position of an information source is the main factor determining the speed of information dissemination via oral communication, the Monte Carlo method was employed to improve the accuracy of results and to avoid the uncertainty caused by different information distribution sources. In this case the simulation time is set to 100.

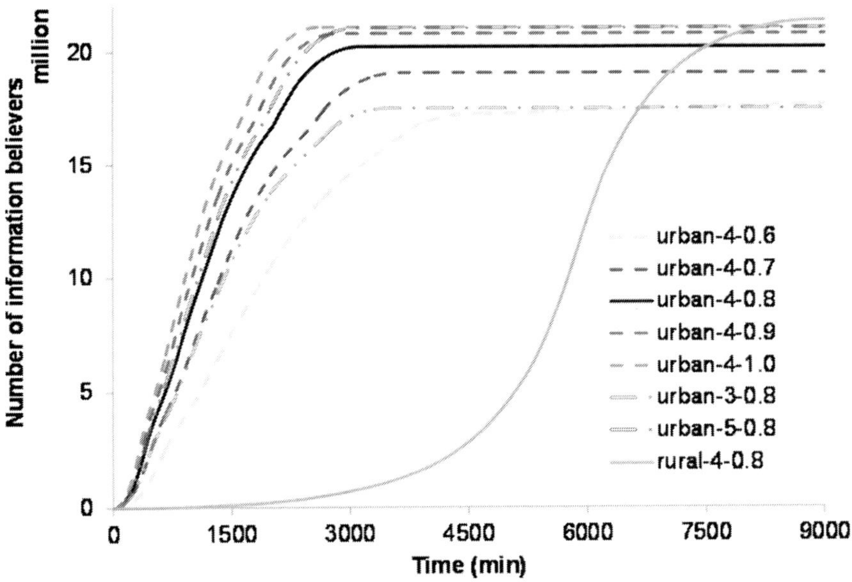

Figure 10. Temporal change of the information believers' number: oral communication.

Information media 5: Television.

Fig. 11 shows the information dissemination by television with different influencing factors. We can conclude that the speed of information dissemination of TV is strongly related to particular time periods: A large number of people are accustomed to watching TV between 6 p.m. and midnight; at other times the speed of information dissemination is more limited. According to the curves of information dissemination, in the first day (1440 min), about 17 million people received the information, and over the following few days the slope of the curve declined. Finally, after ten days, about 22 million people would have been informed via TV because of the high degree of trust. As shown in Fig. 11 (A), the length of time watching TV increases with increasing age, and the speed of information acquisition via TV is faster. Fig. 11 (B) shows that the capability of information dissemination of television in rural areas is, in contrast to all the other five media, stronger than in urban areas. In addition, the effect of gender is very small. Furthermore, the very high information coverage leads to the dominance of TV with regard to information dissemination.

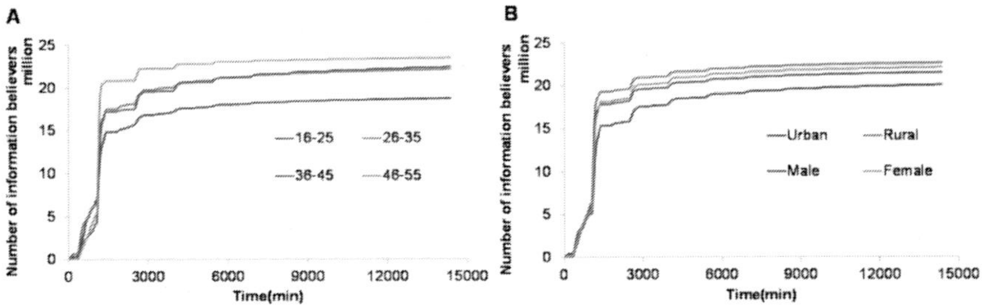

Figure 11. Temporal change of the information believers' number in different groups: television.

(A) age. (B) gender and residential area.

Information media 6: News portal.

The information dissemination of a news portal with three influencing factors is shown in Fig. 12. Statistical data analysis shows that the information dissemination of news portal accords with equation 13.

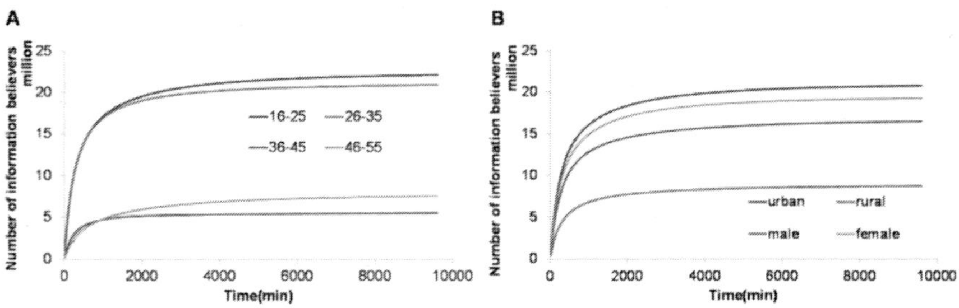

Figure 12. Temporal change of the information believers' number in different groups: news portal.

(A) age. (B) gender and residential area.

$$N_{portal}(t) = -1.531 \times 10^7 e^{-0.001618t} + 1.705 \times 10^7 \quad \textbf{(13)}$$

where t is the time for information dissemination and $N_{portal}(t)$ is the total number of information believers. This curve follow the logistic distribution which R^2=0.9587.

Fig. 12 (A) demonstrates that age is the most important influencing factor. The fact that information acquisition of the younger group (16–35) is much greater than that of the middle-aged group (36–55) shows that information on news portals can be quickly disseminated among young people. Fig. 12 (B) shows that, considering the influencing factors of gender and residential area, a news portal is very fast at disseminating information, potentially reaching 15 million people in just 1700 minutes. However, due to the lower degree of trust, the final number of information believers reached only 17.8 million.

The analysis of the six media under study increases our understanding of different information characteristics. When a serious disaster is approaching, a single information medium cannot manage the dissemination of a large amount of information. A combination of several information dissemination media which is tailored to the specific situation can increase the efficiency of information dissemination and provide people with more time and more accurate information to be informed and make better decisions. Furthermore, governments can make scientific and correct decisions to transmit information, based on different criteria such as information source and characteristics of disaster carriers.

2 Comprehensive assessment of each information dissemination mechanism

Fig. 13 shows the change in the number of information believers over time when using short messages, microblogs, cell phones, television, news portals, and oral communication. In the initial 30 minutes, the news portal is the fastest regarding information dissemination because a large number of users can receive the information at the same time. Between 30 and 500 minutes after information dissemination short messages rank first (ignoring the maximum load carrying ability of the base station). The speed of information dissemination can reach exponential growth in the initial period since messages are transmitted from person to person in a short time. After a period of about 100 minutes, the number of information believers will reach a constant value of 16 million. Cell phones have a lower speed of information dissemination than short message services because information cannot be forwarded to many people in a short time. Fig. 13 shows a logistic curve and illustrates that cell phones increased the number of information believers to 16 million within 720 minutes. Television plays an important role in the evening when the majority of people are watching TV at home. With the highest degree of trust and coverage ratio, TV can inform as many people as possible. The information dissemination ability of a microblog is not high due to a lower coverage ratio and degree of trust. It can be used as an auxiliary tool in information dissemination. Oral communication, albeit slow, is a very important information dissemination medium in disaster situations, particularly in the case of network paralysis. A combination of different information media will improve the effectiveness and speed of information dissemination.

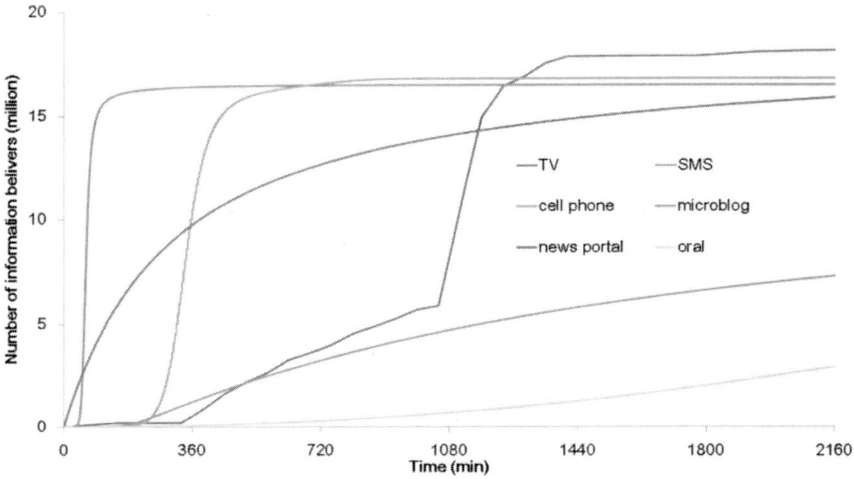

Figure 13. Comprehensive information dissemination comparison of six media.

In this paper six information media were studied. Six indices were established to evaluate the comprehensive capability of each medium regarding information dissemination: total coverage of information reception (TCIR); the time it takes for half of the population to believe the information (THB); frequency of media usage and time (FMU); the degree of trust (TD); total cost (TC); and delay time (DT).

TCIR is defined as the ratio of the number of people who received the information to the total number of people over a long enough period. THB is the time at which half of the people received and believed the information, and it represents the speed of information dissemination during the initial time. TCIR and THB can be calculated using the model process mentioned above. FMU indicates the popularity of the media. Information from official information media has a high degree of trust. The data for these two indices can be directly obtained from questionnaires. The total cost of each information medium was calculated through a price investigation on Taobao which has more than 70% of electronic commerce market share in China [22]. The delay time of the six information media are calculated by the equations mentioned above.

The final scores of the six media are computed using a Min-Max Normalization; they are listed in Table.2. Six indices are classified into two categories. One is positive (+) (capability of information dissemination increases when the value of the index increases), the other is negative (−) (the value is subtracted by 1). According to these six indices, the comprehensive expression of each information medium is reflected in the radar graph shown in Fig. 14.

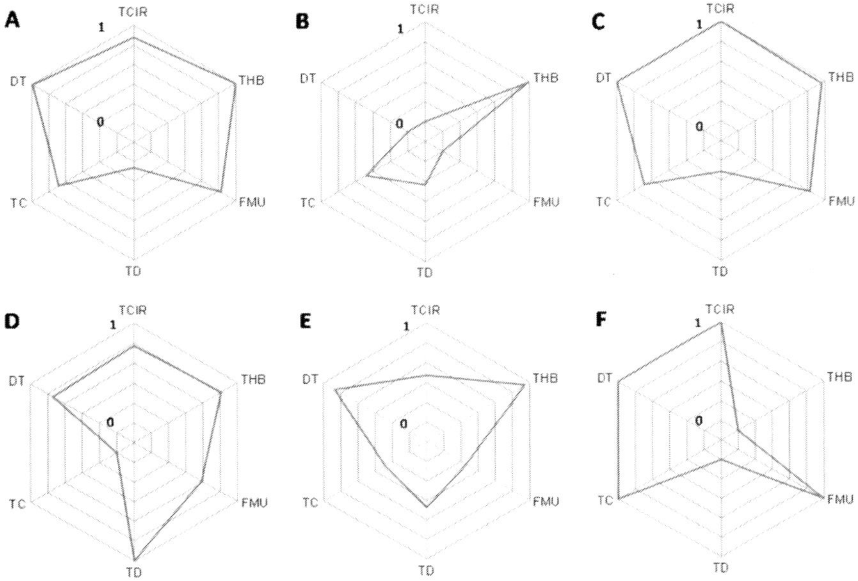

Figure 14. Radar graphs of comprehensive information dissemination assessment of each media.

(A) Short message service; (B) Microblog; (C) Cell phone; (D) Television; (E) News portal; (F) Oral communication.

Table 2. Value of six indices of different information media.

		SMS	Microblog	Cell phone	Television	News portal	Oral
TCIR	(+)	0.879	0	1.000	0.773	0.472	1.000
THB	(−)	1.000	0.986	0.961	0.814	0.947	0
FMU	(+)	0.826	0	0.826	0.583	0.261	1.000
TD	(+)	0.059	0.235	0.110	1.000	0.468	0
TC	(−)	0.682	0.482	0.681	0	0.283	1.000
DT	(−)	0.990	0	0.994	0.737	0.867	1.000

The radar graphs express the information dissemination capability of the six media and the comprehensive characteristics directly. Data analysis reveals that short messages, cell phones, and TV have a higher comprehensive information dissemination capability. Short messages and cell phones have a shorter delay time and higher information coverage ratio as well as information dissemination speed, but the degree of trust in them is lower. Television has the highest degree of trust but longer delay time. Microblogs, which have a very long delay time and moderate degrees of trust and information coverage ratio, have a fast initial information dissemination speed. News portals, as a very popular network media, are a very fast method of information dissemination, particularly during the early periods. Oral communication is also a very important information dissemination medium (no cost, ease of use), especially in high population density areas. Different lengths of pre-warning times allow different choices of information dissemination media. For instance, if the pre-warning time is limited, short messages and news portals should be used. Ultimately, the combination of different media can improve the efficiency of information dissemination. The results above can be useful in making an emergency plan that ensures the safety of lives and properties during a disaster.

3 Information media in disaster pre-warning

Developing information dissemination technology and understanding the mechanisms of each information medium are crucial for disaster pre-warning and management. Tailored to the specific disaster situation, government and victims can use different information dissemination strategies. Cell phones, SMS, microblogs, news portals, and TV usually play the most important role in some conventional disaster pre-warning such as rainstorm and frost because they feature a higher information dissemination effectiveness. However, when a serious earthquake strikes, the majority of networking and station bases will paralyze and the majority of electronic network media cannot be used. Here, oral communication will disseminate emergency information with few words or sentences. A large number of victims would try to notify all the people around them. Our analysis of oral communication mentioned above suggests that information sources positioning strongly determined the effectiveness of information dissemination. Governments can set the optimal source position to improve the information dissemination speed; they also can assess the spreading time through the analysis introduced above to help improve disaster management and save more lives. Data analysis also revealed that TV has a higher degree of trust and that it also has a higher information dissemination effectiveness in the evening. Governments should put their attention to TV rather than microblog or news portal to spread the warning information if a serious disaster occurs in the evening. Generally speaking, by combining different information media characteristics governments can improve disaster pre-warning and reduce casualties and damage to properties in an effective way, and victims can acquire more information to make informed decisions. Summing up, there is a need to analyze information dissemination characteristics of different media to ensure that warning information can be spread to every person with short delay times in a reliable manner.

CONCLUSIONS

In this study models of six information dissemination media, including short messages, microblogs, cell phones, television, news portals, and oral communication, were established. The capabilities of each medium to disseminate information were assessed, using data obtained from the dissemination models, statistical data, and questionnaires collected in Beijing. Based on the information dissemination capability analysis and taking into consideration factors such as age, gender, and residential area, different characteristics of the six media were summarized. Our analysis shows that SMSs have the highest speed while cell phones can disseminate more detailed information because verbal communication allows better explanation of complex situations. People's habits suggest the employment of television be emphasized in the evening.

In case of serious disasters such as earthquakes, electronic networks are prone to paralyze and oral communication will play an important role to disseminate information in a reliable manner. To directly compare and analyze different aspects of the information dissemination capabilities of the six media radar graphs considering six indices were drawn. Short message services and cell phones have more comprehensive information dissemination capabilities than other information media but they have lower degrees of trust. Television is also a good information dissemination medium; it has a higher information coverage and the highest degree of trust. Compared to other information media, oral communication is not outstanding in information dissemination speed; however, it possesses convenience. News portals and microblogs can be used as auxiliary tools, but their information coverage is not very large. Each of the six media has different strength and limitations; therefore, to help improve dissemination of information, reduce losses, and ensure the safety of disaster carriers, their combination should be tailored to the specific disaster situation. The models and simulation methods can be applied to many other regions.

In future works, more ways of information dissemination and more influencing factors will be considered, including the maximum information carrying capacity and the vulnerability of each medium in a disaster. An integrated system covering all recommendable combinations of media will be established to disseminate emergency information timely and accurately under various circumstances.

REFERENCES

1. Basher R (2006) Global early warning systems for natural hazards: systematic and people-centred. Philos Trans R Soc A-Math Phys Eng Sci 364(1845): 2167–2182.

2. 2.Chenglan B (2005) Tsunami Disaster and Its Pre-warning System. Recent Dev World Seismol 1: 14–18.

3. Preis T, Moat HS, Bishop SR, Treleaven P, Stanley HE (2013) Quantifying the digital traces of Hurricane Sandy on Flickr. Sci Rep 1–3.

4. Li Q, Yang T, Zhao E, Xia X, Han ZG (2013) The Impacts of Information-Sharing Mechanisms on Spatial Market Formation Based on Agent-Based Modeling. PloS One 8(3): e58270.

5. Kaplan AM, Haenlein M (2010) Users of the world, unite! The challenges and opportunities of social media. Bus Horiz 53(1): 59–68.

6. Macilwain C (2013) Sharing information is preferable to patenting. Nat 498: 273.

7. Allen HG, Stanton TR, Di Pietro F, Moseley GL (2013) Social media release increases dissemination of original articles in the clinical pain sciences. PloS One 8(7): e68914.

8. Lengel RH, Daft RL (1988) The selection of communication media as an executive skill. Acad Manag Exec 2(3): 225–232.

9. Uchida N, Takahata K, Shibata Y, Shiratori N (2011) Never Die Network Extended with Cognitive Wireless Network for Disaster Information System. Complex, Intell Softw Intensive Syst (CISIS), 2011 International Conference on. IEEE 24–31.

10. Sattler DN, Larpenteur K, Shipley G (2011) Active shooter on campus: evaluating text and e-mail warning message effectiveness. J Homel Secur Emerg Manag 8(1).

11. Wei J, Zhao D, Yang F, Du S, Marinova D (2010) Timing crisis information release via television. Disasters 34(4): 1013–1030.

12. Whittaker S, Bellotti V, Gwizdka J (2006) Microblog in personal information management. Commun ACM 49(1): 68–73.

13. Odeny TA, Bailey RC, Bukusi EA, Simoni JM, Tapia KA, et al. (2012) Text messaging to improve attedance at post-operative clinic visits after adult male circumcision for HIV prevention: a randomized controlled trial. PloS One 7(9): e43832.

14. Zhang N, Huang H, Su B, Zhang B (2013) Analysis of different information dissemination ways for disaster pre-warning: A Case Study of Beijing. Proc 3rd Int Conf Multimedia Technol (ICMT 2013). Springer Berlin Heidelberg: 183–192.

15. Shim JP, Varshney U, Dekleva S, Nickerson RC (2007) Wireless telecommunications issues: Cell phone TV, wireless networks in

disaster management, ubiquitous computing, and adoption of future wireless applications. Commun Assoc Inf Syst 20: 442–456.

16. Katada T, Asada J, Kuwasawa N, Oikawa Y (2000) Development of practical scenario simulator for dissemination of disaster information. J Civ Eng Inf Process Syst 9: 129–136.

17. Zhang N, Huang H, Su B, Zhang H (2013) Population evacuation analysis: considering dynamic population vulnerability distribution and disaster information dissemination. Nat Hazards 69(3): 1629–1646.

18. Lang SY (2012) Research on portal websites of china sports news media credibility—Take the university students audience groups for example. Beijing: Capital University of Physical Education and Sports.

19. Eugster PT, Guerraoui R, Kermarrec AM, Massoulié L (2004) Epidemic information dissemination in distributed systems. Comput 37(5): 60–67.

20. Katada T, Oikawa Y, Tanaka T (1999) Development of simulation model for evaluating the efficiency of disaster information dissemination. J Jpn Soc Civ Eng: 1–14.

21. Beijing Bureau of Statistics (2009) Census information of Beijing: China statistics Press.

22. Li D, Li J, Lin Z (2008) Online consumer-to-consumer market in China–a comparative study of Taobao and eBay. Electron Commer Res Appl 7(1): 55–67.

10

AIDS, CONFLICT AND THE MEDIA IN AFRICA: RISKS IN REPORTING BAD DATA BADLY

Massimo Lowicki-Zucca[1], Paul Spiegel[2] and Filippo Ciantia[3]

[1]Child Protection Section, UNICEF, New York, USA,

[2]Division of Operational Support, UNHCR, Geneva, Switzerland and

[3]Associazione Volontari per il Servizio Internazionale, Kampala, Uganda

ABSTRACT

Background

Conflict, poverty and HIV disproportionately affect people in sub-Saharan Africa. The manner in which governments, national and international organisations and the media report on the HIV epidemic in situations of conflict, post-conflict and reconstruction can have unintended and negative consequences for those affected populations. The media in particular has a huge influence on how the world observes and reacts to the HIV epidemic among conflict-affected and displaced populations.

Discussion

Three case studies focused on Sudan, Uganda and Guinea describe what the media reported and why the reports were incomplete, misleading or incorrect. The exploration of possible ways to ensure that the media do not unwittingly inflame delicate and complicated situations of HIV among conflict-affected and displaced populations is then undertaken using epidemiological and journalistic principles. The discussion is divided into four sections: 1) Avoid stigmatising statements and ensure a balanced view; 2) Avoid accurate but misleading statements; 3) Avoid inaccurate statements by clearly stating sources and verifying their credibility; and 4) Do not repeat data and conclusions from other news sources without checking their accuracy. The aim of this manuscript is to stimulate awareness and debate among persons and organisations working on HIV/AIDS as well as the media in order to improve dialogue and ultimately to reduce stigma and discrimination amongst an already vulnerable group – conflict-affected and displaced persons.

Summary

The media and humanitarian organisations have published misleading and inaccurate HIV data and statements on conflict-affected and displaced populations in Sudan, Uganda and Guinea. Given the unique characteristics of the HIV epidemic and conflict-affected and displaced populations, the media have a special obligation to report in a balanced and non-discriminatory manner that may go beyond the accepted standards of journalism. The media may wish to have the HIV data and their interpretation reviewed by technical experts before going to press. Specific training for reporters and editors regarding ethical issues and basic epidemiological methods may help them to better understand the complexity of the situation and report more accurately; similar training for media watch groups and human rights organisations may improve the monitoring of such situations and possibly reduce misreporting and subsequent discrimination. More rigorous HIV biological and behavioural surveillance should be undertaken in situations of conflict and displacement and humanitarian guidelines should be integrated with guidance on media relations and reporting responsibilities of humanitarian agencies. Finally, humanitarian agencies must ensure the data they release are sound and that any biases are clearly stated. Improved communication with the media will help to ensure more accurate reporting and interpretation.

BACKGROUND

Conflict, poverty and HIV disproportionately affect people in sub-Saharan Africa. In 2004, 25 active armed conflicts occurred worldwide, 69 countries were affected by refugee movements and 48 countries by internal displacement of their populations [1]. Africa was the most affected continent. The current estimated number of refugees and internally displaced persons (IDPs) worldwide are 12 and 25 million, respectively [2, 3]. Their needs are enormous due to the trauma they have suffered and the deplorable conditions in which they live. Furthermore, their vulnerabilities are increased due to destitution, displacement, discrimination and reduction of basic services and coping mechanisms. Significant challenges lie ahead for those who have become displaced, living in new and sometimes hostile environments. Repatriation to their country of origin also poses new challenges as well as problems.

Perceived HIV status, regardless of one's actual status, carries with it a stigma that can destroy individuals, their families and even communities. The manner in which governments, national and international organisations and the media report on the HIV epidemic in situations of conflict, post-conflict and reconstruction can have unintended and negative consequences for those affected populations including the aggravation of xenophobic fears, the imposition of mandatory HIV testing by authorities to regulate immigration or refugee inflows, refoulement (forced return of refugees to their country of origin), the hampering of reconciliation processes and creating obstacles to their integration in host communities and repatriation to countries of origin.

Everywhere in the world, people are very sensitive to the fears of disease being "brought in" by outsiders. Their fears can be exploited by some and used to promote political agendas. A recent example is the measures proposed by the United Kingdom's Conservative Party, after intense public and political debate about the scale and nature of asylum and migration, to affirm that "the [HIV] risk to the population comes primarily from those seeking permanent residency in the U.K, either as an asylum seeker or through the immigration service" [4]. Such arguments have been countered elsewhere, on the basis of limited evidence as well as practical and ethical problems [5, 6].

The media has a huge influence on how the world observes and reacts to the HIV epidemic among conflict-affected and displaced populations. Therefore, as already argued for health and medical reporting in general [7, 8], the media have a special responsibility to report on this sensitive topic knowledgeably and prudently, to consider and report on all sides of this complex issue, and to take into account any harmful implications their reporting may have for such populations [9].

The case studies in three conflict-affected African countries presented below state what the media reported and why the reports were incomplete, misleading or incorrect. The exploration of possible ways to ensure that the media do not unwittingly inflame delicate and complicated situations of HIV among conflict-affected and displaced populations by reporting and repeating misleading or incorrect statements from individuals, organisations and media sources is then undertaken. This article is meant to stimulate awareness and debate among persons and organisations working on HIV/AIDS as well as the media in order to improve dialogue and ultimately to reduce stigma and discrimination against an already vulnerable group – conflict-affected and displaced persons.

Sudan

"The fact that many Sudanese will return to their homes from countries where the HIV/AIDS prevalence is very high, will doubtless increase the likelihood of a further spread of the epidemic" [10].

Conflict in Sudan has displaced millions of people and forced hundreds of thousands to flee across borders. In the south of the country, the 21-year old war between the Government of Sudan and the Sudan People Liberation Movement/Army has caused the internal displacement of approximately 4 million people, to which the more than 1.5 million displaced as a consequence of the more recent conflict in Darfur must be added. As of the end of 2003, more than 500,000 Sudanese refugees were residing mainly in Uganda, Ethiopia, Kenya and Chad [11].

By the end of 2003, the overall HIV prevalence among adults in Sudan was estimated at 2.3% (95% confidence interval (CI) 0.7 to 7.2) [12]. In 2002, the Sudanese government undertook an HIV survey in 14 of 26 states with the following results: pregnant women at antenatal clinics (1.0%), tuberculosis (TB) patients (1.6%), sexually transmitted infections (STI) patients (1.1%), sex workers (4.4%), tea sellers (2.5%), IDPs (1.0%) and Eritrean refugees (4.0%) [13].

Following progress in the negotiations between the Government of Sudan and the Sudan People Liberation Movement/Army, future peace in South Sudan and the consequent return home of refugees and IDPs was reported widely in the media. Particular attention was expressed regarding high infection rates among Sudanese IDPs and refugees, and the fear that refugees living in host countries with high prevalence rates will return and exacerbate the epidemic in South Sudan [14, 15]. The situation was described as "severe", "on the verge of an HIV/AIDS epidemic" and a "disaster" that was going to "doubtless increase the likelihood of a further spread of the epidemic" [10, 15, 16].

Uganda

Headline: *"HIV/AIDS soars in war-torn northern Uganda"* [17].

Northern Uganda is currently devastated by a 19-year old conflict between the Ugandan Government and the Lord's Resistance Army (LRA), which escalated in 1996 causing massive population displacement, further aggravated since the increase of violence in mid-2002. At the end of September 2004, there were 1.4 million IDPs in some 200 camps, living in extremely difficult hygienic and environmental conditions and depending on relief food distribution [18].

Uganda experienced declines in HIV prevalence during the 1990s. National prevalence estimated by antenatal sentinel surveillance peaked in the early 1990s and has fallen to 4.1% (95% CI 2.8 to 6.6) by the end of 2003 [12]. Sentinel surveillance shows that median HIV prevalence in the capital Kampala declined from a high of 29.4% in 1992 down to 8.3% in 2002, while in areas outside major urban centres it decreased from 12.0% to 4.6% [19].

Several reports in the national and international press and information disseminated by international organizations have emphasized that the HIV prevalence in northern Uganda (11.9% in 2002) is nearly twice as high as the national rate (6.2% in 2002) and growing due to conflict [20]. These reports particularly highlighted the high HIV prevalence among IDPs in the camps and the highest prevalence among victims of the LRA [21, 22, 23, 24, 25, 26]. Children, particularly girls, captured by the LRA have been reported to have an HIV prevalence of approximately 50% [17, 23, 27, 28, 29]. In the past, this vulnerable group had already been suggested to be infected with extremely high rates of STIs, including HIV [30]. Furthermore, direct reference to "immorality" among IDPs as explanation for the higher rates of HIV prevalence was attributed to unspecified "NGO (non-governmental organisation) workers" [31].

Guinea

"It's the refugees' fault. AIDS comes with them!" [32].

Since 1990, the republic of Guinea with a population of 7.5 million persons has hosted hundreds of thousands of refugees from primarily Sierra Leone and Liberia. Until late 2000, the refugees lived in small villages scattered throughout the rural south-eastern Forest region. During September to December 2000, attacks by armed factions in Guinea led to the displacement and consequent transfer of the refugees to safer camps in the north-west of the country [32]. By the end of 2004, there were still approximately 150,000 refugees primarily from Liberia, Sierra Leone and Cote d'Ivoire [2]. Due to recent conflict in Cote d'Ivoire, which has the highest HIV prevalence in the West Africa (7.0%) [12] over 100,000 Guineans have returned home, many to the Forest Region [32].

A national HIV seroprevalence survey, undertaken in Guinea in December 2001, showed an overall HIV prevalence of 2.8% among pregnant women with 4.4% in urban areas and 2.2% in rural areas [33, 34]. An HIV prevalence of 7.0% was reported in two towns in the Forest Region, the area where the refugees were located. By the end of 2003, HIV prevalence was estimated at 3.2% [12].

Before the national survey, it was assumed that the overall HIV prevalence in Guinea was lower than 2.8%. The media reported that the higher HIV prevalence in the Forest Region was likely due to the influx of refugees, blaming their "loose morals" that resulted in "flourishing promiscuity and prostitution" [32].

DISCUSSION

The International Federation of Journalists' Declaration of Principles on the Conduct of Journalists is proclaimed as a standard of professional conduct for journalists engaged in gathering, transmitting, disseminating and commenting on news and information in describing events [35]. Of the eight principles stated, two are particularly applicable for this article:

I. The journalist shall report only in accordance with facts of which he/she knows the origin. The journalist shall not suppress essential information or falsify documents.

II. The journalist shall be alert to the danger of discrimination being furthered by media, and shall do the utmost to avoid facilitating such discriminations based on, among other things, race, sex, sexual orientation, language, religion, political or other opinions, and national and social origins.

We discuss below the critical aspects of the coverage of these three case studies by media reports following four main arguments:

1. Avoid stigmatising statements and ensure a balanced view

"The fact that many Sudanese will return to their homes from countries where the HIV/AIDS prevalence is very high will doubtless increase the likelihood of a further spread of the epidemic" [10].

"Infection rates are particularly high among vulnerable groups, such as internally displaced persons (IDPs) and refugees" [10].

Concern regarding stigmatizing statements against refugees living in Sudan and Sudanese refugees living in surrounding host countries began after the Integrated Regional Information Network (IRIN) [10] reported on a UN newsletter [16]. Although refugees often come from countries of origin with lower HIV prevalence and move to live among host country populations with higher HIV prevalence, each case is context specific and must be examined independently [36]. The degree of interaction among refugees and host communities as well as their HIV knowledge and behaviour all contribute to the HIV prevalence in both populations. Sudanese refugees living in Kenya and Uganda still have much lower HIV prevalence than their surrounding host communities despite living among them for over a decade [36]. Furthermore, Sudanese refugees living in Kenya have shown better knowledge and less risky behaviour than some Sudanese living in South Sudan [37]. Blanket statements such as the first one in the text box above are unhelpful and can be damaging. These and other statements in the UN report and IRIN article were published without checking with other sources, such as the United Nations High Commissioner for Refugees, NGOs working with the refugees, or the refugees themselves. After discussion with IRIN, the news organization acted in a rapid and professional manner. They removed the original article from their website, interviewed different experts in the field to provide a more balanced view, and changed the first statement listed above to "The fact that many Sudanese will return to their homes from countries where the HIV/AIDS rate are high *might* increase the likelihood of a further spread of the epidemic" [15].

Headline: "GUINEA: Refugee influx adds fuel to AIDS crisis in southeast Guinea" [32].

Another IRIN report stated that refugees are being blamed for spreading HIV among the local Guinean population. Statements from local Guineans and even refugees provide credence to the assertion that refugees spread HIV. However, the HIV prevalence has never been measured among refugees in Guinea and there is insufficient evidence to know the effect that the mixing of refugees and locals have had on the HIV prevalence in the region. Only near the end of the article does it state that condom use and knowledge of HIV/AIDS were much lower among Guinean youth than Liberian refugees.

2. Avoid accurate but misleading statements

"The HIV-infection rate in Sudan, according to UNFPA, is already considered an epidemic, making Sudan the country with the highest infection rate in North Africa and the Middle East region" [10].

Although Sudan has the highest HIV prevalence in North Africa and the Middle East, it has the lowest prevalence compared with the countries surrounding it to the East, West and South [12]. The former statement was made to buttress the point that Sudan has a serious HIV problem. Indeed, HIV is a very serious issue in Sudan; however, the fact remains that HIV prevalence is much higher in surrounding countries than Sudan itself.

"The rate of HIV/AIDS infection in northern Uganda is nearly double that in the rest of the country..." [29].

HIV prevalence in the Northern Uganda, represented by the surveillance site located in Lacor hospital in Gulu, is often correctly reported as nearly double the national average. This point estimate is then used to 'prove' that the conflict in Northern Uganda has caused the HIV epidemic to flourish. The estimated HIV prevalence for Gulu is however not the only one above the national average and is in fact similar to other urban sentinel sites in areas not affected by conflict (Table 1). Moreover, trends over time actually show that the HIV prevalence in Northern Uganda has decreased over time, similar to many other sentinel surveillance sites in the rest of the country. The decrease in the HIV prevalence in Gulu has been significant from 27% in 1993 to 12.8% in 1998 to 11.9% in 2002 ($p < 0.001$) [19, 38]. The trends in Table 1 clearly show that, from 1993 to 2002, the reduction of HIV prevalence in the sentinel site for Northern Uganda has been larger than that of many other sentinel sites. Despite an increase in the intensity of the conflict from 1996 onwards, trends from 1998 to 2002 show a larger decrease in Gulu than in peaceful southern and eastern Uganda, represented by the sentinel site of Mbarara and Mbale regional hospitals, respectively.

Table 1. Decline in HIV prevalence rates, 1993–2002. Selected sentinel sites, Uganda.

			HIV Prevalence				
Site	District	Urban/ rural*	1993	1998	2002	% change (2002/1993)	% change (2002/1998)
Nsambya	Kampala TC	Urban	26.6	13.4	8.5	50.4%	63.4%
Rubaga	Kampala TC	Urban	24.4	14.2	8.1	58.2%	57.0%
Mbarara	**Mbarara**	**Urban**	**18.1**	**10.9**	**10.8**	**60.2%**	**99.1%**
Jinja	Jinja	Urban	16.7	10.5	5	62.9%	47.6%
Tororo	Tororo	Rural	11.3	10.5	6.3	92.9%	60.0%
Mbale	**Mbale**	**Urban**	**8.7**	**6.3**	**5.9**	**72.4%**	**93.7%**
Soroti	Soroti	Rural	9.1	7.7	4.6	84.6%	59.7%
Matany	Moroto	Rural	2.8	1.3	0.7	46.4%	53.8%
Mutolere	Kisoro	Rural	4.2	2.5	1.5	59.5%	60.0%
Gulu	**Gulu**	**Urban**	**27.0**	**12.8**	**11.9**	**47.4%**	**93.0%**

* Urban population defined as >50,000 persons and rural population as <50,000 persons Source: adapted from [19]

Therefore, basic epidemiological principles must be used when interpreting HIV prevalence data. Trends over time must be examined as opposed to comparing point prevalence estimates as occurred above.

3. Avoid inaccurate statements by clearly stating sources and verifying their credibility

"Data from the mid-1990s onwards suggested the infection rates had risen rapidly in the conflict-affected areas of southern and western Sudan. According to a national prevalence and behaviour survey conducted in 2002, HIV prevalence was already four percent among pregnant women attending clinics in the refugee camps" [10].

There are no data at present suggesting that the HIV prevalence in South and West Sudan is rising rapidly. No source is provided for the statement in the above text box. In South Sudan, IRIN reported that the Sudan Evangelical Mission found HIV prevalence to be 4–10% in Rumbeck and 17–21% in Yambio in their voluntary counselling and testing (VCT) centres [10]. However, VCT data present biases and cannot be used as proxy for HIV prevalence in the general population due to the biases involved in self selection of clients and referrals from medical personnel. As a comparison, HIV prevalence rates from VCT services in both Kitgum and Pader districts in neighbouring north Uganda, are estimated at 20% (AVSI-supported PMTCT sites program data. unpublished), whereas PMTCT results show the HIV prevalence to be 7.9%–9.9% in Kitgum and 4.6% in Pader [39].

The second sentence in the above quotation discusses HIV prevalence among Eritrean refugees living in the Eastern part of the country from the Sudanese National AIDS Control Programme's 2002 report. The comparison, however, should not be among Sudanese pregnant women attending antenatal care (ANC) from all over the country (HIV prevalence of 1.0%) with refugee pregnant women in East Sudan (4.1%) but rather between Sudanese pregnant women from the sentinel site nearest to the refugee camps (El Gedarif). The data provided by the 2002 report does not allow disaggregation by state. However, in 1998, Sudan reported the HIV prevalence in the ANC sentinel surveillance in El Gedarif as 4.0% [37, 40], almost identical to the 4.1% reported among the refugees. There is limited HIV data from Eritrea; one sentinel site outside an urban area in 1994 showed 3% prevalence while one major urban area site in 1999 showed 4%; both are similar to the sites found in El Gedarif in Sudan and among the refugees [41]. Finally, the same IRIN article also claims that HIV infection rates are particularly high among vulnerable groups, such as IDPs and refugees. However, this is also incorrect; the HIV prevalence among IDPs was estimated to be 1.0% [13, 36].

"About half the girls who escape from the rebels are found to be HIV positive, doctors say" [25].

Claims of extremely high HIV prevalence among children abducted by the LRA are not supported by data; no systematic HIV testing has ever been undertaken among this group. The statement reported above, originally made by a Government official [27] and then reported by numerous NGOs and news agencies, was subsequently dismissed by organizations responsible for the major reception centres for these children in the region (personal communications and email exchanges between members of the Psychosocial Working Group and Child Care Centres in North Uganda, August 2004).

4. Do not continuously repeat data and conclusions from other news sources without checking for accuracy

[AIDS is the] "leading cause for death, constituting 69% of deaths in Gulu area, or three times higher than direct killings during military confrontation" [26].

Misleading or false information regarding HIV and AIDS in Northern Uganda has been parroted repeatedly by news agencies, apparently without verification. Figure 1 attempts to trace the origin and the subsequent reporting between July and November 2004 of three main statements: 1) HIV prevalence in Northern Uganda is double that of the whole country; 2) HIV prevalence is 50% among those children abducted and subsequently released by the LRA; and 3) AIDS is the cause of 69% of the total deaths in Northern Uganda.

The first two issues were discussed previously and have been shown to be incorrect. The third issue relates to a recent report on the humanitarian situation of Northern Uganda which claimed AIDS to be the leading cause of death (69%) in the Gulu area, three times higher than direct killings during military confrontation [26]. The source for this statement was not provided, and coverage of HIV testing is limited to few areas within Gulu District. Conversely, Médecins Sans Frontières undertook at the end of 2004 a population-based survey and reported alarmingly high rates of mortality in the insurgent-affected districts of Lira and Pader in Northern Uganda (crude mortality rate of 2.8/10,000/day and under five mortality rate of 5.4/10,000/day) [42]. As in the Democratic Republic of Congo [43], the main causes of death were indigenous communicable diseases that have been exacerbated due to the conflict, such as malaria (47% of all deaths), respiratory disease (28%) and diarrhoeal disease (21%); however, AIDS could be an underlying factor that was not reported.

To further support this point, several months after the initial and incorrect statements were reported, all three re-emerged in the media [44] and, more recently, IDPs in North Uganda have been reported as having an average HIV/AIDS prevalence six times higher than the national average [45].

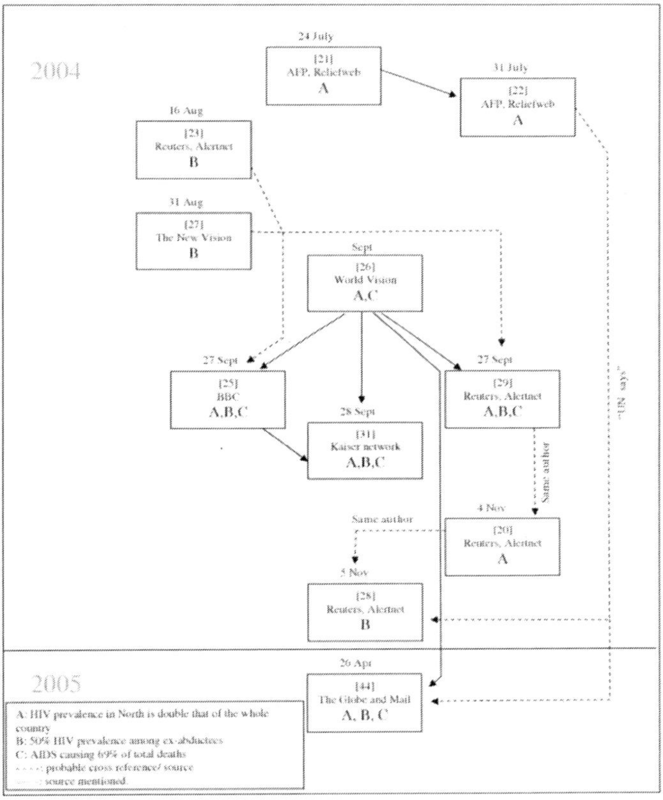

Figure 1. Sequence of reporting of three main incorrect statements on HIV and North-Uganda.

SUMMARY

The relationship between HIV/AIDS and conflict-affected and displaced populations is complicated and is influenced by numerous complex and competing factors, including the HIV prevalence in the area of origin and host communities, the amount of time since displacement, and the interaction between the affected and host communities [36, 46, 47].

This complex relationship is not unidirectional; conflict and displacement does not necessarily translate into higher HIV infection rates among affected persons. However, these situations increase the vulnerability of all persons, affected and host populations, to HIV infection. The incorrect, incomplete or misleading reporting of data and statements does not help to inform HIV policy or programming; rather it may reinforce discriminatory attitudes that stigmatise a population in need of protection and support.

Whilst misinformation in the media may be due to poor understanding and limited interest about disease patterns and measurement, it may also be due to the preference of the media for reporting dramatic stories. This is exemplified by the frequently negative portrayal of Africa by the international press. As a result, basic training for journalists in epidemiology may not be sufficient and alternative channels would need to be explored such as training of media watch groups and human rights organisations.

Given the unique characteristics of the HIV epidemic and conflict-affected and displaced populations, the media have a special obligation to report on this disease in a balanced and non-discriminatory manner that may go beyond the accepted standards of verifying sources. Many of the articles and reports cited in this paper did not provide their sources, the methodologies of collecting the data, or its possible biases.

To ameliorate the situation and avoid such situations in the future, we recommend that the media have HIV data and their interpretation reviewed by technical experts before going to press. Specific training for reporters and editors regarding ethical issues and basic epidemiological methods may help them to better understand the complexity of the situation and report in a more accurate manner. Similar training for media watch groups and human rights organisations may improve the monitoring of such situations and possibly reduce misreporting and subsequent discrimination. More rigorous HIV biological and behavioural surveillance surveys must occur in situations of conflict and displacement as this will provide data for decision makers and help to reduce the likelihood of incorrect, incomplete or misleading statements. The assertion that rigorous data collection is not possible during the acute phase of a crisis or immediately post-conflict is incorrect, as shown by several surveys implemented in such situations: DRC [43], Iraq [48], Kosovo [49], Sudan [50] and Uganda [42]. Humanitarian guidelines should be updated to include details on media relations and responsibilities of humanitarian agencies for reporting on mortality and morbidity; such issues are not included in either the Sphere Project containing the humanitarian charter and minimum standards on disaster response [51] or in the IASC Guidelines for HIV/AIDS Interventions in Emergency Settings [46]. Finally, humanitarian agencies must ensure the data they release are sound and biases are clearly stated. Improved communication with the media will help to ensure more accurate reporting and interpretation.

ACKNOWLEDGEMENTS

The statements in this publication are the views of the authors and do not necessarily reflect the policies or the views of UNICEF or UNHCR.

COMPETING INTERESTS STATEMENT

The authors and their institutions have no financial or other conflicts of interests.

There were no grants or outside funding for this work.

AUTHORS' CONTRIBUTIONS

Author 1 (MLZ) wrote the paper and undertook the literature review.

Author 2 (PS) conceived of the concept, designed the outline, and co-wrote the paper.

Author 3 (FC) participated in the literature review and co-wrote the paper.

REFERENCES

1. Alerta 2005: Informe sobre conflictos, derechos humanos y construcción de paz.[http://www.reliefweb.int/rw/lib.nsf/db900SID/EVIU-6BLCD2?OpenDocument]
2. Refugee Trends: 1 January-30 September 2004. [http://www.unhcr.ch/cgi-bin/texis/vtx/statistics/opendoc.pdf?tbl=STATISTICS&id=41c9863c4]
3. Internal Displacement: Global Overview of Trends and Developments in 2004. [http://www.internal-displacement.org/8025708F004BE3B1/(httpInfoFiles)/D8ECF9078661F05E802570A0003A5081/$file/Global_overview_2004_final_low.pdf]
4. Before It's Too Late: A New Agenda for Public Health. [http://www.conservatives.com/getfile.cfm?file=Policy-PublicHealth-August2003&ref=POLICYDOCUMENT/1664&type=pdf]
5. Coker R: Compulsory screening of immigrants for tuberculosis and HIV. *Bmj.* 2004, 328: 298-300.

6. Coker R: Migration, public health and compulsory screening for TB and HIV. 2003, [http://www.jcwi.org.uk/archives/ukpollcy/Health%20screening%20WP1.pdf] London, Institute for Public Policy Research

7. Schwitzer G: Statement of principles for health care journalists. *PLoS Med.* 2005, 2: e84.

8. Schwitzer G, Mudur G, Henry D, Wilson A, Goozner M, Simbra M, Sweet M, Baverstock KA: What are the roles and responsibilities of the media in disseminating health information?. *PLoS Med.* 2005, 2: e215.

9. Spiegel PB: Differences in world responses to natural disasters and complex emergencies. *Jama.* 2005, 293: 1915-1918.

10. Telemans D: Sudan: HIV/AIDS swell feared when refugees return-UNFPA. [http://www.irinnews.org/print.asp?ReportID=43715]

11. 2003 Global Refugee Trends. 2004 [http://www.unhcr.ch/cgi-bin/texis/vtx/home/opendoc.pdf?tbl=STATISTICS&id=40d015fb4] . Geneva, UNHCR

12. Report on the global AIDS epidemic. July 2004. 2004, UNAIDS, [http://www.unaids.org/bangkok2004/GAR2004_html/GAR2004_00_en.htm]

13. Situation Analysis: Behavioural and Epidemiological Surveys and Response Analysis. HIV/AIDS Strategic Planning Process. Karthoum, Sudan National AIDS Control Program; 2002.

14. With Peace Expected in Sudan, HIV/AIDS Threat Looms. U.N. Wire, 2004. [http://medilinkz.org/news/news2.asp?NewsID=4367]. last accessed: Oct 11, 2005

15. SUDAN: Fears over increase in HIV/AIDS as calm returns to the south. [http://www.plusnews.org/pnprint.asp?ReportID=4083]

16. Sudan Newsletter -Aug 2004. [http://www.unhcr.ch/cgi-bin/texis/vtx/protect/opendoc.htm?tbl=PROTECTION&id=434a73e72]

17. Wallis D: HIV/AIDS soars in war-torn northern Uganda.[http://www.uk.tiscali.com/news/newswire.php/news/reuters/2004/09/27/world/hiv/aidssoarsinwar-tornnorthernuganda.html]

18. Humanitarian Appeal 2005 for Uganda.[http://www.reliefweb.int/w/rwb.nsf/9ca65951ee22658ec125663300408599/1463710c996cedd2c1256f41004aa7f1?OpenDocument]

19. HIV/AIDS Surveillance Report: June 2003. [http://www.health.go.ug/docs/hiv0603.pdf]

20. Wallis D: FEATURE-Refugees from Ugandan war say world forgets them. [http://www.unhcr.ch/cgi-bin/texis/vtx/protect/opendoc.htm?tbl=PROTECTION&id=434a7c142]

21. UN special AIDS envoy in weeklong visit to Uganda.[http://www.reliefweb.int/w/rwb.nsf/437a83f9fa966c40c12564f2004fde87/914c3c39d7e823d1c1256edd0031ee5f?OpenDocument]

22. Northern Uganda under siege from AIDS and rebels: UN special AIDS envoy.[http://www.reliefweb.int/w/rwb.nsf/ 437a83f9fa966c40c12564f2004fde87/b3dc6ae614a87089c1256ee400356466?OpenDocument]

23. Sayagues M: As Uganda AIDS rate falls, orphan ranks swell.[http://www.alertnet.org/thefacts/reliefresources/109266260820.htm]

24. Olara S: Rape: The hidden weapon against women in war-torn northern Uganda. [http://www.unhcr.ch/cgi-bin/texis/vtx/protect/opendoc.htm?tbl=PROTECTION&id=434a7de02]

25. War threatens Uganda Aids success. [http://news.bbc.co.uk/1/hi/world/africa/3694372.stm]

26. Pawns of politics - children, conflict and peace in northern Uganda. [http://www.child-rights.org/PolicyAdvocacy/pahome2.5.nsf/cractionnews/49B263F8D988FD6488256F1C004C960A/$file/Pawns_Of_Politics.pdf]

27. Namutebi J: 50% of freed kids have HIV. [http://www.aegis.com/news/nv/2004/NV040850.html]

28. Wallis D: FEATURE-Children abducted by Uganda rebels face hard times. [http://www.unhcr.ch/cgi-bin/texis/vtx/protect/opendoc.htm?tbl=PROTECTION&id=434a7f3c2]

29. Muleme G: War boosts HIV/AIDS in Northern Uganda. [http://uniformservices.unaids.org/%5Ccountry%5CAfrica%20and%20the%20Middle%20East%5CUganda%5CArticles%5C2004-09-27%20War%20Boosts%20HIV-AIDS%20in%20Northern%20Uganda.txt]

30. Jabweli O: 89% Of Kony Captives Have STDs. [http://www.aegis.com/news/nv/2002/NV020716.html]

31. HIV/AIDS Prevalence in Northern Uganda Almost Double National Average Because of Conflict, Rape as Weapon of War. [http://www.kaisernetwork.org/daily_reports/rep_index.cfm?DR_ID=25951]

32. Guinea: refugee influx adds fuel to AIDS crisis in southeast Guinea.[http://www.aegis.com/news/irin/2004/IR040781.html]

33. Surveillance of mortality during a refugee crisis--Guinea, January-May 2001. *MMWR Morb Mortal Wkly Rep.* 2001, 50: 1029-1032.

34. Lartigue L: National study reveals higher than expected rates of HIV.[http://www.usaid.gov/gn/health/news/021011_hivsurvey]

35. IFJ Declaration of Principles on the Conduct of Journalists. [http://www.ifj.org/default.asp?Issue=ETHICS&Language=EN]

36. Spiegel PB: HIV/AIDS among conflict-affected and displaced populations: dispelling myths and taking action.*Disasters.* 2004, 28: 322-339.

37. Spiegel PB: Using HIV epidemiology to advocate for refugees and returnees.: Apr 14-16; Emory University, Atlanta, GA, USA, 2005.

38. Fabiani M, Accorsi S, Lukwiya M, Rosolen T, Ayella EO, Onek PA, Declich S: Trend in HIV-1 prevalence in an antenatal clinic in North Uganda and adjusted rates for the general female population. *Aids.* 2001, 15: 97-103.

39. Ciantia F: HIV Seroprevalence in Northern Uganda: the Complex Relationship between AIDS and Conflict.[http://www.reliefweb.int/w/rwb.nsf/480fa8736b88bbc3c12564f6004c8ad5/94f00dca140cd12d85256f100072fe29?OpenDocument]

40. Sudan Epidemiological Fact Sheet 2002. [http://www.who.int/GlobalAtlas/predefinedReports/EFS2004/index.asp?strSelectedCountry=SD]

41. Eritrea Epidemiological Fact Sheet 2002. [http://www.who.int/GlobalAtlas/predefinedReports/EFS2004/index.asp?strSelectedCountry=ER]

42. Internally Displaced Camps in Lira and Pader, Northern Uganda: A Baseline Health Survey- Preliminary Report. 2004[http://www.msf.or.jp/news/baseline/Baseline.pdf] Kampala, MSF-H

43. Mortality in the Democratic Republic of Congo: Results from a Nationwide Survey. New York, International Rescue Committee; 2004.

44. Nolen S: Ugandan girl, 16: Abduction, rape, escape ... AIDS.[http://www.theglobeandmail.com/servlet/ArticleNews/TPStory/LAC/20050426/UGANDAAIDS26/TPInternational/?query=ugandan+girl]

45. Oboth T: HIV Prevalence Among IDPs Stands At 35 Percent. The Monitor. [http://www.km-net.org/e-news/2005/jun05/jun07.htm#item5]

46. Guidelines for HIV/AIDS Interventions in Emergency Settings. 2004 [http://www.aidsandemergencies.org/resources.html] IASC Task Force on HIV in Emergencies

47. Mock NB, Duale S, Brown LF, Mathys E, O'Maonaigh H C, Abul-Husn NK, Elliott S: Conflict and HIV: A framework for risk assessment to prevent HIV in conflict-affected settings in Africa. *Emerg Themes Epidemiol.* 2004, 1: 6.

48. Abad-Franch F: Mortality in Iraq. *Lancet.* 2005, 365: 1134.

49. Spiegel PB, Salama P: War and mortality in Kosovo, 1998-99: an epidemiological testimony. *Lancet.* 2000, 355: 2204-2209.

50. Grandesso F, Sanderson F, Kruijt J, Koene T, Brown V: Mortality and malnutrition among populations living in South Darfur, Sudan: results of 3 surveys, September 2004. *Jama.* 2005, 293: 1490-1494.

51. The Sphere Handbook. [http://www.sphereproject.org /handbook /index.htm]

11

COMPARATIVE STUDY ON INTER-ORGANIZATIONAL COOPERATION IN DISASTER SITUATIONS AND IMPACT ON HUMANITARIAN AID OPERATIONS

Mizan Bustanul Fuady Bisri

Department of International Cooperation Policy Studies, Graduate School of International Cooperation Studies, Kobe University, GSICS Building, 2-1 Rokkodai, Nada-ku, Kobe-shi, Hyogo-ken 657-8501, Japan

ABSTRACT

Given the increased numbers of disasters and humanitarian crises which occur in the face of diminishing global resources, the contemporary disaster management and humanitarian fields face greater challenges to optimize cooperation and coordination processes among actors as well as in ensuring and increasing humanitarian aid delivery performance. This research, by using two case studies, will comparatively investigate inter-organizational cooperation and its performance on humanitarian operations during emergency response periods of the West Java Earthquake 2009 and the West Sumatera Earthquake 2009 in Indonesia. A combination of quantitative analysis, social network analysis (SNA), and qualitative analysis is used. SNA has been proven to be instrumental in modeling humanitarian actors' cooperation. In this research, humanitarian operation performance is analyzed in terms of its coherence, coverage, and connectedness. By categorizing results from the SNA in correlation with Gillmann's typology, it is proven that the networks in West Java fit the lead-agency type while in West Sumatra fit the lead-partnership type. In terms of performance, humanitarian operations in West Sumatra performed better in all three criteria compared to those in West Java. Based on the conclusions from this research, recommendations to improve cooperation and coordination among humanitarian actors in disaster situations have been made.

Keywords: Cooperation, Earthquake, Emergency, Humanitarian cluster, Social network analysis

INTRODUCTION: CONTEMPORARY DISCOURSE ON COOPERATION IN DISASTER AND HUMANITARIAN CRISES

The contemporary humanitarian and disaster management field faces several interrelated challenges and problems which make study on coordination and cooperation vital to save as many lives as possible and to lessen impacts. To begin with, there is a growing trend in the number and scale of disasters (UNISDR 2015; Cahill 2012), including that of climate-related and man-made disasters. During the first decade of this century alone, 4000 disasters occurred, significantly jumping from the 900 disasters during the 1970s (Brinkman 2010). In particular, the mortality and economic losses associated with disaster risks in low- and middle-income countries are an uptrend, with the average of economic losses from disasters reaching an average of US$250 billion to US$300 billion each year (UNISDR 2015).

These disasters have happened in the face of diminishing resources for aid relief, humanitarian operations, and reconstruction. For example, there has been a significant reduction in official development assistance from major donors for disaster relief and it is believed that this trend will continue even until the post-2015 period (Cahill 2012). Salvatore (2012) provides more evidence that over the past decade, international governments have spent about $90 billion on humanitarian assistance, although the actual needs were far greater. He further claims that aid spending often covers no more than two thirds of aid needs. At the same time, inter-relationships between multiple humanitarian actors from global to local levels continue to search for optimum cooperation processes and coordination structures (Gillmann 2010; Taylor et al. 2012; Fredriksen 2012) within a complex network of polycentric disaster governance (Lassa 2015) and on how to improve performance on humanitarian aid delivery (Moore et al. 2003; Beck 2006; Tomassini and Wassenhove 2009; Taylor et al. 2012). Therefore, research on networks of actors in a given disaster case and how it affects humanitarian aid operations will contribute to the discourse.

The topic of coordination and cooperation in managing contemporary disasters and other humanitarian emergencies is linked to a broader debate on the relative roles of the state, the private sector, and non-governmental organizations in ensuring collective security. According to Lakoff (2010), the main concern is how lines of responsibility among diverse organizations should be drawn, in terms of both jurisdictional responsibility and technical capacity. Thus, to manage disaster situations, what is in need are either new regulatory norms or new organizational forms, i.e., with the particular role of the government being to design a mechanism in doing so. Furthermore, Jasanoff (2010) also noted a similar notion: contemporary disaster risk and its response have escaped the control of technocratic managers and should be understood more broadly as a problem of democratic governance. Specifically, the ongoing discourse is whether coordination and cooperation during a disaster situation should be centralized or decentralized. Roberts (2010), based on the US Federal Emergency Management Agency, states that governing disaster response requires a networked form of government that links the federal, state, and local levels of the government and private organizations (including non-government organizations (NGOs)). Thus, even though these actors share common goals, they are not subject to direct command; hierarchy alone is a poor tool to respond to disaster. In his view, successful disaster response occurs not through command from above but through loose networks of formal organizations and informal professions that maintain broad agreement about shared goals and responsibilities. Lassa (2015) stated that the observed "tragedy of commons" following the Indian Ocean Tsunami of the 2004 shows the complexity of the network in the post-disaster governance.

In practice, the preceding discourse is evident with the establishment of the humanitarian clusters after the Indian Ocean Tsunami in 2004. The cluster approach is an effort for coordinating humanitarian actors by sector aimed at improving the effectiveness, predictability, and accountability of humanitarian response (Fredriksen 2012). It was launched in 2005 by the Inter-Agency Standing Committee (IASC). A cluster is a group of organizations in a specific sector of humanitarian response that works together to coordinate operational activities (IFRC 2012). It is also a formal humanitarian coordination forum for sectors of the response at the country level (Clarke and Campbell 2015). At the global level, it comprises 11 clusters: (1) camp coordination and management; (2) food security; (3) early recovery; (4) education; (5) emergency shelter; (6) health; (7) nutrition; (8) protection; (9) water, sanitation, and hygiene (WASH); (10) emergency telecommunications; and (11) logistics.

The arrangement of a cluster is applied at both the international level and at the country level in which the latter generally mirrors the global clusters. Indonesia is one of the countries which adopted the cluster approach. The IASC team in Indonesia and the Government of Indonesia produced a national contingency plan in early 2009, a few months before the earthquakes studied here (IASC 2009). However, depending on each country and the emergency itself, some clusters can be combined (IASC 2006) and that the clusters are activated when there is an international response to an emergency upon request of the host government (IFRC 2010).

In each cluster, the IASC has designated a lead agency, i.e., an agency responsible for providing leadership in the cluster which would be accountable to the UN Emergency Relief Coordinator (ERC) through the United Nations Office for Coordinating Humanitarian Affairs (UNOCHA). At the global level, the lead agency manages three areas: standards and policy setting, capacity building, and operational support. The cluster approach encourages the global cluster lead to be proactive in ensuring partners include national and local organizations. Meanwhile, the country-level clusters are tasked with coordinating actors in each sector in specific crisis responses and ensuring that standards for practice set by the global clusters are met during these responses (IASC 2006).

At the country level, national government ministries formally act as co-chairs in cluster meetings, sometimes even acting as cluster co-leads with the appointed lead agency (Fredriksen 2012). The extent to which government ministries participate as true partners in the clusters, however, varies greatly from country to country. In Indonesia, government ministries have been active participants in the cluster-based coordination of humanitarian responses to natural disasters within their territories (Fredriksen 2012). The existence of representatives from the government as co-leads in the cluster is also seen as a source of legitimacy. To this end, whether or not a lead agency in a cluster truly acts as the ultimate leader which governs all government/non-government humanitarian actors is still perceived, by many, as debatable. Furthermore, in reality, even within the same country during the same disaster, cluster hubs can be set up in several locations and a lead agency may be appointed differently in each hub or administrative boundary.

Specific to the IASC clusters, Clarke and Campbell (2015) state that the term "coordination" inside the humanitarian sector often describes loosely a variety of different kinds of relationships and coined that in reality, there are three levels of coordination between complete independence and full merger during humanitarian operations, i.e., communication, alignment and collaboration. According to their research, humanitarian clusters generally fall in to the "alignment level," i.e., organizations retain a high degree of independence but may adjust their activities to create a more effective response on the basis of activities of other organizations. The research was able to showcase that generally, cluster members decided to join a coordinated response since the benefits (access to guidance and information, opportunities to build relationships and see the bigger picture, as well as increased legitimacy for activities) outweigh the cost (time, loss of autonomy, and competitive advantage). However, their concept of coordination levels will not be able to visualize the actual network of multiple organizations engaged in emergency response of a humanitarian crisis. In addition, their work is also limited to the observation of the cluster's work regarding joint strategy development and joint assessments and thus does not looked into actual relationship of cluster members in the implementation of emergency response activities.

Gillmann (2010), on the other hand, used insights from the Darfur Crisis and Indian Ocean Tsunami in 2004 and proposed four typologies for cooperation of humanitarian efforts, i.e., Loose Alliance, Orchestrated Alliance, Lead Partnership, and Lead Agency, whereas the illustration and brief description of each type can be seen in Fig. 1. Among this typology, Gillmann argues that a lead-agency network is the best pattern for inter-organizational cooperation at the time of a disaster, to best meet the standard performance of humanitarian operations. The proposition of the typology is very important and, as she herself suggests, needs to be tested in other cases. Even though her work also originates from network theory, her approach is fully qualitative and only incorporates global humanitarian actors and does not incorporate local actors, which in reality also participate in the humanitarian efforts.

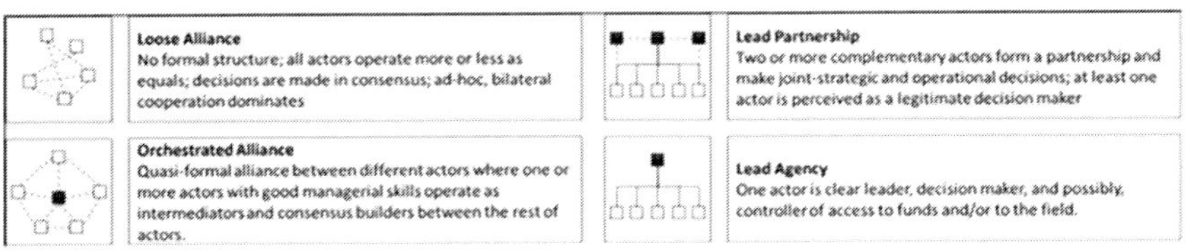

Figure 1. Typology for inter-agency coordination of humanitarian efforts at the time of disaster (Gillmann, 2010)

Therefore, in this paper, the author would like to test the typology proposed by Gillmann (2010) using a larger dataset of actors. For testing, at least two comparable case studies are needed. Accordingly, this paper will comparatively study inter-organizational cooperation of emergency response in two earthquakes in Indonesia, i.e., the West Java Earthquake on 2 September 2009 and the West Sumatra Earthquake on 30 September

2009, and their impact on humanitarian aid delivery operations. Both earthquakes happened at nearly the same time, in the same country, and fall within the same emergency level based on the Indonesian IASC Contingency Plan (IASC 2009). In addition, both earthquakes in their occurrence serve as an early test to the newly established Indonesian Disaster Management system of Law 24/2007 and humanitarian clusters adopted by global humanitarian actors as defined by UN Resolution 46/182. The author agrees with DARA (2010) and Wilson (2010) that both earthquakes provide a stark comparison of response after natural disasters in the same country. The cases are expected to show the difference of network creation, given the different trajectories of political decision of the government in responding to each earthquake, particularly on perception of the strength of the state and decision to activate humanitarian clusters, which include that of international organization.

OBJECTIVES AND RESEARCH QUESTIONS

In general, this paper aims to contribute to the theoretical discourse as well as practical queries in the subject of inter-organizational cooperation arrangement at the time of disaster and humanitarian crisis. The specific research goal is to comparatively investigate inter-organizational cooperation and its humanitarian operation performance during the emergency response of the West Java Earthquake 2009 and the West Sumatra Earthquake 2009. Accordingly, the research objectives include the following: (1) examine the practices of inter-organizational cooperation during the emergency response of both earthquakes; (2) model the networks of inter-organizational cooperation during the emergency response of both earthquakes and explore their characteristics, i.e., by using social network analysis (SNA) performed using UCINET version 6.532 (Borgatti et al. 2002) and categorized based on Gillmann's typology (Gillmann 2010); (3) identify and compare performance of humanitarian aid operations resulting from the given network of actors and its cooperation, i.e., by using some criteria conceptualized by Beck (2006); and (4) identify policy implications and their practical relevance to the humanitarian field, e.g., in the context of Indonesia, Southeast Asia, and international humanitarian system in general.

To meet the aforementioned objectives, the following research questions are addressed: (1) In what ways did inter-organizational cooperation function and create networks during the emergency response of both earthquakes? (2) What were the characteristics of cooperation in humanitarian operations within the networks during the emergency response of both earthquakes? (3) Which type of network performed better in the emergency response of both earthquakes?

METHODOLOGY: SOCIAL NETWORK ANALYSIS AND DATA COLLECTION METHOD

This research includes both quantitative and qualitative approaches. SNA has been chosen as the main approach in this study due to its ability to represent the structure of relations between actors and to analyze a large number of relations within a network (Prell 2012). In short, SNA is the study of the structural relationships among interacting network members (individual, organizations, etc.) and of how those relationships produce varying effects (Varda et al. 2009).

In regard to the utilization of SNA in disaster and humanitarian studies, a variety of research has been conducted. Some research applies SNA for analyzing the individual level of network in disasters, while others are more concerned with organizational issues. Some individual-level research of SNA may give explanations of who is at risk, who has more capacity to recover (Haines et al. 1996), and how individual strategies recover after a disaster (Hulbert et al. 2005). Other research focuses on the organizational level of SNA to analyze inter-organizational cooperation related to a disaster. For example, in organizational-level research on developed countries, Kapucu et al. (2010) give a broader view of aid and emergency response following Hurricane Katrina and by employing full quantitative SNA techniques, they successfully show that further investment in the State Government is needed because it proved to be the key actor. Other studies were able to explain factors which decide organizations' motivations to create, maintain, dissolve, and reconstitute the inter-organizational links during Hurricane Katrina by comparing results from manual and computed social network analysis (Varda et al. 2009). However, both studies have made little contribution to the greater discourse on how to improve global cooperation for humanitarian efforts at the time of disaster, since they primarily concentrate on the case from a developed country, in which there is not much cooperation among international and local actors. Alternatively, another example came from the SNA model of inter-organizational cooperation during the Great East Japan Earthquake and Tsunami 2011 (Bisri 2016). Using the Japan case, Bisri (2016) was able to showcase that multiple actors engage during the emergency response at the time of the 2011 tsunami, ranging from traditional and non-traditional humanitarian actors. However, the effect of the network to the humanitarian operation performance was not within the scope of this paper.

Few studies used SNA to analyze disaster in developing and least-developed countries. Among them, Moore et al. (2003) examine the role of network centrality in humanitarian operations following the 2003 Mozambique Flood in which over 49 countries and 30 international NGOs were involved in the relief effort. They tried to analyze whether organizations with the potential to connect with a number of other organizations were involved in higher impact projects. As a result, they found that international NGOs were highly central to the network of collaborators and that centrality measurement result did affect the number of the project's beneficiaries. On the other hand, Kumar (2011) analyzed inter-organizational networks during the emergency response of the 2007 Peru Earthquake. By analyzing the network of 300 organizations using SNA, he argues that there was a pattern in the collaboration behavior of organizations involved in the earthquake relief effort, i.e., large international organizations played a more central role in the overall relief effort. In addition, he compares the behavior of collaborations at various humanitarian clusters as well as between three municipalities affected.

In Indonesian context, Lassa (2010) uses SNA to identify the relation among institutional features in disaster risk management of Indonesia. He maps out which regulation is the most referred to by the government and which actor is the most central in disaster risk management in Indonesia. Furthermore, by analyzing the polycentric governance using SNA of the post-disaster stage of the Indian Ocean Tsunami 2004, he shows important features of the network of disaster actors, i.e., the degrees of separation on the post-disaster network reflect the "small world" realities, existence of loops in the network that reflect the tendency of some actors not to cooperate, and importance of certain hubs in the network and the humanitarian cluster, while other actors make scattered single principal-client links (Lassa 2015).

In this research, SNA is being performed using the UCINET version 6.532 (Borgatti et al. 2002) to produce network graphs of both cases and analyzes the complete network structure by performing egocentric measurements on degree centrality and betweenness centrality, i.e., which are common disaster research (Moore et al. 2003; Varda et al. 2009; Kapucu et al. 2010; Kumar 2011; Bisri 2016). Degree centrality is a measurement of an actor's level of involvement or activity in the network, and it calculates the number of immediate contacts an actor has in a network (Prell 2012, pp. 96–103). Betweenness centrality is a measurement of to what extent an actor is located in the direct path of exchange between two other actors in the network (Wasserman and Faust 1994). It looks at how often an actor rests between two other actors, i.e., calculates how many times an actor sits on the geodesic (the shortest path) linking two other actors together. The degree centrality and betweenness centrality are the two common measurements used as a proxy of an actor's relative position in the coordination structure. In addition, sociometric measurements were also performed, i.e., density and clique identification. Density refers to the proportion of ties in a network that are actually present, and it counts how many actual ties exist in a network and expresses this number as a proportion of the potential ties that could exist in the network (Prell 2012, pp. 166–167). Lastly, a clique is an informal grouping of actors in the network which indicates the strong cohesiveness in the subgroup; it refers to subgroups of actors consisting of mutual ties (Prell 2012, p. 155). In a disaster situation, a clique is subsets of organizations that develop recurring patterns of interaction (Scott 2000).

In this research, the "nodes" represented in the SNA model are organizations performing emergency response activities, which range from national and local government units, international NGO, local NGO, and agencies of the UN, while the "ties" that link two nodes represent joint delivery of emergency response activities, i.e., combine all possible cooperation from financial support, human resource mobilization, and in-kind contribution. All the measurements were done in "valued" and "directed" mode, meaning that frequency and direction of relationship among actors are detected and become sensitive to each SNA measurement. In the model, the valued network gives weight to each tie; thus, if a tie appears to be thicker, it means more than one cooperation (joint implementation of emergency response) were being done by those connected two organizations.

Given the result of SNA, the model of networks from both cases will be contrasted with the typology suggested by Gillmann (2010). To bridge these two approaches, Gillmann's typology of networks (i.e., loose alliance, orchestrated alliance, lead partnership, and lead agency) is used so that the result of egocentric measurements through SNA (degree centrality, betweenness, closeness, and eigenvector centrality) of networks in both cases, drawn in principal-component network mode, will fall into one category of the typology. The use of principal-component is essential to bridge the visualization of SNA with the typology of Gillmann, as the novelty of this paper.

To further analyze how the inter-organizational cooperation network affects humanitarian aid operation performance, several criteria provided by Beck (2006) will be used. There are seven criteria in evaluating humanitarian action: relevance or appropriateness, connectedness, coherence, coverage, efficiency, effectiveness, and impact. It is positioned as the continuation of DAC criteria in evaluating humanitarian action, whereas Beck (2006) adds another three criteria to merge with the original five criteria and thus the seven aforementioned criteria. Given the nature of this research, which is a more "system-wide" analysis, the most appropriate criteria to assess humanitarian aid operations in both West Java and West Sumatra Earthquakes 2009 are coherence, coverage, and connectedness.

According to Beck (2006), coherence refers to the need to assess humanitarian policies and actions taken by actors, to ensure that there is consistency and that of overlap in actions was avoided. Thus, there will be two indicators in measuring coherence, i.e., (1) existence and timeliness of joint-assessment and/or joint-humanitarian action plan and (2) qualitative performance coordination mechanism and information sharing, while the criterion of coverage concerns on the need to reach major population groups facing life-threatening suffering wherever they are. Thus, indicators of coverage are the total and percentage of beneficiaries, geographical, and timeliness distribution of humanitarian aid in clusters. Connectedness refers to the need to ensure that activities of a short-term emergency nature are carried out in a context that takes longer term and interconnected problems into account. Thus, existence and timeliness of the Damage and Loss Assessment (DALA), Human Recovery Need Assessment (HRNA), and Post-Disaster Need Assessment (PDNA) documents, as well as the continuation of organizational presence from emergency response to the recovery phase, will be used as indicators.

A desk study has been completed, which gathered information regarding emergency response activities in both earthquakes from Situation Reports published by BNPB (National Disaster Management Agency), Indonesian Ministry of Health, and United Nations Office for Coordination of Humanitarian Affairs (UNOCHA), as well as the 3W Matrix (who is doing what and where) compiled by the humanitarian partners. In creating the dataset for SNA on both cases, information gathered from the desk study is reorganized into a "database of emergency response activities." In the database, each activity contains the following fields: organization name and type, location of activity, type of activity, sector in which the project is classified (e.g., shelter), organization(s) responsible for the activity, description, progress of activity, classification of financier/executor, and beneficiaries. Given the information compiled in the database, a relational matrix (proxy of cooperation) of emergency response is developed. Activities included in the dataset are those implemented during the emergency response period, by two or more organizations. An activity that is said to be implemented by a single organization and/or did not clearly state its implementing partner will not be included in the dataset of input to the SNA. The sample of emergency response activities is classified into 12 groups, in relation to humanitarian cluster arrangement, as follows: food distribution (FD); non-food item distribution (NFI); health services (HS); disaster impact rapid assessment (RA); search and rescue (SAR); coordination and communication (CC); cash support and donation (CD); education in emergency time (Edu); water, sanitation, and hygiene (WASH) promotion; shelter (Shelter); logistics (LOG); and others.

In the West Java case, the official emergency period was dated from 2 to 16 September 2009. However, in reality, the response was performed for the whole of September; thus, all emergency response activities until 30 September 2009 were included in the dataset, i.e., accounted for taken into consideration. On the other hand, the official emergency response for the West Sumatra Earthquake 2009 was defined for 1 month. Therefore, activities dated from 30 September until 30 October 2009 were included in the dataset, i.e., accounted for 431 sample of emergency response activities.

The second method of data collection is through semi-structured interviews to key actors identified from the dataset and first iteration of the SNA modeling, i.e., can be said as key organizations. For each organization, author interviewed resource persons who came from ministries of the central government (e.g., National Disaster Management Agency-BNPB), agencies of West Java and West Sumatra Provincial Governments (e.g., Local Disaster Management Office-BPBD), agencies at local governments in affected areas, agencies of the United Nations (e.g., UNOCHA) international and local NGOs, and university/research institutions. Resource persons interviewed are those who are directly involved as responder in the emergency response of the earthquake or knowledgeable of the case. During the interviews, confirmation to the initial findings of preliminary SNA results was addressed to resource persons. In addition, they were asked about the questions related to the humanitarian operation performance (coherence, coverage, and connectedness) of the earthquakes.

THE WEST JAVA AND WEST SUMATRA EARTHQUAKES 2009, AFTERMATH, AND RESPONSE

The West Java Earthquake 2009 occurred on Wednesday, September 2, at 14:55 local time with a magnitude 7.3 on the Richter scale and epicenter located 142 km southwest of Tasikmalaya City, at a depth of 30 km below sea level. This earthquake occurred due to the subduction of plates between the Indo-Australian plate and the Eurasian plate, in the southern part of Java Island. Fifteen municipalities were affected, with 81 people dead, 1287 people seriously injured, and 50,964 households or 194,805 people displaced (Bappenas 2009).

The first official statement was delivered by the West Java Governor at 22:30 on the same day in the form of West Java Governor Decree SK 360/kep.1260-Hukham/2009 regarding Emergency Response Status. It was immediately followed by the formation of Satkorlak West Java (Coordinating Task Force for Disaster Response), and the first emergency response team was dispatched by the provincial government.[1] The response phase was set for a 2-week period, and the priorities were as follows: (1) organizing disaster relief, (2) conducting a study and rapid assessment for disaster impact and victim search and rescue, (3) conducting rescue and evacuation, (4) fulfillment of basic needs, (5) protection of vulnerable groups, and (6) restoration of immediate infrastructure and facilities.[2] Similarly, activation of emergency response activities by agencies at the municipality government level also took place. The central government, BNPB in particular, supported the decision taken by its provincial counterpart, and it sent an assessment and quick response team to West Java and connected them with the other line ministries and agencies, such as the Ministry of Health, army, and police. On 3 September 2009, President Yudhoyono, Minister of Health, Minister of Social Affairs, and Head of BNPB, visited the affected areas.[3]

Meanwhile, UN agencies held a coordination meeting and sent their own joint-assessment team by 3 September 2009, 05:00 in the morning.[4] The purpose was to determine whether they would intervene, i.e., since at that time, there was no formal contact made with the government.[5] In parallel, some local and international NGOs, independently or jointly, started to enter the field and perform immediate rescue activities and disaster-impact assessments. Coordination between government-led humanitarian efforts and those of UN agencies were made later on 5 September 2009, where BNPB and UNOCHA facilitated meetings to update the joint assessments.[6]

Within the first 72 h, the government claimed that the local and national governments had enough resources to respond to the crisis. President Yudhoyono even stated that international assistance was not required and the government remained capable of handling the emergency response given the approximately US$530,000 financial support from the central government.[7]In the subsequent process, the government insisted, under assumption of West Java's capacity and its proximity to Jakarta, that the emergency response could be handled by joint efforts from central, provincial, and local governments, in addition to national and local NGOs on the field. The Indonesian government was keen to demonstrate that 5 years after the Aceh Tsunami, they could respond to a disaster efficiently and effectively (DARA 2010). The earthquake was perceived as a time to show the international community that Indonesia could single-handedly manage the emergency response of a medium-large disaster.[8]

However, the shortage of manpower and organizational capacity in some sectors resulted in slow progress in the emergency response. In terms of organizational capacity, the absence of BPBD (Provincial Disaster Management Agency) in West Java could be the factor, which was actually mandated by Law 24/2007 on Disaster Management. Another factor that could be overlooked by the government was that the emergency response periods coincided with the holiday season of Eid al-Fitr, leaving the capacity to respond lower than initial expectations.[9] In the health and social sectors, the shortage of manpower was compensated through the network of national and local health agencies with numerous universities which have medical faculty. Many of the doctors and nurses volunteered during the emergency response. In addition, the Ministry of Health and Ministry of Social Affairs also has their own national volunteer networks, which were mobilized from neighboring regions. In other sectors, gaps were identified for rapid assessment, water sanitation, and temporary shelter provision, given the lack of skills and manpower from local governments and local NGOs. Therefore, after 1 week, BNPB made a statement that in-country assistance, whether from national or international organizations, was welcomed and would be coordinated under the leadership of BNPB and Satkorlak West Java.[10]

Given the change in the BNPB statement, two UNOCHA staff members were deployed to Satkorlak West Java to help the coordination with humanitarian organizations in the affected areas. Thus, it was agreed that four clusters would be activated through coordination with UNOCHA and Satkorlak West Java, i.e., education and water-sanitation clusters were led by UNICEF, the shelter cluster was led by the International Federation of Red Cross (IFRC), and early recovery (including disaster impact assessment) was led by the United Nations Development Program (UNDP). In addition, UNOCHA routinely convened UN-NGO-Donor Coordination meetings for emergency response of the earthquake. The other humanitarian sectors and health services as well as search and rescue remained under the complete leadership of the government with support from local/national NGOs. To complement these changes, the provincial government issued two additional new decrees, i.e., the formation of the Emergency Response Team for West Java Earthquake (No. 360.05/Kep. 1263-Hukham/2009) and the Allocation of Emergency Response Funds (No.900/Kep 1265-Keu/2009).

In total, during the emergency response periods of the West Java Earthquake 2009, there were 343 activities identified. Distribution of activities can be seen below. The delivery of NFI (e.g., blanket, tent, mats) dominated the emergency response (64 activities), followed by health services and cash donation (each 51 activities), see Fig. 2.

The West Sumatra Earthquake 2009 occurred on 30 September 2009, 17:16 local time, and measured 7.6 on the Richter scale with the epicenter located 45 km southwest of Padang City. As an aftermath, the earthquake caused 1117 deaths and 2902 injuries (BNPB 2009). In addition, there were 250,000 families (around 1,250,000 people or 25 % from total West Sumatra population) being internally displaced and affected by the earthquake. In total, there were 249,653 houses damaged, i.e., 114,797 homes severely damaged, 67,198 moderately damaged, and another 67,658 lightly damaged (BNPB 2009).

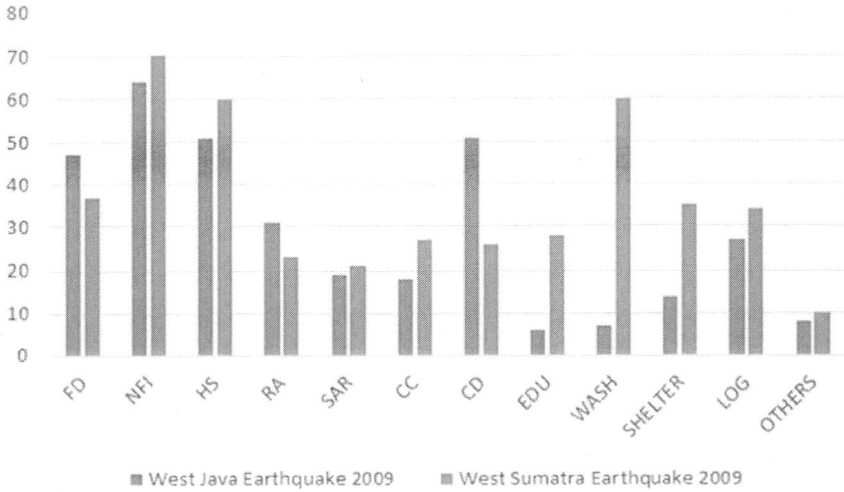

Figure 2. Number of emergency response activities in both earthquakes (Source: author's calculation from various situation reports)

Since the West Sumatra Earthquake 2009 occurred less than a month after the one in West Java, it placed a second wave of demands on the Indonesian disaster management authorities. Given this situation, after a high-level ministerial meeting, BNPB announced that emergency response to the earthquake and relief provisions would take place for 2 months,[11] i.e., although it was later reduced to 1 month given the performance of emergency response activities from both local and international organizations.[12] Along with the decision from BNPB, President Yudhoyono announced that the Government of Indonesia welcomed international assistance but needed to be coordinated through the government.[13]

In the first 24 h, different from the approach in West Java, the Governor of West Sumatra, Satkorlak West Sumatra, and under approval from BNPB, invited the UNOCHA to become their counterpart in managing coordination and cooperation for humanitarian aid delivery in both emergency response and early recovery[14]; even the governor provided an office for UNOCHA in his residence (DARA 2010). As an immediate response, a joint mission from the UN, led by UNOCHA and comprised of officers from FAO, UNDP, UNFPA, UNICEF, and WHO, was deployed to Padang City within the first 18 h. Later on, the UN mission was empowered by the arrival of the UNDAC team (UN Disaster Assessment and Coordination). Also, in the evening of the quake day, BNPB coordinated deployment of its own personnel and other national ministries; they reached West Sumatra in the dawn of 1 October 2009 and were perceived timely by the provincial government and its city counterpart.[15] On the other hand, some international NGOs independently also started to send their teams to West Sumatra, in particular those affiliated with the ECB Consortium, which in this earthquake was led by Mercy Corps. It seems that local authorities did not want to repeat the same mistakes made in West Java.

Although it was not fully operational within the first week, less than 48 h after the earthquake, it was agreed that the humanitarian cluster approach would be activated.[16] There were ten humanitarian clusters: (1) agriculture with FAO and UNDP as lead agencies; (2) coordination and safety and early recovery with UNDP and Bappeda West Sumatra as lead agencies; (3) education with UNICEF, Save the Children (STC), and Education Agency of West Sumatra as lead agencies; (4) food and nutrition with WFP and UNICEF as lead agencies; (5) health with WHO and Health Agency of West Sumatra as lead agencies; (6) logistic and telecommunications with WFP as lead agency; (7) protection with UNICEF, UNFPA, and Social Agency of West Sumatra as lead agencies; (8) shelter with IFRC as lead agency; (9) water, sanitation, and hygiene (WASH) with UNICEF as lead agency; and (10) emergency telecommunications with WFP as lead agency. Members of each cluster were comprised of both local and international actors.

During emergency response periods in West Sumatra, 431 sample activities were identified, which took place from 30 September to 30 October 2009. As can be seen from Fig. 2, activities related to NFI distribution to disaster victims and refugees ranked the highest (70 activities), followed by health service and WASH (each 60 activities). Variations of activities not categorized in the preceding 11 groups include debris removal activity, a cash-for-work program, distribution of disaster-risk-reduction booklets, and economic recovery programs for small-medium enterprises.

NETWORK OF INTER-ORGANIZATIONAL COOPERATION IN WEST JAVA AND WEST SUMATRA

As can be seen in Fig. 3, in the 2009 West Java Earthquake, there were 192 organizations involved in emergency response, and most organizations were national/local NGO (50) and local government agencies (45). There were also 22 international NGOs identified, of which some of them were already in West Java due to their operations in the recovery of the 2006 Pangandaran Tsunami. Also, there were 21 universities involved, most of which were represented by their medical faculty in the health cluster. There were 18 agencies from provincial governments and 10 agencies/ministries from central governments. In addition, 16 private companies contributed by giving cash or in-kind assistance. In terms of UN agency deployment, there were eight, and only two foreign government agencies involved. On the other hand, in West Sumatra, there were 223 organizations involved. Record showed involvement of 63 international NGOs (28 %) and 40 local government agencies (18 %). The number of foreign governments which provided assistance was also quite high, accounting for 35 agencies (16 %). In terms of national/local NGOs, there were 29 organizations (13 %). On the other hand, 17 agencies and ministries of the central government also intervened directly (8 %), and so did 18 agencies of the provincial government (8 %). Lastly, there were 12 agencies of the UN (5 %), three universities (only 1 %), and six private companies (only 3 %) involved.

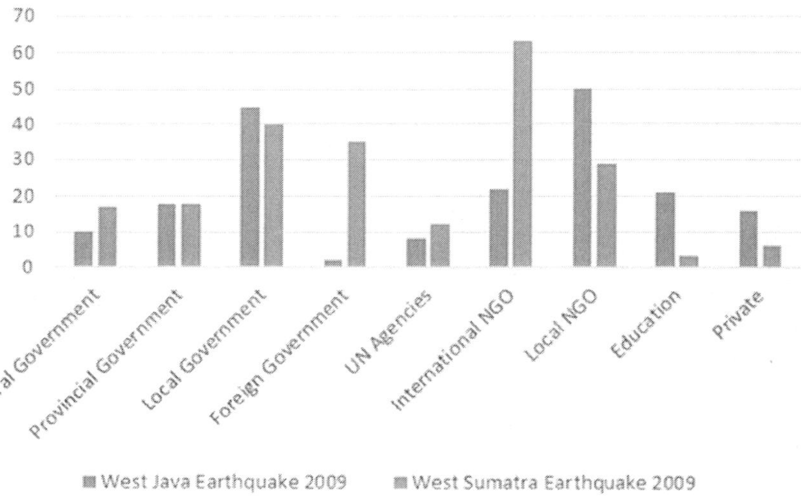

Figure 3. Number of agencies involved during emergency response of both earthquakes (Source: author's calculation from various situation reports)

Based on the data of actors and emergency response activities, network analysis was performed. The network in West Java comprises 192 nodes (identified actors) and 729 ties which resulted from 343 identified activities, while the network in West Sumatra comprises 223 nodes and 865 ties resulted from 431 identified activities. Furthermore, calculation on degree and betweenness centrality of all actors in both networks was performed, and the result of the top-15 actors with the highest centrality can be found in Fig. 4.

WEST JAVA EARTHQUAKE 2009

DEGREE CENTRALITY				BETWEENESS CENTRALITY			
Rank	Organization	Degree	Normalized Degree	Rank	Organization	Betweeness	Normalized Betweeness
1	Satkorlak West Java	128.000	6.702	1	Satkorlak West Java	25322.410	69.293
2	BNPB	52.000	2.723	2	BPBD Cianjur	4540.551	12.512
3	Dinkes West Java	45.000	2.356	3	Dinkes West Java	2126.770	5.860
4	UN OCHA	42.000	2.199	4	BNPB	1608.035	4.409
5	PMI	33.000	1.728	5	PMI	1453.605	4.006
5	Kemenkes	33.000	1.728	6	Oxfam	834.854	2.300
7	PKPU	26.000	1.361	7	ITB	824.974	2.273
8	UNICEF	23.000	1.204	8	UNICEF	774.560	2.134
9	BPBD Cianjur	21.000	1.099	9	Disdik West Java	654.177	1.803
10	WVI	17.000	0.890	10	Jabar Peduli	636.871	1.760
	YTBI	17.000	0.890	11	UN OCHA	603.093	1.662
12	Oxfam	16.000	0.838	12	PKPU	593.128	1.635
13	TNI	14.000	0.733	13	Kemenkes	410.452	1.131
14	WFP	13.000	0.681	14	ASB	362.113	0.998
15	CRS	12.000	0.628	15	Satkorlak Tasikmalaya	358.563	0.988
15	Hope	12.000	0.628				
15	Basarnas	12.000	0.628				

WEST SUMATRA EARTHQUAKE 2009

DEGREE CENTRALITY				BETWEENESS CENTRALITY			
Rank	Organization	Degree	Normalized Degree	Rank	Organization	Betweeness	Normalized Betweeness
1	UN OCHA	64.000	4.762	1	IOM	4254.889	11.601
2	UNICEF	53.000	3.943	2	IFRC	3091.425	8.430
3	IOM	40.000	2.976	3	BNPB	2951.556	8.054
4	BNPB	39.000	2.902	4	Satkorlak West Sumatra	2851.284	7.775
5	Satkorlak West Sumatra	34.000	2.530	5	UNICEF	2806.304	7.652
5	IFRC	34.000	2.530	6	WHO	2093.680	5.709
7	STC	33.000	2.455	7	UN OCHA	1921.928	4.968
8	UNDP	27.000	2.009	8	Kemenkes	1758.225	4.794
8	WFP	27.000	2.009	9	STC	1681.196	4.584
10	Bappeda West Sumatra	25.000	1.860	10	UNDP	1489.933	4.063
11	UNFPA	22.000	1.637	11	PMI	936.380	2.553
12	WHO	21.000	1.563	12	CRS	772.258	2.106
13	Kemenkes	20.000	1.488	13	FAO	710.395	1.937
14	SIDA	19.000	1.414	14	Mercy Corps	659.186	1.798
15	FAO	18.000	1.339	15	Bappeda West Sumatra	648.318	1.768
15	Bappenas	18.000	1.339				

Figure 4. Result of degree centrality and betweenness centrality measurements (Source: author's analysis)

In comparing networks created in both earthquakes to fit in Gillmann's typology, the principal-component-mode visualization was performed, based on the value of degree and betweenness centrality above. This step visualizes the result of degree and betweenness centrality measurements in a graph and clarifies better which organizations served as leader(s) or as follower(s) in the network. As can be seen in Fig. 5, the network in West Java fits the lead-agency type of network in Gillmann's typology, with one provincial government body ranked significantly as the network's leader having clear authority as a decision maker and controlled access to the field, which was also supported closely by BNPB, the central government. At the same time, several organizations leading four clusters in West Java had a distant position with the lead agency, i.e., PMI (Indonesian Red Cross), IFRC, UNICEF, Ministry of Health (*Kemenkes*), and Health Agency (*Dinkes*) of West Java. Based on degree centrality measurement, as can be seen in Fig. 4, the network was very centralized and linked to Satkorlak West Java with its normalized degree centrality 6.702. As a national agency, BNPB thus ranked second in terms of degree centrality, which mainly supported and supervised Satkorlak West Java, since the province did not have their own BPBD. Dinkes West Java also ranked third with high degree centrality since the agency mostly bridged the Kemenkes and health agencies at the municipality level. Afterwards, UNOCHA ranked fifth in terms of centrality due to its network with INGOs and local NGOs and the late introduction of cluster arrangement. There are two national NGOs which scored high in terms of degree centrality, i.e., PMI, ranked fifth, and PKPU, ranked seventh. PMI has pre-established branches at provincial and local levels, while PKPU was involved in several humanitarian clusters at one time.

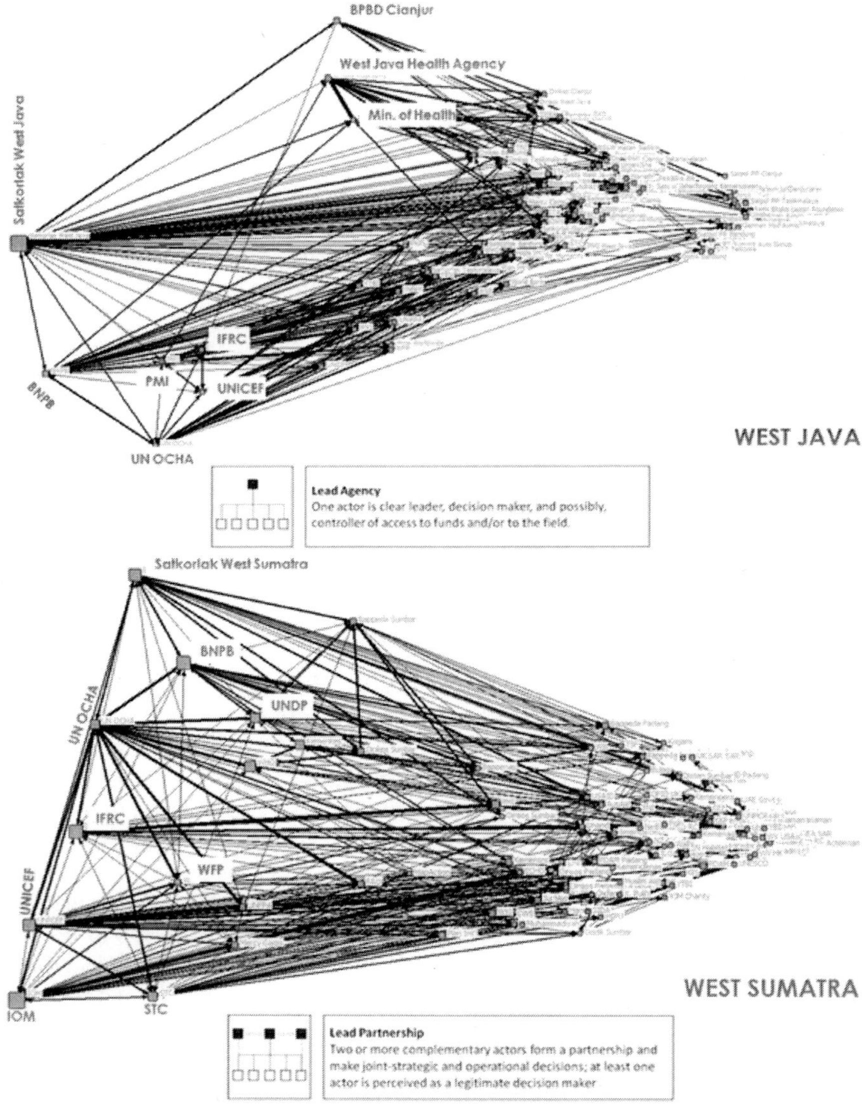

Figure 5. Comparison of principal-component networks in West Java and West Sumatra (Source: author's analysis)

While viewed from the principal-component network mode, the network of actors in West Sumatra fits the lead-partnership type. As can be seen from Fig. 5, Satkorlak West Sumatra, UNOCHA, UNICEF, IOM, IFRC, BNPB, STC, WFP, and UNDP are identified as principals of the network. Those organizations were the focal points of the network, BPBD West Sumatra, BNPB, and UNOCHA, with the remaining organizations all humanitarian cluster lead agencies. It is seeming that the "cluster approach" did function in orchestrating emergency response during the West Sumatra Earthquake 2009. In addition to UNOCHA, BNPB, and Satkorlak West Sumatra, among the top-15 organizations with the highest degree centrality, almost all of them are the lead agency in each cluster. As the betweenness measurement reveals, organizations which play an important role in bridging other humanitarian actors ranked within the top ten. Most notably is IOM, which provided ground-transportation support for all organizations to deliver food, non-food items, and any other disaster relief aid to the affected areas. In the process, IOM later joined WFP to share the leading role in the logistic cluster. It was then followed by UNICEF, which bridged many members in education, food and nutrition, protection, and WASH clusters. Specifically, in the health cluster, the WHO also played an instrumental role in bridging international NGOs and local organizations through the Ministry of Health and Health Agency of West Sumatra and thus ranked third in terms of betweenness centrality. As for IFRC, it had an instrumental role in bridging PMI with other Red Cross teams.

As a whole, the network density in West Java is 5.005 with 37 inter-organizational cliques detected, while in West Sumatra, the network density is 5.259 with 40 inter-organizational cliques detected. Clique analysis was completed with a minimum set size of four organizations, performed in directed measurement. Although the number of cliques is somewhat similar, the membership characteristic shows some differences. In the West Java case, out of 37 cliques identified, 10 of them purely consist of national-local organizations. Furthermore, 8 out of those 10 cliques are related to emergency response in the health cluster, which as described in the "The West Java and West Sumatra Earthquakes 2009, aftermath, and response" section initially did not invite activation of the health cluster under international humanitarian partner. The remaining 27 cliques are characterized as having a combination of at least national government agencies (e.g., BNPB, Basarnas, Indonesian Army, or Ministry of Health), at least one agency of the UN or international NGO, and at least one agency of the West Java provincial government or national NGO. On the other hand, in the case of West Sumatra, only two cliques that purely consist of national-local agencies, i.e., a clique of BNPB, West Sumatra Province, Indonesian Police, and Indonesian Army, as well as a clique of the Ministry of Education, West Sumatra Education Agency, Bandung Institute of Technology, and Andalas University. The rest of the 38 cliques are a combination of international and national/local organizations, with at least one out of the two cluster lead identified in the clique.

It should be noted that although both provinces have a similar level of organizational capacity, a different approach was taken in terms of how to orchestrate coordination and cooperation of emergency response and the statement of welcoming international assistance. By saying organizational capacity, it mainly refers to the fact that by September 2009, both provincial governments had not formed their BPBD and at the municipality level, their BPBDs were neither non-existence nor still infant. In West Java, BNPB supported centralization of coordination to Satkorlak West Java and initially neither requested for international assistance nor encouraged activation of the humanitarian cluster system, while in West Sumatra, from the very beginning, the provincial government and BNPB welcomed international assistance and instantly agreed on activating the humanitarian cluster system. Consequently, Satkorlak West Sumatra, under supervision from BNPB, partnered with UNOCHA and other humanitarian clusters lead agencies.

HUMANITARIAN AID OPERATION PERFORMANCE IN WEST JAVA AND WEST SUMATRA

Humanitarian operations in West Sumatra performed better in all criteria of coherence, coverage, and connectedness compared to West Java. As noted by Pranoto (2011), the UNDAC team praised Indonesia's capability in managing evacuation stages during emergency response in West Sumatra. While commenting on response in West Java, UNOCHA (2009) and DARA (2010) called the West Java Earthquake 2009 as a "forgotten disaster." In terms of coherence, West Sumatra's network was more cohesive, as indicated from the calculated network density (5.259) and number of cliques found (37). All nine humanitarian clusters were activated faster, within 48 h, and legitimate, whereas humanitarian clusters were clearly being led by government agencies and UN agencies/INGOs, as in contrast with the four clusters activation 1 week after the earthquake with unclear appointments of government agencies to become counterpart of the cluster's lead agency in West Java. There were also more joint assessments identified, as opposed to the many uncoordinated assessments with delay in the official assessment found in West Java. Humanitarian aid operation in West Sumatra is also more coherent with the existence of the West Sumatra Earthquake 2009 Humanitarian Response Plan, whereas no similar document existed in West Java. These situations are indeed affected greatly by the initial statement of the government in responding to both earthquakes. In West Java, as mentioned by Wilson (2010), many NGOs felt confused and hesitant to intervene. While in West Sumatra, many actors appreciated the coordination of the humanitarian operations.

Humanitarian operations in West Sumatra also performed better from coverage criterion. During the first 72 h until the end of the first week, SAR activities in West Java ended with inadequate manpower to continue the remaining relief activities, while such a situation was not found in

West Sumatra since, at the same period, international SAR teams already arrived and provided additional manpower. In West Sumatra, the emergency response was finished earlier than scheduled, shortened from 2 to 1 month, given the fast distribution of aid, while in West Java, it was extended from 2 weeks to 1 month. The time when external emergency relief started and the time needed until it reached beneficiaries were also faster than those in West Java (BNPB 2009), i.e., 4 to 7 days in West Sumatra and 7 to 9 days in West Java. Based on DARA's calculation (2010), 90 % of needs in West Sumatra were actually being met even with only 37 % fulfillment of the budget in the West Sumatra Humanitarian Response Plan, as opposed to only 60 % in West Java. Based on the author's calculation, on average, 85 % from total IDPs in West Sumatra covered or gained benefit from emergency provisions, while in West Java, only around 60 %. However, in terms of percent beneficiaries receiving health services and food aid in both West Java and West Sumatra, on average, 80 % of the total affected people in each municipality did receive benefit.

Lastly, in terms of connectedness, humanitarian operations in West Sumatra also performed better. First, all DALA, HRNA, and PDNA documents which needed to ensure orchestrated emergency response and transition to recovery were published faster in West Sumatra than in West Java, i.e., the process was activated timely 2 weeks the after disaster and the documents were published less than 5 weeks after the earthquake, while in West Java, it was published after 7 weeks from the earthquake. In this sense, even when measured against current BNPB regulations (BNPB 2011), which at that time were not in operation, efforts in West Sumatra were already in compliance with the regulations. Humanitarian operations in West Sumatra also provided a strong base for recovery, mainly with its timely and high coverage of temporary shelter, while in West Java, even as of February 2010, people still reported living in tents. Further connectedness with the recovery plan saw preparation processes in West Sumatra being conducted jointly with other local stakeholders and international partners, while in West Java, only by the government. As a consequence, West Sumatra has greater organizational retention towards the recovery period, e.g., five out of seven ECB agencies remained on the field, more than 50 INGOs continued the recovery process, the humanitarian clusters transformed into working groups and legitimized by the government, and the early recovery efforts led legitimately and operationally by UNDP and Development Planning Agency of West Sumatra (Bappeda). While in West Java, only two out of seven ECB agencies remained, there was no clear role of clusters in recovery, and although early recovery was said to be led by UNDP, there was no clear coordination with the West Java government.

CONCLUSIONS AND RECOMMENDATIONS

This research, through SNA measurements and qualitative analysis, complements specific findings regarding the emergency response of the West Java Earthquake 2009 and the West Sumatra Earthquake 2009 made by Wilson (2010) and DARA (2010). Although both provinces have similar levels of organizational capacity, different approaches were taken in terms of how to orchestrate coordination and cooperation of emergency response and on statement of welcoming international assistance. By saying organizational capacity, it mainly refers to the fact that by September 2009, both provincial governments have not formed their BPBD and at the municipality level, their BPBDs were neither non-existence nor still infant. In West Java, BNPB supported centralization of coordination to Satkorlak West Java and initially neither requested for international assistance nor encouraged activation of the humanitarian cluster system, while in West Sumatra, from the very beginning, the provincial government and BNPB welcomed international assistance and instantly agreed on activating the humanitarian cluster system. Consequently, Satkorlak West Sumatra, under supervision from BNPB, worked in tandem with UNOCHA and other humanitarian cluster lead agencies. The network of inter-organizational cooperation formed on the ground is indeed not isolated from one another, i.e., the response in West Sumatra was also modified given the performance of emergency response in West Java. However, this research specifically compared networks in both cases, as a result of a conscious political decision by the government, as to test Gillmann's typology. By performing a lead-partnership mode of network which was comprised of all nine humanitarian clusters and activated timely, it was proven that humanitarian operations in West Sumatra performed better in all criteria of coherence, coverage, and connectedness.

This research, however, found a different conclusion than Gillmann's typology that the lead-agency type of network will always perform better if planned to be in operation; while at the same time supported Gillmann's pre-statement to her own typology that without adequate capacity and legitimacy of a lead agency, it is better to return and perform inter-organizational cooperation in emergency response activities by using the lead-partnership mode of network. Lastly, although still needing to be tested with other case studies, one of the possible implications from this research is that in a country or disaster-affected areas where the remaining governmental capacity exists but is still in infancy or developing their institutional capacity, lead partnership in humanitarian operations is better; while a lead-agency type of network led by UN agencies or NGOs is more appropriate for disaster situations and humanitarian operations where the remaining governmental capacity is weaker.

Given the findings of this research, the network of actors in a humanitarian operation should not only be fully associated with a lead-agency type of network but also can be strengthened in the operation through a lead-partnership type of network. Therefore, for some regulations in Indonesia, it is vital to add another criterion which regulates regarding at what level of disasters in association with the remaining local (or national) government capacity; thus, the command system for humanitarian operations will be implemented through a lead agency or a lead partnership, i.e., in relation to Indonesian Government Regulation 23/2008 regarding The Role of International Agencies and International Non-Government Organizations in Disaster Management, BNPB's Regulation Number 14/2010 regarding Guideline in Creating Command Post for Disaster Emergency Response, and BNPB's Regulation 22/2010 regarding the Role of the International Organization and Non-governmental International Organizations during Emergency Response.

The same applies to the risk of regional-level disasters, for example, in the Southeast Asian region. Alternatives on whether to perform a lead-agency or a lead-partnership type of network in an emergency situation can enrich the detailed implementation of the ASEAN Coordinating Center for Humanitarian Assistance on disaster management (AHA Centre), on facilitating regional standby arrangements for disaster relief and emergency response. The AHA Centre is recommended to identify the level of disasters and the remaining capacity of the government in order to determine whether it should intervene as lead agency or maintain lead partnership among national governments in managing emergency response to regional-level disasters. Lastly, as can be learned from this research, basically, the humanitarian cluster arrangement functioned with various capacities and levels of engagement between international/domestic and government/non-government actors. In the future, the various cluster arrangements should take into consideration when deciding whether the inter-cluster coordination should use lead-agency or lead-partnership type of network. Where in-country IASC exist, like in Indonesia, this consideration can be introduced to the inter-agency contingency plan managed by IASC.

For further scholarly purposes, the author would like to also recommend further research suggestions; first, there is merit to conduct research which detects networks of actors involved in not only humanitarian operations during emergency response but also those of which participated in disaster risk reduction and the development field in general, both before and after a disaster or the long-term recovery phase. Second, it is also recommended to conduct similar research for other types of disasters, especially with a slow-onset disaster characteristic, e.g., volcanic eruptions and climate-related disasters, and politically sensitive humanitarian crises, such as domestic conflict or civil war. By doing so, a broader view can be seen whether the current system and organizations which are actively involved in disaster management are able to perform regardless of the disaster type. Third, the author would like to suggest the utilization of SNA for enriching the ongoing innovation of real-time evaluation (RTE) in disaster situations or humanitarian crises. At the same time, a better record of emergency response activities in all humanitarian clusters in an RTE will improve network modeling and will measure humanitarian aid delivery performance more accurately. Lastly, it is also worth to perform an ethnographic approach and network census in creating input for a dataset, i.e., not solely depending on recorded data in Situation Reports. With this, it will also be possible to distinguish between formal networks among organizations and informal network among agencies of organizations.

FOOTNOTES

1 Daily Report Pusdalops (Crisis Operation Center) BNPB—3 September 2009

2 Summarized from Governor Decree SK 360/kep.1260-Hukham/2009 on Emergency Response Status

3 Daily Report Pusdalops (Crisis Operation Center) BNPB—4 September 2009

4 West Java Earthquake 2009 Situation Report #2, 3 September 2009, UNOCHA

5 Interview with Key Person P, March 2012

6 West Java Earthquake 2009 Situation Report #3, 4 September 2009, UNOCHA

7 Ibid

8 Interview with Key Person X, March 2012

9 Confirmed in interviews with Key Person D and Key Person L, both in March 2012

10 BNPB West Java Earthquake Situation Report 7 September 2009

11 West Sumatra Earthquake 2009 Situation Report #1 (UNOCHA 2009)

12 West Sumatra Earthquake 2009 Situation Report #8 (UNOCHA 2009)

13 West Sumatra Earthquake 2009 Situation Report #2 (UNOCHA 2009)

14 In the interview with Key Person A in February 2013, after the earthquake, by 18:00, the provincial government started their first rapid assessment; thus, by 23:00, they sent a request to BNPB based on the assessment result, and later, by 03:00, the provincial government has set

up a command center in the Governor's office and was ready to host incoming officials from the Central Government and UN Agencies.

15 Confirmed in interviews with key person A, E, T, and U in February 2013

16 Summarized from documentation by Pranoto (2011) and West Sumatra Earthquake 2009 Situation Report #3, UNOCHA

ACKNOWLEDGEMENTS

The author would like to acknowledge Professor Jun Matsunami of the Graduate School of International Cooperation Studies, Kobe University, Japan, for his guidance on this research and review on the manuscript. In addition, the author is also indebted to the Asian Development Bank-Japan Scholarship Program and later MEXT scholarship which facilitate author position in GSICS, Kobe University, and support the finance of the data gathering process and fieldwork for this research. Lastly, the author would like to extend gratitude to two blind-reviewers and the editor at the Journal of International Humanitarian Action, whose inputs contribute greatly to the improvement of this manuscript.

COMPETING INTERESTS

The author declares that he has no competing interests.

AUTHOR'S INFORMATION

Mizan Bustanul Fuady Bisri (Mizan) is a PhD Candidate in the Department of International Cooperation Policy Studies, Graduate School of International Cooperation Studies (GSICS), Kobe University, Japan. Prior to his PhD position, he received MA in political science from GSICS-Kobe University and M.Sc. in urban planning from Bandung Institute of Technology (ITB) in Indonesia. As a young scholar, Mizan has published several international academic articles, research reports, and a book chapter. He also has received several prestigious research grant and scholarship, such as Asian Development Bank—Japan Scholarship Program and UNOCHA Humanitarian Research and Innovation Grant Program in 2013. He is also assuming the position of Regional Focal Point for North and South East Asia in Disaster Risk Reduction at the United Nations Major Group for Children and Youth (UN-MGCY).

REFERENCES

1. Bappenas (2009) Rencana Aksi Rehabilitasi dan Rekonstruksi Wilayah Pasca Gempa bumi di Provinsi Jawa Barat dan Kabupaten Cilacap, Provinsi Jawa Tengah 2 September 2009 (Action Plan Rehabilitation and Reconstruction of Post West Java Earthquake 2 September 2009). Bappenas (Ministry of Development Planning), Jakarta
2. Beck T (2006) Evaluating humanitarian action using the OECD-DAC criteria. ALNAP, London
3. Bisri MBF (2016) Observing Partnership Innovation through Inter-organizational Network Analysis on Emergency Response of the Great East Japan Earthquake and Tsunami 2011. Japan Social Innovation Journal, 27–41.
4. BNPB (2009) West Sumatra and Jambi natural disasters: damage, loss, and preliminary needs assessment. BNPB, Jakarta
5. BNPB (2011) Head of BNPB Regulation Number 15/2011 about guideline for post disaster need assessment. BNPB, Jakarta
6. Borgatti S, Everett MG, Freeman L (2002) Ucinet 6 for Windows: software for social network analysis. Analytic Technologies, Harvard
7. Brinkman H-J (2010) World Food Program: fighting hunger with an updated tool-box. WFP, Rome
8. Cahill K (2012) More with less: disasters in an era of diminishing resources. Fordham University Press, New York
9. Clarke PK, Campbell L (2015) Exploring coordination in humanitarian clusters. ALNAP/ODI, London
10. DARA (2010) Humanitarian Response Index 2010: crisis reports Indonesia. DARA, Madrid
11. Fredriksen A (2012) Making humanitarian spaces global: coordinating crisis response through the cluster approach. Columbia University, Graduate School of Arts and Sciences. Columbia University (Dissertation), New York
12. Gillmann N (2010) Interagency coordination during disaster: strategic choices for the UN, NGOs, and other humanitarian actors in the field. Nomos, Baden-Baden
13. Haines V, Hurlbert JS, Beggs JJ (1996) Exploring the determinants of support provision: provider characteristics, personal networks,

community context, and support following life events. J Health Soc Behav 37(3):252–264

14. Hulbert JS, Beggs JJ, Haines V (2005) Bridges over troubled waters: what are the optimal networks for Katrina's victims? Social Science Research Council. Available via http://understandingkatrina.ssrc.org/Hurlbert_Beggs_Haines/. Accessed 10 Dec 2015.

15. IASC (2006) Guidance note on using the cluster approach to strengthen humanitarian approach. IASC (Inter-Agency Standing Committee), Geneva

16. IASC (2009) Indonesia Inter-Agency Contingency Plan. IASC (Inter-Agency Standing Committee), Jakarta

17. IFRC (2010) Operation update Indonesia: West Sumatra earthquakes. IFRC, Geneva

18. IFRC (2012) Shelter coordination in natural disasters. IFRC-International Federation of Red Cross and Red Crescent Societies, Geneva

19. Jasanoff S (2010) Beyond Calculation: a Democratic response to Risk. In A. Lakoff, Disaster and the Politics of Intervention. New York: Columbia University Press

20. Kapucu N, Arslan T, Collins ML (2010) Examining intergovernmental and inter-organizational response to catastrophic disasters: towards a network-centered approach. J Adm Soc 42(2):222–247

21. Kumar A (2011) Collaboration networks in disaster relief and humanitarian aid: a case study of Peru. Northwestern University (Master thesis), Illinois

22. Lakoff A (2010) Disaster and the politics of intervention. Columbia University Press, New York

23. Lassa J (2010) Institutional vulnerability and governance of disaster risk reduction: macro, meso, and micro scale assessment (with case studies from Indonesia). UNU – EHS (Dissertation), Bonn

24. Lassa J (2015) Post disaster governance, complexity and network theory: evidence from Aceh, Indonesia after the Indian Ocean Tsunami 2004. PLoS Curr Disasters.

25. Moore S, Eng E, Daniel M (2003) International NGOs and the role of network centrality in humanitarian aid operation: a case study of coordination during the 2000 Mozambique floods. Disasters 27(4):305–318

26. Pranoto S (2011) Lessons Learned Pembelajaran Rehab Rekon Pasca Gempa di Sumatra Barat 30 September 2009 (Lessons learned rehabilitation and reconstruction in post West Sumatra Earthquake 2009). Pilar Karya, Padang

27. Prell C (2012) Social network analysis—history, theory, and methodology. Sage Publications, London

28. Roberts PS (2010) Private choices, public harms: the evolution of national disaster organizations in the United States. In: Lakoff A (ed) Disaster and the politics of intervention. Columbia University Press, New York

29. Salvatore D (2012) Globalization, growth, poverty, governance, and humanitarian assistance. In: Cahill KM (ed) More with less: disaster in era of diminishing resources. Fordham University Press, New York

30. Scott J (2000) Social Network Network Analysis. London: Sage Publications.

31. Taylor G, Stoddard A, Harmer A, Haver K, Harvey P, Barber K, Wilhelm C (2012) The State of the Humanitarian System 2012. ALNAP, London, Available via http://www.alnap.org /resource/6565. Accessed 20 Dec 2015

32. Tomassini R, Wassenhove LV (2009) Humanitarian logistics. Palgrave Macmillan, Londin

33. UNISDR (2015) Global Assessment Report on Disaster Risk Reduction 2015. UNISDR, Geneva

34. UNOCHA (2009) West Sumatra Earthquake 2009: humanitarian response plan. UNOCHA, Jakarta

35. Varda D, Forgette R, Banks D, Contractor N (2009) Social network methodology in the study of disasters: issues and insights prompted by post-Katrina research. Popul Resolution Policy Rev 28:11–29

36. Wasserman S, Faust K (1994). Social Network Analysis: Methods and Applications. Cambridge: Cambridge University Press.

37. Wilson P (2010) Report of the joint evaluation of the Indonesian ECB consortium's responses to the West Java and West Sumatra earthquakes. Indonesia Emergency Capacity Building Consortium, Jakarta, Available via http://www.alnap.org/resource/5957. Accessed 5 Dec 2015

12

THE IMPACT OF MEDIA REPORTING ON THE EMERGENCE OF CHARCOAL BURNING SUICIDE IN TAIWAN

Ying-Yeh Chen[1,2], Feng Chen[3], David Gunnell[4], Paul S. F. Yip[5,6]

[1] Taipei City Psychiatric Center, Taipei City Hospital, Taipei City, Taiwan,

[2] Institute of Public Health and Department of Public Health, National Yang-Ming University, Taipei City, Taiwan,

[3] Department of Statistics, University of New South Wales, Sydney, Australia,

[4] School of Social and Community Medicine, University of Bristol, Bristol, United Kingdom,

[5] Hong Kong Jockey Club Center for Suicide Research and Prevention, University of Hong Kong, Hong Kong, China,

[6] Department of Social Work and Social Administration, University of Hong Kong, Hong Kong, China

ABSTRACT

We investigated the association of the intensity of newspaper reporting of charcoal burning suicide with the incidence of such deaths in Taiwan during 1998–2002. A counting process approach was used to estimate the incidence of suicides and intensity of news reporting. Conditional Poisson generalized linear autoregressive models were performed to assess the association of the intensity of newspaper reporting of charcoal burning and non-charcoal burning suicides with the actual number of charcoal burning and non-charcoal burning suicides the following day. We found that increases in the reporting of charcoal burning suicide were associated with increases in the incidence of charcoal burning suicide on the following day, with each reported charcoal burning news item being associated with a 16% increase in next day charcoal burning suicide ($p<.0001$). However, the reporting of other methods of suicide was not related to their incidence. We conclude that extensive media reporting of charcoal burning suicides appears to have contributed to the rapid rise in the incidence of the novel method in Taiwan during the initial stage of the suicide epidemic. Regulating media reporting of novel suicide methods may prevent an epidemic spread of such new methods.

INTRODUCTION

A rapid increase in suicides by burning barbecue charcoal changed the epidemiology of suicide in Taiwan in the first decade of the 21st century [1], [2]. The incidence of charcoal burning suicide increased from 0.1 to 5.1 per 100,000 population between 1998 and 2010, making it the second most common method of suicide (after hanging) in Taiwan, accounting for more than 30% of suicides in 2010 [3].

Previous reports have suggested that media glamorization of this novel method was responsible for the dramatic increase in charcoal burning suicide [4], [5]. The first widely-reported case of charcoal burning suicide occurred in Hong Kong in 1998 where a middle-aged woman was depicted as having a peaceful and painless death by burning barbecue charcoal in a small sealed room [4], [6]. It is believed the method was subsequently adopted in Taiwan because the same written language (i.e. traditional Chinese characters) is used in both countries, thus reports of its use were accessible to the whole population. The shared cultural belief on the importance of maintaining the appearance of the body for a better next life may also contribute to its spread in these two regions. An interview-based study in Taiwan found that 87% of individuals who survived a suicide attempt where charcoal burning was used said that media reporting contributed to their choice of this method [5]. However, no previous studies have systematically examined the intensity of reporting of this new method when it first appeared in Taiwan and whether the intensity of media reporting was associated with the increasing incidence of suicides by charcoal burning.

The aim of the current analysis is to explore the role of the newspaper reporting in the dissemination of charcoal burning suicide in Taiwan during 1998–2002. We assessed whether the intensity of newspaper reporting was associated with subsequent increases in charcoal burning suicides.

METHODS

Ethics Statement

Because no personal data were involved, this study was exempted from ethical review by the Human Research Ethics Committee, Taipei City Hospital, Taiwan.

Data

During 1998–2002, three major newspapers, China Times (CT), United Daily (UD) and Liberty Times (LT) accounted for more than 90% of newspaper sales in Taiwan with approximately equal market shares for these three newspapers [7]. The content of two (UD and CT) of these three papers from the late 1990s/early 2000s was available in electronic archives. Using online search tools, the United Daily News Dataset (for UD), and Knowledge Media Winner (for CT), were searched for news articles containing Chinese key words related to suicide and suicide method (see appendix) published between1998–2002 (N=9675 for UN; N=11468 for CT). Editorials commentaries, fictional stories, suicide terrorism, and articles providing general information about suicide prevention were excluded. A total of 1898 and 3689 suicide news items for UD and CT were retrieved respectively. Articles were then read individually to identify those that reported charcoal burning suicide vs. other methods of suicide. Altogether 176 and 158 news items for UD and CT respectively on charcoal burning suicide and 1722 (UD) and 3531 (CT) on other methods of suicide were identified.

The electronic archives for LT did not cover the study period. To assess possible bias from the exclusion of this paper, we randomly selected two months in 2001/2002 and hand searched the newspaper archives to investigate the concordance of suicide reporting in LT with UD and CT. The reporting of charcoal burning suicides in the LT was lower than the other two daily newspapers. In the two months selected in 2001, we identified a total of ten news items on charcoal burning suicide in UD, seven in CT and only one news item in LT. In 2002, 23 news items on charcoal burning suicide were identified for UD and 19 for CT, but only 3 news items on charcoal burning suicide were reported in LT, indicating the reporting of charcoal burning suicide in LT was probably lower than in the other two newspapers. Throughout the study period, suicide news stories (including those of charcoal burning suicides) were never reported on the front pages of the papers reviewed.

Data on suicide deaths, classified according to the International Classification of Disease (ICD-9) were obtained from official death records in Taiwan. The ICD-9 codes used were deaths registered in E950–959 (intentional self-harm) and E980–989 (intent undetermined). Deaths certified as undetermined intent were also included because previous research indicated that many suicide deaths were included in this category [8]. There is no specific ICD-9 code for charcoal-burning suicide. Such deaths are coded as E952/E982 (suicide or undetermined death by poisoning using nondomestic gas). Before 1998, E952/E982 accounted for less than two percent of suicide deaths in Taiwan. Hence, we assumed that most of the suicides coded E952/E982 subsequent to 1998 were by charcoal burning [9]. Therefore, E952/E982 was used to denote charcoal-burning suicide in our analysis.

Analytic Strategy

The cumulative number of charcoal burning (or non-charcoal burning) news items about suicide from time 0 (beginning of 1998) up to time t was modeled by a counting process $N(t)$. The intensity process $\lambda(t)$ of $N(t)$ is assumed to be $\lambda(t) \equiv \lim_{\delta t \to 0+} [N(t+\delta t) - N(t) | Y(t)] / \delta t = Y(t)\alpha(t)$, where $\mathrm{E}[\cdot \mid \cdot]$ denotes conditional expectation [10]–[13]. In this model the exposure process $Y(t)$ represents the number of charcoal burning (or non-charcoal burning) suicide cases on the day before t, and the intensity function $\alpha(t)$ represents the ratio of the expected daily number of reports to the number of charcoal burning (or non-charcoal burning). The time-varying reporting intensity $\alpha(t)$ and its first order derivative $\alpha'(t)$ were then estimated using a nonparametric curve estimation method, the local polynomial method [10]–[12]. The crude charcoal burning (or non-charcoal burning) incidence rate in cases per day (=intensity), and its first order derivative – a measure of the rate of change in incidence – were also estimated using this method with $Y(t) \equiv 1$. These estimated incidences and rates of change in incidence (first order derivatives) curves were then plotted against aligned calendar time (in days) to illustrate the relationship between suicide reporting and suicide incidence graphically.

To formally assess the potential impact of news reporting of charcoal burning suicides on suicide incidence, analyses using conditional Poisson generalized linear autoregressive models were performed. We first fitted an unadjusted Poisson generalized linear autoregressive model to examine the effect of newspaper reporting of charcoal burning suicide on the incidence of charcoal burning deaths. In this model only lag terms of the predictor (i.e. daily number of newspaper reports of charcoal burning suicide) and outcome (i.e. daily count of charcoal burning suicide) were included. We then fitted an adjusted model by adding potential confounders to the model. The potential confounders were the daily count of non-charcoal burning suicide (which served as an indicator of background suicide rate) and day of the week (as the number of newspaper pages and suicide count could vary according to different days of the week). Equivalent models for the impact of news reporting of non-charcoal burning suicide on non-charcoal burning suicide deaths were fitted as well. Specifically, the Poisson generalized linear autoregressive model we used for the count of charcoal burning suicides y_t^C is

$$\begin{cases} y_t^C \sim \text{Poisson}(\mu_t^C); \\ \log(\mu_t^C) = \beta_0^C + \beta_{11}^C y_{t-1}^C + \ldots + \beta_{1q}^C y_{t-q}^C + \beta_{21}^C x_{t-1}^C + \ldots + \beta_{2q}^C x_{t-q}^C \end{cases} \quad (1)$$

where x_t^C denotes the amount of newspaper reports of charcoal burning suicides on day *t*. The same approach was used for suicides by methods other than charcoal burning. The adjusted models are obtained by including *q* lagged terms (up to one week) of the corresponding covariates. Our primary hypothesis concerned the impact of news reporting on the incidence of charcoal burning suicides, but of course if there were no suicides there would be no reporting, so we also investigated the strength of association between the incidence of suicides and subsequent reporting of these deaths. To do this we used a Poisson generalized linear autoregressive model similar to (1) except that the number of reported news items acted as the dependent variable. For interpretability, the lag parameter *q* was set to 7 in all the aforementioned models as prior studies tended to assume that the effect of news reporting of non-celebrity suicides lasted for about 1 week [14], [15].

RESULTS

The incidence of charcoal burning suicide began to increase in 2000, with a more rapid and prominent rise in 2001, whereas the incidence of suicide using all other methods was relatively stable during the study period with a slight fall towards the end of 2002 (top panel, Figure 1) indicating some degree of method substitution. Newspaper reporting intensity of charcoal burning suicide (the number of reports per death) started to rise after 2000, a sharp increase occurred midway through 2001 and reporting peaked on 24th Feb. 2002 and subsequently declined (second panel, Figure 1). The reporting intensity for other methods of suicide was higher than charcoal burning suicide before the end of 2001, but the reporting intensity of charcoal burning suicide surpassed the reporting of suicides using other methods at the end of 2001 and the early 2002. As can be seen from the top two panels of figure 1, the rapid rise in the reporting intensity of charcoal burning suicide coincided with a rapid rise in the incidence of charcoal burning suicides. The peak for the reporting of charcoal burning preceded the peak for the incidence of charcoal burning deaths. However, when the reporting intensity of charcoal burning suicide decreased in early 2002, the number of charcoal burning suicides remained high.

The 3rd and 4th panels of figure 1 plot the derivatives of suicide incidence (panel 3) and news reports per suicide (panel 4). The derivatives indicate the rate of change. When the value is greater than 0, it suggests that the intensity is increasing and when the value is less than 0, it indicates the intensity is decreasing. The period when the reporting of charcoal burning suicide accelerated (2001 to early 2002, when the derivatives are >0) coincided with the time period when charcoal burning suicides began to increase exponentially in Taiwan (panel 3 and panel 4, figure 1). When the reporting intensity of charcoal burning suicide declined in early 2002 (panel 4, figure 1), the incidence of charcoal burning suicide remained at a high level (panel 1, figure 1), although this period coincided with a fall in the rate of increase in charcoal burning deaths (panel 3, figure 1).

As illustrated in the figure (see top panel), the peak of charcoal burning suicide (June 2002) occurred after the peak of reporting of charcoal burning suicide (Feb. 2002), suggesting that news reporting could have contributed to the momentum for the spread of charcoal burning suicide in the community. Furthermore, when the rate of change of charcoal burning suicide increased, the rate of change of other methods declined (panel 3) indicating some possible substitution of methods; similarly, when charcoal burning suicide was excessively reported, the reporting intensity (number of reports per case) of other methods of suicide decreased and vice versa (panel 4). It is important to note that the incidence of charcoal burning remained at a high level even after the reporting intensity has reduced. This suggests that by this stage the method of charcoal burning suicide had penetrated into the community and become self-perpetuating, regardless of further reporting.

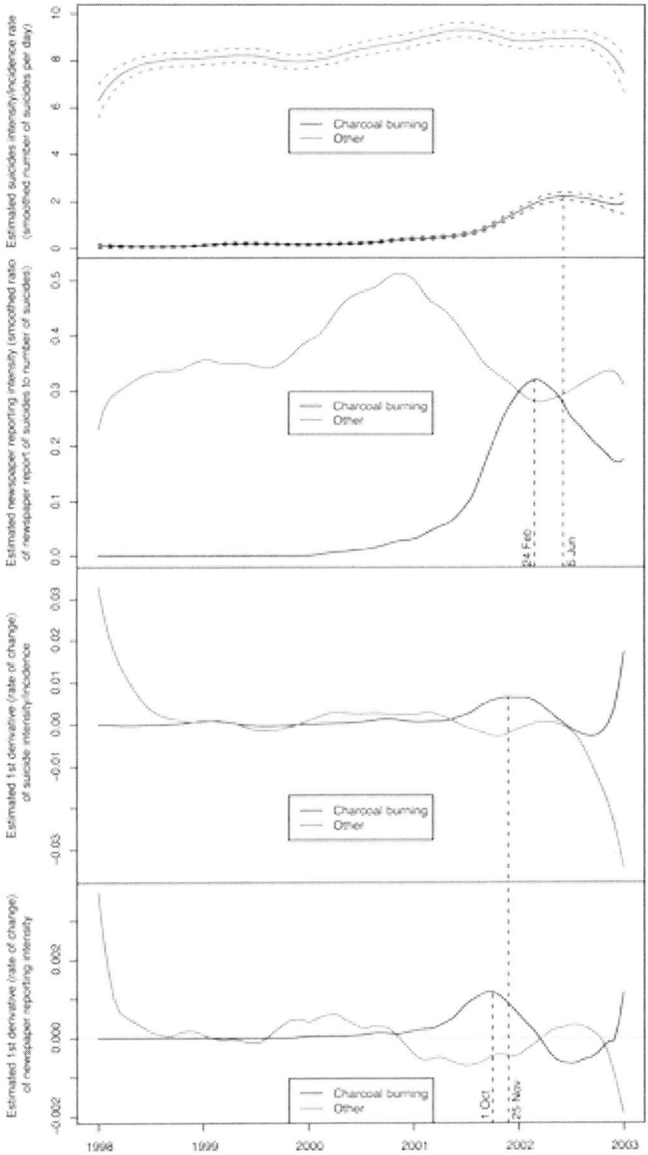

Figure 1. The relationships between newspaper reporting intensity of charcoal burning suicides and suicide incidence in Taiwan, 1998–2002.

Table 1 presents the Poisson regression analysis investigating the impact of news reporting intensity of charcoal and other methods of suicide on the incidence of method-specific suicide rates. The reporting of charcoal burning suicide was positively associated with an increase in the next day occurrence of charcoal burning suicide, each reported news item on charcoal burning suicide was associated with a 16% increase in charcoal burning suicide in the following day (p<.0001) (see footnote under Table 1 for detailed explanations). In contrast, the reporting of other methods of suicide was not related to the occurrence of such suicides on the next day. The association between news reporting and actual suicide did not attenuate when potential confounders were controlled for. Our presentation and the findings of the Poisson regression analysis were restricted to suicides on the following day, whereas we know the effect of any single report is likely to last more than this [16]. Our time series data indicated that altogether, three of the seven p values for lags from day 1 to day 7 for charcoal burning suicide were <0.01 (lag 1, lag 6 and lag 7), whereas the lowest of the seven p-values for the other methods of suicide was 0.41, indicating effects of reporting were not restricted to suicides occurring on the following day.

Table 1. The impact of suicide news reporting (charcoal burning and non-charcoal burning respectively) in the previous day on suicide incidence in the following day in Taiwan, 1998–2002.

	Charcoal burning (CB) suicide			
	Unadjusted[a]		Adjusted[b]	
	estimate (s.e.)	p value	estimate (s.e.)	p value
News reporting of CB suicide in the previous day	0.14 (0.03)	<0.0001	0.15 (0.04)	<0.0001
	Non-Charcoal burning (non-CB) suicide			
	Unadjusted[a]		Adjusted[c]	
	estimate (s.e.)	p value	estimate (s.e.)	p value
News reporting of non-CB suicide in the previous day	−0.00 (0.00)	0.74	0.00 (0.00)	0.60

*Note: [a]Poisson generalized linear autoregressive model controlling for secular trend;
[b]Poisson generalized linear autoregressive model controlling for secular trend, secular trend of non-charcoal burning suicide count and days of the week;
[c]Poisson generalized linear autoregressive model controlling for secular trend, secular trend of charcoal burning suicide count and days of the week.
*Note: The Poisson estimates can be transformed to proportions by exponentiation of the estimate and minus 1. For example, in the unadjusted models, the Poisson estimates 0.14 and −0.00 can be transformed to exp (0.14) − 1 ≈ 15% and exp (−0.00) − 1 ≈ 0% respectively. These estimates mean that before adjusting for potential confounders, each news article on charcoal burning suicide was associated with a 15% [95% CI = 0.08, 0.22] increase in charcoal burning suicide on the following day; whereas news reporting of non-charcoal burning suicide was not associated with an increase in non-charcoal burning suicide. After adjusting for potential confounders, for each reported news article on charcoal burning suicide was associated with a 16% (exp (0.15) − 1 ≈ 16%) [95%CI = 0.07, 0.26] increase in charcoal burning suicide on the following day.

To assess potential mutual causation (i.e. increased suicide led to increased reporting), Table 2 presents the results of the Poisson regression analysis assessing the influence of charcoal burning and other suicides on newspaper reporting of method-specific suicide rates. The results suggest that the occurrence of both charcoal burning and non-charcoal burning suicides are strongly related to the reporting of method-specific suicide rates on the following day (P<.0001). However, the effect size for charcoal burning deaths was much larger indicating that charcoal burning suicide was considered more 'newsworthy'. Increase in one case of charcoal burning suicide was associated with an increase of 31% in the rate of news reporting on charcoal burning suicide (P<0.0001); whereas the increase in one case of non-charcoal burning suicide was associated with an increase in

4% of news reporting on non-charcoal burning suicide (see footnote under table 2 for detailed explanations).

Table 2. The impact of actual suicides (charcoal burning and non-charcoal burning) on news reporting of charcoal burning and non-charcoal burning suicide in the next day.

	News reporting on charcoal burning (CB) suicide			
	Unadjusted[a]		**Adjusted[b]**	
	estimate (s.e.)	**p value**	**estimate (s.e.)**	**p value**
CB suicide in the previous day	0.27 (0.04)	<0.0001	0.27 (0.04)	<0.0001
	News reporting on non-charcoal burning (non-CB) suicide			
	Unadjusted[a]		**Adjusted[c]**	
	estimate (s.e.)	**p value**	**estimate (s.e.)**	**p value**
Non-CB suicide in the previous day	0.04 (0.00)	<0.0001	0.04 (0.00)	<0.0001

CB: charcoal burning. Non-CB: Non-charcoal burning.
*Note: [a] Poisson generalized linear autoregressive model controlling for secular trend;
[b]Poisson generalized linear autoregressive model controlling for secular trend, secular trend of non-charcoal burning suicide count, secular trend of news reporting on non-charcoal burning suicide and days of the week;
[c]Poisson generalized linear autoregressive model controlling for secular trend, secular trend of charcoal burning suicide count, secular trend of news reporting on charcoal burning suicide and days of the week.
*Note: For each case of charcoal burning suicide was associated with an increase of 31% (exp (0.27) − 1≈ 31%) in the rate of news reporting on charcoal burning suicide; whereas the increase in one case of non-charcoal burning suicide was associated with an increase in 4% (exp (0.04) − 1 ≈ 4%) of news reporting on non-charcoal burning suicide.

DISCUSSION

Main Findings

Newspaper reporting of charcoal burning suicide was associated with an increase in the number of charcoal burning suicides in Taiwan during the early period of the epidemic. Based on our estimation, each reported charcoal burning news item was associated with a 16% increase in next day charcoal burning suicide; whereas the reporting of all other methods of suicide was unrelated to their incidence on the following day. The period when the rate of increase in the newspaper reporting of charcoal burning suicides was at its highest preceded the peak rate for charcoal burning suicide, providing some evidence for a causal effect of news reporting, although other explanations are possible. The reporting intensity of charcoal burning suicide decreased after early 2002 but the incidence of charcoal burning suicide remained high, although the rate of increase of charcoal burning suicides decreased slightly during this period. This finding indicates that when a novel method is made well known, it may become self-sustaining and further reporting may not influence its relative incidence.

Strengths and Limitations

Our study provides the first empirical evidence of the possible role of newspaper reporting on the charcoal burning suicide epidemic in Taiwan. This is also the first report that illustrates the dynamic and competitive relationships of news coverage for different types of suicide news. However, our study results should be interpreted in light of the following limitations. First, a challenge in the assessment of the association between media reporting and suicide incidence is the problem of reverse causation, i.e. media reporting of suicide events is in part a reflection of its increasing incidence, rather than media 'causing' the increase in suicide rates. We assessed the causal direction by exploring the temporal association between media reporting and suicide incidence, i.e. whether rises in reporting preceded rises in suicide and found some evidence that this was the case. Second, suicide rates in Taiwan have been rising since 1993, it is possible that the increasing use of charcoal burning suicide is a reflection of underlying trends in suicide rather than an effect of media reporting, although the rise in charcoal burning deaths occurred 5 years after the more general increase in Taiwan's suicide rates. Third, ICD codes did not allow us to distinguish charcoal burning suicides from other suicide by gassing, but as the great majority of such suicides were by charcoal burning [9], this will not have a major impact on our analysis. Fourth, suicide news reporting has been measured by counting news items, a content analysis of the articles has not been performed, it is likely that the prominence and content of the articles may influence uptake of the method [17]. However, the quantity of report is in itself an important dimension of media influence on suicide in terms of raising public awareness of a new suicide method. In addition, other types of media channels such as the electronic media and TV stations have not been included in the analysis. Lastly, there are no accurate newspaper circulation data available for all the newspapers in Taiwan; reported sales were based on a telephone survey on a limited sample of Taiwanese. As mentioned earlier, one major newspaper, Liberty Times (LT), was not included to the analysis, as the electronic archives for the newspaper was not available. However, our hand search indicated that LT reported few suicides during the study period, hence may not have affected our results substantially.

Interpretations and Implications

Although charcoal burning suicide has become one of the most common methods of suicide in some Asian countries [18], it is still not well-understood why the method became so popular in such a short period of time. Our analysis has provided valuable empirical evidence on the possible contribution of extensive newspaper reporting of charcoal burning suicide in the spreading of the novel method. The rapid diffusion of charcoal burning was not associated with reports of a particular celebrity who used this method or other key death, rather, the increase in the quantity of news reporting of the method appeared to be followed by a significant rise in the use of the method. Throughout the study period, charcoal burning suicides were never reported on the front pages of the papers reviewed. Of note, in 1994, before the well-recognized 1998 Hong Kong charcoal burning case, Taiwanese media reported extensively on a suicide pact of two teenage girls who died together by burning barbecue charcoal in a sealed hotel room [19]. The media suggested that they were lesbians who killed themselves because such relationships are not approved by Taiwanese society. Charcoal burning suicide did not spread at that time even though the reporting of the suicide pact persisted for about one week. It is possible that suicide by socially "deviant" figures may be less likely to lead to a modeling effect [17]. Additionally, at that time, the news media focused on the deaths of two smart teenage lesbians rather than the use of a novel method. For example, the headlines of this suicide pact on CT on July 26 1994 read " Two gifted students from Taipei First Girls High School, Lin and Shi, were found dead on the 25th"; on UD the news read "Two students from Taipei First Girls High School left death notes and said goodbye to the world together". Our finding suggests that cumulative media reporting of a new method adopted by the general population may have the potential to induce a suicide epidemic through a gradual diffusion process.

The finding that after Feb. 2002, the reporting intensity of charcoal burning suicide decreased (second panel, Figure 1) whilst the occurrence of charcoal burning suicide continued to rise (top panel, Figure 1) suggests that the spread of the novel method had become self-sustaining. A likely explanation is that after a while, everyone in a population is aware of the new suicide method (through media exposure, word of mouth and knowledge of friends/family who have used the method). At this point, the media no longer plays a role in increasing awareness of the method. Thus, responsible reporting of novel methods of suicide may be more effective at the very early stage of a potential epidemic.

Our analysis demonstrates the mutual causation between news reporting of charcoal burning suicide and its actual incidence; i.e. the incidence of charcoal burning suicide was associated with its reporting and the reporting of the novel method was related to its future incidence. The process of self-perpetuation through mutual causation may have been a crucial factor for the emergence and the diffusion of the novel method in Taiwan.

Our analysis reveals that reporting of different types of suicide news are competitive. When one type of suicide news gets media attention, other types of suicide news items get less reported.

CONCLUSIONS

This analysis indicates that newspaper reporting may have fuelled Taiwan's charcoal burning suicide epidemic. Repetitive reporting appears to be harmful, despite the fact that the news items were not placed in the front page, and no celebrity suicides were linked to the use of the method at the early stage of the epidemic. However, once the method had become rooted in the community, the impact of media reporting becomes less prominent; the method takes its own path and becomes self-sustaining. Hence, working proactively with the media to improve the quality of reporting of these tragic deaths and regulate potential harmful reporting are particularly important in the early stage of a suicide epidemic. When a new method becomes widely used, prevention focusing only on regulating media reporting is not adequate. Other intervention measures such as method restriction, gatekeeper training and improve mental health of high risk groups should all be considered.

AUTHOR CONTRIBUTIONS

Conceived and designed the experiments: Y-YC DG PSFY. Performed the experiments: Y-YC PSFY FC. Analyzed the data: FC PSFY. Contributed reagents/materials/analysis tools: FC PSFY. Wrote the paper: Y-YC FC DG PSFY.

REFERENCES

1. Chang SS, Gunnell D, Wheeler BW, Yip PSF, Sterne JA (2010) The evolution of the epidemic of charcoal-burning suicide in Taiwan: a spatial and temporal analysis. PLoS Med 7: e1000212.

2. Chen YY, Yip PSF, Lee C, Fan HF, Fu KW (2010) Economic fluctuations and suicide: a comparison of Taiwan and Hong Kong. Soc Sci Med 71: 2083–2090.

3. Taiwan Suicide Prevention Center (2009) Survey and research. Taiwan Suicide Prevention Center. Available: http://www.tspc.doh.gov.tw/tspc/portal/center/index.jsp . Accessed 2012 October 1.

4. Yip PSF, Lee DTS (2007) Charcoal-burning suicides and strategies for prevention. Crisis 28 (suppl 1)21–27.

5. Tsai CW, Gunnell D, Chou YH, Kuo CJ, Lee MB, et al. (2011) Why do people choose charcoal burning as a method of

suicide? An interview based study of survivors in Taiwan. J Affect Disord 131: 402–407.

6. Liu KY, Beautrais A, Caine E, Chan K, Chao A, et al. (2007) Charcoal burning suicides in Hong Kong and urban Taiwan: an illustration of the impact of a novel suicide method on overall regional rates. J Epidemiol Community Health 61: 248–253.

7. Lin LY (2008) A historical experiment with deregulation: the changes and challenges of the press after the lifting of the press ban in Taiwan. Mass Commun Res 95: 183–212.

8. Chang SS, Sterne JA, Lu TH, Gunnell D (2010) 'Hidden' suicides amongst deaths certified as undetermined intent, accident by pesticide poisoning and accident by suffocation in Taiwan. Soc Psychiatry Psychiatr Epidemiol 45: 143–152.

9. Lin JJ, Chen LH, Huang SM, Lu TH (2008) Problems in estimating the number of suicides by charcoal burning in Taiwan. J Epidemiol Community Health 62: 566.

10. Chen F, Huggins RM, Yip PSF, Lam KF (2008) Nonparametric estimation of multiplicative counting process intensity functions with an application to the Beijing SARS epidemic. Commun Stat - Theo M 37: 294–306.

11. Chen F, Yip PSF, Lam KF (2011) On the local polynomial estimators of the counting process intensity function and its derivatives. Scand J Stat 38: 631–649.

12. Chen F (2011) Maximum local partial likelihood estimators for the counting process intensity function and its derivatives. Stat Sinica 21: 107–128.

13. Chen YY, Chen F, Yip PSF (2011) The impact of media reporting of suicide on actual suicides in Taiwan, 2002–05. J Epidemiol Community Health 65: 934–940.

14. Pirkis JE, Burgess PM, Francis C, Blood RW, Jolley DJ (2006) The relationship between media reporting of suicide and actual suicide in Australia. Soc Sci Med 62: 2874–2886.

15. Niederkrotenthaler T, Voracek M, Herberth A, Till B, Strauss M, et al. (2010) Role of media reports in completed and prevented suicide: Werther v. Papageno effects. Br J Psychiatry 197: 234–243.

16. Sisask M, Varnik A (2012) Media roles in suicide prevention: a systematic review. Int J Environ Res Public Health 9: 123–138.

17. Niederkrotenthaler T, Till B, Kapusta ND, Voracek M, Dervic K, et al. (2009) Copycat effects after media reports on suicide: a population-based ecologic study. Soc Sci Med 69: 1085–1090.

18. Wu KCC, Chen YY, Yip PSF (2012) Suicide Methods in Asia: Implications in Suicide Prevention. Int J Environ Res Public Health 9: 1135–1158.

19. Guan RJ (2010) The aftermath of the suicide of an intelligent young girl from an elite senior high school. PC home Personal News Channel [in Chinese]. Available: http://mypaper.pchome.com.tw/kuan0416/post/1320901966. Accessed 2012 October 1.

13

USING SOCIAL MEDIA FOR ACTIONABLE DISEASE SURVEILLANCE AND OUTBREAK MANAGEMENT: A SYSTEMATIC LITERATURE REVIEW

Lauren E. Charles-Smith[1], Tera L. Reynolds[2], Mark A. Cameron[3], Mike Conway[4], Eric H. Y. Lau[5], Jennifer M. Olsen[6], Julie A. Pavlin[7], Mika Shigematsu, Laura C. Streichert[2], Katie J. Suda, Courtney D. Corley[1]

[1] Data Sciences and Analytics Group, Pacific Northwest National Laboratory, Richland, Washington, United States of America,
[2] International Society for Disease Surveillance, Boston, Massachusetts, United States of America,
[3] Commonwealth Scientific and Industrial Research Organization Digital Productivity Flagship, Canberra, Australia,
[4] Department of Biomedical Informatics, University of Utah, Salt Lake City, Utah, United States of America,
[5] School of Public Health, The University of Hong Kong, Hong Kong Special Administrative Region, People's Republic of China,
[6] Skoll Global Threats Fund, San Francisco, California, United States of America,
[7] Henry M. Jackson Foundation for the Advancement of Military Medicine, Bethesda, Maryland, United States of America,

ABSTRACT

Objective

Research studies show that social media may be valuable tools in the disease surveillance toolkit used for improving public health professionals' ability to detect disease outbreaks faster than traditional methods and to enhance outbreak response. A social media work group, consisting of surveillance practitioners, academic researchers, and other subject matter experts convened by the International Society for Disease Surveillance, conducted a systematic primary literature review using the PRISMA framework to identify research, published through February 2013, answering either of the following questions:

1. Can social media be integrated into disease surveillance practice and outbreak management to support and improve public health?
2. Can social media be used to effectively target populations, specifically vulnerable populations, to test an intervention and interact with a community to improve health outcomes?

Examples of social media included are Facebook, MySpace, microblogs (e.g., Twitter), blogs, and discussion forums. For Question 1, 33 manuscripts were identified, starting in 2009 with topics on Influenza-like Illnesses (n = 15), Infectious Diseases (n = 6), Non-infectious Diseases (n = 4), Medication and Vaccines (n = 3), and Other (n = 5). For Question 2, 32 manuscripts were identified, the first in 2000 with topics on Health Risk Behaviors (n = 10), Infectious Diseases (n = 3), Non-infectious Diseases (n = 9), and Other (n = 10).

Conclusions

The literature on the use of social media to support public health practice has identified many gaps and biases in current knowledge. Despite the potential for success identified in exploratory studies, there are limited studies on interventions and little use of social media in practice. However, information gleaned from the articles demonstrates the effectiveness of social media in supporting and improving public health and in identifying target populations for intervention. A primary recommendation resulting from the review is to identify opportunities that enable public health professionals to integrate social media analytics into disease surveillance and outbreak management practice.

INTRODUCTION

Social media communication is an increasingly utilized outlet for people to freely create and post information that is disseminated and consumed worldwide through the Internet. News media, traditional scientific outlets, and social media create a platform for minority viewpoints and personal information, which is not being captured by other sources. Social media can create a sense of anonymity, allowing for unadulterated personal expression when compared to traditional face-to-face meetings, especially among young people and about intimate matters [1]. In this respect, social media provide an additional informal source of data that can be used to identify health information not reported to medical officials or health departments and to reveal viewpoints on health-related topics, especially of a sensitive nature.

In the past 10 years, research articles connecting disease surveillance with Internet use have increased in number, most likely due to the increase in availability of health-related information from various Internet sites. For example, Wikipedia article hits [2], Google search terms (Google Flu Trends) [3], and online restaurant reservation availability (OpenTable) [4] were modeled against the number of patients with influenza-like illness (ILI) reported by the Centers for Disease Control and Prevention (CDC). Several literature reviews have looked at the potential of this type of research to benefit human health.

Moorhead et al. conducted a review of research studies to identify potential uses, benefits, and limitations of social media to engage the general public, patients, and health professionals in health communication [5]. Although articles identified benefit from using social media in health communications, the authors note a lack of research focused on the evaluation of short- and long-term impacts on health communication practices. Bernardo et al. provided a scoping review of the use of search queries and social media in disease surveillance [6]. First reported in 2006, the reviewed literature highlighted accuracy, speed, and cost performance that was comparable to existing disease surveillance systems and recommended the use of social media programs to support those systems.

Velasco et al. defined their literature review to contain only peer-reviewed articles on event-based disease surveillance [7] in which they identified and described 12 existing systems. Walters et al. described numerous systems implemented and dedicated to biosurveillance, defined as "the discipline in which diverse data streams such as these are characterized in real or near-real time to provide early warning and situational awareness of events affecting human, plant, and animal health," many of which center around human disease outbreaks [8]. The paper points out that including emerging media, such as blogs and Short Message Service (SMS), into these systems along with standardized metrics to evaluate the performance of different surveillance systems is crucial to the advancement of these early warning systems.

As members of the International Society for Disease Surveillance (ISDS), we established a social media working group (henceforth called the workgroup) to develop research, technology, and operational innovations in electronic public health surveillance. We proposed to evaluate the use of social media to enable public health professionals to realize positive, valuable, and timely community health outcomes at the local, state, regional, national, and global levels. To address these goals, we followed the PRISMA process [9] by systematically compiling and analyzing literature that demonstrates innovation in electronic public health surveillance through the use of social media.

By focusing on how research on social media data (further defined below) can be used for actionable disease surveillance, we are able to bring to light the best ways of using these tools to target vulnerable populations and improve public health in the broad spectrum from identifying and monitoring disease outbreaks to addressing traditionally intractable health concerns, such as adolescent drug and alcohol use.

METHODS

This systematic review builds upon the preferred reporting items outlined in the PRISMA Statement in effort to properly assess the quality and quantity of health-related research using social media analytics for active surveillance, S1 Checklist. A social media application was defined for this review as, "an Internet-based application where people can communicate and share resources and information, and where users can activate and set their own profiles, have the ability to develop and update them constantly, and have the opportunity to make such profiles totally or partially public and linked with other profiles in a network." Examples of social media included in this review are Facebook, MySpace, microblogs (e.g., Twitter), blogs, and discussion forums. Articles using data sources, such as Internet searches, ProMed-mail, and citizen-generated data were not included. In March 2013, a query of scientific literature databases (PubMed, Embase, Scopus, and Ichushi-Web) was conducted for all literature published through February 2013 to determine potential publications for review by the workgroup (Table 1).

Table 1. The databases (PubMed, Embase, Scopus, and Ichushi Web) that were queried and the search terms applied to identify potential publications for review.

Database	Type of Search	Search Terms
PubMed database (http://www.ncbi.nlm.nih.gov/pubmed/)	Medical Subject Headings (MeSH)	"Internet," "social media," "blogging," "biosurveillance," "disease outbreaks," "epidemics," "communicable diseases," "population surveillance," "sentinel surveillance," "public health"
Embase database (http://www.elsevier.com/online-tools/embase)	Emtree (Elsevier Life Science thesaurus)	"social media," "Internet," "social network," combined with "biosurveillance," "epidemic," "pandemic influenza", "pandemic," "infection," "communicable disease," "outbreak"
Scopus (http://www.scopus.com/)	General terms	Combination of PubMed and Embase search terms
Ichushi-Web (http://www.jamas.or.jp/personal_web/login.html)	General terms	Japanese translated combination of PubMed and Embase search terms

Searches were further refined to include only human subjects and to exclude review (i.e., meta-analysis or other systematic reviews) and editorial articles. Articles published in Italian, German, Dutch, English, Spanish, and Japanese were included in the search check box because of multilingualism within the workgroup. In addition to these searches, other articles reviewed for potential inclusion were the ISDS research committee monthly literature review collection (http://www.syndromic.org/cop/research) and references from relevant articles, systematic reviews, and meta-analyses found through initial literature searches. The online bibliographic service Zotero (https://www.zotero.org/) was used for citation management.

The workgroup was formed from members of the ISDS with diverse background specialties, (e.g., public health physician, doctor of veterinary medicine, data scientist, public health professor, biomedical informatics) and countries of residence (e.g., USA, Australia, China, Japan). Within the group, a pair of members evaluated each collected abstract in detail for possible inclusion in the systematic review. Each member recorded the following information from each potential publication: author(s), date of publication, publication type (e.g., journal, conference proceedings, white or gray literature), data source type (e.g., social networking sites, microblogs, or open source databases). Requirements were that each study must be published as original researchand must analyze social media. The initial review was done for all documents containing an abstract, including peer-reviewed conference proceedings or white papers. An article was excluded if the full text was not available, if only methods were described (i.e., building an application programming interface, but no results), or if it did not directly address one of the two following research questions:

1. Q1. Can social media be integrated into disease surveillance practice and outbreak management to support and improve public health?
2. Q2. Can social media be used to effectively target populations, specifically vulnerable populations, to test an intervention and interact with a community to improve health outcomes?

Any differences of opinion about whether to include a paper were resolved through discussion until the workgroup achieved a consensus on inclusion or exclusion.

For each article fitting the review inclusion criteria, one workgroup member was assigned to extract and record specific details from the full-text article. This information included background (e.g., study objective, sample population and size, and the location, setting, time, and duration of the study), methods (e.g., study design, keywords, classification methods), outcomes measured (e.g., population, disease studied, intervention or exploratory (i.e., whether the study evaluates the impact of or observes the use of social media, respectively), hypothesis, outcomes related to either research question), results, and conclusions. To assess involvement of a public health jurisdiction in the study or intervention, a reviewer searched the acknowledgements for funding agency and methods for direct public health involvement. In addition, the reviewers included any information they believed might have introduced bias into the study. Note that to date, this study protocol has not been registered.

RESULTS

Study Selection

We identified 1,405 English language studies published through February 2013 in peer-reviewed journals, conference proceedings, and white/gray literature through Embase, PubMed, and Scopus database searches, as well as 8 articles through the Japanese database, Ichushi-Web (Fig 1). An additional 181 studies were identified from citation lists of relevant reviews or editorials and the workgroup's private collections. After removing duplicates, 1,499 studies remained for the abstract screening step. We excluded 1,205 of these studies because they were reviews, letters, commentaries, or did not address either of the research questions. An additional 8 studies were excluded because the full-text publications were not available. These excluded study abstracts or presentations reported promising preliminary research addressing active disease surveillance. Topics ranged from targeting sexually transmitted diseases in traditionally hard-to-reach populations [10–13] to detecting unusual events, anomalies, and social disruption for early warning systems [14].

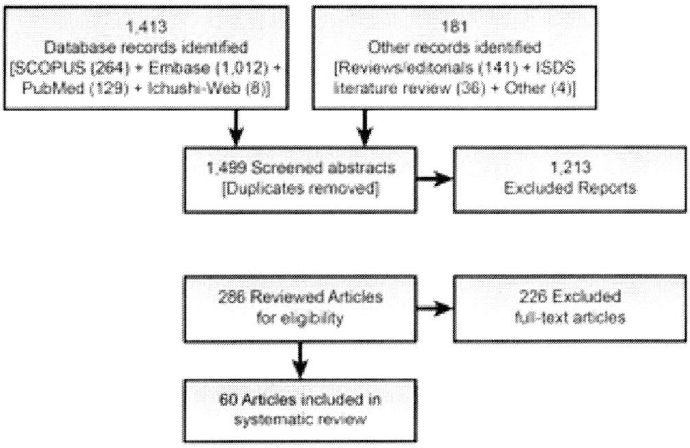

Figure 1. Flow diagram for the selection of literature reviewed.

The abstract screening process resulted in 286 studies identified for detailed review of full-text articles. After this review, we further excluded studies that did not meet our definition of social media (e.g., Internet search, ProMED-mail) or discussed methods exclusively. We identified a total of 60 studies that met our eligibility criteria and addressed at least one of the two research questions. This process took over a year to complete because the authors donated their free time to review and analyze the literature.

Study Characteristics

Question 1 –Intervention into Surveillance Practice and Outbreak Management.

Of the 33 studies concerning disease surveillance and outbreak management, 48% (n = 16) were conducted in North America [15–30], 24% (n = 8) in Europe [31–37], 15% (n = 5) in Asia [38–42], 9% (n = 3) in an unspecified location [43–45], 3% (n = 1) in South America [46], and 3% (n = 1) on a global scale [47]. Twitter was used as the primary data source in 81% (n = 27) of the studies although Facebook, various blogs, and health-related discussion forums were also investigated [15–17,19–23,26,27,29–40,43–47]. The studies examined data from January 2006 [46] to January 2012 [38] with the majority focused on 2009. The collection period spanned the 2009 H1N1 influenza pandemic, and 45% (n = 15) of the papers focused on influenza monitoring [15,16,19,27,31–33,38–40,43–45,47]. Comparison to CDC reports were most commonly used to evaluate the effectiveness of the various surveillance techniques presented. Most Twitter-based studies identified study populations through automatic means, i.e., Twitter keyword searches such as "influenza," "H1N1," and "swine flu" to target influenza-related tweets. The articles reported that study sizes were measured either by the number of tweets, ranging from 150 thousand [38] to 2 billion [22], or the number of unique social media users, ranging from 118 users [28] to 24.5 million [33]. Most studies were published in English (2 in Japanese), and all were exploratory in nature.

Question 2 –Targeted Vulnerable Populations.

Thirty-two studies were identified as targeting a vulnerable population to improve health outcomes. These studies emphasized interaction with users rather than automatic algorithms and therefore typically contained focused populations and smaller datasets. The study sizes ranged from 19 post-partum women [48] to 155,508 Twitter users from 9 distinct areas [26]. All of the studies included were published in English and 66% (n = 21) were conducted in North America [20,21,25,26,49–65], 12% (n = 4) in Australia [48,66–68], 9% (n = 3) in Asia [41,69,70], and 6% (n = 2) in Europe [1,71]. Most of the studies were classified as exploratory, although 24% (n = 8) of studies did include some type of intervention [1,55,56,58,60,64,69,71]. Populations studied were generally more focused than Question 1 studies, e.g., pregnant smokers in Australia. The study populations dated from January 2000 [1] to February 2012 [66], although many do not disclose study periods. Interestingly, the studies addressing Question 2 first appeared in 2000, but published literature on Question 1 does not appear until 2010. Also, there is a spike in addressing both questions during 2011 (Fig 2).

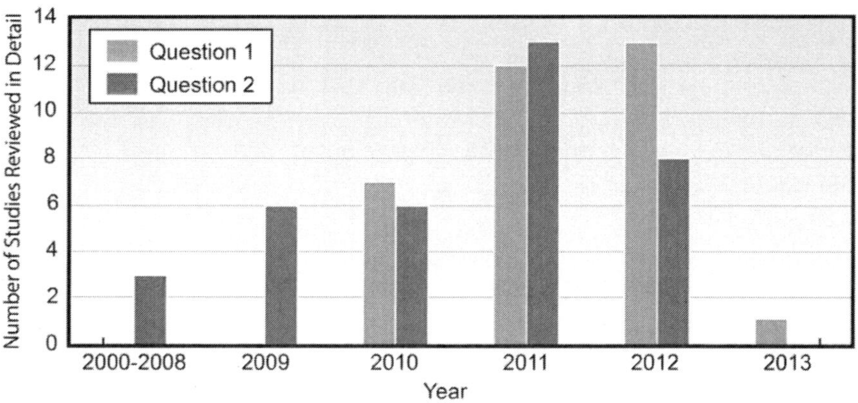

Figure 2. Number of Studies Addressing Questions 1 and 2, Reviewed in Detail by Year Published (January 2000 –February 2013).

Bias Across and Within Studies

The spectrum of studies selected for review were subject to publication bias because only primary literature was included and, therefore, other non-published information collected by state or federal health agencies was not incorporated. The choice of data search engines may have excluded valid studies that may not have been published in journals exposed through this process. In addition, there may be more recent articles published since our collection end date of March 2013.

Within the 60 studies reviewed, no important bias was identified by the authors and workgroup reviewers in 43% (n = 26) of the studies [1,19–21,23,24,29,31,34–36,38,39,41,43–45,49,53,57,61–63,66,70,72]; 56% (n = 34) displayed some degree of bias risk. The types of bias can be broken down into six different categories. Selection bias (n = 17) was the most prevalent as data was often collected out of convenience [25,51,52,60], at focused locations [15,46], or within specific social groups [65] and, therefore, was often not representative of the total population [15,26,28,30,46–48,51,54,58,59,65,71,73]. There were 14 articles displaying a faulty study design due to the choice of time period [16,17,27,33,37,40,42,47], data source [18,42,60], study scope [37,42], reporting of results [37,54], or lack of result measure [50,51]. Temporal relationship and directionality bias within 8 studies caused issues in the ability to extrapolate data [16,65,67] or infer directionality or causality [28,32,55,69]. A few studies had sample sizes that were too small to draw conclusions, i.e., sample size bias [17,30,55,64,67]. Other biases present in the reviewed articles were reliability bias [22,28,54,68] and selective interpretation bias [32,40].

Public Health Involvement

There was a small number of local (3%, n = 2) and state (15%, n = 9) governmental public health agencies involved in the studies reviewed for actionable health and disease surveillance (Table 2). These supportive agencies reside in England (London) and the United States of America (USA) (California, Louisiana, Michigan, and Washington State). Public health involvement was mainly in monetary support on a national level (n = 30) from Brazil, Canada, Germany, Japan, Netherlands, Switzerland, Taiwan, and USA. One research paper, funded by the University of Maryland, USA, described the implementation of social media communication by a local Taiwan government for disaster management, which showed promise over current national awareness and response protocols [69]. Other universities showing interest in support of social media research were located in Australia, Germany, Italy, Japan, United Kingdom (UK), and USA. The private funding agencies that supported reviewed literature are found in the UK and USA. Only 3 papers contained a co-author who was affiliated with a public health agency, i.e., Public Health Agency of Canada [24], Governmental Institute of Public Health of Lower Saxony in Germany [37], and National Cancer Institute in USA [60].

Table 2. Counts of Funding Agency Types and Their Direct Involvement in the Review Studies.

	Funding Agency Question 1	Funding Agency Question 2	Funding Agency Total	Direct Involvement Question 1	Direct Involvement Question 2	Direct Involvement Total
Private	3	5	8	0	0	0
University	8	12	20	0	0	0
Local	1	1	2	0	1	1
State	5	4	9	0	0	0
National	20	10	30	0	0	0
Total	37	32	69	0	1	1

For both research questions, this table records the number of articles in which private organizations, universities, and governments (local, state and national) contributed as funding agencies and/or organizations with direct involvement in each study or intervention reviewed. Note that some articles contained more than one funding agency.

Question 1: Can social media be integrated into disease surveillance practice and outbreak management to support and improve public health?

The key to our systematic literature review of Question 1 was to identify if, when, and how social media have been applied for disease surveillance and outbreak management to support and improve public health. Within the 33 manuscripts identified as addressing this question, we found an overwhelming number focused on influenza-like illnesses (45%, n = 15). For the remaining articles, we classified the instances into Infectious Diseases (n = 6), Non-infectious Diseases (n = 4), Medication and Vaccines (n = 3), and Other (n = 5) to understand the extent and focus of current research. All of these studies were exploratory research and did not contain any type of intervention analysis.

Influenza-like Illness.

Influenza-like illness (ILI) was the first disease to be modeled using social media data in our review (Table 3). We identified 15 original, exploratory studies on ILI targeting social media users (e.g., Twitter and other blogs) from the USA, UK, and Japan between 2008 and 2012. From simple text searches, (e.g., flu or influenza [32,40,45]) to more specific influenza subtypes (e.g., H1N1, Swine Flu [16,44,47]) and symptomatic disease sets [15,17,19,31,32,38,39], all of the studies claimed to be able to use the social media data in real-time disease surveillance. A study by Sadilek, Kautz, and Silenzio (2012), applied their technique to identify the health of any person through geo-tagged Twitter microblogs in an effort to predict disease transmission [15]. In general, correlation between social media data and national health statistics, e.g., from the CDC, ranged from 0.55 [18] to 0.95 [43] and was shown to predict outbreaks before the standard outbreak surveillance method favored by each country [19,31,32,38,39].

Table 3. Characteristics of 15 influenza-like illness studies addressing research question 1[a].

Author (et al.)	Social Media Type	Location	Sample Population	Study Type	Population/ Disease Studied	Time Period	Intervention/ Exploratory
Achrekar [16]	Twitter	North America	1.9 million Twitter users	Retrospective	Influenza	Not specified	Exploratory
Aramaki [40]	Twitter	Asia	300 million tweets	Retrospective	Influenza (H1N1)	2008–2010	Exploratory
Chew [47]	Twitter	North America	Over 2 million tweets	Retrospective	Influenza	May–Dec 2009	Exploratory
Collier [44]	Twitter	Asia/Europe	5283 tweets	Retrospective	Influenza	2010	Exploratory
Corley [18]	Blogs, forums	North America	158,497,700 English language	Retrospective	Influenza	2008–2009	Exploratory
Culotta [17]	Twitter	North America	574,643 tweets	Retrospective	Influenza	Feb–Apr 2010	Exploratory
Culotta [43]	Twitter	North America	500 million tweets	Other	Influenza	2009/10 flu season	Exploratory
De Quincey [45]	Twitter	Europe	135,000 tweets	Retrospective	Influenza	2009	Exploratory
Doan [33]	Twitter	Europe (UK)	24.5 million Twitter Users	Retrospective	Influenza	2009–2010	Exploratory
Ishikawa [38]	Twitter	Asia (Japan)	157,007 tweets	Prospective cohort	Influenza	July 2011–Jan 2012	Exploratory
Lampos [31]	Twitter	Europe (England & Wales)	200,000 geolocated tweets; Urban centers	Correlation study	Influenza	2009/10 flu season	Exploratory
Okamura [39]	Twitter	Asia (Japan)	716,417 tweets	Retrospective	Influenza	Dec 2010–Jan 2011	Exploratory
Sadilek [15]	Twitter	North America (NYC area)	6237 tweets	Prospective cohort	Influenza	2010	Exploratory
Signorini [19]	Twitter	North America	Twitter users	Retrospective	Influenza (H1N1)	2009	Exploratory
Szomszor [32]	Twitter	Europe	3 million tweets	Retrospective	Influenza (H1N1)	May–Dec 2009	Exploratory

[a]Q1: Can social media be integrated into disease surveillance practice and outbreak detection management to support and improve public health and outbreak management?

Infectious Diseases.

We identified 6 studies that used different social media programs to determine if the timeliness and sensitivity of detection for other infectious disease outbreaks (e.g., dengue fever, cholera, human immunodeficiency virus (HIV), and *Escherichia coli*) could be improved (Table 4). In a study by Chunara, Andrews, and Brownstein (2013), the volume of cholera-related Twitter posts and HealthMap news media reports were compared to official Haiti cholera case reports during the first 100 days of the 2010 outbreak [23]. The changes in social media and news data trends were detected up to 2 weeks earlier than official case data, which they believe could have had direct implications on the disease outbreak and control measures taken [23]. After analyzing 7 million tweets on medical conditions during the 2011 *Enterohaemorrhagic E. coli* (EHEC) outbreak in Germany, Diaz-Aviles et al. (2012) found over 450,000 posts related to the outbreak and determined that this information would have detected the outbreak 1 day earlier than other warning systems [34]. Gomide et al. (2011) showed a correlation between Twitter posts in Brazil and dengue outbreaks (e.g., reported dengue cases correlated with the word "dengue" (0.78) and personal experience with dengue (0.96)) [46]. However, they reported that only 40% of tweets included location, which limited spatial analysis [46].

Although the breadth of studies is limited and most often retrospective, detection of outbreaks through social media tracking appears to provide a timeliness advantage in a variety of infectious disease outbreak settings.

Table 4. Characteristics of 6 infectious disease studies addressing research question 1[a].

Author (et al.)	Social Media Type	Location	Sample Population	Study Type	Population/Disease Studied	Time Period	Intervention/ Exploratory
Stuart Chester [24]	Web forums	North America	Mountain biking forum	Cohort	Campylo-bacteriosis outbreak during race	2007	Exploratory
Chunara [23]	Twitter	North America (Haiti)	Twitter data	Not specified	Cholera outbreak	Oct 2010–Jan 2011	Not specified
Díaz-Aviles [34]	Twitter	Europe (Germany)	Twitter data	Case study	*E. coli* outbreak	May–Jun 2011	Exploratory
Díaz-Aviles [35]	Twitter	Europe (Germany)	Twitter data	Algorithm development	*E. coli* outbreak	May–Jun 2011	Exploratory
Gomide [46]	Twitter	South America (Brazil)	Twitter data	Retrospective	Dengue fever outbreak	2006–2011	Exploratory
Ku [41]	Yahoo forums	Asia (Taiwan)	Yahoo knowledge public health forums	Retrospective	HIV/AIDS content	2007–2009	Exploratory

[a]Q1: Can social media be integrated into disease surveillance practice and outbreak detection management to support and improve public health and outbreak management?

Non-infectious Diseases.

The 4 studies identified as targeting non-infectious diseases were purely exploratory and focused on alcohol, tobacco, and sexual activity (Table 5). Facebook [25] and Twitter [27] were used to identify associations between alcohol references and misuse in college students or alcohol sales, respectively. It was shown that social media references to alcohol correlated with college students' self-reported alcohol use, including alcohol-related injuries, and the U.S. Census Bureau's alcohol sales volume. Therefore, social media data can enhance alcohol use surveillance and target specific audiences in need of health support. Another study, directed at college freshmen's Facebook use, found a positive correlation between displaying sexual references online and reporting the intention to become sexually active, providing a new forum to target prevention or education messages to adolescents [28]. Prier et al. (2011) examined different tools available to most effectively identify public health topics on Twitter [26]. They found that the Latent Dirichlet Allocation (LDA) topic modeling method was successful in identifying broad topics, e.g., physical activity, obesity, substance abuse, and attitudes towards healthcare, whereas a smaller, more focused dataset created by query selection and theme analysis is necessary to detect lower-frequency topics such as tobacco use. Overall, the study showed that social media can be used to promote both positive and negative heath behaviors.

Table 5. Characteristics of 4 non-infectious disease studies addressing research question 1[a].

Author (et al.)	Social Media Type	Location	Sample Population	Study Type	Population/Disease Studied	Time Period	Intervention/ Exploratory
Culotta [27]	Twitter	North America	Twitter data	Retrospective	Influenza rates and alcohol sales volume	2009–2010	Exploratory
Moreno [25]	Facebook	North America	Undergraduates from to U.S. universities	Cross-sectional survey	Problem drinking	2009–2010	Exploratory
Moreno [28]	Facebook	North America	U.S. university students (ages 18 and 19 years)	Cross-sectional	Sexual reference displays	2008–2011	Exploratory
Prier [26]	Twitter	North America	Twitter data	Retrospective	Tobacco use	2010	Exploratory

[a]Q1: Can social media be integrated into disease surveillance practice and outbreak detection management to support and improve public health and outbreak management?

Medication and Vaccines.

Social media discussions can be used to determine attitudes, misinformation, and adverse events related to medications, vaccines, and other drug uses (Table 6). Salathé and Khandelwal (2011) identified an increase in Twitter data between August and November 2009 related to the launch of the 2009 influenza H1N1 vaccine [20]. Tweets among opinionated users most often shared similar positive or negative sentiments towards vaccine use. As a result, simulation studies of disease transmission result in clusters of individuals with negative vaccine sentiments being unvaccinated and, therefore, at a higher risk of infection. This evidence may assist in targeting public health interventions of unvaccinated people at risk of disease. Another study reported that negative sentiment is more contagious than positive and, therefore, an increase in positive attitudes may predict an even greater increase in negative sentiment, which can be useful in modeling the diffusion of health behavior on social networks [21]. Twitter feeds provide a forum for discussions regarding medications and, therefore, can be targeted to improve information dissemination. Bian et al. scanned Twitter feeds for 5 different drugs and found 239 drug users with 27 drug-related adverse event tweets [22]. This study identifies support for pharmacovigilance through social media analysis, especially concerning new drug releases.

Other.

Many researchers have evaluated ways to best access and use health information on Twitter for disease surveillance (Table 7). A group in Germany retrospectively reviewed tweets that contained keywords of infectious disease symptoms and found 51% contained headlines that were linked to news websites regarding outbreaks and determined that a potential exists for using Twitter for real-time disease surveillance [37]. Sofean and Smith (2012) designed and evaluated a real-time architecture for collecting and filtering disease-related postings on Twitter and found

Table 6. Characteristics of 4 medicine or vaccine studies addressing research question 1[a].

Author (et al.)	Social Media Type	Location	Sample Population	Study Type	Population/Disease Studied	Time Period	Intervention/ Exploratory
Bian [22]	Twitter	North America	2 billion tweets	Retrospective	Adverse drug events	May 2009 –Oct 2010	Exploratory
Salathé [20]	Twitter	North America	Twitter data	Prospective cohort	Sentiment towards new vaccine	Aug 2009 –Feb 2010	Exploratory
Salathé [21]	Twitter	North America	Twitter data	Prospective cohort	Sentiment towards new vaccine	Aug 2009 –Feb 2010	Exploratory

[a]Q1: Can social media be integrated into disease surveillance practice and outbreak detection management to support and improve public health and outbreak management?

they could track health status in real time [36]. Other researchers developed methods for pulling social media, including using a Badu search engine [42] and the Ailment Topic Aspect Model (ATAM) [29]. ATAM introduces prior knowledge into the model from articles on diseases, reports model behavior in new settings, tracks illnesses over time and location, correlates risk factors with ailments, and then analyzes the correlations of symptoms and treatments. The ATAM is able to discover any coherent ailments, symptoms and treatment and does not have to be disease-specific [30]. Using a variety of search engines and new tools, it is possible to detect and track a variety of health ailments using social media.

Table 7. Characteristics of 5 "other" topic studies addressing research question 1[a].

Author (et al.)	Social Media Type	Location	Sample Population	Study Type	Population/ Disease Studied	Time Period	Intervention/ Exploratory
Krieck [37]	Twitter	Europe (Germany)	Twitter data	Retrospective	Fever, swine flu & H1NI-related	Sep 2010 – Feb 2011	Exploratory
Paul [30]	Twitter	North America	2 billion tweets	Not specified	Not specified	2010	Exploratory
Paul [29]	Twitter	North America	2 billion tweets	Not specified	Not specified	2010	Explanatory
Sofean [36]	Twitter	Europe	Twitter data	Algorithm development	Twitter data	Not specified	Exploratory
Yang [42]	Weblogs, microblogs, wikis, etc.	Asia	Weblogs, microblogs, wikis, etc.	Case study	Chinese social media data	Not specified	Not specified

[a]Q1: Can social media be integrated into disease surveillance practice and outbreak detection management to support and improve public health and outbreak management?

Question 2: Can social media be used to effectively target populations, specifically vulnerable populations, to test an intervention and interact with a community to improve health outcomes?

For question 2, we identified if, when, and how social media have been used to target populations and transform information gleaned from this data into action. The majority of studies within this group used social media to identify health risk behaviors (n = 10) and evaluate use of virtual communities to aid in risk reduction. For the remaining articles, we classified the instances into Infectious Diseases (n = 3), Non-infectious

Diseases (n = 9), and Other (n = 10) to get a better overview where exploratory research (n = 25) and intervention efforts (n = 7) have been focused.

Health Risk Behaviors.

Social media, especially Facebook [25,49,68] and MySpace [56,57], have been used to target adolescents displaying health risk behaviors associated with substance abuse and sexual activities (Table 8). Specialized chat rooms, websites, and Twitter have been targeted for adult health risk behavior with tobacco use [26,48,60], substance abuse [53], and sexual activities [58]. The specific populations, located in the USA and Australia, include college students [49,56,68], post-partum women [48], men who have sex with men (MSM) [58], and low-income youth [57]. These studies show that social media can be effective at identifying adolescent populations displaying substance abuse, especially alcohol [25,49,68], in addition to sexual behavior [57], and that social media can improve community health outcomes in at-risk adolescents [56] and MSM [58]. Interestingly, tobacco-related subjects posed an issue for researchers who tried to use topic modeling in Twitter [26] and found that the use of a virtual community bulletin board to reduce smoking behavior was ineffective [60]. As proposed by Prier et al. (2011), the use of low-frequency topics, such as tobacco use, may require human intervention for selection of query terms and relevant subsequent analysis to properly address health concerns [26].

Infectious Diseases.

Two of the 3 social media studies focusing on infectious diseases (67%), investigated the use of social media to reach target populations for protection against sexually transmitted infections (STI) (Table 9). For example, Sullivan et al. (2011) identified factors behind the underrepresentation of black and Hispanic MSM in online research studies (ORS) despite this group experiencing the largest increase in HIV case reports [62]. Targeted banner advertisements were posted in MySpace, displaying an ethnicity-matched model. This approach increased the odds of click-through of the ORS (adjusted odds ratios 1.7–1.8), but with limited effect on reducing dropouts. In the 2009 H1N1 pandemic, Szomszor, Kostkova, and de Quincey found that health communication via official Twitter feeds and trusted news organizations (e.g., BBC) was most effective in reaching the public; however, timeliness of health information may not directly translate to site popularity among these trusted sources [72]. In addition, they found 40% of appreciable health-related information identified on the Internet containing poor scientific merit was directly linked to spam. Overall, the studies showed potential in reaching populations concerning socially stigmatized or sensitive health conditions, but time and effort are needed to build up a trusted channel for information dissemination.

Table 8. Characteristics of 10 health risk behavior studies addressing research question 2[a].

Author (et al.)	Social Media Type	Location	Sample Population	Study Type	Population/ Disease Studied	Time Period	Intervention/ Exploratory
Frost [53]	PatientsLikeMe	North America (USA)	Patient members of PatientsLikeMe	Retrospective	Self-reported outcomes of off-label drug use	2010	Exploratory
Litt [49]	Facebook	North America (DC area)	89 Adolescents (ages 13–15 years); spend at least 1 hour on Facebook/week	Randomized	Perceptions of alcohol	2011	Exploratory
Lowe [48]	Any type of social media	Australia	Women who visited an ante-natal clinic	Prospective cohort	Pregnant smokers	2011	Exploratory
Moreno [25]	Facebook	North America	Undergraduates from 2 U|S. universities	Cross-sectional survey	Problem drinking	2009–2010	Exploratory
Moreno [56]	MySpace	North America	Ages 18–20 years; at least 1 risk behavior (sexual or substance abuse)	Randomized controlled intervention trial	Adolescent risk behavior (sexual and substance)	2007	Intervention
Prier [26]	Twitter	North America	Twitter data	Retrospective	Tobacco use	2010	Exploratory
Ralph [57]	TeenSMART and MySpace	North America (California)	Teens in lower-income areas	Survey, interviews, focus groups	General sexual health	July–Sept 2008	Exploratory
Rhodes [58]	Chat room	North America (North Carolina)	1,851 users; 210 users online assessment	Trained interventions and questionnaire	HIV risk behaviors for MSM	2004–2005	Both
Ridout [68]	Facebook	Australia	158 university students	Retrospective	Alcohol use	2009–2010	Exploratory
Stoddard [60]	Web-based Bulletin board	North America (USA)	1375 adult federal employee or contractors	Randomized	Willing to quit smoking	2006–2007	Intervention

[a]Q2: Can social media be used to effectively target populations, specifically vulnerable populations, to test an intervention and interact with a community to improve health outcomes?

Table 9. Characteristics of 3 infectious diseases studies addressing research question 2[a].

Author (et al.)	Social Media Type	Location	Sample Population	Study Type	Population/Disease Studied	Time Period	Intervention/ Exploratory
Ku [41]	Yahoo forums	Asia (Taiwan)	Yahoo knowledge public health forums	Retrospective	HIV/AIDS content	2007–2009	Exploratory
Sullivan [62]	MySpace banner ad	North America (USA)	MySpace MSM	Online survey	MSM at risk for HIV	2009	Exploratory
Szomszor [72]	Twitter	Global	English language users	Retrospective	Swine flu outbreak	2009	Exploratory

[a]Q2: Can social media be used to effectively target populations, specifically vulnerable populations, to test an intervention and interact with a community to improve health outcomes?

Non-Infectious Diseases.

Social media could potentially be used to target populations with illnesses of high prevalence and public health impact (e.g, depression, cancer, obesity, diabetes, and asthma) with an intervention to improve health outcomes. In a 16-week study of 32 women with breast cancer, an intervention using an electronic support group reported a significant decrease in depression symptoms and reaction to pain, and a trend towards increasing posttraumatic growth, zest for life, and deepening of spiritual lives [55]. There were some dropouts in participation, which was attributed to different personalities' response to the electronic support group. Similarly, researchers set up a chat room to provide an educational tool for adolescents with Type 1 diabetes and found that it significantly increased compliance and decreased HbA(1c) concentrations (from 8.9% to 7.8%) over a period of 3 months [1]. Mobile support programs used to increase dietary self-monitoring and improve weight loss resulted in body weight changes; however, a similar study using Twitter did not find any differences [64]. Therefore, the types of social media and the populations who will use and benefit from this type of information are key factors in how they impact health.

Multiple studies attempted to determine whether the potential exists for social media to reach vulnerable populations (Table 10). For mental health, a study of college freshmen showed that 46% of female and 21% of male students referenced stress, depression, or stress-related conditions, e.g., weight issues or drinking alcohol, on Facebook, and those who referred to stress were significantly more likely to mention weight concerns or depression [51]. These researchers concluded that Facebook may provide a mode of distribution of targeted stress reduction information. Similarly, researchers in Australia found that 44% of students reported the need for mental health support; within this group, 50% of them already use the Internet and 47% said they would use online social networks for mental health problems [67]. Social media could be used to identify those with non-infectious diseases and provide education and support to improve public health.

Table 10. Characteristics of 9 non-infectious diseases studies addressing research question 2[a].

Author (et al.)	Social Media Type	Location	Sample Population	Study Type	Population/ Disease Studied	Time Period	Intervention/ Exploratory
Baptist [50]	Facebook, MySpace, Twitter, etc.	North America	Asthma patients, ages 12–40 years	Cross-sectional	Asthma	2010	Exploratory
Egan [51]	Facebook	North America	300 U.S. university students, ages 18–19 years	Prospective cohort	Stress-related conditions	2009–2010	Not specified
Iafusco [1]	Chatline	Europe (Italy)	Young people with type 1 diabetes	Not specified	Diabetes care	2000	Intervention
Lieberman [55]	Discussion forums	North America	32 women with breast carcinoma	Clinical trial	Benefits of discussion forum for breast cancer	Not specified	Intervention
O'Dea [67]	MySpace, Facebook, others	Australia	Convenience sample of rural Australian high school students	Mixed methods	Social media for mental health	Not specified	Exploratory
Song [59]	Other (social networking site)	North America (Los Angeles, CA)	14 childhood cancer survivors (ages 18–25 years)	Content analysis (video clips)	Quality of life issues for childhood cancer survivors	Not specified	Exploratory
Takahashi [70]	Japanese social network	Asia	105 participants	Observational cross-section study	Depression-oriented social networking site	2007	Exploratory
Tsaousides [63]	Facebook	North America	96 individuals (60% female, ages 23–70 years) with traumatic brain injuries	Qualitative (online survey)	Use among individuals with traumatic brain injuries	Not specified	Exploratory
Turner-McGrievy [64]	Mobile Pounds Off Digitally (POD)	North America (USA)	Men and women users of POD	Randomized	Overweight and obese adults	July 2010 –Feb 2011	Intervention

[a]Q2: Can social media be used to effectively target populations, specifically vulnerable populations, to test an intervention and interact with a community to improve health outcomes?

Other.

Social media was used to identify "other" target populations, e.g., low-income groups [61] and older people in need of physical activity [71], to assess vaccination sentiments [20] and misuse of antibiotics [73] (Table 11). Salathé et al. (2011) found a strong correlation (r = 0.78) between vaccination sentiments on Twitter and vaccination rates reported by the CDC across U.S. Department of Health and Human Service regions [21]. Clusters of unprotected individuals with negative vaccination sentiments can be identified and targeted for tailored interventions. Scanfeld, Scanfeld, and Larson (2010) identified individuals from Twitter who may have misused antibiotics for treating viral infections who could be targeted for health-related education [73]. Dissemination of valid health information among the identified groups may promote behavioral change towards a healthier lifestyle.

Table 11. Characteristics of 10 "other" topic studies addressing research question 2[a].

Author (et al.)	Social Media Type	Location	Sample Population	Study Type	Population/ Disease Studied	Time Period	Intervention/ Exploratory
Dumbrell [66]	Twitter	Australia	Tweets from 114 health organizations	Case study	Various public health issues	2012	Exploratory
Fisher [52]	Various	North America (Utah)	111 patients at outpatient facility	Survey	Interests of patients in social media	2011	Exploratory
Huang [69]	Plurk	Asia (Taiwan)	>24,000 people displaced after extreme weather event	Case study	Locate displaced people after extreme weather	Aug 2009	Exploratory
Idriss [54]	Forum for psoriasis	North America	260 subjects from 5 online psoriasis support groups	Case study (online survey)	Demo-graphics, usage patterns and experiences	2006–2007	Exploratory
Peels [71]	Discussion forums	Europe (Netherlands)	> 7000 participants over 50 years old	Mixed methods	Increasing physical activities	2005–2010	Intervention
Salathé [20]	Twitter	North America	Twitter data	Prospective cohort	Sentiment towards new vaccine	Aug 2009 –Feb 2010	Exploratory
Salathé [21]	Twitter	North America	Twitter data	Prospective cohort	Sentiment towards new vaccine	Aug 2009 –Feb 2010	Exploratory
Scanfield [73]	Twitter	North America	Twitter data	Content analysis	Antibiotic information	2009	Exploratory
Stroever [61]	Facebook	North America	Low-income parents	Qualitative (focus group)	Value of child health information to low-income parents	2010	Exploratory
Wicks [65]	PatientsLikeMe	North America (80% USA)	7000 PatientsLikeMe members	Cross-sectional study	PatientsLikeMe Usefulness	2009	Exploratory

[a]Q2: Can social media be used to effectively target populations, specifically vulnerable populations, to test an intervention and interact with a community to improve health outcomes?

DISCUSSION

This systematic primary literature review on the use of social media to support public health practice has identified many evidence gaps and biases in the current knowledge on this topic. There are few studies to date on interventions and a lack of use of social media in practice despite the high potential for success identified in exploratory studies. This mirrors the lack of scientific reports published (n = 16) on performance assessment of disease surveillance methods found by Babaie et al. (2015), regardless of their necessity to public health response [74]. Our findings may suggest that it is particularly challenging to translate research using social media for biosurveillance into practice. This challenge may be amplified by the lack of an ethical framework for the integration of social media into public health surveillance systems [75]. In addition, the focus of many studies, especially on infectious diseases, is done retrospectively, potentially highlighting the ease in prediction post outbreak rather than implementation of social media prospectively. The under-representation of social media analytics in active surveillance may be due to a lack of resources or technical skills necessary for successful execution in the public health domain. Alternatively, public health departments may be using social media as a tool but not publishing their efforts. Due to the number of heterogeneous data sources used in analysis, a comparison and evaluation of techniques was not possible. However, this review demonstrates some evidence that the use of social media data could provide real-time surveillance of health issues, speed up outbreak management, and identify target populations necessary to support and improve public health and intervention outcomes.

Social media can impact the public health surveillance domain, bringing the wider media landscape to the public health community. This impact has been particularly important in the context of public health emergencies, such as after Haiti's post-earthquake cholera outbreak, where the utility of using social media as a data source in rapidly changing and dynamic situations was clearly shown [23]. Pharmacovigilance is another key area where social media have demonstrated value. Traditional methods of reporting adverse drug events rely on gatekeepers (e.g., clinicians and pharmaceutical companies) to alert authorities of these events. Social media, in particular Twitter, have shown significant potential for creating real-time access to firsthand reports of adverse drug events, thereby bypassing the gatekeeper bottleneck [22,76].

Traditionally hard-to-reach groups, e.g., MSM and adolescents, may be more likely to engage with social media rather than with more conventional public health communication channels, creating a new avenue to address sensitive health issues. A significant proportion of the interventions reviewed (40%) concentrated on targeting populations with increased risk of STIs, a topic often avoided in public settings [11,12,56,58]. Mental health intervention studies suggested that young people would be willing to use social media to address mental health issues [51,65,67,70]. In this context, the type of mediations must fit the social media outlet targeted. For example, mental health interventions conducted via Twitter, with a 140 character limit, are likely to be very different from the kinds of interventions conducted through the more discursive communication possible with Internet discussion forums.

Different target groups, e.g., age groups, may prefer different social media outlets. Consequently, knowing the population and how they use social media can be a critical part of successful intervention and surveillance. For example, in the articles reviewed focusing on health risk behaviors, we found that adolescents were targeted using Facebook [25,49,68] and MySpace [10,56,57], while adults were targeted within Twitter and specialized chat rooms and websites [26,48,53,58,60]. However, to our knowledge, there is no directed health-related scientific research addressing which social media outlet should be targeted for specific populations. For health surveillance, the impact of the potential lack of population representativeness in the use of social media to detect and track disease outbreaks has not been adequately researched.

In addition, different topics may require different search techniques to identify targeted populations. In the study by Prier et al. (2011), they were successful at identifying broad topics in social media, e.g., physical activity and obesity, using the LDA method, yet for lower-frequency topics, such as tobacco use, human intervention was required for selection of query terms to create a smaller, more focused data set in which subsequent analysis was possible [26]. Similarly, the type of social media platform used in analyses may change based on the target population and the years being studied. For example, the use of social media has evolved from blogs and discussion forums pre–2005 to social networking platforms as new technologies came to market. In this respect, the field of surveillance would benefit from a study classifying topics of concern and appropriate analysis techniques to achieve the greatest number of results or largest audience for intervention.

Since February 2013, the last search date reported in this review, there has been an increase in the number of articles published per year using a similar initial search query to this review. Estimating an 80% exclusion rate based on the results discussed above, around 90 new articles per year were published in 2013 and 2014. This number is higher than previous years, although many of the new literature focus is on previously described sources (e.g., google flu) and methods being applied to a different disease. Regardless, an upward trend in publications suggests an increase interest in understanding social media's role in disease surveillance. This literature review demonstrates the effectiveness of social media in supporting and improving public health and identifying target populations for intervention. Coupled with the increased interest in social media analytics, opportunities to integrate this novel data source into disease surveillance and outbreak management should arise for public health professionals.

ACKNOWLEDGMENTS

This work was supported by the International Society for Disease Surveillance. The authors thank Christine Noonan at Pacific Northwest National Laboratory (PNNL) for project support, as well as Amy Ising, University of North Carolina at Chapel Hill, William Storm, Ohio Department of Health, and Silvia Valkova, IMS Institute for Healthcare Informatics, for their contributions to the project. Participation of Courtney D. Corley and Lauren E. Charles-Smith was supported in part by the PNNL's Laboratory Directed Research and Development Program. Pacific Northwest National Laboratory is operated for the U.S. Department of Energy by Battelle under Contract DE-AC05-76RL01830. The views expressed in this article are those of the authors and do not necessarily represent the views of the U.S. Department of Defense, U.S. Department of Veterans Affairs, or Health Services Research and Development Service.

AUTHOR CONTRIBUTIONS

Conceived and designed the experiments: LECS TLR MAC MC EHYL JAP MS LCS KJS CDC. Performed the experiments: LECS TLR MAC MC EHYL JMO JAP MS LCS KJS CDC. Analyzed the data: LECS TLR MAC MC EHYL JMO JAP MS LCS KJS CDC. Contributed reagents/materials/analysis tools: LECS TLR MAC MC EHYL JMO JAP MS LCS KJS CDC. Wrote the paper: LECS TLR MAC MC EHYL JMO JAP MS LCS KJS CDC.

REFERENCES

1. Iafusco D, Ingenito N, Prisco F. The chatline as a communication and educational tool in adolescents with insulin-dependent diabetes: preliminary observations. Diabetes Care. 2000;23: 1853–1853. doi: 10.2337/diacare.23.12.1853b.

2. McIver D, Brownstein J. Wikipedia Usage Estimates Prevalence of Influenza-Like Illness in the United States in Near Real-Time. PLoS Comput Biol. 2014;10: 1–8. doi: 10.1371/journal.pcbi.1003581.

3. Ginsberg J, Mohebbi MH, Patel RS, Brammer L, Smolinski MS, Brilliant L. Detecting influenza epidemics using search engine query data. Nature. 2009;457: 1012–1014.

4. Nsoesie E, Buckeridge D, Brownstein J. Guess Who's Not Coming to Dinner? Evaluating Online Restaurant Reservations for Disease Surveillance. J Med Internet Res. 2014;16.

5. Moorhead S, Hazlett D, Harrison L, Carroll J, Irwin A, Hoving C. A New Dimension of Health Care: Systematic Review of the Uses, Benefits, and Limitations of Social Media for Health Communication. J Med Internet Res. 2013;15. d

6. Bernardo TM, Rajic A, Young I, Robiadek K, Pham MT, Funk JA. Scoping Review on Search Queries and Social Media for Disease Surveillance: A Chronology of Innovation. J Med Internet Res. 2013;15: e147.

7. Acera E, Agheneza T, Denecke K, Kirchner G, Eckmanns T. Social Media and Internet-Based Data in Global Systems for Public Health Surveillance: A Systematic Review. Milbank Q. 2014;92: 7–33.

8. Walters R, Harlan P, Nelson N, Hartley D. Data Sources for Biosurveillance. Wiley Handbook of Science and Technology for Homeland Security. John Wiley & Sons, Inc.; 2009. pp. 1–17.

9. Moher D, Liberati A, Tetzlaff J, Altman D. Preferred Reporting Items for Systematic Reviews and Meta-Analyses: The PRISMA Statement. PLoS Med. 2009;6.

10. 10.Moreno MA, Brockman L, Christakis DA. "Oops, I Did It Again": A Content Analysis of Adolescents' Displayed Sexual References on Myspace. J Adolesc Health. 2009;44: S22–S23.

11. Read R, Ewalds T, Singh A. Web 2.0 and [Nexopia.com]: Direct-To-Teen STI Interaction via a social networking site. 18th International Society for STD Research Conferences. London; 2009.

12. Schmidt M, Currie M, Bertram S, Bavinton T, Bowden F. Promoting Chlamydia Testing to Young Women, Their Partners and Their GPs using modern and social media. SEXUAL HEALTH. 2009. pp. 369–369.

13. Yamauchi E. MYMsta: Using Mobile Social Networking in HIV Prevention. Sex:: Tech Conference 2010. San Francisco; 2010.

14. Vaillant L, Barboza P, Arthur R. Epidemic Intelligence: Assessing event-based tools and users' perception in the GHSAG community [Internet]. Presentation presented at: IMED; 2011; Vienne, France. Available: http://www.isid.org/events/archives/IMED2011/Downloads/IMED2011_Presentations/IMED2011_Vaillant.pdf.

15. Sadilek A, Kautz H, Silenzio V. Predicting disease transmission from geo-tagged micro-blog data. AI Access Foundation; 2012. pp. 136–142.

16. Achrekar H, Gandhe A, Lazarus R, Yu SH, Liu B. Twitter improves seasonal influenza prediction. SciTePress; 2012. pp. 61–70. Available: http://www.cs.uml.edu/~bliu/pub/healthinf_2012.pdf.

17. Culotta A. Towards detecting influenza epidemics by analyzing Twitter messages. Association for Computing Machinery; 2010. pp. 115–122. Available:

18. Corley CD, Cook DJ, Mikler AR, Singh KP. Text and Structural Data Mining of Influenza Mentions in Web and Social Media. Int J Environ Res Public Health. 2010;7: 596–615.

19. Signorini A, Segre AM, Polgreen PM. The Use of Twitter to Track Levels of Disease Activity and Public Concern in the U.S. during the Influenza A H1N1 Pandemic. PLoS ONE. 2011;6: e19467.

20. Salathé M, Khandelwal S. Assessing Vaccination Sentiments with Online Social Media: Implications for Infectious Disease Dynamics and Control. PLoS Comput Biol. 2011;7.

21. Salathé M, Vu DQ, Khandelwal S, Hunter DR. The Dynamics of Health Behavior Sentiments on a Large Online Social Network. arXiv:12077274. 2012; Available: http://arxiv.org/abs/1207.7274.

22. Bian J, Topaloglu U, Yu F. Towards large-scale twitter mining for drug-related adverse events. Association for Computing Machinery; 2012. pp. 25–32. Available:

23. Chunara R, Andrews JR, Brownstein JS. Social and news media enable estimation of epidemiological patterns early in the 2010 Haitian cholera outbreak. Am J Trop Med Hyg. 2012;86: 39–45.

24. Stuart Chester TL, Taylor M, Sandhu J, Forsting S, Ellis A, Stirling R, et al. Use of a Web Forum and an Online Questionnaire in the Detection and Investigation of an Outbreak. Online J Public Health Inform. 2011;3. d

25. Moreno MA, Christakis DA, Egan KG, Brockman LN, Becker T. Associations between displayed alcohol references on Facebook and problem drinking among college students. Arch Pediatr Adolesc Med. 2012;166: 157–163.

26. Prier KW, Smith MS, Giraud-Carrier C, Hanson CL. Identifying health-related topics on twitter an exploration of tobacco-related tweets as a test topic. Springer Verlag; 2011. pp. 18–25. Available:

27. Culotta A. Lightweight methods to estimate influenza rates and alcohol sales volume from Twitter messages. Lang Resour Eval. 2013;47: 217–238.

28. Moreno MA, Brockman L, Wasserheit J, Christakis DA. A Pilot Evaluation of Older Adolescents' Sexual Reference Displays on Facebook. J Sex Res. 2012;49: 390–399.

29. Paul MJ, Dredze M. A model for mining public health topics from Twitter. Health (N Y). 2012;11: 16–6.

30. Paul MJ, Dredze M. You Are What You Tweet: Analyzing Twitter for Public Health. ICWSM. 2011.

31. Lampos V, Cristianini N. Tracking the flu pandemic by monitoring the social web. IEEE Computer Society; 2010. pp. 411–416. Available:

32. Szomszor M, Kostkova P, De Quincey E. #Swineflu: Twitter predicts swine flu outbreak in 2009. Springer Verlag; 2011. pp. 18–26. Available: .

33. Doan S, Ohno-Machado L, Collier N. Enhancing Twitter Data Analysis with Simple Semantic Filtering: Example in Tracking Influenza-Like Illnesses. 2012 IEEE Second International Conference on Healthcare Informatics, Imaging and Systems Biology (HISB). 2012. pp. 62–71. doi: 10.1109/HISB.2012.21.

34. Diaz-Aviles E, Stewart A. Tracking Twitter for Epidemic Intelligence. Case study: EHEC/HUS outbreak in Germany, 2011. Association for Computing Machinery; 2012. pp. 82–85. Available:

35. Diaz-Aviles E, Stewart A, Velasco E, Denecke K, Nejdl W. Towards personalized learning to rank for epidemic intelligence based on social media streams. Association for Computing Machinery; 2012. pp. 495–496. Available:

36. Sofean M, Smith M. A real-time architecture for detection of diseases using social networks: Design, implementation and evaluation. Association for Computing Machinery; 2012. pp. 309–310. Available:

37. Krieck M, Dreesman J, Otrusina L, Denecke K. A new age of public health: Identifying disease outbreaks by analyzing tweets. Proceedings of Health Web-Science Workshop, ACM Web Science Conference. 2011.

38. Ishikawa T. Evaluation of microblog as influenza surveillance source. J Natl Inst Public Health. 2012;61.

39. Okamura N, Seki K, Uehara K. Using Microblog for Syndromic Surveillance. IPSJ SIG Tech Rep. 2011;

40. Aramaki E, Maskawa S, Morita M. Twitter catches the flu: Detecting influenza epidemics using Twitter. Association for Computational Linguistics (ACL); 2011. pp. 1568–1576.

41. Ku Y, Chiu C, Zhang Y, Fan L, Chen H. Global disease surveillance using social media: HIV/AIDS content intervention in web forums. IEEE Computer Society; 2010. p. 170. Available: doi: 10.1109/ISI.2010.5484749.

42. Yang M, Li YJ, Kiang M. Uncovering social media data for public health surveillance. Pacific Asia Conference on Information Systems; 2011.

43. Culotta A. Detecting influenza outbreaks by analyzing Twitter messages [Internet]. 2010 Jul. Report No.: 1007.4748. Available: http://arxiv.org/abs/1007.4748

44. Collier N, Son NT, Nguyen NM. OMG U got flu? Analysis of shared health messages for bio-surveillance. J Biomed Semant. 2011;2: S9.

45. De Quincey E, Kostkova P. Early warning and outbreak detection using social networking websites: The potential of Twitter. Springer Verlag; 2010. pp. 21–24. Available:

46. Gomide J, Veloso A, Meira W Jr, Almeida V, Benevenuto F, Ferraz F, et al. Dengue surveillance based on a computational model of spatio-temporal locality of twitter. ACM Web Science Conference (WebSci). 2011. pp. 1–8.

47. Chew C, Eysenbach G. Pandemics in the Age of Twitter: Content Analysis of Tweets during the 2009 H1N1 Outbreak. PLoS ONE. 2010;5: e14118.

48. Lowe JB, Barnes M, Teo C, Sutherns S. Investigating the use of social media to help women from going back to smoking post-partum. Aust N Z J Public Health. 2012;36: 30–32.

49. Litt DM, Stock ML. Adolescent alcohol-related risk cognitions: the roles of social norms and social networking sites. Psychol Addict Behav J Soc Psychol Addict Behav. 2011;25: 708–713.

50. Baptist AP, Thompson M, Grossman KS, Mohammed L, Sy A, Sanders GM. Social media, text messaging, and email-preferences of asthma patients between 12 and 40 years old. J Asthma Off J Assoc Care Asthma. 2011;48: 824–830.

51. Egan KG, Moreno MA. Prevalence of stress references on college freshmen Facebook profiles. Comput Inform Nurs CIN. 2011;29: 586–592.

52. Fisher J, Clayton M. Who Gives a Tweet: Assessing Patients' Interest in the Use of Social Media for Health Care. Worldviews Evid Based Nurs. 2012;9: 100–108.

53. Frost J, Okun S, Vaughan T, Heywood J, Wicks P. Patient-reported Outcomes as a Source of Evidence in Off-Label Prescribing: Analysis of Data From PatientsLikeMe. J Med Internet Res. 2011;13.

54. Idriss SZ, Kvedar JC, Watson AJ. The role of online support communities: benefits of expanded social networks to patients with psoriasis. Arch Dermatol. 2009;145: 46–51.

55. Lieberman MA, Golant M, Giese-Davis J, Winzlenberg A, Benjamin H, Humphreys K, et al. Electronic support groups for breast carcinoma. Cancer. 2003;97: 920–925.

56. Moreno MA, Vanderstoep A, Parks MR, Zimmerman FJ, Kurth A, Christakis DA. Reducing at-risk adolescents' display of risk behavior on a social networking web site: a randomized controlled pilot intervention trial. Arch Pediatr Adolesc Med. 2009;163: 35–41.

57. Ralph LJ, Berglas NF, Schwartz SL, Brindis CD. Finding Teens in TheirSpace: Using Social Networking Sites to Connect Youth to Sexual Health Services. Sex Res Soc Policy. 2011;8: 38–49.

58. Rhodes SD, Hergenrather KC, Duncan J, Vissman AT, Miller C, Wilkin AM, et al. A Pilot Intervention Utilizing Internet Chat Rooms to Prevent HIV Risk Behaviors Among Men Who Have Sex with Men. Public Health Rep. 2010;125: 29–37. pmid:20408385

59. Song H, Nam Y, Gould J, Sanders WS, McLaughlin M, Fulk J, et al. Cancer survivor identity shared in a social media intervention. J Pediatr Oncol Nurs Off J Assoc Pediatr Oncol Nurses. 2012;29: 80–91.

60. Stoddard JL, Augustson EM, Moser RP. Effect of Adding a Virtual Community (Bulletin Board) to Smokefree.gov: Randomized Controlled Trial. J Med Internet Res. 2008;10.

61. Stroever SJ, Mackert MS, McAlister AL, Hoelscher DM. Using social media to communicate child health information to low-income parents. Prev Chronic Dis. 2011;8: A148. pmid:22005641

62. Sullivan PS, Khosropour CM, Luisi N, Amsden M, Coggia T, Wingood GM, et al. Bias in Online Recruitment and Retention of Racial and Ethnic Minority Men Who Have Sex With Men. J Med Internet Res. 2011;13: e38.

63. Tsaousides T, Matsuzawa Y, Lebowitz M. Familiarity and prevalence of Facebook use for social networking among individuals with traumatic brain injury. Brain Inj BI. 2011;25: 1155–1162.

64. Turner-McGrievy G, Tate D. Tweets, Apps, and Pods: Results of the 6-Month Mobile Pounds Off Digitally (Mobile POD) Randomized Weight-Loss Intervention Among Adults. J Med Internet Res. 2011;13.

65. Wicks P, Massagli M, Frost J, Brownstein C, Okun S, Vaughan T, et al. Sharing Health Data for Better Outcomes on PatientsLikeMe. J Med Internet Res. 2010;12.

66. Dumbrell D, Steele R. What are the characteristics of highly disseminated public health-related tweets? Association for Computing Machinery; 2012. pp. 115–118.

67. O'Dea B, Campbell A. Healthy connections: online social networks and their potential for peer support. Stud Health Technol Inform. 2011;168: 133–140. pmid:21893921

68. Ridout B, Campbell A, Ellis L. "Off your Face(book)": alcohol in online social identity construction and its relation to problem drinking in university students. Drug Alcohol Rev. 2012;31: 20–26.

69. Huang C- M, Chan E, Hyder AA. Web 2.0 and Internet Social Networking: A New tool for Disaster Management? Lessons from Taiwan. BMC Med Inform Decis Mak. 2010;10: 57.

70. Takahashi Y, Uchida C, Miyaki K, Sakai M, Shimbo T, Nakayama T. Potential Benefits and Harms of a Peer Support Social Network Service on the Internet for People With Depressive Tendencies: Qualitative Content Analysis and Social Network Analysis. J Med Internet Res. 2009;11: e29.

71. Peels DA, van Stralen MM, Bolman C, Golsteijn RHJ, de Vries H, Mudde AN, et al. Development of web-based computer-tailored advice to promote physical activity among people older than 50 years. J Med Internet Res. 2012;14: e39.

72. Szomszor M, Kostkova P, St Louis C. Twitter informatics: Tracking and understanding public reaction during the 2009 Swine Flu pandemic. IEEE Computer Society; 2011. pp. 320–323.

73. Scanfeld D, Scanfeld V, Larson EL. Dissemination of health information through social networks: Twitter and antibiotics. Am J Infect Control. 2010;38: 182–188.

74. Babaie J, Ardalan A, Vatandoost H, Goya MM, Akbarisari A. Performance Assessment of Communicable Disease Surveillance in Disasters: A Systematic Review. PLOS Currents Disasters. 2015;Edition 1.

75. Vayena E, Salathé M, Madoff L, Brownstein J. Ethical Challenges of Big Data in Public Health. PLoS Comput Biol. 11: e1003904.

76. Sarker A, Ginn R, Nikfarjam A, O'Connor K, Smith K, Jayaraman S, et al. Utilizing Social Media Data for Pharmacovigilance: A Review. J Biomed Inform. 2015;54: 202–212.

14

EARLY FLOOD DETECTION FOR RAPID HUMANITARIAN RESPONSE: HARNESSING NEAR REAL-TIME SATELLITE AND TWITTER SIGNALS

Brenden Jongman [1], Jurjen Wagemaker [2], Beatriz Revilla Romero [3,4] and Erin Coughlan de Perez [1,5,6]

[1]Institute for Environmental Studies, VU University Amsterdam, De Boelelaan 1085, Amsterdam 1084HC, The Netherlands

[2]Floodtags, The Hague 2516 BE, The Netherlands

[3]European Commission Joint Research Centre, Ispra 21027, Italy

[4]Faculty of Geosciences, Utrecht University, Utrecht 3512 JE, The Netherlands

[5]Red Cross/Red Crescent Climate Centre, The Hague 2521 CV, The Netherlands

[6]International Research Institute for Climate and Society, Palisades, NY 10964, USA

ABSTRACT

Humanitarian organizations have a crucial role in response and relief efforts after floods. The effectiveness of disaster response is contingent on accurate and timely information regarding the location, timing and impacts of the event. Here we show how two near-real-time data sources, satellite observations of water coverage and flood-related social media activity from Twitter, can be used to support rapid disaster response, using case-studies in the Philippines and Pakistan. For these countries we analyze information from disaster response organizations, the Global Flood Detection System (GFDS) satellite flood signal, and flood-related Twitter activity analysis. The results demonstrate that these sources of near-real-time information can be used to gain a quicker understanding of the location, the timing, as well as the causes and impacts of floods. In terms of location, we produce daily impact maps based on both satellite information and social media, which can dynamically and rapidly outline the affected area during a disaster. In terms of timing, the results show that GFDS and/or Twitter signals flagging ongoing or upcoming flooding are regularly available one to several days before the event was reported to humanitarian organizations. In terms of event understanding, we show that both GFDS and social media can be used to detect and understand unexpected or controversial flood events, for example due to the sudden opening of hydropower dams or the breaching of flood protection. The performance of the GFDS and Twitter data for early detection and location mapping is mixed, depending on specific hydrological circumstances (GFDS) and social media penetration (Twitter). Further research is needed to improve the interpretation of the GFDS signal in different situations, and to improve the pre-processing of social media data for operational use.

Keywords: climate risk; social media; flood risk; forecasting; GFDS: early detection; Twitter; humanitarian response

1. INTRODUCTION

Flooding of river systems caused over US$1 trillion in damages and 220,000 fatalities, globally, since 1980 [1]. Many low-income countries are especially vulnerable to floods, given the generally low standards of flood protection and the limited capacity of disaster response, social protection, and healthcare facilities [2,3]. National and international humanitarian organizations, therefore, have an important role in supporting both *ex ante* disaster risk reduction and *ex post* disaster response of these countries. The need for disaster response was exemplified recently during the recent 2015 Malawi floods, when the Red Cross/Red Crescent Movement alone launched an emergency appeal of over CHF 2 million within days of the event to assist over 40,000 affected people [4]. Humanitarian aid is offered daily on a smaller scale for the hundreds of flood events that happen around the world each year [5].

The effectiveness of these disaster response efforts is contingent on accurate and timely information regarding the geographical location and impacts of the ongoing flood event. Decisions on the deployment of emergency aid and the distribution of supplies should be based on insights in where impacts are faced and what the nature of these impacts is [6].

Here, we consider three questions that are of interest to humanitarian organizations in the immediate aftermath of a flood:

(1) Where is the flood?

(2) When can we know about the flooding?

(3) What do we know about the impacts?

Traditionally, such information reaches humanitarian organizations through a network of field stations, employees, and volunteers, as well as through common news outlets, such as radio and television [7,8]. However, the intelligence that is received through these channels often reaches the right people only with a delay of many hours or even several days, and cannot always fully capture the three key parameters: timing, location, and impacts of the event. Innovative systems for early flood detection are recently being developed to provide additional spatial and intensity information that could be used in disaster response [9]. In this paper, we focus on two such innovative systems, the first based on near-real-time satellite data and the other on near-real-time Twitter data, and analyze how these systems sources may support effective humanitarian response. We perform the analysis based on case-studies in Pakistan and the Philippines.

Global satellite-based early detection systems are often able to identify riverine flood-induced water coverage from space within 24 h. Examples of such systems are the flood maps based on MODIS [10,11] and the Global Flood Detection System (hereinafter refer as GFDS) [12]. MODIS uses an optical signal to estimated inundated areas, which was used successfully for near-real-time inundation mapping in the 2012 Pakistan floods [13]. GFDS uses daily passive microwave satellite observations for rapidly identifying inundated areas, and has been applied for this purpose in recent floods; for example, in Bolivia 2014 and in India 2014. During these events, GFDS was proven useful in disaster response by providing flood extent, and time series of satellite observations for the current and the three previous years, in order to provide information about the importance of the flood event in relationship to potential previous events. Examples of disaster response assistance maps produced using daily GFDS data can be found at the Emergency Response Coordination Centre (ERCC) ortal [14].

Separate from the developments in satellite observation, past years have seen a spur of development in the use of near-real-time data streams from (social) media platforms such as Twitter, Facebook, Instagram, and news websites during and after disasters. Whereas satellite information has a typical delay of 24 h or more, social media messages can already be accessed within minutes of publication. Recent advances have made it possible to attribute social media information to geographic locations by extracting the body text (e.g., "New York City") and linking this to the location on a map [15,16,17]. One of the first times that social media was used on a large scale for disaster monitoring was after the earthquake in Haiti in 2010 [18]. A team lead by Patrick Meijer collected tweets of observers and placed them on a map using the Ushahidi platform, assisting rescue operations [9]. Since then, social monitoring tools have been used regularly during or after disasters, including wildfires [19], earthquakes [20], floods [21], winter storms [22], heavy snowfall [23], and typhoons [24]. Several platforms have been designed to support these efforts, such as Twitter Alerts and GeoFeedia. The Operations Centre of the Philippine Red Cross, for example, uses Twitter for disaster tracking. They both pay close attention to the messages in which they are called upon ("@philredcross") and search for keywords and hashtags to track known incidents (e.g., #flood, #insurgency, #earthquake, *etc.*). In addition, the Operations Centre use Twitter to follow agencies such as PAGASA (*Philippines Atmospheric, Geophysical and Astronomical Services Administration*), USGS and others, to monitor typhoons and earthquakes.

The main uses of social media in disaster situations have been improving situational awareness throughout the post-event response phase, two-way communication with affected people, psychological analysis [25], and relief coordination [24]. Earle *et al.* (2010) show that Twitter can also be used for the rapid mapping of disasters. Their results demonstrate that Twitter messages can be used to delineate earthquake-affected areas within several minutes, before official earthquake observations are available.

Whereas the use of satellite information and social media data for disaster response is gaining an increasing amount of attention, the ways in which these methods compare to one another and how they could complement current best practice in humanitarian organizations, remains largely undiscussed. For floods, specifically, the usability and accuracy of these distinct types of information sources has, furthermore, never been assessed comparatively. The aim of this paper is to provide a first comparison of these three channels of early detection information, in terms of the timing of the signal, as well as the type and value of the information. For this purpose, we analyzed data for a range of major and smaller flood events in Pakistan and the Philippines, all of which occurred in 2014. For all of these events we have had access to disaster response information from the local Red Cross National Societies, data from the near-real-time satellite flood detection system GFDS, and social media reporting through Twitter.

This paper continues as follows. Section 2 describes the methodologies and data sources used for the analysis. Section 3 presents the results of the flood mapping, early detection and event understanding. Section 4 provides discussion and conclusions.

2. METHODS AND DATA

We assess the effectiveness and usability of the near-real-time satellite and (social) media data for disaster response, by analyzing a range of flood events reported in Pakistan and the Philippines. For Pakistan, we focus on one single major flood event in September 2014, whereas for the Philippines we analyze 80 smaller flood events. For each of the events, we combine information on flood detection from three data sources: disaster response organizations (Section 2.1), the GFDS satellite signal (Section 2.2), and Twitter (Section 2.3). We analyze the potential added value of the remote sensing and Twitter data for each of the humanitarian questions regarding flood response (Section 2.4): location, timing, and impacts.

2.1. Disaster Reporting and Response Information

As a baseline, we consider the reported flood impact information that existed at the time of the flooding events in Pakistan and the Philippines, from January 2014 onwards.

For Pakistan, we focused on the major September 2014 floods. These floods were caused by monsoon rains in the catchment areas of the eastern rivers of Jhelum, Sutlej, Ravi, and Chenab. The floods affected over 2.5 million people, causing 367 fatalities and destroying over 100,000 houses. We considered a range of documents that detailed the information available post-flood, including (1) Daily Emergency and Response Situational Reports, produced by USAID and iMMAP (2–4 September); (2) Weather Report and Flood Advisory documents produced by the NDMA [26]; (3) Internal communications kindly made available by the International Federation of the Red Cross/Red Crescent office in Islamabad; and (4) post-event analysis documents of flood extent and impacts dated late September or early October 2014, including the official NDMA Recovery and Needs Assessment [27].

For the Philippines, we analyzed flood events as reported to the Philippines Red Cross Society (PRC) between January 2014 and January 2015. This database contains 80 individual events, which can be attributed to 21 individual hydro-meteorological extremes (intense rainfall events, tropical typhoons, dam bursts, *etc.*). For each of the 80 events, the database contains information on the event cause; geographical location, date of the event, date of event reporting to the PRC, and date and type of intervention by the PRC. See Table 1 for an example entry from this dataset. The dataset clearly outlines the timeline in event occurrence, reporting, and action, and is therefore ideally suited for the range of analytics pursued in this study.

Table 1. Extract from event occurrence and response dataset provided by the PRC (date: day/month year).

WHAT Kind of Flood (Floods, Flash Floods, and Flooding Caused by the Opening or Failure of Dams)	WHERE did the Event Happen (Village/Region)	WHEN did the Event Happen?	WHEN Was the Event Reported/Known to the PRC (and by What Media, if Possible)?	WHEN Was Action Undertaken by PRC in Response to the Event?	Event Type
Overflowing of rivers due to TD Lingling (Local name: Agaton)	Compostela Valley	11/1/2014	11/1/2014 (Online news and local PRC Chapter report)	11/1/2014—Deployed volunteer for assessment 13/1/2014—Served Hot meals to 530 persons	Tropical Depression
Overflowing of river due to Typhoon Rammasun (Local name: Glenda)	Northern Samar	15/7/2014	15/7/2014 (Chapter Report/Volunteers on the ground)	Alerted volunteers to the area and mobilised 35 volunteers and staff. 16/7/2015—Served hot meals to 620 individuals, Distributed Non Food Items to 202 Families, and Food Items to 788 Families.	Typhoon

2.2. Near-Real-Time Satellite Data

Near-real-time information from satellite observation is recently becoming available to disaster response organizations during ongoing floods. The Global Flood Detection System (GFDS) is one of the main systems used for this purpose. GFDS is an experimental system set up to detect and map in near-real-time major river floods based on daily passive microwave satellite observations. The purpose of this system is to identify and measure floods with potential humanitarian consequences after they occur. In order to quantify the magnitude of the flood event, GFDS calculates the "flood magnitude" product as the number of standard deviations (sd) from the mean (avg): $M = (signal - avg)/sd$. Floods appear typically for anomalies of two (small and regular flood) or above four (large and unusual flood). All data are available as global raster maps at a spatial resolution of 0.09° × 0.09° (~10 km at the equator).

In this project, we retrieved the geospatially explicit GFDS signal for seven days before until seven days after the reported date of the event. We then used this data to analyze the development of the signal over time for the impact locations as specified by the disaster response data (Section 2.1), as well as for national-level analytics (see Section 2.4).

The reasoning behind using GFDS for this analysis, is because: (1) the GFDS data are published openly through a user-friendly web interface; (2) the raw pre-processed images can be freely accessed; (3) the system provides consistent outputs with short intervals of one day; (4) in addition to flood location and extent (which is also possible using MODIS imagery), GFDS allows for the analysis of time series; and (5) the system is based on observations rather than hydrological model outputs (a flood detection methodology used for example by the Global Flood Monitoring System [28]). A disadvantage of the GFDS system is its relatively coarse resolution. Data from MODIS-based flood detection products such as produced by the Dartmouth Flood Observatory (DFO) provide flood extents at higher resolution, but these do not allow for time series analysis, nor can they provide a signal under cloud-covered conditions.

2.3. Near-Real-Time Twitter Data

The biggest challenge in effectively using social media information for disaster response is the systematic and rapid analysis of often vast amounts of data. In this study, we use the automated social media analytics platform *Floodtags* [29], which enables the filtering, visualization, and mapping of social media content based on location and keywords. We retrieve Twitter content for the September 2014 flood event in Pakistan and a selection of nine out of the 80 reported flood incidents in the Philippines. These nine incidents are linked to five individual flood events, and were selected to cover a range of different types of flooding (small, large, rain-induced, dam failure, *etc.*).

We retrieved the data for Philippines and Pakistan from the streaming API from Twitter. We searched for the words "baha", "bumabaha", "apaw", "pagbaha", "pag-apaw", "guho", "سیلاب", "flood", "floods", "flooding", "inundation", "inundations". Next, we enriched the tweets with Open Street Map data in order to get more location-specific detail, we filtered out place names with four or less characters and we excluded ambiguous English words (e.g., college, villa, *etc.*). This analysis of message body text is the methodology used for assigning a location to each Twitter message where possible. Whereas the metadata that comes with Twitter messages posted by a mobile device also include information on the geographical location of that device at the time of posting, this information is not used in this study. The first reason for this choice is the fact that the majority of tweets report second-hand information, *i.e.*, they discuss events that do not happen at the location of the person publishing the tweet [24]. Second, even when a tweet refers to a first-hand observation, it is not obvious that this observation has happened at the same time and place of the sending of the tweet [30]. If a flood happens in a remote area of the country without Internet access, it can be expected that observations are only tweeted as soon as the person reaches an area with Internet access, e.g., a larger town, causing more noise in the location data coming directly from Twitter. Uncertainty in the location detection remains, however, because certain place names may be featured multiple times in the same country [31], for example. See Discussion and Conclusions for a more extensive discussion of these challenges.

Wherever a specific tweet referred to a web page (URL), we also downloaded that web page as additional information. See Table 2 for the number of tweets for Pakistan and Philippines in the selected timeframes (September 2014 for Pakistan and the entire year 2014 for Philippines). Note that the temporal coverage and number of tweets vary strongly between the two case-study countries. We do not aim to conduct a comparative assessment, but rather use the data for different purposes throughout this paper.

The penetration rate of social media is relatively low in Pakistan, at 4% of the population; in the Philippines the penetration is higher at 29% [32]. A relatively large share of the Twitter users in both countries can be expected to reside in larger towns and cities. Therefore, the spatial variation displayed by a Twitter based *heat map* (*i.e.*, a map of absolute Twitter activity on a specific subject) will have a bias to showing floods in densely populated places [33]. Further research efforts are needed to develop methods for normalizing the data for population or social media penetration.

Table 2. Filtered flood-related tweets between 1 September 2014 and 31 January 2015.

Language	Flood Tweets Containing Pakistan Places (September 2014; One Event)	Flood Tweets Containing Philippine Places (July 2014–January 2015; Multiple Events)
English	197,651	458,689
Urdu	74,141	0
Filipino	0	36,055

2.4. Analytics and Outputs

In this paper, we bring the information from disaster response organizations, the GFDS satellite signal, and Twitter activity together in an analytical framework, to produce three types of analyses: *location mapping* (*i.e.*, "where is the flood?"); *early detection* (*i.e.*, "when can we know about the flooding?"); and *event understanding* (*i.e.*, "what do we know about the causes and effects?"). These specific analyses are chosen to assess the diverse potential of the near-real-time data for disaster response activities. We conduct the three analyses using a selection of the satellite and Twitter datasets for Pakistan and the Philippines, without aiming to analyze all three questions for both countries and for both data types.

2.4.1. Location mapping

Accurate information about the spatial extent of the ongoing flood at a given point in time is essential for effective disaster response. We assess the use of GFDS and online media information for near-real-time flood mapping, using the extracted data for Pakistan.

By analyzing the GFDS signal, we can produce an estimated significance of the flood at each gridded pixel of about 10 by 10 km. In this study, in order to show the detected spatial flood extent and for clarity, we selected those pixels with a magnitude value above four as the threshold of a flood occurrence in an analogous way as the experimental global flood maps uses the GFDS data.

Similarly, the real-time analysis of online (social) media content can be used to produce "heat maps" of online activity surrounding a specific topic [34,35], such as flooding. Such maps show the spatial intensity of tweets in a color scheme, at a given time interval (min, h, days, months). For consistency with the GFDS data, which is available on a daily basis, we also derived daily heat maps in this study.

2.4.2. Early detection

We assessed the effectiveness of GFDS and Twitter signals to be used for the early detection of floods, using the datasets extracted for the Philippines. For both data types we studied the temporal trend in the signal strength (*i.e.*, flood magnitude for GFDS, and tweet count for Floodtags data). These signals were then compared to the timing of the reporting of the flood event by the PRC. The results of this exercise are displayed as a graphical overlay of the timing graphs of GFDS and Floodtags data. For Floodtags data, this method is illustrated in Figure 1.

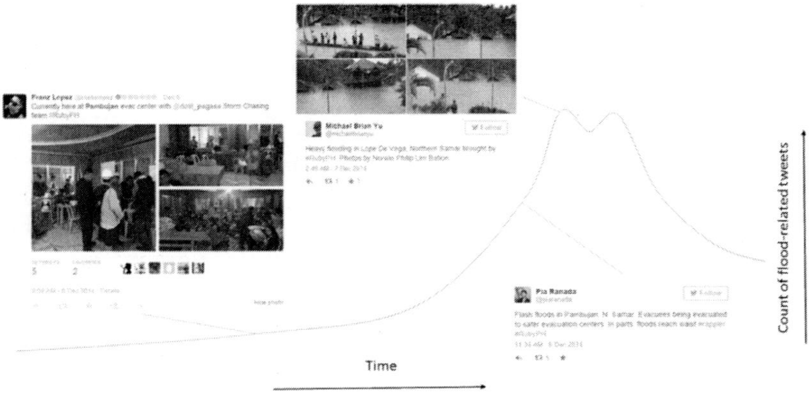

Figure 1. Schematic display of a typical Twitter count pattern leading up to a flood event (graph is illustrative; tweets are actual messages derived from flood events in the Philippines in 2014).

In addition, we analyzed the GFDS signal across all events, to draw a statistical distribution of the signal strength across all cases. The main purpose of this analysis is to assess the performance of the GFDS signal in the case of the Philippines events *versus* the Pakistan flood.

2.4.3. Event understanding

Twitter information provides almost unlimited scope for qualitative situational analysis right before, during, and after disasters [9]. This may include sentiment analysis, photograph analysis, as well as impact assessment. In this study, we argue that information from social media may be especially useful to improve the understanding of, and response to, unexpected or controversial flood occurrences. Within the flood episode in Pakistan, we handpicked a number of such occurrences for which we retrieved and analyzed qualitative Twitter information. These occurrences include an intentional breaching of flood defenses to protect selected areas, and the downstream flooding following the opening of hydropower dams. For both these types of events we analyze the timeline as well as the content of Twitter data, to evaluate its use in disaster response. For hydropower dam openings, we also analyze the GFDS signal to analyze the potential of the satellite system to detect such events. These are selected to provide insights in the timeline, cause, and effects of such controversial events, using information that is available in near-real-time.

3. RESULTS AND DISCUSSION

3.1. Rapid Flood Mapping

Figure 2 shows the estimated daily flood affected areas in Pakistan for 6th, 9th, and 12th September, as estimated from the GFDS satellite signal (Figure 2A) and the Twitter activity (Figure 2B). Figure 2C shows the flood affected areas as published by UN-OCHA two weeks after the end of the flooding episode [36].

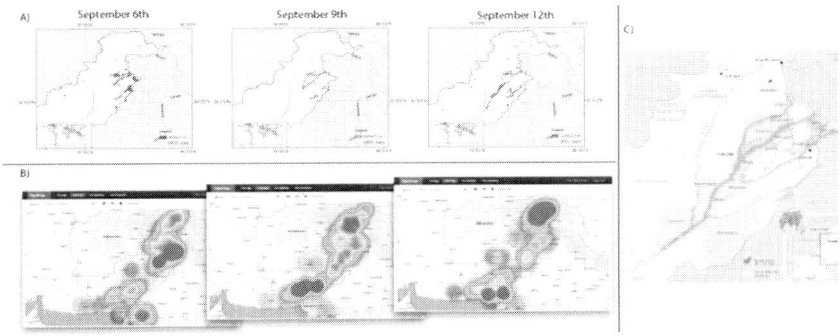

Figure 2. Affected flood areas as derived from different sources: (**A**) flood signal from GFDS for 6, 9 and 12 September. (**B**) heat map based on flood related Twitter activity for 6, 9 and 12 September; and (**C**) inundation map published by UN-OCHA in October 2014, outlining all areas that were inundated at some point in September 2014.

The results demonstrate that the daily flood extents identified in near-real-time by the GFDS signal (Figure 2A) agree well with the detailed assessment that was produced weeks after the ending of the flooding. Furthermore, these maps highlight that detail on the spatial development of the flooding, *i.e.*, the gradual change in inundated areas across the region, can be tracked with a delay of less than a day.

The spatial mapping of the twitter activity using the Floodtags platform (Figure 2B) shows a substantially different pattern from the GFDS data, highlighting that spatial information derived from social media is more complex to assess than satellite-based data. First of all, in contrast to the satellite-based inundation identification, flood-related tweets are not necessarily an indication of an ongoing flood at the same time and place as where the tweet was posted. Research has shown that less than 5% of the disaster related tweets during Typhoon Haiyan dealt with personal observations, whereas 40% reflected second-hand information (*i.e.*, re-tweets, or tweets about news reports) [24]. Second, the heat maps are strongly biased towards urban areas, both those affected from floods and those outside of the flood plain. This bias is caused by a higher penetration of Internet and social media in urban areas. The result from both of these effects is clear from the heat maps, which show a large concentration of tweets in urban centers, such as Islamabad (in the north of the country), Hyderabad, and Karachi (in the south of the country). These centers of Twitter activity are not directly affected by major flooding, highlighting a clear mismatch between the event location and signal location in this case.

3.2. Rapid Flood Detection

We assessed the capabilities of the GFDS and Twitter data to rapidly detect flood events, by comparing the timing of those signals to the moment on which the flood events were reported by the disaster management organizations (PNDA in Pakistan; and PRC in the Philippines). Figure 3 shows the results of this analysis for three selected flood events, numbered 63 (Figure 3A); 33 (Figure 3B), and 32 (Figure 3C). These three examples highlight the mixed performance of both the Twitter and satellite signal for flagging the reported flood events.

Event #63 (Figure 3A) was a local flood event in Pambujan, in Northern Samar region, caused by the landfall of Typhoon Ruby. Disaster management organizations in the Philippines, including the PRC, were well-prepared for the landfall of this typhoon. For this specific location, flooding due to overflowing of a dam was reported to the national PRC on December 8th and acted upon shortly after, according to the information available to the authors (red vertical line). On Twitter, however, over 200 tweets and photos testifying and discussing the start of the flooding were already posted starting two days earlier (6 December). Small-scale evacuations shown in these tweets emphasized that local disaster response organizations (including the Municipal Disaster Risk Reduction Management Office) were aware of the ongoing event between the 6 and 8 December. A high GFDS satellite signal was also recorded between the 4 and the 6 December, suggesting that high rainfall and flooding may have taken place in that period. In the case of this event, therefore, monitoring of the Twitter and GFDS signals may therefore have had potential for earlier detection and more rapid disaster response by national-level humanitarian organizations.

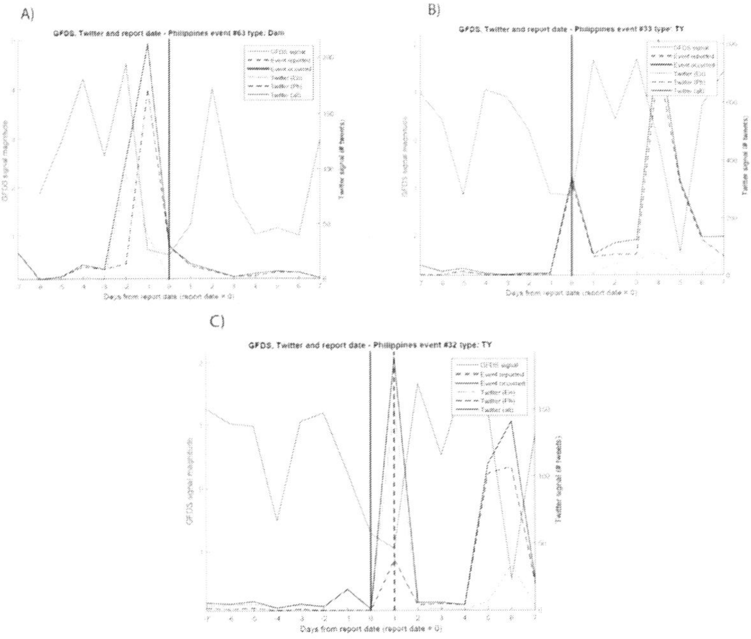

Figure 3. Flood signal from GFDS (blue line) and Twitter analysis (black lines for tweets in English language (fine dash); Filipino language (coarse dash); and both languages (solid line). The red lines indicate when the event occurred (solid) and was reported (dashed). If only one red line is shown, the dates of occurrence and reporting are the same. Flood types refer to dam break ("Dam") and typhoon ("TY"). The individual graphs are for different events that occurred throughout 2014, including (**A**) one dam overtopping and (**B**,**C**).two typhoon-triggered river floods.

A consistent early signal based on the analysis of both Twitter and satellite data like this, however, is not found for most of the events under analysis. Since the PRC already uses Twitter and other (social) media sources to some extent for disaster detection and monitoring, the peak in the Twitter signal can often be found on the same day the disaster was known to the PRC (Figure 3B). In the case of event #32 (Figure 3C), the information received from the PRC indicated that the event was reported (dashed red line) one day after it occurred (solid red line). Again, a small signal in the Twitter count data (black lines) and GFDS data (blue lines) was recorded 1–2 days earlier. However, the biggest peak in the Twitter signal is recorded on the day of reporting (*i.e.*, one day after the event occurred). This emphasizes that the majority of flood-related tweets are generally reporting second-hand information, by retweeting eye witness reports or news items [24].

The performance of the GFDS signal in these three flood events visualised in Figure 3 is mixed. In the case of event #63 (Figure 3A), the system seemed to have performed well, and there was a strong (>4 magnitude) signal several days before the event was reported. In the other two events (Figure 3B,C), however, there was no clear peak before the event and the magnitude remained low (<3) between seven days before and seven days after the event.

We analyzed the statistical distribution of the GFDS signal for this 15 day period surrounding each of the 80 flood events in the Philippines, and for 17 different locations during the September 2014 Pakistan floods. For comparability across events, we analyzed the deviation of the GFDS signal compared to the average value for each pixel, rather than the absolute GFDS magnitude values. The results of this analysis are displayed in Figure 4, for the Philippines (Figure 4A) and Pakistan (Figure 4B). Note that a single event date of 4 September is assumed for Pakistan (which is the first date on which flooding was reported), whereas the 21 individual event dates are used for the Philippines events. In places where GFDS performs well, we would expect a relatively high magnitude signal (compared to average) on the days right before and after a reported flood ("day 0" in Figure 4).

The results in Figure 4A show that, across all reported flood events in the Philippines, the GFDS signal fluctuates without a clear pattern. In general, there is no strong signal of higher magnitudes directly before or after reported flood events, although for few locations the relative magnitude values are high. There does seem to be a trend in the outliers prior to events in the Philippines, perhaps indicating that some events were well-captured, whereas many were not. In contrast, the results for Pakistan show a clear pattern of increasing signal for all locations right before the date of first flooding (4 September), which continues to rise and then slowly decreases. This shows that for most locations in the Pakistan analysis, the GFDS signal performs well in showing relative changes in flood magnitude. These findings emphasize that the performance of the GFDS system depends on the hydrological situation, as well as the land-use. The microwave satellite signal is generally better able to detect changes in water cover in dry areas (e.g., Pakistan) than in the irrigated agricultural lands, wetlands and coastal areas that characterize most of the Philippines. Obviously, the Pakistan floods were also a more extreme event than the Philippines event and, therefore, easier to detect by satellite observation. A full comparison of a wide range of similar-sized events in both countries would be needed to assess the effectiveness in early detection in different circumstances.

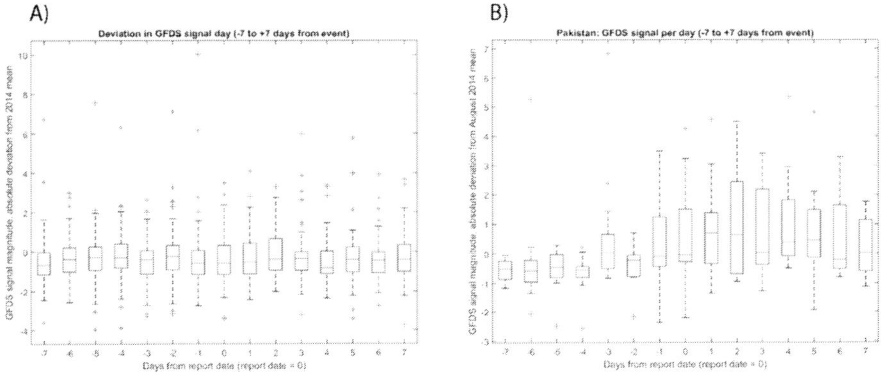

Figure 4. Box plots showing the distribution of signal deviation from the mean, for (**A**) all 80 flood events (*i.e.*, 80 locations) reported throughout 2014 in the Philippines; and (**B**) the September 2014 floods in Pakistan at 17 locations. For the event date ("day 0" on x-axis), we used the specific reported event date for each individual event for the Philippines; and 4 September 2014 for Pakistan.

3.3. Improving Event Understanding

Satellite early detection signals provide a quantitative indication of the location and possible magnitude of an ongoing event. In addition to providing insights in these aspects, near-real-time data from social media platforms can also provide qualitative insights in the situation on the ground [9]. These insights may include public discussions about risk prevention and evacuation measures (either pre-emptive, forced or voluntary evacuation); picture evidence of ongoing floods; and requests for emergency aid.

In order to assess the use of such data for disaster response, we analyzed tweets surrounding the flooding near the town of Athara Hazari, in north-eastern Pakistan. This specific case was noticed due to the particular and long-lasting pattern of flood-related Twitter messages over the period 4–29 September, with a number of activity peaks. By analyzing the content of these messages, a reconstruction of the events during this period can be made (Figure 5). This reconstruction shows a following timeline of events: starting on 4 September, people are increasingly worried about rising water levels; on September 8th, public discussions start about potential management strategies of the government, which include intentionally undermining flood protection around Athara Hazari in order to protect the headworks at Trimmu and the city Jhang; on September 10th, a range of tweets indicate that these dykes are actually blown without warning to the local population, inundating at least 100 villages; in the period after 10 September, these decisions and their implications were heavily discussed within the affected region and beyond. The discussions largely considered questions of why this had happened, including speculation that flood protection was jeopardized in order to protect the sugar mills owned by the family of the Prime Minister.

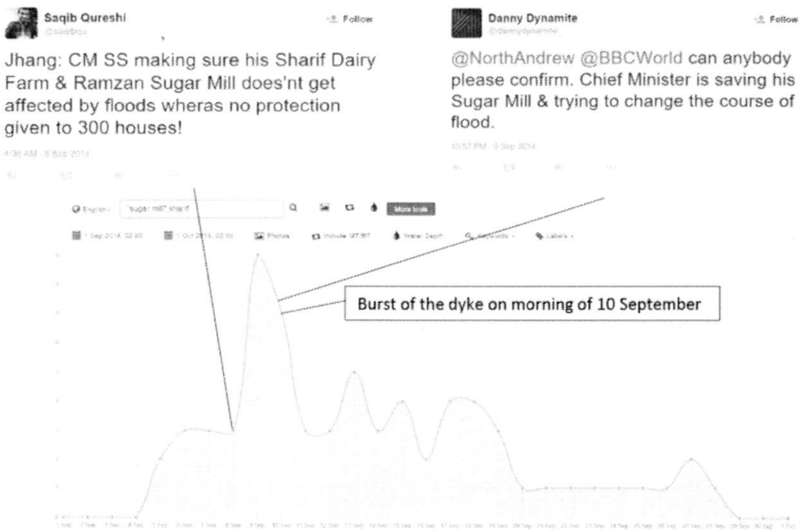

Figure 5. Twitter activity in Pakistan surrounding the blowing of flood defenses around Athara Hazari for the protection of the Sugar Mills at Trimmu and the city Jhang.

The sudden flooding of lands by blowing of levees and opening or breaking of dams can also be identified using the GFDS satellite signal. Figure 6 shows the GFDS signal for two locations downstream (Figure 6A) and upstream (Figure 6B) of the Tarbella dam in Pakistan, for seven days before and seven days after the 4 September. Figure 6A shows a very strong peak (>8) in the flood magnitude signal downstream of the Tarbella dam on the 1 September, indicating a sudden opening of this dam. Figure 6B indicates that the water cover upstream of the dam did not see a similar peak, and indeed dropped steeply 2–3 days later.

Pakistan has more than 20 major dams and barrages, which have an important role in the occurrence and management of floods. Twitter is an important platform for the population to discuss issues surrounding these dams, such as full reservoirs; sudden dam openings; and barrage overtopping. We analyzed the twitter signal about a range of dams in the affected areas in Pakistan, as well as a range of dams located further upstream in India (districts Jammu, Kashmir, Himachal Pradesh, and Punjab) and immediately downstream in Pakistan (districts Jhelum and Mandi Bahaudin) (Figure 7). The peaks in the Twitter activity follow the flow of the river. Tweet counts in Indian districts peak around mid-August; the Mangla dam in North-Eastern Pakistan shows a small peak on 5 September; four days later, a peak is recorded in the Jhelum district further downstream; and another few days after, the Mandi Bahauddin district peaks. As noted previously, only part of the Twitter messages can be attributed to direct observations, whereas a majority of tweets are reflecting upon these observations.

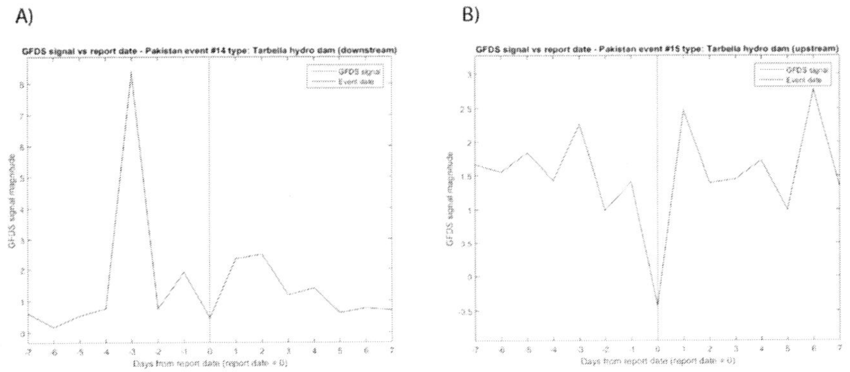

Figure 6. GFDS signal for locations directly (**A**) downstream and (**B**) upstream of the Tarbella Dam, in North-Eastern Pakistan.

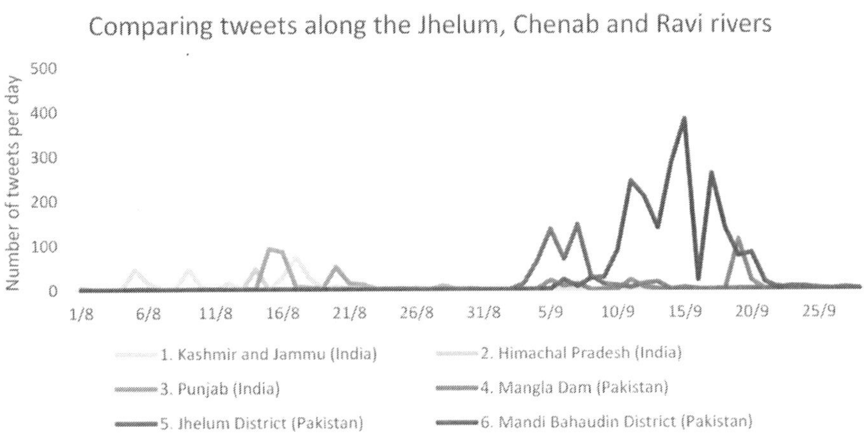

Figure 7. Tweet count related to dams and barrages, along the Jhelum, Chenab, and Ravi rivers. The locations are roughly ordered from upstream to downstream (numbered 1 to 6).

Analyzing the content of the tweets, we find that the small peak at Mangla Dam on the 5 September includes Twitter users discussing their worry about the full capacity of Mangla Reservoir. Later in the month (20 September) Twitter users discuss the fact that the Meteorological Department in Pakistan advised Mangla Dam to release water as early as mid-August. According to Twitter users, this warning had not been followed up, leading to the Mangla Dam being full despite warnings. A full dam capacity is hazardous when high rainfall is expected in the upstream area, since it may force the dam operator to open the dam for the release of substantial amounts of water. Actively following these dam-related conversations on social media could give humanitarian organizations enhanced insights in the potential for a dam opening upon high rainfall upstream, and could therefore be useful in preparing for potential flood impacts. Twitter could also be used as a medium for two-way communication with people living downstream of the dam, to gain further intelligence and to advise these people on possible preparedness activities.

4. CONCLUSIONS AND RECOMMENDATIONS

In this research we analyzed the potential value of near-real-time satellite and social media information for improving the understanding of the location, timing, causes, and impacts of floods, in order to enhance the speed and effectiveness of disaster response. Both the GFDS satellite data and the Twitter data that we analyzed in this paper have huge potential for enhancing disaster response, whereas both also have issues. In this section we will discuss some of these issues and propose further research directions.

4.1. GFDS satellite information

In general, GFDS is suited for monitoring and measuring large riverine floods and less so for small floods of short duration. In particular, GFDS provides unique information to assess the dynamic aspects of floods and for the quantitative measurement of flood impact. However, there are some known errors in the signal [37], including: (1) in agricultural areas, irrigation of the measurement and comparison pixels can affect the signal, as was shown by the relatively weak performance of the signal in the Philippines compared to Pakistan (Section 3.2); (2) intermittent instrument noise occasionally produce intermittent positive spikes in discharge (here work by the Dartmouth Flood Observatory is ongoing to solve this issue); (3) snow gives a similar signal as water and is not filtered out in the current version; and (4) due to the methodology applied to calculate the signal, GFDS may give erroneous results in coastal areas. The GFDS signal is therefore less suited for use in delta regions and islands.

Furthermore, care should be taken when interpreting the absolute magnitude values from GFDS. For the flood maps shown is this study (Section 3.1), we used only those flood magnitude values above four, because we wanted to spatially focus on the areas with more extreme flood anomaly detected by GFDS. However, values between two and four are typically associated a small and regular floods. From a humanitarian action point of view, these values could be combined with field knowledge of the vulnerability of specific areas. Values above two can then be used to set up monitoring and prepare for the potential development of a large flood. This can be complementary to analysis of forecasted extreme precipitation or flood forecasts from national meteorological services and global systems such as the Global Flood Awareness System. In addition, the GFDS offers the possibility to facilitate monitoring by displaying areas of interest in a (pre-) operational manner into the website, as is done for Bangladesh [38].

As research and technology progresses, additional satellite products should be considered as alternatives to GFDS. At this point, GFDS and MODIS (see Section 2.1) are the only sources of satellite water detection which are publicly available with a daily time step. One separate development that may be a promising alternative is the progress in global flood forecasting models [39], such as GloFAS (Global Flood Awareness System) [40] and GFMS (Global Flood Monitoring System) [28]. The performance of these systems for taking DRM actions prior to flood events is currently being tested by the Uganda Red Cross, together with the German Red Cross and the Red Cross/Red Crescent Climate Centre [41]. Currently, the uncertainty in the predictions is still large, and such forecast products cannot be considered as reliable as detection products, such as GFDS. However, the lack of adequate ground truth for most of the flood events that occurs, makes the evaluation of both (prototype) flood forecasting and satellite monitoring systems challenging [42]. Nevertheless, there are several studies that have tested the impact of using satellite-derived flood inundation products for calibration [43,44] or data assimilation [45,46] within hydrological models to improve its skill, showing promising results.

4.2. Twitter Analysis

In contrast to the GFDS signal, which is better suited for monitoring large floods, Twitter can be used to monitor floods of any size, as long as the observations and discussions are shared by people on social media. This analysis was shown to have several challenges. First, the consistent and accurate geographical allocation of the Twitter messages is complex [24,47,48]. In assessing the geographical location, we are looking for the impact location, rather than the geographical location of reporting, by analyzing place indications in the body of the tweet text. This is complex, since body texts may contain many ambiguous words, including place names, which may cause a substantial share of the messages that cannot be confidently georeferenced. In addition, there may be place names that are featured multiple times within the same country [31]. Georeferencing messages outside of the affected area is a key priority, given that the majority of tweets is discussing second hand information rather than observations [24].

A second challenge is analyzing the spatial distribution of tweet intensity. For densely populated areas, results showed that we can easily find large numbers of tweets about (upcoming) floods. However, for rural areas, such as Northern Samar in the Philippines, we found only two eye witnesses tweeting. Such a small tweet intensity is unlikely to alarm observers from humanitarian organizations, unless these are specifically called upon in the tweet (e.g., by using "@philredcross"). In addition, such small numbers of eye-witness reports raise questions about false-alarm rates. Given the costs associated with disaster response, one or two eye-witness reports are unlikely to trigger action on the side of the humanitarian organization. However, they could trigger further investigation, for example by responding directly to the specific Twitter user.

Third, there are challenges surrounding the selection of tweets that are relevant for the issues we need answers to. For this study, we conducted the assessment using a relatively simple query and using its statistics. Whereas the results are already promising, the accuracy could improve if we would improve the processing of data, for example by classifying the data using clusters [49]. Clustering according to subjects may enable the user to distinguish the different types of observations and use them accordingly.

Finally, when monitoring social media, it may be interesting to distinguish individual messages from the "wisdom of the crowds" [50]. While a single tweet may not say much (e.g., one person worries about a flood), the crowd may indicate that something will actually happen (e.g., many people worry about a flood and with it, predict the flood). This effect could be nourished by making people aware that their messages are used effectively for disaster response, which may lead to more responsible and informative tweets.

4.3. Recommendations for further research

In this study we have identified a number of recommendations for further research on the use of near-real time satellite and Twitter data for disaster response.

- **Post-processing and filtering**: further research efforts are needed to develop comprehensive near-real-time post-processing and filtering methodologies for social media content. These methodologies, which may include more sophisticated textual, geographical, and sentimental analyses, should aim for improving the accuracy of the location and impact analytics that are derived from this data, making the information more useful for humanitarian organizations.

- **Near-real-time action trigger analysis**: this study has shown that many of the flood events can be traced in the GFDS and Twitter signal, as a relative increase in signal compared to the baseline. However, there is currently no link between a certain signal magnitude and the probability or intensity of a flood and, therefore, with certain preparedness or response measures. Further research efforts are needed to analyze the signal magnitude during floods in various geographical settings, to link these magnitudes to relevant preparedness measures at the side of humanitarian organizations, and to establish the communication links between the data producers and humanitarian organizations to enable these actions to be taken.

- **Linking signals with vulnerabilities**: humanitarian organizations such as the PRC are conducting regular Vulnerability Capacity Assessments (VCAs) in order to understand the vulnerability of communities [51]. There is a potential for linking the flood signals from satellite observation and social media to detailed knowledge of the vulnerabilities in the area, to make a more substantiated judgment about potential humanitarian actions in the region.

- **Citizen reporters**: there are currently initiatives ongoing in the Philippines to deploy "citizen reporters", which are civilians who are asked for real-time information of ongoing events which is then used publicly by TV news stations. The system of citizen reporters may be equally valuable for humanitarian organizations, who could follow and support their volunteers during ongoing events, using social media such as Twitter. Research is needed to assess how such an approach could be implemented in the work flow of humanitarian organizations, and how this could be used to improve disaster response.

- **Partnerships**: Easy access to information generated by social media, and using it accordingly, can be a way forward towards new partnerships in disaster preparedness and response, and towards evolving approaches of working together. Research is needed to establish which partners are currently involved in disaster reduction and response, and how harnessing social media could change their relationships.

ACKNOWLEDGMENTS

We are grateful to Gwendolyn Pang and Maycarol Layugan (Philippines Red Cross), Muhammad Qaswar Abbas (IFRC Pakistan Country Delegation) and Donna Lagdameo (Red Cross/Red Crescent Climate Centre) for the data, support and technical assistance which they provided and which made this study possible. We acknowledge ESRC-DFID-NERC for providing funding for this research under the Big Data for Resilience programme. Further funding was provided by an NWO-VICI Grant (Grant Agreement 45314006).

AUTHOR CONTRIBUTIONS

Brenden Jongman, Jurjen Wagemaker, Beatriz Revilla Romero and Erin Coughlan de Perez jointly designed the research. Jurjen Wagemaker and Beatriz Revilla Romero extracted Twitter and satellite data, respectively. Brenden Jongman, Jurjen Wagemaker and Beatriz Revilla Romero analyzed the data and produced maps and figures. All authors jointly interpreted results and wrote the manuscript.

CONFLICTS OF INTEREST

The authors declare no conflict of interest.

REFERENCES

1. Munich Re. NatCatSERVICE Database; Munich Reinsurance Company Geo Risks Research: Munich, Germany, 2014.
2. Jongman, B.; Winsemius, H.C.; Aerts, J.C.J.H.; Coughlan de Perez, E.; van Aalst, M.K.; Kron, W.; Ward, P.J. Declining vulnerability to river floods and the global benefits of adaptation. Proc. Natl. Acad. Sci. USA 2015, 112. [PubMed]
3. The United Nations Office for Disaster Risk Reduction (UNISDR). Global Assessment Report on disaster risk reduction 2015: Making Development Sustainable: The Future of Disaster Risk Management;

The United Nations Office for Disaster Risk Reduction: Geneva, Switzerland, 2015.

4. International Federation of Red Cross and Red Crescent Societies (IFRC). Emergency Appeal: Malawi Floods 2015; International Federation of Red Cross and Red Crescent Societies (IFRC): Geneva, Switzerland, 2015.

5. Kellett, J.; Caravani, A. Financing Disaster Risk Reduction: A 20 Year Story of International Aid; Global Facility for Disaster Reduction and Recovery (GFDRR): Washington, DC, USA, 2013.

6. Coughlan de Perez, E.; Monasso, F.; van Aalst, M.; Suarez, P. Science to prevent disasters. Nat. Geosci. 2014, 7, 78–79.

7. Zhang, D.; Zhou, L.; Nunamaker, J.F., Jr. A knowledge management framework for the support of decision making in humanitarian assistance/disaster relief. Knowl. Inf. Syst. 2002, 4, 370–385.

8. Asplund, M.; Nadjm-Tehrani, S.; Sigholm, J. Emerging information infrastructures: Cooperation in disasters. In Critical Information Infrastructure Security; Setola, R., Geretshuber, S., Eds.; Springer: Berlin, Germany, 2009; pp. 258–270.

9. Meier, P. Digital Humanitarians: How Big Data Is Changing the Face of Humanitarian Response; Taylor and Francis Press: Abingdon, UK, 2015.

10. NASA NRT. Global Flood Mapping. Available online: http://oas.gsfc.nasa.gov/floodmap/ (accessed on 13 Junuary 2015).

11. Brakenridge, R.; Anderson, E. MODIS-based flood detection, mapping and measurement: The potential for operational hydrological applications. In Transboundary Floods: Reducing Risks Through Flood Management; Marsalek, J., Stancalie, G., Balint, G., Eds.; Springer: Rotterdam, The Netherlands, 2006; pp. 1–12.

12. De Groeve, T.; Riva, P. Global real-time detection of major floods using passive microwave remote sensing. In Proceedings of the 33rd International Symposium on Remote Sensing of Environment, Stresa, Italy, 4–8 May 2009.

13. Memon, A.A.; Muhammad, S.; Rahman, S.; Haq, M. Flood monitoring and damage assessment using water indices: A case study of Pakistan flood-2012. Egypt. J. Remote Sens. Sp. Sci. 2015, 18, 99–106.

14. European Commission Humanitarian Aid & Civil Protection ERCC Portal. Available online: http://erccportal.jrc.ec.europa.eu/Maps/Daily-maps# (accessed on 18 August 2015).

15. Ao, J.; Zhang, P.; Cao, Y. Estimating the locations of emergency events from Twitter streams. Procedia Comput. Sci. 2014, 31, 731–739.

16. Abdelhaq, H.; Gertz, M. On the locality of keywords in Twitter streams. In Proceedings of the 5th ACM SIGSPATIAL International Workshop on GeoStreaming, Dallas, TX, USA, 4 November 2014.

17. Leetaru, K.H.; Perkins, T.K.; Rewerts, C. Fulltext geocoding versus spatial metadata for large text archives: Towards a geographically enriched wikipedia. D-Lib Mag.2012, 18.

18. Muralidharan, S.; Rasmussen, L.; Patterson, D.; Shin, J.H. Hope for Haiti: An analysis of Facebook and Twitter usage during the earthquake relief efforts. Public Relat. Rev.2011, 37, 175–177.

19. Goodchild, M.F.; Glennon, J.A. Crowdsourcing geographic information for disaster response: A research frontier. Int. J. Digit. Earth 2010, 3, 231–241.

20. Earle, P.; Guy, M.; Buckmaster, R.; Ostrum, C.; Horvath, S.; Vaughan, A. OMG earthquake! Can Twitter improve earthquake response? Seismol. Res. Lett. 2010, 81, 246–251.

21. Vieweg, S.; Hughes, A.L.; Starbird, K.; Palen, L. Microblogging during two natural hazards events: What Twitter may contribute to situational awareness. In Proceedings of the 2010 ACM Conference on Human Factors in Computing Systems, Atlanta, GA, USA, 10–15 April 2010.

22. Muller, C.L.; Chapman, L.; Johnston, S.; Kidd, C.; Illingworth, S.; Foody, G.; Overeem, A.; Leigh, R.R. Crowdsourcing for climate and atmospheric sciences: Current status and future potential. Int. J. Climatol. 2015, 35, 3185–3203.

23. Muller, C.L. Mapping snow depth across the West Midlands using social media-generated data. Weather 2013, 68, 82.

24. Takahashi, B.; Tandoc, E.C.; Carmichael, C. Communicating on Twitter during a disaster: An analysis of Tweets during Typhoon Haiyan in the Philippines. Comput. Hum. Behav. 2015, 50, 392–398.

25. Neubaum, G.; Rösner, L.; Rosenthal-von der Pütten, A.M.; Krämer, N.C. Psychosocial functions of social media usage in a disaster situation: A multi-methodological approach. Comput. Hum. Behav. 2014, 34, 28–38.

26. Monsoon Weather Situation Report 2014; North Dakota Medical Association (NDMA): Islamabad, Pakistan, 2014.

27. Pakistan Floods 2014: Recovery Needs Assessment and Action Framework 2014–2016. Available online: http://www.ndma.gov.pk/new/Documents/Recovery_Needs_Assessment.pdf (accessed on 26 June 2015).

28. Wu, H.; Adler, R.F.; Tian, Y.; Huffman, G.J.; Li, H.; Wang, J. Real-time global flood estimation using satellite-based precipitation and a

coupled land surface and routing model. Water Resour. Res. 2014, 50, 2693–2717.

29. FloodTags. Available online: https://www.floodtags.com/ (accessed on 8 September 2015).

30. Hahmann, S.; Purves, R.; Burghardt, D. Twitter location (sometimes) matters: Exploring the relationship between georeferenced tweet content and nearby feature classes. J. Spat. Inf. Sci. 2014, 2014, 1–36.

31. Leetaru, K.; Wang, S.; Cao, G.; Padmanabhan, A.; Shook, E. Mapping the global Twitter heartbeat: The geography of Twitter. First Monday 2013, 18.

32. 30 m Internet Users in Pakistan, Half on Mobile: Report. Available online: http://tribune.com.pk/story/567649/30m-internet-users-in-pakistan-half-on-mobile-report/ (accessed on 21 May 2015).

33. Guan, X.; Chen, C. Using social media data to understand and assess disasters. Nat. Hazards 2014, 74, 837–850.

34. Gove, R.; Gramsky, N.; Kirby, R.; Sefer, E.; Sopan, A.; Dunne, C.; Shneiderman, B.; Taieb-Maimon, M. NetVisia: Heat map & matrix visualization of dynamic social network statistics & content. In Proceedings of the 2011 IEEE Third International Conference on Privacy, Security, Risk and Trust and 2011 IEEE Third International Conference on Social Computing (SocialCom), Boston, MA, USA, 9–11 October 2011; pp. 19–26.

35. Schreck, T.; Keim, D. Visual analysis of social media data. Computer 2013, 46, 68–75.

36. UN Office for the Coordination of Humanitarian Affairs. Pakistan: Humanitarian Snapshot—Floods (as of 2 Oct 2014); UN Office for the Coordination of Humanitarian Affairs: Geneva, Switzerland, 2014.

37. Brakenridge, G.R.; Kettner, A.; Syvitski, J.; Overeem, R.; de Groeve, T.; Cohen, S.; Nghiem, S.V. River Watch 2. Satellite River Discharge and Runoff Measurements: Technical Summary; University of Colorado: Boulder, CO, USA.

38. European Commission Joint Research Centre. Global Flood Detection System: Flood status report for Bangladesh. Available online: http://www.gdacs.org/flooddetection/monitoringregion.aspx?filter=Bangladesh (accessed on 14 September 2015).

39. Ward, P.J.; Jongman, B.; Salamon, P.; Simpson, A.; Bates, P.; de Groeve, T.; Muis, S.; de Perez, E.C.; Rudari, R.; Trigg, M.A.; et al. Usefulness and limitations of global flood risk models. Nat. Clim. Chang. 2015, 5, 712–715.

40. Alfieri, L.; Burek, P.; Dutra, E.; Krzeminski, B.; Muraro, D.; Thielen, J.; Pappenberger, F. GloFAS-global ensemble streamflow forecasting and flood early warning. Hydrol. Earth Syst. Sci. 2013, 17, 1161–1175.

41. Coughlan de Perez, E.; van den Hurk, B.; van Aalst, M.K.; Jongman, B.; Klose, T.; Suarez, P. Forecast-based financing: An approach for catalyzing humanitarian action based on extreme weather and climate forecasts. Nat. Hazards Earth Syst. Sci. 2015, 15, 895–904.

42. Revilla-Romero, B.; Hirpa, F.A.; Thielen, J.; Salamon, P.; Brakenridge, G.R.; Pappenberger, F.; de Groeve, T. Evaluation of global flood forecasting and satellite monitoring systems in data-sparse regions—A challenge. Remote Sens 2015. under review.

43. Di Baldassarre, G.; Schumann, G.; Bates, P.D. A technique for the calibration of hydraulic models using uncertain satellite observations of flood extent. J. Hydrol.2009, 367, 276–282.

44. Milzow, C.; Krogh, P.E.; Bauer-Gottwein, P. Combining satellite radar altimetry, SAR surface soil moisture and GRACE total storage changes for hydrological model calibration in a large poorly gauged catchment. Hydrol. Earth Syst. Sci. 2011, 15, 1729–1743.

45. Zhang, Y.; Hong, Y.; Wang, X.; Gourley, J.J.; Gao, J.; Vergara, H.J.; Yong, B. Assimilation of passive microwave streamflow signals for improving flood forecasting: A first study in Cubango River Basin, Africa. IEEE J. Sel. Top. Appl. Earth Obs. Remote Sens. 2013, 6, 2375–2390.

46. Giustarini, L.; Matgen, P.; Hostache, R.; Montanari, M.; Plaza, D.; Pauwels, V.R. N.; de Lannoy, G.J. M.; de Keyser, R.; Pfister, L.; Hoffmann, L.; et al. Assimilating SAR-derived water level data into a hydraulic model: A case study. Hydrol. Earth Syst. Sci.2011, 15, 2349–2365.

47. Van Laere, O.; Schockaert, S.; Dhoedt, B. Georeferencing Flickr resources based on textual meta-data. Inf. Sci. 2013, 238, 52–74.

48. Dunkel, A. Visualizing the perceived environment using crowdsourced photo geodata. Landsc. Urban. Plan. 2015, 142, 173–186.

49. Hürriyetoğlu, A. Tweet stream analysis for flood time estimation. In Proceedings of the 25th Meeting of Computational Linguistics in the Netherlands, Antwerp, Belgium, 5–6 February 2015.

50. Galton, F. Vox Populi (The wisdom of the crowds). Nature 1949, 75, 450–451.

51. Van Aalst, M.K.; Cannon, T.; Burton, I. Community level adaptation to climate change: The potential role of participatory community risk assessment. Glob. Environ. Chang. 2008, 18, 165–179.

INDEX